A History of Political Thought

A History of Political Thought

A Thematic Introduction

John Morrow

NEW YORK UNIVERSITY PRESS
Washington Square, New York

First published in the U.S.A. in 1998 by
NEW YORK UNIVERSITY PRESS
Washington Square
New York, N.Y. 10003

This book is printed on paper suitable for recycling and
made from fully managed and sustained forest sources.

Library of Congress Cataloging-in-Publication Data
Morrow, John, Ph. D.
The history of political thought : a thematic introduction / John
Morrow.
p.   cm.
Includes bibliographical references and indexes.
ISBN 0–8147–5448–1 (hardcover). — ISBN 0–8147–5597–6 (pbk.)
1. Political science—History.   I. Title.
JA81.M757 1998
320'.01'1—dc21   97–23354
                                                                          CIP

Printed in Malaysia

For Ruth Cook and in memory of Bill

Contents

Preface

This book is designed to provide an introduction to the history of
political thought that will be useful for students studying this subject in
both history and politics programmes. It considers the full range of Western political thinking from the ancient world until the middle decades of
the twentieth century and concludes with some brief indications of
important developments in contemporary political theory. Although the
book focuses on Western thought, it also contains a few side-glances at
non-Western treatments of similar or related issues.

Unlike many introductory surveys that present a series of chronological
chapters discussing the ideas of a more or less exhaustive list of important thinkers, this book focuses on themes and explores the ways in which
the issues raised by them have been addressed by a range of historically
significant political thinkers. This approach has been chosen with a view
to identify varying responses to common or at least related concerns that
have been of lasting significance to Western political thinkers. Each chapter discusses a number of thinkers who have had interesting points to
make about the issues under consideration. An attempt has been made to
identify the relationship between various thinkers and to trace patterns of
development across extensive periods of time. Some thinkers are discussed in a number of chapters while others make a more fleeting
appearance.

Three charts reflecting the conventional distinction between the ancient
and medieval (*c.* 400 BC–1500 AD), early modern (1500–1800) and modern (1800–) periods (see pp. 7, 8, 11–12) provide a chronology that relates
thinkers to one another and to major historical events. Boxes located
within the text present biographical information on a wide range of
important thinkers discussed in the book: the location of these is indicated by bold entries in the personal name index.

While working on this book I enjoyed a period of research leave in Cambridge. I am most grateful to the Leave Committee of Victoria University for granting me leave, and to the Warden and Fellows of Robinson College who, by electing me into a Bye Fellowship, provided a congenial environment during my stay in Cambridge. Staff of the Robinson College Library, the Cambridge University Library and the Victoria University Library have dealt courteously and efficiently with many enquiries. Miles Fairburn of the History Department at Victoria and Patrick Maloney of the Politics Department at that University have read various chapters of this books. My wife Diana Morrow has read the whole work in a number of forms and has helped me correct the proofs. Members of the Politics Department at the University of Keele responded to a seminar outlining the project, and I have also benefited greatly from the insightful and patient comments of my publisher's three anonymous readers. Adrienne Nolan has cheerfully provided valuable secretarial assistance. In thanking these people for their efforts on my behalf, and in acknowledging Steven Kennedy's efficient and encouraging editorial oversight, I do not, of course, absolve myself of responsibility for any of the shortcomings of this work.

Victoria University of Wellington, New Zealand   John Morrow

List of 'Thinker' Boxes

Introduction

This book is intended to provide a succinct but comprehensive treatment of a range of thinkers, issues and debates that have been of central importance in the Western tradition of political thought. Many introductions to the history of political thought survey the ideas of an extensive number of 'great thinkers' who are presented as representing the high-points of a tradition jokingly referred to as extending 'from Plato to Nato'. While this approach provides a convenient way of outlining the ideas of particular thinkers, one that has the virtue of chronological coherence and allows for a consideration of the biographical and historical background in which their works were produced, it makes it difficult to include considerations of a range of less commonly noted but historically significant political thinkers, and prohibits identification of thematic patterns in the history of political thought.

In order to overcome these difficulties while at the same time taking account of chronological and contextual considerations, this book is organised around themes that extend across wide tracts of European history and provide a framework for chronological accounts of the aspects of thinkers' writings that relate to them. The purpose of this approach is to highlight questions about politics that have played an important role in Western political thinking, and to present a consideration of them that identifies continuities and changes in the ways in which these questions have been posed and answered over long periods of time. It also allows for consideration of a wider range of thinkers than could be accommodated in a manageable book organised along 'Plato to Nato' lines.

Changing perspectives on issues of enduring concern and the appearance of questions that would not have occurred to earlier thinkers are related to developments – in economic and social structures, in forms of political organisation, in religious beliefs and in ways of viewing human beings and the world – that have occurred in the West in the two and a half thousand years that separate the ancient and modern worlds. These changes mean that it would be anachronistic to treat Western political thinking as a homogeneous whole. At the same time however, it is important to acknowledge that Western political thinkers have been aware of at least aspects of their past and have often formulated their ideas by reference to the ideas of their predecessors. These considerations explain why it makes sense to talk of patterns of change and continuity, and they also explain why this book makes only passing reference to non-Western political thought. For the most part, Western political thinkers have not reflected on systematic statements about politics developed in other cultures.

Periodisation

The two and a half thousand year span of European history with which this book deals is conventionally divided into a number of periods. These periods do not form absolutely discrete historical entities, but they are useful because they reflect distinctive features of the political, economic and social structures of Western societies at different stages in their development, and the sets of intellectual, religious and political beliefs that correspond to them. The first thousand years, that is, from about 500 BC until 500 AD, is referred to as the 'ancient' period. During this period Western political thought focused on the city states of Greece, and on the Roman Republic and the Empire that succeeded it. There were some similarities between the governments of the Greek city states and that which emerged during the history of the Roman Republic, and thinkers who reflected on the experience of the latter were aware of the ideas of their Greek predecessors. For most of this period political thinking focused on pre-Christian societies, but in late antiquity it had to come to grips with the growing influence of Christian ideas in the Roman Empire.

The medieval period extends from the sixth century to the late fifteenth century. Medieval political thought reflected the Christian basis of Western culture, the erosion of the authority of the Holy Roman Empire, the emergence of the complex system of economic, political and social organisation known as 'feudalism', and the appearance in the late medieval period of the increasingly unified nation states. These states dominated the political history of the 'early modern' period, which extends from the early sixteenth to the late eighteenth century. The first two centuries of the early modern period were dominated by the religious and political ramifications of the division of Western Christendom into two camps as a result of the Protestant Reformation, which began in 1517 in Germany and quickly spread throughout Europe. This challenge was met by a counterreformation conducted by rulers who remained attached to Roman Catholicism.

These events stimulated an upsurge in speculation on political questions, and they overlapped the reappearance, particularly in Italy, of forms of government that focused on city states and the recovery of philosophical works from the ancient world. These developments meant that late medieval and early modern political theory was set in a framework that capitalised to some degree on ideas derived from the Greek and Roman worlds. Sometimes the use of ancient works produced conceptions of politics that ran counter to lessons derived from the Christian tradition. The influence of the latter was also blunted to some degree in the seventeenth century by the burgeoning interest in scientific investigation, and in the eighteenth century by the stress placed on human reason by the 'enlightenment' movements in a number of European countries. Taken together, these movements in Western intellectual culture prepared the ground for the more secular perspectives on politics that were developed by a number of 'modern' writers in the nineteenth and early twentieth centuries.

In the modern period political theory not only became increasingly, although not exclusively, secular in orientation, but it also focused on issues that were distinctive to the experience of Western societies and the other countries of the world that were influenced by them. Unprecedented developments in the economic life of these societies, conventionally categorised as the 'industrial revolution', and the democratisation of social and political relationships had a marked impact on the way that people thought about politics. The modern period witnessed the appearance of a wide range of complex political theories, elements of which were incorporated into the political ideologies that were attached to the perceived interests of distinct groups or classes within society. Thus while the political thinking of the modern world exhibited some continuity with that of earlier periods, it was also marked by the appearance of theories of mass politics, and those promoting deliberate, revolutionary change. Both of these developments involved a significant departure from the approaches to politics that had characterised earlier periods.

The Focus of the Book

For the most part, this book focuses on ideas of *rule* and sets this issue within the framework of the *state*. Central to this conception of politics is a series of questions concerning the purposes of political authority, the persons who should possess it and the ways in which it should be exercised. The perspective adopted here does not provide a framework that exhausts the subject matter of 'politics'. It focuses on the internal aspect of politics rather than its international dimensions or alternative perspectives that bear on class, gender and race. Nonetheless the latter are not excluded from consideration – gender issues play a limited role in the discussions that follow, as do those of class. As we shall see, theories of class politics have posed important challenges to a tradition that has been largely concerned with rule and the state, and conceptions of gender and race politics seem set to have the same effect. The fact remains, however, that the perspective on politics employed here has been at the centre of Western political thinking from the time of the ancient Greeks until the modern era. Alternative conceptions of politics have been developed in critical reaction to traditional concerns.

As is made apparent throughout this book, political thinking has always had a strongly prescriptive tendency. That is, attempts to arrive at an understanding of the nature of politics and of particular political problems have almost invariably given rise to arguments that favour certain political institutions, ideas and practices, and question the alternatives to them. The themes used to structure the following chapters identify sets of prescriptions relating to the purpose and nature of political rule and the structures within which it takes place. Part I of the book examines a number of responses to the question: to what ends should political authority be directed? In Parts II and III the focus of the discussion shifts to arguments about *who* should exercise supreme authority and *how* such authority should be exercised. Finally, Part IV examines theories that justify resistance to political superiors and those that promote revolutionary challenges both to rulers and to the systems of government in which they are located.

These themes are divided between a number of chapters that explore a distinct set of answers to the general questions posed in Parts I–IV. Although the positions discussed in each chapter exhibit fundamental similarities, they vary to some degree. These variations can be explained by reference to the particular contexts in which the theories in question were produced, and to the common tendency for writers to use the ideas of their predecessors as starting points from which to develop new approaches to issues that have been of ongoing importance in the history of political thought. Each chapter follows a chronological line of development, and its historical scope is determined by the richness of the material available and by the extent to which a particular theme has persisted over time. Major thinkers appear in a number of chapters, but consideration of their ideas is supplemented by and placed within the context of a range of ideas produced by historically significant but less prominent writers. In common with many introductory surveys, this book presents a series of accounts of the ideas of those who are conventionally seen as 'great names' and are accorded pride of place in the history of Western political thought. However, the approach adopted here also allows us to consider arguments developed by thinkers who fall outside this august company but were significant in their own times.

As we shall see, writers' contributions to the history of political thought have been influenced strongly by their understanding of the problems facing their own societies, by their perception of the strengths and weaknesses of other treatments of them, and by presuppositions about human nature and social life grounded in fundamental religious or metaethical assumptions. Recent scholarly studies of the history of political thought have stressed the importance of these contextual and situational factors. They have warned of the need to avoid anachronism and to treat the past in a way that takes account of its distinctive character. The past, it has been said, is a foreign country: they do things differently there.

While recognising the force of these strictures, one must also bear in mind that historical thinkers have rarely adhered to them. They have often formulated their ideas by drawing on, or reacting against, the arguments of their predecessors, and they have tended to treat the past as a treasure trove from which they can draw for their own purposes. Seen from this point of view, in a sense we can think of the study of political thought as involving an analysis of the ideas of a fairly limited number of thinkers who have made a conscious attempt to grapple with a definable range of issues in markedly different political and intellectual environments, and have brought significantly different preoccupations to bear upon them. In other words, while recognising the historical specificity of political theories, it is still useful to identify general themes that have played an enduring role in the history of political thought. Of course the historical reach of the themes addressed in this book and the approaches that form the subject matter of its chapters vary greatly, but provided these variations are given due recognition their existence does not preclude a thematic treatment of issues over long periods of time.

Western Political Thinking: A Brief Overview

The earliest systematic statements of political theory to survive in a relatively complete form were produced in the fourth century BC by the Greek writer Plato and his pupil Aristotle. These works focus on the type of state that was common in the Greek world in that period: the *polis*, or city state. The *polis* was not merely an administrative unit, nor even just the source of protection or material well-being. For the Greeks the *polis* was, quite literally, a way of life. It provided the focus of identification for a complex web of artistic, economic, intellectual, moral, political and religious aspirations. In short it embraced and reflected the culture of the community and provided the framework within which individuals realised their aspirations. A large proportion of early political theory was

produced in Athens, a city state whose government was based on democratic principles. Positive accounts of Athenian democracy appear in fragmentary statements ascribed to Protagoras and Democritus, while aspects
of this way of thinking were subjected to critical scrutiny by Plato and
Aristotle.

While ancient political theories focused on the *polis*, or in the case of
the Roman writer Cicero, on the more extensive type of republican
regime that emerged in the second and first centuries before Christ, medieval political theorists had to come to grips with an environment that
contained a range of political institutions. These writers knew about the
polis and from the thirteenth century they also had access to fairly complete versions of ancient political writings. However, medieval political
thinkers considered empires and kingdoms as well as city states. They
also explored the relationship between political institutions and ideas,
and the conception of human life that was determined by the implications
of Christianity. For example St Augustine of Hippo, writing in the fifth
century AD, was highly critical of Greek and Roman assumptions about
the ultimate value of political institutions and drew a sharp distinction
between 'earthly cities' (such as the Roman Empire) and the 'heavenly
city', which embraced the destiny of Christians. In the late medieval period, however, the growing interest in Aristotle encouraged a reassessment
of the classical heritage. A number of writers, of whom the most important was the thirteenth-century philosopher and theologian St Thomas
Aquinas, identified a close and positive relationship between political
institutions and the realisation of Christian values. Much of Aquinas'
theory focused on kingdoms rather than empires or city states. He sought
to relate the exercise of political authority to the need for human beings
to be subjected to systems of political regulation that embody fundamental principles derived from divine governance of the universe. In developing his position Aquinas drew upon many of the details of Aristotle's
political and moral philosophy. He also claimed that the state is fundamental to human existence within the strictures of Christianity.

The appearance of a number of rich and powerful city states in late
medieval and early modern Italy caused political thinking to focus anew
on the problems encountered in this form of political organisation. The
major issues facing these states, stability and survival, raised questions
about the value systems of republics, as well as their internal organisation
and external relations. The most original and influential thinker to emerge
in this context was Niccoló Machiavelli, who produced a number of
important works in the early sixteenth century. Machiavelli drew on the
classical past, and particularly the example of the Roman Republic, to
develop a specification for a popular republican state. A striking feature
of Machiavelli's work is that he treated politics in relation to the requirements of a distinctly political morality, and was openly critical of the

Chronology: Ancient and Medieval Periods c.400 BC–1500AD

Thinkers		Works	Contemporary events	
BC				
d. 399	Socrates	No writings	431–404:	The Great Peloponnesian War.
	Protagoras		404–403.	Rule of the Thirty Tyrants at Athens.
	Democritus			
d. 347	Plato	*Republic* (c. 380)		
		Laws (unfinished)	333:	Defeat of Greek forces by Alexander the Great.
d. 322	Aristotle	*Ethics*		
		Politics		
d. 264	Zeno	No writings		
d. c. 125	Polybius	*The Histories* (c. 146)	146:	Greek states fall under Roman control.
			133:	Gracchian land reforms attempted at Rome.
			123:	Second attempt at Gracchian land reform.
			88–82:	Civil war in Rome.
d. 43	Cicero	*The Republic*	63:	Cicero consul.
		The Laws	44:	Assassination of Julius Caesar.
			31–14AD:	Rule of Augustus, end of Roman Republic.
AD				
d. 397	Ambrose	*De Officiis Ministrorum* (386)	306–337:	Rule of Constantine the Great.
			312:	Constantine's conversion to Christianity.
d. 430	Augustine	*The City of God* (413–27)	410:	Sack of Rome by Alaric.
d. 496	Gelasius	*Address* (494)		
d. 565	Justinian I	*Digest* (533)	527–565:	Rule of Justinian I.
		Institutes (533)		
			c. 1000:	Venice established as a major naval and trading port.
			1066:	Norman conquest of England.
d. 1085	Gregory VII	*Decree Against Lay Investitures* (1075)		
d. 1180	John of Salisbury	*Polycraticus* (1159)	1075–1122:	The Investiture Controversy.
			1215:	Magna Carta.
			c. 1240:	Latin texts of Aristotle's writings circulated in the West.
d. 1268	Bracton, Henry	*Of the Laws and Customs of England* (1268)		
d. 1274	Aquinas	*Summa Theologiae* (c. 1266–73)		
d. 1342	Marsilius of Padua	*Defender of the Peace* (1324)		
d. 1349	William of Ockham	*A Short Discourse* (1346)		
d. 1357	Bartolus of Sassoferrato	*Tract on City Government*		
d. c. 1430	Pizan, Christine de	*Book of the Body Politic* (1604)		
			1337–1453:	The Hundred Years War.
			1450–1550:	Renaissance in Italy.
			1494–5:	French Invasion of Italy.
			1517:	Start of the Protestant Reformation.

Chronology: Early Modern Period, c.1500–1800AD

Thinkers		Works	Contemporary events	
d. 1520	de Seyssel, Claude	*The Monarchy of France* (1519)	1512:	Restoration of Medici at Florence.
d. 1527	Machiavelli, Nicoló	*The Prince* (1513) *The Discourses* (1513–19)	1527:	Florentine Republic reestablished.
d. 1540	Guicciardini, Francesco	*Dialogue on the Government of Florence* (1523)		
d. 1546	Luther, Martin	*On Secular Authority* (1523) *Against the Murderous Thieving Hordes of Peasants* (1525)	1517: 1524–5:	Protestant Reformation begins. The Peasants' War in Germany.
d. 1560	Melanchthon, Philippe	*Philosophiae Moralis Epitome* (1550)		
d. 1564	Calvin, John	*Institutes of Christian Religion* (1559)	1536:	Calvin at Geneva.
d. 1572	Knox, John	*Letter to the Commonalty* (1558)	1562–98:	French Wars of Religion.
d. 1590	Hotman, François	*Francogallia* (1573)	1572:	Massacre of St. Bartholomew.
d. 1596	Bodin, Jean	*Six Books of the Commonwealth* (1576)		
d. 1600	Hooker, Richard	*Laws of Ecclesiastical Polity* (1593–7)		
d. 1605	Beza, Theodore	*The Right of Magistrates* (1574)		
d. 1617	Suarez, Francisco	*Tractatus de Legibus ac Deo Legislatore* (1611)		
d. 1623	Mornay, Philippe du Plessis	*Vindiciae Contra Tyrannos* (1579)	1625:	Charles the First, King of England; beginning of his troubles with parliament.
d. 1645	Grotius, Hugo	*The Law of War and Peace* (1625)		
d. 1653	Filmer, Sir Robert	*Patriarcha* (1632–42)	1642–6, 1648:	Civil War in England.
d. c. 1663	Overton, Richard	*An Appeal to the People* (1647)	1649:	Execution of Charles.
d. 1679	Hobbes, Thomas	*Leviathan* (1651)	1649–1660:	English Commonwealth.
d. 1677	Harrington, James	*Oceana* (1656)	1660:	Restoration of Charles II.
d. 1674	Pufendorf, Samuel	*The Law of Nature and of Nations* (1672)		
d. 1704	Locke, John	*Two Treatise of Government (1689)*	1688;	Glorious Revolution in England.
d. 1704	Bossuet, Jaques	*Politics Drawn from the Very Words of Holy Scripture* (1709)		
d. 1776	Hume, David	*Essays Moral and Political* (1741, 1742)		
d. 1755	Montesquieu, Charles	*The Spirit of the Laws* (1748)		
d. 1771	Helvetius, Claude	*De L'Esprit* (1758)		
d. 1778	Rousseau, Jean-Jacques	*Discourses* (1749–55) *Social Contract* (1762)		
d. 1780	Blackstone, William	*Commentaries on the Laws of England* (c. 1769)		
d. 1794	Beccaria Ceasar	*On Crimes and Punishments* (1764)	1775–83:	American Revolutionary War.
d. 1784	Diderot, Denis	*The Encyclopaedia* (1776) (with others)		
d. 1836	Madison, James	*The Federalist* (1787–8)		
d. 1832	Bentham, Jeremy	*Fragment on Government* (1776) *Introduction to the Principles of Morals and Legislation* (1789)		
d. 1836	Sièyes, Abbé	*What is the Third Estate?* (1789)	1789:	French Revolution.
d. 1796	Burke, Edmund	*Reflections on the Revolution in France* (1791) *Appeal from the New to the Old Whigs* (1792)	1793:	Execution of Louis XVI of France.
d. 1809	Paine, Thomas	*Rights of Man* (1791, 1792)		
d. 1797	Wollstonecraft, Mary	*A Vindication of the Rights of Men* (1791) *A Vindication of the Rights of Women* (1792)	1793–4:	The Reign of Terror
d. 1832	Godwin, William	*An Enquiry Concerning Political Justice* (1793)	1795–99:	The Directory in France.
d. 1797	Babeuf, Francois	*Tribune of the People* (1795)	1799–1804	Consulate in France.
d. 1821	de Maistre, Joseph	*Considerations on France* (1796)		
d. 1804	Kant, Immanuel	*Metaphysics of Morals* (1797)		

effect of Christian ideas on political practice. These issues played an important role in his account of republics, and also in his treatment of the problems faced by single rulers, or 'princes'.

Machiavelli's works were produced at a time when many city states were falling prey to larger, more powerful nation states. From the early sixteenth century the focus of Western political thinking shifted finally and irrevocably to this form of state, but it did so against a backdrop of bitter religious controversy engendered by the Protestant Reformation and Catholic reactions to it. The sixteenth and seventeenth centuries were marked by new and important departures in political theory. On the one hand, a number of important early-modern writers developed theories of absolute sovereignty, which gave rulers more or less complete control over their subjects. On the other hand these developments were resisted by those who were concerned about the effect that theories of absolute sovereignty would have on subjects' fulfilment of their religious obligations.

Absolutism developed in response to uncertainties about the relationship between subjects and rulers in the new nation states. These uncertainties resulted from concern about the bearing that traditional ('customary') systems of regulation and those derived from divine command ('natural law') would have on laws formulated by the person or persons who held supreme power in the state (the 'sovereign'). It was argued that productive forms of political organisation should be subject to the unquestioned authority of an absolute ruler. Early formulations of this theory incorporated ideas derived from medieval political theory. For example the important late-sixteenth-century French writer Jean Bodin remained attached to ideas of natural law, and attempted to reconcile an absolute sovereign with the conventional constitutional structure of the French state. In contrast his seventeenth-century English successor, Thomas Hobbes, regarded these ideas as a major source of intellectual and practical confusion and sought to construct what he termed a 'scientific' account of politics. Hobbes dismissed past political thinkers and was particularly critical of the influence of Aristotle. Hobbes took it upon himself to purge his contemporaries of the dangerous illusions they had inherited from the past. He wished to provide his readers with a clear and incontestable understanding of politics that would allow them to see that their safety and welfare could only be secured by an absolute sovereign. These theories were designed to deprive subjects of the right to challenge the actions of rulers. They thus rejected the ambivalently formulated but tenaciously held idea that the exercise of political authority should be subject to constraint.

But while Bodin and Hobbes caused these ideas to be seriously challenged, they did not drive them from the field. To the contrary, the development of theories of absolute government within the early modern context prompted a restatement and refinement of traditional arguments that pushed them in new, and potentially radical, directions. The turmoil that accompanied the emergence of a number of early modern states was caused at least in part by the breakdown of a unified view of Christianity during the Reformation. Rulers were themselves embroiled in these disputes, so their claim to absolute authority had far-reaching religious implications. Consequently, from the late sixteenth century until the end of the next century, theories of absolute government were challenged by a number of writers who argued that these theories conflicted with what they saw as their fundamental obligations to God. An important result of these concerns was the development of a vigorous tradition of resistance theory. In their attempt to justify resistance to unjust rulers, some writers resuscitated traditional political ideas such as those which held that rulers should be subject to legally defined constraints, or to those embodied in systems of regulation (the 'laws of nature') that were derived from God and were binding because of his supreme authority over his creation.

Some statements of these positions, like that advanced by Hobbes' young contemporary, John Locke, placed great weight on the fact that human beings are endowed with 'natural rights'. These rights belong to *all* human beings, and the interests specified by them have important implications for the ways in which political authority is structured and exercised. In both the mid-seventeenth and the late eighteenth century, ideas of natural rights played an important role in arguments about the regulation of political power. For example natural right theory played a significant role in justifying the revolutions in Britain's North American colonies in the 1770s and in France after 1790.

The fact that individuals possess natural rights does not mean that the only way their rights can be protected is through political participation. Nevertheless there is an important tradition in the history of political thought that relates natural rights to democratic forms of government. This argument was made by a very limited number of participants in the English revolution of the seventeenth century, but it assumed a more central place in Western political thinking from the second half of the eighteenth century. However, while writers such as the radical Anglo-American thinker Thomas Paine justified democracy by appealing to natural rights, and argued that contemporary forms of monarchical government were incompatible with the protection of these rights, democracy was also justified on other grounds. In the early nineteenth century Jeremy Bentham and other proponents of 'utilitarianism' argued that democracy is necessary to 'good government', that is, political authority should be exercised in such a way that it promotes the interests of *all* members of the community. This assumption has underwritten many nineteenth- and twentieth-century accounts of democracy, but in some important cases it has been given a distinctive cast by socialist thinkers. Socialists have

Chronology: Modern Period, c.1800—

Thinkers		Works		Contemporary Events
d. 1830	Constant, Benjamin	*Principles of Politics Applicable to All Representative Governments (1815)*	1804–14:	Napoleon I Emperor of France.
d. 1848	Chateaubriand, François	*Monarchy According to the Charter(1816)*	1815: 1815:	Defeat of Napoleon at Waterloo. Restoration of French monarch and many other rulers deposed during the revolutionary period.
d. 1831	Hegel, G.W.F.	*Elements of the Philosophy of Right(1821)*		
d. 1836	Mill, James	*Essay on Government (1820)*		
d. 1848	Wheeler, Anna	*Appeal (1825)*		
d. 1833	Thompson, William	*Appeal (1825)*		
d. 1858	Owen, Robert	*A New View of Society (1813)*		
d. 1834	Coleridge. S. T.	*Church and State (1831)*		
d. 1859	Austin, John	*Province of Jurisprudence Determined (1832)*		
d. 1881	Carlyle, Thomas	*Chartism (1839)* *Latter Day Pamphlets (1850)*	1848:	Revolutions in various European countries; establishment of Second French Republic.
d. 1858	Taylor, Harriet	*Enfranchisement of Women (1851)*		
d. 1859	de Tocqueville, Alexis	*Democracy in America (1835)*		
d. 1862	Thoreau, Henry	*Civil Disobedience (1849)*	1861–5:	American Civil War.
d. 1865	Proudhon. J.-P.,	*What is Property? (1840)* *Poverty of Philosophy (1846)* *Federation (1863)*		
d. 1873	Mill, John Stuart	*On Liberty (1859)* *Representative Government (1861)* *On the Subjection of Women (1869)*	1870:	Paris Commune; establishment of Third French Republic.
d. 1876	Bakunin, Michael	*Statism and Anarchy (1873)*		
d. 1882	Green, T. H.	*Lectures on the Principles of Political Obligation (1882)*		
d. 1883	Marx, Karl and	*The German Ideology (1845/7)*		
d. 1895	Engels, Friedrich	*The Communist Manifesto (1848)* *Capital (1867–)*		
d. 1900	Nietzsche, Friedrich	*Beyond Good and Evil (1886)* *The Genealogy of Morals (1887)*		
d. 1900	Sidgwick, Henry	*Elements of Politics (1891)*	1914–18:	First World War.
d. 1938	Kautsky, Karl	*The Class Struggle (1892)*	1917:	Revolution in Russia.
d. 1923	Bosanquet, Bernard	*Philosophical Theory of the State (1899)*	1918:	Abdication of German Emperor; creation of German Republic.
d. 1932	Bernstein, Eduard	*Evolutionary Socialism (1899)*	1919:	Adoption of Weimar Constitution by German Republic.
d. 1947	Webb, Sidney	*Industrial Democracy (1897)*	1922:	Mussolini becomes dictator of Italy.
d. 1921	Kropotkin, Peter	*Mutual Aid (1897)*	1927:	Consolidation of Stalin's position in Russia's Communist Party.
d. 1952	Maurras, Charles	*Enquiry into Monarchy (1900)*	1927:	Mao Tse-tung joins Communist Party.
d. 1923	Pareto, Vilfredo	*Socialist Systems (1902)*	1933:	Stalinist purge of Communist Party.
d. 1920	Luxemburg, Rosa	*Social Reform or Revolution (1950)*	1933:	Hitler Chancellor of Germany
d. 1940	Goldman, Emma	*Anarchism (1910)*	1935–39:	Civil War in Spain.
d. 1929	Hobhouse, L. T.	*Liberalism (1911)*	1937:	Japanese invasion of China.
d. 1920	Weber, Max	Various essays (c. 1919)	1939–45:	Second World War.
d. 1938	Bukharin, Nikolai	*ABC of Communism (1921)*	1945:	Fall of fascist regime in Italy and Third Reich in Germany.
d. 1940	Trotsky, Leon	*The Permanent Revolution (1928)*	1947:	Independence of India
d. 1941	Mosca, Gaetano	*The Ruling Class (1923)*	1949:	Creation of People's Republic of China.
d. 1945	Hitler, Adolf	*Mein Kampf (1925)*	1950:	Korean War.
d. 1945	Mussolini, Benito	'The Doctrine of Fascism' (1930)		
d. 1948	Gandhi, M.	*Nonviolent Resistance (1935)*		
d. 1973	Kelsen, Hans	*General Theory of Law and State (1945)*	c1950:	Civil Rights movements in United States.
d. 1937	Gramsci, Antonio	*Prison Note-books (1947)*	b. 1921	Rawls, John
d. 1961	Fanon, Frantz	*The Wretched of the Earth (1961)*	b. 1938	Nozick, Robert
d. 1964	King, Martin Luther	*A Letter from Birmingham Jail (1963)*		
d. 1976	Mao Tse-tung	Numerous essays		
d. 1992	Hayek, F. A.	*The Constitution of Liberty (1960)* A Theory of Justice (1971) Anarchy, State and Utopia (1974)		

argued that popular control of political institutions is necessary to eliminate the grossly inegalitarian and oppressive consequences of the development of modern capitalist economic structures. It should be noted, however, that socialists' understanding of these problems varies greatly. While some theorists have looked to a democratised state to regulate economic activity in such a way that it produces general benefits, others – most notably those influenced by the writings of the nineteenth-century founders of modern communism, Karl Marx and Friedrich Engels – maintain that capitalism is incompatible with true democracy. They have therefore promoted a revolutionary transformation that will destroy capitalism and the forms of political organisation that support it.

The movement towards democracy in the nineteenth century prompted a number of responses. Some writers (for example Edmund Burke and Joseph de Maistre in the late eighteenth and early nineteenth centuries, and Charles Maurras a hundred years later) sought to preserve benefits identified with traditional, monarchical forms of government. Others questioned the moral and practical desirability of democratic politics. For writers such as John Stuart Mill, democracy seemed likely to produce a morally and culturally stultifying 'tyranny of the majority', expressed in a legal form or through 'public opinion'. Mill thought that the conformist tendencies of unenlightened mass opinion would stifle intellectual discussion and 'experiments in ways of living' that are essential to human progress. He thus sought to insulate those whose intelligence and originality would contribute to social and moral progress from the impact of mass opinion by preserving individual freedom. Mill also favoured systems of government that gave a prominent role to enlightened elites.

While Mill thought that democracy posed a threat to individual freedom, a number of nineteenth- and twentieth-century writers rejected democracy because it conflicted with their ideas about the need for authority in human life. For them, authority was necessary to sustain social and political order, and to compensate for the intellectual and moral failings of ordinary members of the population. In the past the principle of state authority had been embedded in monarchs, but in the modern world it was necessary to identify new elites who could provide leadership in cultures that could no longer sustain traditional forms of government. Some conceptions of elite rule coexisted with political systems that were formally democratic, but others, such as fascism and national socialism, looked to new authority structures that were appropriate for mass societies. Aspects of fascism and national socialism bear a passing resemblance to traditional conceptions of authoritarian monarchical government, but they were underwritten by ideas that were a product of the democratic and modern cultures they rejected.

Themes

This book opens with a consideration of the *ends* of politics, that is, it examines a range of responses to the question: what is the primary goal of political institutions and particularly of the state? Consideration of this question allows us to explore views about the values that are fundamental to political life. Although accounts of the ends of politics vary greatly, almost all political theorists identify the state with the definition and maintenance of *order*. They argue that regardless of the specific purposes the state fulfils, it is necessary to provide a degree of regulation and coordination in human affairs that would not be possible in the absence of authoritative institutions such as the state. As we shall see, theorists of order often stress the need to impose acceptable patterns of behaviour on wilful individuals, but there is also an important tradition that has a more positive conception of order, one that focuses on its role in facilitating human cooperation.

Having surveyed these ideas, the remaining chapters in Part I will examine theories that specify the particular values that are to be realised by political institutions. While some theorists argue that politics should provide the means to foster human *virtue*, others have as their primary concern the protection and/or promotion of individual *freedom* or *happiness*, and use these to evaluate particular political forms and modes of political conduct.

Part II deals with arguments about the *location* of political power. It addresses a range of answers to the question: who should rule? Consideration of this issue raises the question of whether claims concerning the ends of politics have any implications for the distribution of political power within the community. The chapters in this part examine arguments about the desirability of placing power in the hands of a *single person*, a *restricted group*, or the *whole community*. Many treatments of these themes are framed in terms of preference for monarchy, aristocracy or democracy. However, ideas of single-person rule and rule by a restricted group are not confined to the types of government that are captured in conventional images of monarchy and aristocracy, but are extended to include modern conceptions of dictatorship and elite rule.

Those who argue in favour of rule by one, a few or many, hold that a particular way of distributing political power is markedly superior to others. Various writers thus identify particular types of regime with 'good government', that is, with systems of rule that are likely to be most conducive to the ends of government. But while accounts of the location of political authority are often seen as closely related to the possibility of good government, they are at most a *necessary* rather than a *sufficient* condition for its realisation.

In any case, claims about *who* rules are conceptually distinct from those that specify the *ways* in which political power should be exercised. Approaches to this issue are addressed in Part III. The general question to be considered there is: how should power be exercised if it is to promote the ends of politics? Many treatments of this issue are underwritten by the assumption that even those who are ideally suited to exercise power (and are therefore entitled to do so) may not always act in ways that promote the purposes for which political authority exists. Having recognised this possibility, a number of political theorists have sought to identify normative and/or institutional means of evaluating, and where necessary regulating, the exercise of political power. Three theories that address this issue are discussed in Part III. Various thinkers have relied on ideas of natural law and natural rights, while others have placed their trust in constitutional arrangements that prevent officeholders from acting unilaterally. In addition, it has been argued that those who exercise political power must do so within systems of legal regulation that are beyond their control. These regulations provide a framework that prevents governors from acting in ways that run contrary to the purposes for which government exists. All these accounts stress the need to constrain rulers, and thus they may be contrasted with those that regard supreme governors (or sovereigns) as the source of law, and rely on them to impose systems of self-regulation that are consistent with their responsibilities to those whom they rule.

Finally, Part IV examines a number of theories that deal with responses to the persistent misuse of political power by rulers. These theories address the question: to what extent, and in what ways, may the exercise and possession of political authority be challenged by those who are subjected to it? Answers to this question may be divided into two categories. Those is the first category, which will be discussed in the context of resistance to unjust rulers and theories of civil disobedience, present a challenge to particular lines of conduct or to particular aspects of public policy. In so doing, however, they do not question the general legitimacy of a particular form of government. The purpose of resistance and civil disobedience is to try to ensure that the exercise of political authority accords with the values that are thought to be inherent in particular political systems. These theories may be contrasted with theories of revolution (whether conducted by violent or non-violent means) since they hold that particular forms of government are inherently unjust. They then proceed to show that appropriate forms of human regulation can only be established after the existing political framework has been destroyed. The chapters in Part IV of this book examine medieval and early modern theories of resistance, various important statements of revolutionary political theory, particularly those produced by nineteenth- and twentieth-century socialists and anarchists, and theories of civil disobedience and non-violent resistance developed by a range of nineteenth- and twentieth-century thinkers. While some theories of civil disobedience and non-violent resistance seek to eliminate improper use of political power within generally acceptable political systems, others utilise non-violence to promote the overthrow of inherently unsatisfactory forms of rule and to facilitate the creation of systems of government that are capable of pursuing desirable ends.

PART I

The Ends of Politics

One of the key concerns of political theorists has been to specify the objectives of politics and to establish criteria against which political actions and institutions should be evaluated. This process is of great importance because it provides the basis for identifying institutions and practices that are seen as legitimate and to which individuals can be said to be obliged to conform. Legitimacy and obligation are closely related because it is assumed that human beings are more likely to regard themselves as being bound, or obliged, to accept outcomes produced by regulatory systems that satisfy primary values. When political theorists seek to explain and justify the exercise of political authority and the institutions in which it is embodied, they do so by relating them to objectives that are endowed with supreme moral and practical significance. These objectives may be seen as constituting the 'ends' of politics; that is, they are fundamental goals that can only be realised, or approached, through political means.

The following four chapters deal with a range of historically important theories that give pride of place to order, virtue, freedom and happiness as goals of politics. These themes have been central to the interests of political theorists over long periods of time, and they are sufficiently general to embrace a range of significant secondary values. This point can be illustrated by considering alternative values such as 'justice' or 'equality'. These ideas have played an important role in the history of political thought but they are often defined by reference to other, more fundamental ends. 'Justice' rests on a conception of rightness that can be related to the general order of society, to the primacy of individual freedom, or to the requirement that just institutions foster the well-being or happiness of those who are subjected to them. Similarly the idea of equality (the equal recognition of the claims and interests of all members of society) has been considered important because it promotes happiness, secures freedom and is necessary to the pursuit of human perfection or virtue, or because it is a prerequisite for the maintenance of a beneficial social and political order.

Order, virtue, freedom and happiness are distinct themes, but it is important to recognise that they are not mutually exclusive. Indeed it is common for political thinkers to associate a properly ordered state with a variety of values. However, for the purposes of analysis and exposition it is useful to identify a key value that forms the basis of particular thinkers' perceptions of the end of politics and to treat other values as derivative of, or dependent upon it. For example, while most writers think that human happiness is an important product of politics, many of them regard this value as a consequence of the pursuit of virtue: to live a virtuous life is itself conducive to happiness.

Although it is useful to identify a primary and distinctive end at the heart of a particular thinker's position, in a sense one end – the attainment of order – is of central concern to virtually all political theorists. This is true even of anarchists and Marxists, who look beyond politics to the creation of a state-less condition. Consequently Part I opens with an examination of a range of accounts of the relationship between politics and order. These theories specify how order should be achieved, and identify the central features of a desirable order. The subsequent chapters – dealing with virtue, freedom and happiness – examine ideas concerning ends of politics that go beyond the attainment of order.

Politics and Order

Political theorists have produced three general sets of arguments about the relationship between order and politics. First, the issue of order has been related to the need for coercive regulatory agencies to repress behaviour that threatens the stability of society and jeopardises beneficial human interaction. Secondly, order has been treated in more positive terms, and has been identified with establishing a basis from which human beings can reap the material, moral and psychological benefits of cooperation. Finally, one can identify a perspective on order that has played a prominent role in Marxist and anarchist political theory. Writers in these traditions view the state as an instrument of order, but they argue that it is necessary only because tensions between individuals and classes have resulted from oppressive and exploitative tendencies within modern societies. Marxists and anarchists believe that once the social and political structures of society have been transformed, a beneficial order based upon voluntary cooperation will emerge. This condition will be social, but it will not be political because it will lack both the state and the forms of coercive regulation that are central to politics.

This chapter opens with an examination of aspects of Greek and Roman political theory presented by Democritus, Protagoras, Plato, Aristotle and Cicero. The focus of ancient political theory was the *polis* or city state. Classical thinkers believed that a properly regulated *polis* formed an order that was directed towards the common good of its members and enabled them to cooperate in the pursuit of ideals that were fundamental to humanity. Although ancient writers recognised that the state played a regulatory and, where necessary, repressive role, their political thought emphasised the positive potentialities of politics.

The late-medieval writings of St Thomas Aquinas show how aspects of Greek and Roman political thought could be incorporated within a Christian framework. In the transition from the medieval to the early modern worlds, Machiavelli and other renaissance writers drew upon classical models when formulating largely positive statements about the appropriate type of order for city states. Neither Aquinas nor Machiavelli conformed to the general tendency for medieval and early modern thinkers to emphasise the repressive role of the state. A strong statement of this position appeared in the writings of the early medieval figure St Augustine, and his influence can be seen in the political ideas of Protestant reformers such as Martin Luther and John Calvin at the beginning of the early modern period. In the late sixteenth and seventeenth centuries the political turmoil that had marked the histories of France and England prompted a number of important thinkers to clarify the relationship between politics and order, and to stress the need for a unified agency or 'sovereign' that was not subject to any authority within the state. This largely negative perspective on order will be discussed here by refering to the writings of Jean Bodin, Hugo Grotius and Thomas Hobbes.

Since these accounts insist on the need for a single source of authority in the state, they are sometimes seen as actually or potentially authoritarian. It is important to note, however, that Bodin and his successors were making a point about the *logic* of government rather than promoting the harsh and repressive attitude towards the exercise of power that characterises conventional accounts of authoritarian rule. The latter reflect an aversion to popular government, a contempt for the intellectual and moral qualities of the bulk of the population, and a fixation with personal leadership that is not part of sovereignty theory. Development of this strongly repressive conception of order can be seen in the writings of a range of nineteenth- and twentieth-century theorists, including Thomas Carlyle, Charles Maurras, Benito Mussolini and Adolf Hitler. It is important to bear in mind, however, that some modern thinkers have advanced more positive accounts of politics that reflect earlier assumptions about order and cooperation. A range of writers, from Rousseau in the mid-eighteenth century to the late-nineteenth-century liberal thinker T. H. Green, will be discussed in the penultimate section of this chapter. The chapter will conclude with a brief preliminary discussion of Marxist and anarchist writers, who identify a positive conception of order with a non-political condition.

Cooperative Order in Ancient Political Theory: Protagoras, Democritus, Plato and Aristotle

The earliest surviving statements of Greek political theory were produced by Athenian writers in the fourth and fifth centuries BC. At that time Athens possessed a democratic structure, one in which all free, native-born, male adults were entitled to participate in the political life of the community. As can be seen in the accounts of Protagoras' political ideas in Plato's *Protagoras*, and in surviving fragments of Democritus's writings (see p. 22), the tradition of democratic politics in Athens produced a political and social order that related individual well-being to opportunities for cooperation. Protagoras argued that a shared sense of respect (*aidos*) and justice (*dike*) made it possible for human beings to compensate for their individual weaknesses by cooperating with one another (Plato, 1991, pp. 13–14). The fact that these qualities were possessed by *all* human beings provided the basis of a democratic order that was sustained by and fostered the distinctive attributes of its members (Farrar, 1992, p. 23).

Protagoras (born c. 485 BC)

Born in Thrace, Protagoras was a successful teacher of rhetoric. He travelled widely throughout the Greek world. He is said to have been a student of Democritus, but this claim is controversial. Protagoras's political ideas are presented in the dialogue by Plato that bears his name.

Like Protagoras, Democritus traced the origin of the state to the need for protection or security. Initially this goal was realised by the specification and enforcement of simple rules by individuals who saw that the maintenance of social order required the elimination of those whose selfish conduct was a threat to it:

If a thing does injury contrary to right
it is needful to kill it.
This covers all cases.
If a man do so
he shall increase the portion in which he partakes of right and security
in any [social] order (Havelock, 1964, p. 128).

From this exclusively negative conception of order emerged a growing appreciation that enforcement of basic rules by individuals served the interests of others, and this in turn gave rise to the sense of 'community' or shared interest that was embodied in the democratic *polis*. Both Democritus and Protagoras believed that because participation in the political life of the state fostered fruitful cooperation between all members of the community, it helped to legitimate the state in the eyes of its members.

The *polis* thus enjoyed the support of those whose individual excellence gave them a leading role in it, and of those ordinary members of the population who attended popular assemblies.

Democritus (c. 460–380 BC)

Like Protagoras, Democritus was a native of Thrace. An important scientific and political thinker, his ethical and political ideas are preserved in a number of fragmentary statements.

Identification of the *polis* with the satisfaction of fundamental human needs was endorsed by Plato, but he argued that a legitimate political order must have a hierarchical structure. Plato deduced this requirement from the division of labour, that underlies all human societies. In order to satisfy their basic needs, human beings cooperate with one another by engaging in specialised production and exchanging goods and services. These arrangements reflect what Plato took to be a primary fact about human beings, that is, they possess differing natural capacities, which equips them to fulfil only *some* of the functions required to supply their basic material needs. By restricting themselves to these functions, and by exchanging the products of their activity with others, individuals can satisfy their needs in the most efficient way. Plato claimed that the division of labour is a general principle of social organisation: it applies to political as well as to social functions and provides the basis for allocating them. Consequently he insisted that only limited sections of the population possess the necessary attributes to participate in the political life of the state. Plato's ideal state has a hierarchical structure based upon two distinct and exclusive classes: the 'producers', who engage in economic activity, and the 'guardians'. The latter are subdivided into two groups: the 'auxiliaries', who perform military and executive functions, and the 'guardians proper', who rule. Political functions are the sole preserve of the guardians because only they possess the necessary intellectual and moral qualities to exercise political power.

But while Plato rejected the premise of contemporary Athenian justice – that political order is based upon the participation of all members of the citizen body – he saw his ideal republic as an order that integrates humans with their fellows and makes the realisation of individual and collective aspirations interdependent. However, his insistence on a strict and exclusive division of functions – the guardians must dedicate themselves to ruling, and the producers should be excluded from any role in the political life of the state – means that most of the population are excluded from the political order, or at least experience it only as a form of external regulation. The type of order necessary to secure social cooperation therefore does not extend to *political* cooperation between all members of the community. This implication is reinforced by Plato's insistence that an erosion of the strict separation of functions will result in corruption of the ideal republic and inaugurate a slide towards dissolution and anarchy, that is, towards chronic disorder.

In addition to the politically truncated aspects of Plato's ideal republic, one should note that this structure is built on individual rather than social or political attributes. Thus while Plato appeared to subjugate individual aspirations to the requirements of what he took to be a just political order, his ideal republic actually rests upon assumptions concerning the psychology of individuals. The allocation of duties reflect what Plato regarded as the full range of distinctive individual attributes, and by this means he was able to claim that individuals realise their own nature by taking their appropriate place within a cooperative social order (Farrar, 1992, pp. 30–1). In other words, Plato argued that hierarchical order satisfies both the needs of the *polis* and those of its members.

Plato (427–347 BC)

The Greek philosopher Plato was born into the upper classes of Athens. He was a follower of Socrates, the principal figure in his philosophic dialogues. *The Republic* (c. 380 BC) and *The Laws* (unfinished), are the main sources of Plato's political theory. Except for brief periods in 367 BC and 361 BC, when he was invited to serve as a philosophical guide to Dionysius II, the ruler of Syracuse in Sicily, Plato lived in his native city. In the 380s BC he founded the Academy to provide an appropriate philosophical education for young members of the Athenian ruling class. Aristotle was among his pupils. Plato's ideas have been a source of inspiration throughout the history of Western political philosophy, all of which was once described as a 'footnote' to Plato.

While Plato's analysis in *The Republic* focused on an ideal state, his pupil Aristotle examined the relationship between different forms of political order and the differing socioeconomic bases of various communities (see p. 61). Aristotle thought that in some circumstances a strictly exclusive, hierarchical order may be appropriate, but he was far less sanguine than Plato about the difficulty of legitimising these arrangements in the eyes of those who are permanently excluded from office. Aristotle's identification of a most practical form of government was closely related to these empirically informed aspects of his political theory. He argued that in states with a mixture of classes, the most appropriate form of government – one that will be generally acceptable and will form an order that facilitates the pursuit of the good life – is 'polity'. Polity gives weighted recognition to various claims, thus reducing the risk of revolution and chronic disorder. It also minimises the risk of misuse of power by mechanisms that combine elements of aristocratic, oligarchic and democratic forms of government (see p. 172). Arrangements of this kind will provide the degree of stability and justice necessary to create an order in which the good life can be pursued in ways that are appropriate to the character of the community and of its individual members.

Aristotle (384–322 BC)

A native of northern Greece and a student at Plato's Academy, Aristotle established his own philosophical school in Athens in 335 BC. Between 343–340 BC Aristotle was tutor to the son of Philip II, King of Macedonia, later known as Alexander the Great. Aristotle's interests were wide-ranging. His major political work, *The Politics*, was compiled after his death from his lecture notes. This work bears the stamp of Aristotle's extensive research into different systems of government, and reflects his belief that questions about ultimate values can be answered by reference to the world of human experience, and not, as in Plato's theory, to a world of perfection to which human affairs should be brought into correspondence.

Despite the differences between Plato's and Aristotle's conceptions of order, they both emphasised its positive role and sought to identify political structures that would satisfy this fundamental goal of politics. Their general position on this question was endorsed by their Roman successor, Marcus Tullius Cicero (see p. 206). In his *Of the Republic* (c. 54 BC) the state (or 'commonwealth') was distinguished from 'any collection of human beings brought together in any sort of way', and defined as 'an assemblage of people in large numbers associated in an agreement with respect to justice and a partnership for the common good' (Cicero, 1970, p. 65). Subsequent discussions confirm the necessary relationship between justice and the form of order created by appropriate political structures (ibid., p. 219). For Cicero, as for his Greek predecessors, the order created through political means and embodied in the state is of fundamental significance to human beings because it produces a form of common life that is central to human fulfilment.

Negative and Positive Conceptions of Order in Medieval Political Theory: St Augustine and St Thomas Aquinas

The classical understanding of the centrality of order in politics was originally rejected by Christians because their aspirations were focused on the world to come. Unlike the writers discussed above, early Christians did not think that membership of a political community contributed to their pursuit of the ultimate goal of human existence. Nevertheless they still had to face the issue of how they should understand the political institutions with which they came into contact. During the course of the first four centuries after Christ, consideration of this problem gave rise to two distinct perspectives on order. By the early fourth century some Christians had begun to think that certain forms of political order were of great positive significance. Within a century however, this view was challenged by one that ascribed to political institutions a negative and largely repressive role in the pursuit of Christian goals.

The first of these positions marked a significant shift away from the originally antagonistic relationship between Christians and the political world of the Roman Empire. The conversion of the Emperor Constantine in 312 AD, seemed to mark a significant, even miraculous, shift in the relationship between the 'earthly' and 'heavenly' cities. It was argued that Christianised states have a special place in God's creation because, in cooperation with the Church, they embody the natural principles laid down by God and are thus of direct and ultimate value in terms of human salvation (Markus, 1991, pp. 94–102).

This general perspective was originally endorsed by St Augustine, the leading Christian philosopher of the early medieval period, but from about 390 AD he adopted a position that departed radically from the Christian version of the Greco-Roman perspective on order. This change is attributable to two developments. In the first place, following his ordination in 391 AD, Augustine's views were transformed by St Paul's account of the indelible and deep-seated implications of the sinful nature of humanity since the fall of man in the garden of Eden. The disobedience of Adam means that the order that leads to God cannot be found in human affairs. Harmony and just order will not be restored until humanity is 'saved', an event that will mark its reabsorption into the timeless realm of true divinity. The conclusion that Augustine derived from this conception of the status of temporal existence is that depravity and conflict are ineradicable features of human life. They can be tempered to some degree, but they will never be overcome.

St Augustine (354–430 AD)

Born into a middle-class family from Thagaste in Roman North Africa,
Augustine was educated in Carthage and Rome. He subsequently taught
rhetoric in Milan. Baptised in 387 AD, the following year Augustine returned
to Africa, where he was ordained priest in 391 and consecrated bishop of
Hippo in 395. His political ideas were presented in the *City of God* (413–27),
a wide-ranging work dealing with the relationship between paganism and
Christianity in the context of the late Roman Empire.

The political bearing of these theological insights was driven home to
Augustine by contemporary developments within the Roman Empire.
From 406 AD the western provinces of Rome were subjected to a series of
attacks by the Goths, which culminated in the sack of Rome in 410
AD. These events sparked dissension among the population over the
relationship between the decline of Rome and the increasing importance
of Christianity within the Empire. In particular it was claimed that
Rome was being punished for neglecting its traditional gods. As a
result of the apparent failings of what they had come to see as a God-
ordained political order and the controversies sparked by it, Christians
were compelled to reexamine the relationship between their faith and
political institutions. This issue was explored by Augustine in his *City of
God*.

Augustine's mature views on the political order can be divided into
discrete but related parts. He drew a sharp distinction between the
rational 'natural' order and the order of human existence through which
all must pass. The characteristics of the latter reflect God's response to
human sinfulness; it deals not with the rational and unchanging, but with
the fluctuating effects of the exercise of human will, often unguided by
any attachment to Christian values (Markus, 1991, pp. 109–12). Neither
political institutions nor such things as systems of law are part of the
cosmic order. In place of the orthodox idea of a Christian commonwealth,
Augustine advanced the idea that government is, and can only be, a
human product. He denied that states can embody true justice, and
offered a neutral account that relates the moral status of particular states
to the values adhered to by its members. The state is an 'association of a
multitude of rational beings united by a common agreement on the
objects of their love' (Augustine, 1972, p. 890). Since Augustine stressed
the sinful nature of humanity, he assumed that no earthly community can
be based on the love of God, nor can it be regarded as part of the natural
order that leads to God.

This general conception of political order underwrites Augustine's theory of the 'two cities': the 'city of God' and the 'earthly city'. Augustine saw these as distinct entities, each distinguished by the 'object of its love'. The city of God is timeless, does not correspond with any earthly realm, and provides a positive framework for the realisation of the supreme end for humanity. This city is coterminus with the 'earthly city', a term that Augustine applied to all political entities, including of course the Roman Empire. But while Augustine insisted that this city is not part of the order that leads to God, he argued that since Christians must, of necessity, spend their allotted time in the world, the earthly city is of some limited and passing benefit to them. Social life is natural, and Christians cannot withdraw from the company of their fellows. Because of sin, however, even the minimal degree of order necessary to ensure sociability cannot be secured without the controlling and guiding influence of the state. Political institutions can contain sin to some extent and can punish manifestations of sin when they occur. Moreover the earthly city can help to secure the enjoyment of what Augustine called 'temporal things'. Above all states can ensure a degree of peace and security, which is a prerequisite of social existence. The earthly city thus contributes indirectly to the realisation of Christian values, even though it is not positively related to the city of God:

> that part [of the Heavenly City] ... which is on pilgrimage in this condition of mortality... needs make use of this peace... until this mortal state, for which this kind of peace is essential, passes away. And therefore, it leads what we may call a life of captivity in this earthly city as in a foreign land, although it has already received the promise of redemption (ibid., p. 877).

The order maintained by the earthly city is negative in the sense that it focuses on the repression of conflict and the other disruptive consequences of sin; it is also negative because it has no place in God's cosmic order. Augustine stressed, however, that the political order is essential for members of both cities and insisted that members of the heavenly city must 'not hesitate to obey the laws of the earthly city by which those things which are designed for the support of this mortal life are regulated ...' (ibid., p. 877). Obedience is even due to cruel and tyrannical rulers as they produce a modicum of order and their harsh and arbitrary rule, a consequence of the sin of the tyrant, form part of God's providence. Thus while Augustine divorced political order from the natural order that leads to God, he gave it an important auxiliary role. He thus insisted that political authority is legitimate, and argued that Christians have an obligation to obey their political superiors.

Augustine's identification of political order with the need to repress at least some of the consequences of human sinfulness was very influential

in the medieval period and beyond. For example Martin Luther, the leading figure in the sixteenth-century Protestant Reformation, adhered to an
Augustinian conception of the relationship between government and
coercive regulation. This aspect of his thought brought him into conflict
with some of his more radical coreligionists (see pp. 309, 324–5). In the
late medieval period, however, there had developed an alternative to the
Augustinian position, one that not only revived aspects of the classical
tradition, but also involved the formulation of a far more positive view of
order. This development is associated particularly with the Italian monk
known to us as St Thomas Aquinas (see p. 29).

Aquinas' political theory was informed by first-hand knowledge of a
number of classical works that had been rediscovered in the late twelfth
century. Aristotle's influence was particularly important. Given Augustine's denial that politics forms part of the natural order, Aquinas' endorsement of the Aristotelian claim that humans are by nature political
animals is particularly significant. Aquinas regarded government as a
necessary consequence of sociability: 'The fellowship of society being …
natural and necessary to man, it follows with equal necessity that there
must be some principle of government within society'. Government is
necessary to provide an 'ordered unity' among groups of human beings
to ensure that 'in addition to the motives of interest proper to each individual there must be some principle productive of the good of the many'
(Aquinas, 1959, p. 5). A central point about Aquinas' understanding of
this requirement is that government is seen as a means of fostering effective cooperation, rather than a mainly repressive institution charged with
dealing with sin and its consequences. These aspects of Aquinas' thought
are brought together in the observation that government would be necessary even if the Fall had never occurred:

> because man is naturally a social animal … men would have lived in
> society, even in a state of innocence. Now there could be no social life
> for many persons living together unless one of their number were set in
> authority to care for the common good (ibid., p. 105).

As a Christian, Aquinas could not accept the idea that human fulfilment
takes place within the state, but he nevertheless believed that the order
created by politics is directly related to the cosmic order that leads to God.

The positive conception of order that appeared in Aquinas' writings
was echoed in a number of important late medieval and early modern
accounts of politics. Many of these theories were closely related to the
theological perspective that underlay Aquinas' philosophy. For example
the late medieval Italian thinker Marsilius of Padua stressed the cooperative features of an order produced within an appropriately structured city
state. The purpose of such an order – to ensure the peace and security of

those who participated in it – was directly related to their destiny as Christians. The city state also provided the focal point for Niccoló Machiavelli, but he related political order to a conception of human fulfilment that is in many ways overtly antagonistic towards the political implications of Christianity. Like the classical writers upon whom he drew, Machiavelli regarded participation in the political life of a republic as a way of both creating and enjoying the benefits of a political order that provides the basis for human fulfilment. Unlike earlier Christian writers such as Marsilius, Machiavelli insisted that the values enshrined in a popular republic are largely independent of, and in some ways hostile to, notions of politics that relate it to divine providence (see pp. 63–5).

St Thomas Aquinas (c. 1225–74)

Aquinas, a native of Sicily and a member of the Dominican Order, was educated in Naples, Paris and Cologne. He taught in the latter before returning to Italy, where from 1259–68 he wrote the first part of his major work, *Summa Theologiae*; the second part, which was never completed, was written in Paris between 1269 and 1274. Aquinas' political thought was part of a large-scale system of Christian ethics and was informed by his appreciation of Aristotle's writings. In addition to the *Summa*, Aquinas also wrote a treatise *On Princely Government* and commentaries on Aristotle's ethics and politics.

In addition to developing an account of a system of popular order created within a republic, Machiavelli also analysed 'princely' government, or rule by a single person. In this context, however, he stressed the need for the prince to maintain his supremacy over the state and to ensure that he is the sole active force in an order where the rest of the population is essentially passive. For example Machiavelli advised princes that it is better to be feared by their subjects than to rely on their love:

> whether men bear affection depends on themselves, but whether they are afraid will depend on what the ruler does. A wise ruler should rely on what is under his own control, not on what is under the control of others (Machiavelli, 1988, pp. 60–1).

By emphasising the negative rather than the positive aspects of an order appropriate to a principality, Machiavelli advanced a conception of the ends of politics that is similar to the one produced by a number of important early modern thinkers. In the one hundred years after 1570 the Frenchman Jean Bodin, the Dutchman Hugo Grotius and his English contemporary Thomas Hobbes each developed a theory of sovereignty that gave a new and distinctive expression to a conception of politics that emphasises the state's repressive role. These writers identified the need for an order that is created and maintained by a single orderer, and related government to the 'sovereign' or supreme authority within the state.

Order and Sovereignty in Early Modern Political Theory: Bodin, Grotius and Hobbes

Jean Bodin's most important work, *The Six Books of the Commonwealth*, was produced in the midst of the series of civil wars that broke out in 1562 and continued for the next thirty years. In these wars, fought between a French Protestant faction (the Huguenots) and Roman Catholics, the French crown often aligned itself with the Catholic cause. From 1571 Bodin was closely associated with the King's younger brother, the Duke of Alençon, who led a group called the *politiques*. The *politiques* were committed to the toleration of Protestantism, a policy that from time to time was pursued by the crown. However in an environment where armed fanatics roamed at will, toleration would have to have been enforced, and for much of the late sixteenth century the French crown was unable to achieve this. Its failure was, of course, largely a product of inadequate political will and restricted military capability, but these were in turn related to the prevailing understanding of the nature and extent of sovereign power, and of the purposes for which such power existed. Bodin was particularly concerned with appeals to 'customary law' (regulations based on cutomary practice), and with claims that certain officials and grandees could legitimately resist the crown. The *Six Books* reflected the *politiques'* belief that political authority exists to maintain order, not to realise particular conceptions of true religion. (Tooley, n.d., p. xi). It also advanced the claim that order cannot be preserved if there is more than one source of human authority in the state.

Bodin's treatment of the state reflects the influence of Christian accounts of the 'good life', which built upon Aristotle's theory. It is important to note, however, that he premised his position on the claim that the purpose of political authority is to maintain order. This concern is signalled in the title of the first chapter of Bodin's book ('The Final End of the Well-ordered Commonwealth') and in the sentence with which his work opens: 'A commonwealth may be defined as the rightly ordered government of a number of families, and of those things which are their common concern, by a sovereign power' (Bodin, n.d., p. 1). These statements make the relationship between politics and order and the need for an orderer a matter of definition, but in the course of his analysis Bodin provided some justifications for these claims.

Jean Bodin (1529/30–1596)

Bodin – a French legal official attached to the household of the religiously moderate Duke of Alençon from 1571 – wrote on historical, legal, political and religious topics. Although he was a firm supporter of the authority of the French crown during the wars of religion, he believed that royal power should not be used to promote particular religious views. Bodin's principal political work, *The Six Books of the Commonwealth* (1576), presented his theory of absolute sovereignty.

One of these arguments depends on a parallel being drawn between the family and the state. For Bodin (and for many of his contemporaries) the family forms a system of 'natural' order with a patriarchal structure, one in which fathers exercise supreme authority over the members of their families. (Schochet, 1975). The patriarchal family corresponds to historically and biblically sanctified patterns of authority that are replicated in an extended form in the state. Bodin thought that the assignment of supreme power to a single source is necessary to sustain the unity of both the family and the state, although he regarded this point as such an obvious one that he presented no arguments in direct support of it. However, to this vague (but no doubt effective) claim about the implications of patriarchal power, Bodin added a more cogent one relating to natural law.

The doctrine of natural law identifies a system of binding regulation that enables human beings to live in conformity with God's intentions (see pp. 199ff). Bodin accepted this general view of natural law, but he justified his claims about order by stressing the need for regulations to cover matters upon which the laws of nature are silent. Some issues must be decided by human authority, by what Bodin called 'will' not reason. Consequently there is a need for a human arbiter, one who can choose between morally indifferent alternatives that have to be determined and enforced if they are not to become causes of dissension. Bodin ascribed this role to the sovereign, and he stressed its importance if order is to be maintained in human affairs. He also identified a number of powers, or 'attributes', which he regarded as being exclusive to sovereigns because they are necessary for the maintenance of the commonwealth (see p. 254)

Given the circumstances in which he wrote, it is not surprising that Bodin gave precedence to the harmful effects of disorder, going so far as to imply that oppression is likely to be far less damaging than the conflict produced by insubordination and a weak or non-existent order. (Bodin, n.d., p. 14). At the same time, however, he was fully aware of the dangers arising from the misuse of political power, and he stressed that legitimate sovereigns are subject to natural law and answerable to God. He also argued that a wise ruler will seek the advice and assistance of officials, corporate bodies and representative 'estates'. These laws and institutions buttress sovereignty rather than detracting from it because they facilitate the 'right ordering' of the commonwealth and are not imposed upon the sovereign by his subjects. Representative or advisory bodies derived their legitimacy from the sovereign and for this reason can be seen as self-imposed constraints or safeguards (ibid., pp. 79, 106–7).

Hugo Grotius (1583–1645)

Grotius, a Dutch jurist and philosopher, served in the Dutch administration but was imprisoned when his patron Oldenbarnevelt fell from power. After escaping from prison Grotius entered the Swedish service, serving as Swedish ambassador to Paris from 1634. He wrote important works on natural law, including *Of the Law of War and Peace* (1625).

The idea that order will be jeopardised by subjects who think they are entitled to challenge their sovereign's right to rule, found its most thoroughgoing statement in the political theory of Thomas Hobbes. However important features of Hobbes' analysis were foreshadowed in Hugo Grotius' *The Law of War and Peace* (see pp. 214–16). Grotius' argument that legitimate government is created through the consent of those who are subject to it was a consequence of his contention that human beings possess 'natural rights', that is, rights that belong to them as individuals and are not the product of social recognition or political enactment. These rights consist of the power to prevent other individuals interfering with life, liberty and body, and with those material goods that are required for the sustenance of life. The right to these things implies also that prepolitical individuals have a right to punish those who infringe their other rights. If human beings act strictly in accordance with their rights, the human world will be naturally harmonious; it will form an ideal moral order in which there will be no need for government. However this ideal state of affairs is constantly threatened by malicious or ignorant behaviour that infringed natural rights and gives rise to conflict. Consequently Grotius identified a need for a political order, one regulated by a sovereign who promulgates and enforces laws to prevent individuals from improperly and immorally pursuing their rights. For Grotius, therefore, the necessity for a regulatory order is a consequence of human wrong-doing, and the purpose of government is to create an orderly environment in which individuals can safely and properly exercise rights that are intrinsic to them as human beings.

Grotius' position can be contrasted with that of Hobbes. Hobbes did not trace conflict to the *improper* exercise of rights. To the contrary, he argued that it is a necessary consequence of individuals acting on the basis of their rights in the absence of an overarching authority (Haakonssen, 1985, pp. 239–41). In the *Leviathan*, Hobbes produced an account of politics that was coloured by his experiences of the English Civil War and the events leading up to it. He made direct reference to contemporary disorders, particularly those produced by attempts to base political claims upon religious doctrines, or to give an independent political role to any person or institution other than the sovereign. The first of these objections applied as much to proponents of conventional ecclesiastical power as to radical sectarians; the second was directed at the pretensions of over-mighty aristocratic subjects of the crown and at those who claimed that the English parliament had an independent representative role. As Hobbes put it:

> If there had not first been an opinion received of the greatest part of England that these powers were divided between the King and the Lords and the House of Commons, the people had never been divided and fallen into this civil war; first between those that disagreed in politics; and after between the dissenters about the liberty of religion (Hobbes, 1960, p. 119).

These points of reference are important, but one must also bear in mind that Hobbes' *Leviathan* was presented as a generally valid, 'scientific' account of politics.

Hobbes' views on this matter reflect deep scepticism about the possibility of arriving at any elaborate and generally accepted account of moral truth (Tuck, 1984, pp. 104–5). This insight explains the range and intractability of the religious opinions that so exercised his contemporaries; it also shows why attempts to use these as the basis of politics were bound to produce conflict. The starting point of Hobbes' argument is an account of what life would be like in the 'state of nature', that is, a condition in which individuals are subject neither to the constraints of law nor to the effective influence of shared moral ideas. State of nature theory is an analytical rather than an historical tool. For Hobbes, as for a number of other political theorists, the location of human beings in a state of nature provides a way of specifying the benefits of political authority by identifying the problems that arise in its absence. By highlighting the features of the state that are necessary to eliminate these problems, state of nature theory identifies the key elements of a legitimate political order.

Thomas Hobbes (1588–1679)

Hobbes was a classical scholar, mathematician, philosopher and scientist, and was identified with the royalist cause during the English Civil War. He was tutor to the young Charles II when he was exiled in France in the late 1640s, but returned to England in 1652 and lived undisturbed under the Commonwealth and Protectorate. Hobbes' most famous political work, *Leviathan*, advanced a scientifically based defence of absolute government that was neutral on the question of who should rule, and was treated with great suspicion by many of his royalist colleagues. This book is often regarded as the most important English contribution to political philosophy.

In formulating a plausible account of natural human beings, Hobbes was obliged to moderate his scepticism by advancing a minimal (and he thought uncontroversial) assumption about human aspirations. Hobbes argued that because human knowledge of the afterlife is uncertain, and since death would put an end to human hopes, we can safely assume that people will agree to the proposition that death is an evil that is to be avoided for as long as possible. If death *is* an evil, it follows that avoidance of death is a 'right', that is, it is a goal that people will agree is legitimate for them and others to pursue. On the basis of this assumption, Hobbes built a set of moral propositions that he thought would be generally accepted. If individuals agree that it is right for human beings to preserve themselves, they will also recognise that it is right for them to do what is necessary to secure this end. Since this right extends only to what individuals think is necessary for their self-preservation, gratuitous damage to others is illegitimate because it contravenes this condition. In the state of nature, however, there are no authoritative agencies, so individuals must themselves judge what actions are necessary for their self-preservation (Hobbes, 1960, p. 84).

These three minimal rights (to self-preservation, to whatever is necessary for self-preservation, and to decide what is necessary) are the only certain points in a moral world beset by the uncertainty produced by scepticism. This lack of knowledge applies not only to normative beliefs – for example those concerning God's intentions for humanity or fundamental notions of justice – but also to the ideas and aspirations of other human beings. In these circumstances, private judgements that relate to self-preservation produce what Hobbes calls a 'state of war', a condition that carries misery and deprivation in its train:

> [D]uring the time men live without a common power to keep them all in awe, they are in that condition which is called war, and such a war, as is of every man against everyman.... In such condition, there is no place for industry, because the fruit thereof is uncertain: and consequently no culture of the earth; no navigation, nor use of the commodities that may be imported by sea; no commodious building; no instruments of moving and removing, such things as require much force; no knowledge of the face of the earth; no account of time; no arts; no letters; no society; and, which is worst of all, continual fear and danger of violent death; and the life of man, solitary, poor, nasty, brutish, and short (ibid., p. 82).

Hobbes' writings are sprinkled with grimly witty asides on human nature, but it should be noted that his analysis of the state of nature is not premised on human depravity. Even if people are moderate in their ambitions and generally good natured, a rational assessment of how they can best preserve themselves in a state of nature will inevitably propel them towards a state of war. In sharp contrast to the position advanced by Grotius, Hobbes argued that it is the exercise of rights that leads to conflict, not their abuse or disregard of the rights of others. Hobbes thought that this outcome is unavoidable because each individual has a right to judge the conduct of others and to respond in appropriate ways. Because natural individuals are roughly equal in the state of nature, Hobbes thought that they will be sanguine about their capacity to take what they want from others, and painfully aware of other's ability to take from them. Under these conditions

> there is no way for any man to secure himself, so reasonable, as anticipation; that is, by force, or wiles, to master the persons of all men he can, so long, till he see no other power great enough to endanger him: and this is no more than his own conservation require, and is generally allowed (ibid., p. 81).

Hobbes' account of life in the state of nature raises a number of complex and interesting questions that have exercised the ingenuity of his readers since *Leviathan* first appeared. These issues cannot be addressed here, but it is important to identify the general bearing of Hobbes' argument and to isolate the central problem with which he grapples. By stripping natural humans of any particular aspirations or ideas, Hobbes was being true to his radical scepticism. He was also making the point that the unavoidably subjective and relativistic nature of people's moral beliefs makes it impossible to rely on them to provide the basis for establishing beneficial human interaction. Elaborate moral and religious ideas, conceptions of virtue and so on, cannot provide a reliable basis for human life since they vary so greatly. But neither can those very minimal and uncontentious moral ideas that Hobbes derived from his basic axiom concerning widespread agreement on the desirability of sustaining human life. Indeed, in the state of nature the exercise of rights produces bitter conflict and misery, not peace and beneficial order.

Where private judgement reigns, where there is chronic behavioural uncertainty and no generally accepted rules of conduct, there can be no order, no stability, no certainty of outcomes. Since the unacceptable features of the state of nature are a consequence of its lack of order, Hobbes argued that its evils can only be avoided if humans place themselves in an orderly condition. This requirement means that they must abandon their right to private judgement on matters pertaining to self-preservation. It also necessitates the creation of an unquestioned and unquestionable source of public judgement. Hobbes dubbed this agency the 'Leviathan', an artificial creature (that is, one created by human beings rather than being found in nature) whose power establishes a system of certainty and peace to replace the uncertainty and discord of the state of nature. Hobbes' Leviathan is in fact the state, that is, a sovereign individual or collection of individuals that act 'in those things which concern the Common Peace and Safetie' and to whom individuals 'submit their wills, every one to his will, and their judgements, to his judgement' (ibid., p. 112). Once the state is created the sovereign is the source of all law, and rights are a matter of legal definition.

According to Hobbes, because a system of government based upon the principle of absolute sovereignty is the only way to avoid the evils of the state of nature, it is the only legitimate form of political authority. This state is fundamental to human well-being and is created by the voluntary actions of those who become the subjects of it. Individuals are therefore obliged to retain their place within this order and can be justly punished by the sovereign for failing to do so. Significantly, Hobbes believed that the consequences of a lack of order are so alarming that the threat of a return to the state of nature is far more to be feared than subjection to any conceivable sovereign. He observed that those who complain about the exercise of sovereign power fail to consider that

> the state of man can never be without some incommodity or other; and that the greatest [incommodity] that in any form of government can possibly happen to the people in general, is scarce sensible in respect of the miseries and horrible calamities, that accompany a civil war, or that dissolute condition of masterless men, without subjection to laws, and a

coercive power to tie their hands from rapine and revenge (ibid., p. 120).

In other words, the need for order is a fundamental requirement of human life, one that can only be satisfied by political institutions that replace private judgement with the authoritative and binding power of a sovereign.

The writings of Hobbes and his predecessors provide a series of trenchant and theoretically significant statements of the role that political institutions played in creating an orderly structure that provides the basis for human life. Despite the repressive aura surrounding Hobbes' Leviathan, and despite his insistence on the unquestionable supremacy of the sovereign, it is a mistake to identify his conception of order with the systems of authoritarian and totalitarian rule that have played such a devastating role in the twentieth century. While Hobbes thought that sovereigns should possess supreme coercive power, he saw no need for them to intrude into all aspects of the lives of their subjects. Moreover the rationale of sovereignty means that individual subjects need not obey sovereigns whose acts or omissions threaten their fundamental safety (see p. 261).

Seen in light of these considerations, Hobbes' work is best regarded as a theoretical statement of the need for a definitive political order in which the final right of determination rests with a clearly identified figure. One product of this conception of sovereignty was the 'command theory' of law, that is, the idea that law has a precise source and that this source creates an order that is subject to a unified agency (the sovereign). In the late eighteenth and early twentieth centuries this theory was an important element in the radical reformulation of political thinking promoted by 'utilitarian' philosophers in England (see p. 271). Utilitarians held that the actions of government should promote the 'greatest happiness of the greatest number', and they adopted Hobbes' command theory of law because it would serve to undercut extrapolitical claims (such as those derived from natural law or natural rights) and ensure that sovereigns would have both the right and capacity to frame systems of law that would conform to the requirements of the principle of utility. For these writers a political order with Hobbesian characteristics was necessary to produce good law, that is, a series of clear and unequivocal commands that would produce the greatest happiness of the greatest number. In the writings of the leading exponent of utilitarianism, Jeremy Bentham, the relationship between sovereignty and utility is made quite clear, but in those of his disciple, the jurist John Austin, there is a tendency to treat sovereign authority as a good in itself. This feature of Austin's position is apparent in his definition of law as 'a rule laid down for the guidance of an intelligent being by an intelligent being having power over him' and in his identification of this power with sovereignty (Austin, 1995, p. 18; Francis, 1980).

Bentham's and Austin's conception of law is similar in some important respects to that developed by the Austrian-American jurist Hans Kelsen in the middle of the twentieth century. Kelsen had strongly democratic sympathies but he deliberately avoided incorporating non-legal principles into his definition of law. He insisted that such a definition should rest upon a purely descriptive account of legal systems in terms of 'positive law', that is, law laid down and enforced by the sovereign. This approach led Kelsen to identify the state with its laws and to consider politics in terms of its relationship to a coercive order recognised by law. Kelsen acknowledged that states may adopt a variety of ends, but he argued that their distinctive and general characteristics derive from the fact that they comprise an order created and maintained though positive law (Kelsen, 1949).

Order, Authoritarianism and Totalitarianism in Modern Political Theory: Carlyle, Maurras, Mussolini and Hitler

The theories discussed in this section focus on an alleged incompatibility between the requirements of order and the tendency towards democratic or 'popular' government. Arguments of this kind became increasingly important in the nineteenth and twentieth centuries. Nineteenth-century examples of an overtly authoritarian perspective on order can be seen in the writings of Thomas Carlyle and Charles Maurras (see p. 40). Carlyle and Maurras were influential men of letters rather than systematic political philosophers, but their widely circulated writings contained lengthy and significant treatments of political themes.

Thomas Carlyle (1795–1881)

Born and educated in Scotland, Carlyle was one of the leading literary figures of the Victorian period. A non-traditional critic of democracy and parliamentary government, Carlyle urged his contemporaries to accept the need for new forms of elite leadership in modern societies. His political ideas are advanced in *Chartism* (1839), *Past and Present* (1843), *Latter Day Pamphlets* (1850) and elsewhere in his voluminous literary output.

Carlyle's political ideas were produced in response to the intellectual and spiritual uncertainties, and the resultant disorders, that he thought characterised English life in the 1820s and 1830s. He argued that these difficulties showed that human beings had lost touch with the modern requirements of a system of natural law that regulated the universe in line with God's intentions for humanity. Foremost among Carlyle's concerns was the credence his contemporaries gave to theories of government that minimised the guiding and regulating role of the state, and their tendency to look for the perfection of representative government and the advance towards democracy as solutions to the 'condition of England question'. In Carlyle's view, endorsement of a minimal state and working-class demands for full political rights are closely related: in the absence of effective elite leadership, the mass of the population are driven to find alternatives to what has, in effect, become a system of 'non-government'. Democracy is the epitome of this tendency because it places political control in the hands of those most in need of guidance and regulation. Carlyle did not deny that people have 'natural rights', but he gave a distinctive and authoritarian meaning to this idea. Their fundamental right is to appropriate leadership, 'the right of the ignorant man to be guided by the wiser, to be, gently or forcibly, held in the true course.' (Carlyle, 1980, p. 189). Carlyle insisted that the masses have to be *governed*; that is, they need to be placed within an order in which the more able few have a recognised claim to regulate human conduct so that it corresponds to the requirements of natural law. Carlyle attributed the disorderly condition of the working classes to their realisation of this necessity, and to their understandable yet futile attempts to find an alternative to a system that institutionalises elite self-interest and dereliction of duty. He assumed that humans' awareness of the need for direction will ensure their willing conformity to an appropriately structured hierarchical order.

In response to the weaknesses that he perceived in contemporary political culture, Carlyle placed increasing emphasis on the 'heroic' dimensions of effective political leadership. He argued that in times of rapid and destabilising change, society needs to be under the control of a 'heroic' statesman whose claim to preeminence is recognised by the general population. In his later writings (dating from the 1840s) Carlyle applauded powerful and decisive rulers such as Oliver Cromwell and Frederick the Great of Prussia, and implied that determination to subjugate the population is a significant indicator of political greatness. These features of Carlyle's later political writings obscure his consistent belief that political authority exists for the intellectual, material and moral benefit of the ruled.

Like Carlyle, the French writer Charles Maurras waged war on the liberal and democratic assumptions that were prevalent in modern European culture. Maurras' primary targets were the ideas of individual autonomy and equality espoused by radical republicans in France. In response to these doctrines, Maurras reiterated conventional right-wing ideas that had first been formulated by Joseph de Maistre in the late eighteenth and early nineteenth centuries (see p.141). Maurras insisted that inequality and dependence are inescapable features of the human condition, and he argued that they require human relationships to be ordered in a hierarchical pattern. Republican ideas of liberty, equality and fraternity thus fly in the face of the requirements of nature, and give rise to conditions of moral and practical anarchy. 'Revolutionary legality has broken up the family, revolutionary centralism has killed community life, the elective system has bloated the state and burst it asunder' (Maurras, 1971b, p. 254). Republican systems of government undermine the idea of order by ignoring the hierarchical principles embodied in the patriarchal family and also in the social and political structures of the most long-lived and successful European states (Maurras, 1971c, p. 266). Maurras believed that these insidious ideas were so ingrained in the mass mind of European societies that it was almost impossible even to 'propagate the notion of order' (Maurras, 1971b, p. 256).

Charles Maurras (1868–1952)

Maurras was a journalist, literary figure and central player in the right-wing movement *Action Française*. His love for the monarchy and the French Catholic Church was matched by his unremitting hatred of democracy, republicanism and individualism. In common with a number of right-wing contemporaries in France and national socialist and fascists movements elsewhere in Europe, Maurras' political thought contained a strong thread of anti-Semitism.

Maurras' original preference was for the restoration of absolute monarchy (see p. 143), but towards the end of his life he threw his support behind Marshall Pétain, the leader of the regime established in the southern part of France following the defeat of the Third French Republic by the Germans in 1940. As the royalist tradition in France had shown itself to be impotent, Maurras was forced to look for an alternative source of authority. Thus while aspects of Maurras' conception of order harked back to Maistre, others looked forward to the political ideas that became commonplace in the fascist and national socialist movements that emerged in Italy and Germany in the 1920s.

These movements were virulently antiliberal and antidemocratic, and sought to establish a new order that would form a distinctive kind of authoritarian state. This point was made quite explicit in the definitive statement of fascist doctrine written jointly by the political head of the Italian movement, Benito Mussolini, and by the academic philosopher Giovanni Gentile. In this essay Mussolini and Gentile warned that 'One does not go backwards. The Fascist doctrine has not chosen Maistre as its prophet. Monarchical absolutism is a thing of the past' (Mussolini, 1935, p. 25). Although fascists rejected the nineteenth-century tradition of liberal democracy, they conceived of the state as an 'organised, centralized, authoritarian democracy', the purpose of which was to forge the population into a system of order that was 'collectivist' and 'spiritual' rather than 'individualistic' and 'materialist' (ibid., p. 24). Mussolini and Gentile's rejection of these features of modern democratic political culture is clear enough, but their positive statements on the goals of the fascist state are expressed as broad-ranging, vague generalities that conjure up a vision of radical national revitalisation, a process that would recapture the heroism of the Roman Empire for the modern Italian state.

Benito Mussolini (1883–1945)

Originally a left-wing journalist, in the years after the First World War Mussolini led the Italian Fascist Party in their successful attempt to gain control of the government formally headed by the King of Italy. Mussolini took the title of 'Il Duce'.

Redefinition of the relationship between the state and its members was central to this vision. Gentile and Mussolini rejected any idea that the state is an instrument that merely serves the interests of individuals or groups. To the contrary, the process of national renewal necessitates the realisation of the primacy of the state itself: it is an 'absolute before which individuals and groups are relative' (ibid., p. 25). Its primary purpose is to impose order through the efforts of an authoritative leader: 'Empire calls for discipline, co-ordination of forces, duty and sacrifice' (ibid., p. 30). These qualities had ossified under liberal democracy, and the proponents of Italian fascism made the recreation of order the prime objective of their political practice and a prominent theme in their political thinking.

While Italian fascism assumed a national political and cultural focus, the key theme of German national socialism was 'race'. National socialist thought and practice was ambiguous about whether the state or the party was the embodiment of its world view (*weltanschauung*), but its ideologists made it clear that political institutions were to be regarded as the handmaidens of race. Thus Adolf Hitler claimed that 'In the state [national socialism] sees on principle only a means to an end and construes its end as the preservation of the racial existence of man' (Hitler, 1969, p. 348). Alfred Rosenberg, the leading formal ideologist of the national socialist movement, made much the same point (Rosenberg, 1971, p. 192). However, since the national socialists insisted that controlled breeding, territorial expansion and the elimination and/or subjugation of allegedly 'inferior' but biologically and morally threatening racial groups was necessary to preserve the interests of the 'master race', they believed that political institutions were of central importance. The alleged 'master race' was superior to all others, but its members varied in their capacities to such an extent that the vast majority of them had to be placed under the control of 'creative minds' who possessed the insight and determination needed to protect the interests of their race. These individuals had a right to control the state and to impose 'disciplined obedience' on the masses. In short, the leaders of the national socialist state were responsible for creating an order that would ensure the survival of its 'superior' racial elements. The hierarchy of racial groups could only be maintained if the principle of hierarchy structured the political life of the 'master race' (see p. 146).

Cooperation and Order in Modern Political Theory: Rousseau, Kant and Green

The ideas discussed in the previous section represent an extreme version of a largely negative and repressive conception of order. Although this conception has played a significant role in the history of modern political thought, it has not gone unchallenged. Important strands in modern political thinking mirror those of the ancient and medieval periods in presenting strongly positive accounts of the relationship between politics and order that focus on their role in promoting cooperation. This point can be illustrated by refering to the works of Jean-Jacques Rousseau, a key figure in the late eighteenth century whose ideas had a profound influence on later political thinking.

In *The Social Contract* (1762) Rousseau rejected accounts of government (identified with both Hobbes and Grotius) that explain order and obedience by reference to fear. Rousseau objected to these theories because they at best describe the basis of many political regimes rather than providing moral justification for them. Rousseau argued for forms of political association that respect the personal interests of their members while providing a way of furthering a new and distinctly cooperative interest that is formed by the creation of the association itself. This interest is directed towards matters of common concern, or those things people share as members of the community. Rousseau argued that while the particular wills of individuals are directed towards their interests, the common interest is promoted by the 'general will'.

The idea of the general will is central to Rousseau's cooperative conception of political order. For Rousseau the primary issue in politics is to identify and maintain a form of order that will allow human beings to reap the benefits of interdependence while avoiding domination and manipulation. These tendencies are inherent to situations where human interaction and dependence are not subject to regulations that are directed towards the pursuit of common interests. Rousseau believed that human interdependence makes order a necessity; the choice is between an order that serves the interests of only some sections of the population, and one that is designed to further those aspects of human life in which the benefits of cooperation have given rise to common interests. Rousseau argued that an appropriate order can be created by a process of 'contract', or agreement, between free beings. By renouncing their natural, prepolitical freedom, individuals can create

> a form of association which defends and protects with all common forces the person and property of every associate, and by means of which each one while uniting with all, nevertheless obeys only himself and remains as free as before.... [T]his act of association produces a moral and collective body (Rousseau, 1987, p. 148).

Jean-Jacques Rousseau (1712–78)

A native of the Swiss city-state Geneva, Rousseau's philosophical reputation developed after he moved to France in 1742. Although closely associated with leading figures in the French Enlightenment, Rousseau was sceptical of the assumptions about human progress to which these writers subscribed. Rousseau's writings deal with the arts, education, science, literature and philosophy. His most important political writings are *Discourse upon the Origin and Foundation of Inequality Among Mankind* (1755) and *The Social Contract* (1762). The ambiguities of Rousseau's legacy are apparent in the writings of Hegel, Marx, T. H. Green and Lenin.

An important feature of Rousseau's position is that political institutions form an order that enables a new form of human existence: the pursuit of shared values means that humans can be both *individual* and *social* beings. The transformative implications of political order are also apparent in the

contrast that Rousseau's German successors drew between the potentialities of a regulated environment and the limitations of a situation where
people seem to be free to follow their own inclinations. For example the
late-eighteenth-century philosopher Immanuel Kant (see p. 69) wrote that
while human beings are obliged to interact with their fellows in order to
satisfy their needs,

> their inclinations make it impossible for them to exist side by side
> forlong in a state of wild freedom. But once enclosed within a precinct
> like that of civil union, the same inclinations have the most beneficial
> effect ... All the culture and art which adorn mankind and the finest
> social order man creates are fruits of his unsociability. For it is com-
> pelled by its own nature to discipline itself, and thus, by enforced art,
> to develop completely the germs which nature implanted (Kant, 1971,
> p. 46).

If human beings are naturally social, political order will be unnecessary,
but since they are not, their inclinations oblige them to establish a
rational legal order to satisfy their needs, and to ensure that they
perform their moral duty by satisfying the requirements of justice.
Kant distinguished a union 'of many individuals for some common
end which they all *share*' from one in which they 'all *ought to share*'. He
identified the latter with a system of 'public right' that is the
subject matter of politics. (ibid., p. 73). It is necessary for human beings to
cooperate in the creation and maintenance of a system of public right in
order to minimise the risk of unjustly infringing the freedom of individuals.

The creation of a political order thus makes it possible for humanity to
pursue what Kant took to be its moral mission. While he gave due weight
to the coercive dimensions of systems of public law, Kant's perspective
on order is a generally positive one. The same point can be made
about some of his successors. Thus in early-nineteenth-century Germany,
G. W. F. Hegel (see p. 87) developed an elaborate account of the modern
state that stresses the extent to which it provides a moral, psychological
and political framework for realising the conceptions of personal and
collective well-being that are characteristic of the modern world. Hegel
argued that the 'essence of the modern state is that the universal should
be linked with the complete freedom of particularity and the well-being
of individuals' (Hegel, 1991, p. 283). That is, it forms an order that
expresses humans' conceptions of both the individual ('particular') and
social ('universal') dimensions of their lives and integrates these into a
harmonious whole (see p. 88).

Aspects of both Kant's and Hegel's political philosophy played an
important role in the thought of the late-nineteenth-century British

writer T. H. Green. In stating his position Green focused explicitly on what he regarded as the inadequacies of the positions formulated by Hobbes and Austin. Green rejected Hobbes' account of sovereignty on the grounds that he could only explain the sovereign's possession of 'powers' not rights, and that he had misconstrued rights as something that individuals can possess as individuals (Green, 1986, pp. 44–5). For Green, in contrast, rights rest on *social* recognition: they are necessary if individuals are to contribute freely to the common good they share with their fellows. Rights are thus of crucial importance in allowing individuals to realise a conception of well-being that relies upon freely made contributions to shared aspects of their existence. In a clear reference to Hobbes' position, Green insisted on the common nature of the good and the need for rights to be recognised by all members of the community:

> Until the object generally sought as good comes to be a state of mind or character of which the attainment, or approach to attainment, by each is itself a contribution to its attainment by every one else, social life must continue to be one of war (ibid., p. 279).

T. H. Green (1836–82)

Sometimes viewed as the first professional political philosopher in England, Green made a career as a teacher at Oxford University. He reformulated liberal values and their political implications to take account of the importance of the interpersonal conditions of moral autonomy. Green's most important political work, *Lectures on the Principles of Political Obligation*, appeared posthumously, but he exerted a profound influence over those who came into contact with him at Oxford.

Green thus argued that the idea of order and the obedience rendered to the political superiors who create and maintain it, have to be explained by reference to a widely held perception that the sovereign embodies the general will of the community and upholds a system of rights that is recognised by its members (ibid., p. 68). Sovereignty was as important to Green as it had been to Hobbes and Austin, but he understood it in relation to the role it plays in creating an order that enables human beings to coordinate their activities and thus realise aspirations that are necessarily social. Consequently,

It is more true to say that law, as the system of rules by which rights are maintained, is the expression of a general will than that the general will is the sovereign. The sovereign, being a person or persons by whom in the last resort laws are imposed and enforced in the long run and on the whole, is an agent of the general will – contributes to realise that will (ibid., p. 75).

Rousseau, Kant, Hegel and Green all ascribed a central role to the state in defining and maintaining an order that will enable human beings to realise the potentialities for cooperation that they regard as fundamental to human well-being. Unlike those thinkers who focused on the repressive and regulatory role of the state, these writers related order to the necessarily social dimension of human life, and treated politics as reflections of this dimension rather than being responsible for it. This conception of politics is epitomised in Green's claim that 'will not force is the basis of the state', and in his related argument that for those with a developed sense of moral and social responsibility the coercive character of law is displaced by its role as a guide and coordinator of human actions. (ibid., p. 89ff).

Order without Politics: Anarchism and Marxism

In concluding our consideration of order as an end of politics it is useful to highlight the distinctive and pervasive character of this position by glancing at a rival tradition that has become significant in nineteenth- and twentieth-century political theory (see pp. 94ff). Anarchists and Marxists were bitter opponents in the history of modern revolutionary socialism, but despite the intractable nature of their rivalry they had a similar view of the relationship between politics and order. Both in terms of its stress upon community as the central agency through which individuals realise their potentialities, and its historical connections with both Rousseau's and Hegel's thought, this tradition developed in overt opposition to that sketched in the previous section.

Like Rousseau's successors, anarchists and Marxists believed individual well-being to be materially, morally and psychologically dependent upon social cooperation, and they sought to specify an order in which these aspirations could be satisfied. However they argued that cooperative order is an exclusively *social* phenomenon, and considered that political institutions, and above all the state, are incompatible with it. Indeed opponents of the state justified its role by reference to tendencies to disorder that are integral to it, and will not occur in its absence .

Anarchists and Marxists offered a variety of explanations for the existence of the state, all of which point to its lack of legitimacy and the absence of any true basis for subjects' obligations to it. 'Social' anarchists and Marxists believed that the exploitative and antisocial implications of private property create tensions that can only be constrained by political authority, but they denied that such authority is a neutral force. To the contrary, the inequalities of power produced through the exploitation of property is reflected in the domination of the state by those who control the material resources of society. While individualistic anarchists were not generally opposed to private property, both they and social anarchists launched radical critiques of all ideas of imposed authority, including those associated with conventional expressions of religion, with all forms of external political leadership and with conventional ideas of law.

The various targets of anarchist criticism were neatly summarised by Emma Goldman:

Religion, the dominion of the human mind; Property, the dominion of human needs; and Government, the dominion of human conduct, represent the stronghold of man's enslavement and all the horrors it entails (Goldman, 1911, p. 59).

Goldman characterised anarchism as 'the philosophy of a new social order' (ibid., p. 56). and contrasted its natural basis with the artificial and counterproductive impositions of government. Government created a tenuous order 'derived through submission and maintained by terror', while anarchism held out the prospect of a 'true social harmony' that grew 'naturally out of solidarity of interests' (ibid., p. 65).

Emma Goldman (1869–1940)

Born in Lithuania (then part of the Russian Empire) and educated in Prussia, Goldman lived in St Petersburg until 1885, when she moved to the United States. Goldman was active in socialist and anarchist politics and was imprisoned in 1917 for her part in an anticonscription campaign. Upon her release from prison in 1919, Goldman was deported to Russia. She quickly became disillusioned with the course of the revolution, and in 1921 she left Russia to spend the rest of her life in exile in various European states. A number of Goldman's anarchist writings were published in 1910 under the title *Anarchism and Other Essays*.

Features of anarchism and Marxism will be examined more closely in subsequent chapters. At this stage, however, it is important to note aspects of the relationship between these rejections of political order and some of the views discussed above. First, there is a sense in which anarchists and Marxists saw the state in terms that echo aspects of Hobbes' theory. Given the implications of private property and other sources of coercion, there *is* a need for a coercive state to keep in check those tendencies that Hobbes associated with the state of nature, and that both anarchists and Marxists thought lay just below the surface of the order maintained by the state. Second, given the inequalities and exploitation that make the state necessary, the idea that individuals can create a political structure that reflects their shared interests is illusory. These inequalities are merely embedded in the political order. In any case, the whole idea of the social contract is flawed because it assumes that individuals can be something other than social beings. Far from creating the basis of a viable social order, the creation of the state negates it. As the Russian anarchist Michael Bakunin put it, 'there is no room in this theory for society, only for the State ... society is totally absorbed by the State' (Bakunin, 1973, p. 137). Finally, Marxists and many anarchists offered a backhanded endorsement of Hegel's conception of the state, but they insisted that it merely sustains an uneasy balance between intractably conflicting interests rather than resolving them. Paradoxically, the elevated idea of the political order advanced by Hegel was necessary only because of the irresolvable tensions created within its underlying social structure. As Marx argued, the illusory qualities of Hegel's state are necessary if it is to fulfil its role in a corrupt environment. In place of the order created by the state, both anarchists and Marxists sought to identify a social order based on true sociability and in no need of the state.

Conclusion

The writers discussed in this chapter believed that identification and maintenance of an appropriate order was a precondition for worthwhile forms of human existence. Except in the case of anarchist and Marxist views of a post-revolutionary condition, the coercive and persuasive capacities of the state were thought to be essential for the creation of order. Order was usually related to human benefit, but in some cases the need for it was seen as a requirement imposed upon humanity in fulfilment of its obligations to God, or as being necessary for the realisation of goals that are fundamental to human beings. The latter of these positions played an important role in ancient political thought, while the former has been central to a long tradition of Western thinking within a Christian framework.

The claim that the state is necessary to produce order gave rise to related ideas about the *form* the state should take. That is, it is argued that only certain types of political organisation are conducive to the maintenance of an appropriate order. In many cases, a focus upon order resulted in the rejection of popular government and the promotion of hierarchical political and social structures. As a modern scholar has remarked of seventeenth-century political thought, 'order theory was a statement of the immutably hierarchical nature of the political world' (Burgess, 1992, p. 134). The need for the state was justified by the wilfulness of ordinary human beings and their inability to subject themselves voluntarily to effective forms of regulation. It should be noted, however, that order was not necessarily seen as incompatible with popular government. Both Bodin and Hobbes thought that democratic institutions are capable of producing order provided they conform to the requirements of an absolutist conception of sovereignty, while Rousseau and his successors sought to identify the main characteristics of forms of government based on egalitarian rather than hierarchical principles.

Finally, it is useful to distinguish 'negative' conceptions of order from those with a 'positive' orientation. As we have seen, theorists such as Augustine, Luther, Hobbes and modern proponents of authoritarian government treated political order as a means of repressing wrongdoing and/or compensating for the moral and intellectual shortcomings of large sections of the population. In contrast thinkers such as Plato, Aristotle, Aquinas, Rousseau, Hegel and Green took a more positive approach that related particular forms of order to the desirability of establishing cooperative conditions in which human beings could pursue other fundamental values.

CHAPTER 2

Politics and Virtue

This chapter will focus on the ideas of a number of important thinkers who identified politics and the most central of political institutions – the state – with the pursuit of ultimate moral values. For these thinkers, politics itself, and the organisation of political institutions, played a crucial role in the practice of the virtue, and contributed thereby to the pursuit of human perfection. In other words, politics was seen as an activity that was centrally concerned with the promotion of human goodness. Some of the writers discussed in this chapter argued that a properly ordered state would directly promote the moral goodness of its members, while others saw political authority as a means of facilitating the pursuit of moral goodness by members of the state. In both cases, however, the focus on virtue did not mean that other ends, for example happiness and freedom, were ignored. As we shall see, a number of important political philosophers argued that virtue and freedom are closely related, and it was generally held that true happiness is dependent upon a proper appreciation of moral goodness. However, in the conceptions of politics discussed in this chapter, values such as freedom or happiness were treated in relation to the pursuit of virtue: that is, they were valued because of their connection with moral goodness.

The chapter will open with a discussion of Plato's and Aristotle's political thought. Both these thinkers examined the relationship between virtue and the distinctive form of political existence that was made possible by membership of the city state or *polis*. Aspects of ancient political thinking played an important role in medieval and early modern Europe, the focus of the second section of this chapter. In these periods the idea of virtue was applied to nation states as well as city states and was set within a Christian framework. This last consideration meant that discussions of the relationship between politics and virtue were coloured by developments such as the Protestant Reformation. One consequence of the turbulence produced by the interaction of religious and political aspirations was the rejection of 'virtue politics' by a number of important seventeenth- and eighteenth-century political thinkers. However, as will be shown in the last section of this chapter, the late-eighteenth-century German philosopher Immanuel Kant and a group of late-nineteenth-century English writers revived this way of thinking about the ends of politics. Yet they focused on the role that political institutions could play in facilitating the development of the moral character of members of the community. In these theories the promotion of moral goodness provides the ultimate justification for political life, but external agencies such as the state can only play an indirect role in its promotion.

Politics and Virtue in Ancient Political Theory: Plato and Aristotle

Identification of a direct relationship between politics and virtue is one of the central themes of the Western tradition of political thought. This tradition originated in the writings of Plato and Aristotle, the foremost political philosophers of the ancient world. These writers are identified closely with the flowering of philosophical activity that marked the high point of the intellectual and political predominance of Athens among the city states of the Greek world in the late fifth and early fourth century BC. It is significant, however, that their lives spanned a period when the political and military status of Athens underwent a great and painful change. Plato (see p. 23) was born in 428–27 BC, shortly after the start of the great Peloponnesian War, and by the time of his death in 348/47 BC he had witnessed Athens' defeat by its rival Sparta in 404 BC, and the temporary overthrow of its democratic form of government in the same year. Nine years after his death the city states of Greece were absorbed into the Macedonian Empire of Alexander the Great, a figure with whom Plato's pupil Aristotle was closely associated.

The political structure of Sparta was based on a numerically restricted, hereditary class that dedicated itself to military duties and to controlling a large slave population. In contrast, although neither slaves, resident aliens nor women possessed political rights in Athens, the political culture of this state was relatively liberal and open. Free adult males exercised a range of political rights and were entitled to play a role in the public life of the city. Athenians' pride in their political institutions and way of life was exemplified in the funeral oration given in 431 BC by the political and military leader Pericles at a ceremony in honour of those who had fallen in the first year of the Peloponnesian War:

Our constitution does not copy the laws of neighbouring states; we are rather a pattern to others than imitators ourselves ... If we look to the laws, they afford equal justice to all in their private differences.... We celebrate games and sacrifices all the year round, and the elegance of our private establishments forms a daily source of pleasure.... We throw open our city to the world, and never by alien acts exclude foreigners from any opportunity of learning or observing;... while in education, where our rivals from their very cradles by a painful discipline seek after manliness, at Athens we live exactly as we please, and yet are as ready to encounter every legitimate danger.... In short, I say that as a city we are the school of Hellas; while I doubt if the world can produce a man, who where he has only himself to depend upon, is equal to so many emergencies, and graced by so happy a versatility, as the Athenian (Thucydides, 1968, pp. 93–5).

The *polis* of Periclean rhetoric reflected its distinctive qualities at the high point of its development. Even allowing for the nervous exaggeration that often marks contemporary reactions, it is generally acknowledged that Plato and his contemporaries confronted a rapidly changing world. The rise of Athens as a regional power transformed the character, direction and scale of political activity in the city, and during Plato's life the impact of this transformation was aggravated by the experience of war, defeat and revolution. The instincts that Plato brought to bear on these developments were generally conservative. One indication of this orientation was his initial enthusiasm when rule by 'the many' (the *demos*) was replaced by a dictatorship of thirty men identified with the long-established, well-to-do Athenian families from which Plato came. This coup, which took place in 404 BC, was shortlived, and so too was Plato's endorsement of it. But although 'the thirty's' cruelty, illegality and self-interest led Plato to withdraw his support for them, his initial approval of the overthrow of popular government in Athens reflected a deepseated disenchantment with contemporary democratic politics and the moral attitudes that underwrote it.

Plato's views on the moral basis of political corruption are apparent in his critical treatment of two sets of relative newcomers in Athenian politics: the 'sophists', specialised, professional teachers, epitomised in the figure of Gorgias, after whom one of Plato's dialogues is named; and the 'demagogues', ambitious politicians, often from the *nouveau riche*. The sophists, who first made their appearance in Athens in the fifth century BC, prided themselves on imparting skills of a general, non-specialised nature to those who wished to make their mark upon the public life of their city. In Plato's works (and one should note that these do not necessarily provide a reliable guide to anything other than Plato's perceptions) Gorgias and his colleagues are closely identified with the art of rhetoric, and with a moral viewpoint that may be described as 'relativistic'. Moral relativists argue that conceptions of justice reflect the requirements of particular groups of people, not immutable, universally applicable ideas. Since there are a variety of such groups, one must accept that basic behavioural norms will vary from place to place and from time to time. As we shall see, this view was anathema to Plato. In any case, he tended to impute to the sophists the idea that moral standards are merely a matter of expediency and may quite accurately (and perhaps more honestly) be specified in the language of self-interest or power.

Plato associated moral relativism and rhetoric with the theory and practice of contemporary Athenian democracy. He thought that demagogues were ingratiating themselves to the least enlightened and most numerous members of the citizen body by pandering to their partial and narrow conception of their own self-interest. In the *Gorgias*, Plato likened oratory to the 'false art' of cookery:

> [it] pays no regard to the welfare of its object, but catches fools with the bait of ephemeral pleasure and tricks them into holding it in the highest esteem.... Now I call this sort of thing pandering and I declare that it is dishonourable ... because it makes pleasure its aim instead of good, and I maintain that it is merely a knack and not an art because it has no rational account to give of the nature of the various things that it offers (Plato, 1960, p. 46).

Orators debase the populace (in much the way that an unscrupulous medical attendant debases a self-indulgent patient) and hasten the ruin of the state. This process of corruption is made possible by the politically effective but morally dehabilitating potentialities of rhetoric. Demagogues trained in this false art displace true statesmen, that is, those who are distinguished by their virtue and their determination to use political power to promote virtue in the state. Rhetoric persuades; it induces belief rather than conviction founded on reason, and is thus ideally suited to encourage human beings to do that for which no ultimately binding reason can be given. Of course persuasion may appeal to people's perception of their self-interest, but it does so by distracting their attention from ultimate standards of moral goodness.

Plato's critical reaction to sophists and demagogues reflected his assessment of their role in corrupting the Athenian state; it also provided the basis for general statements on appropriate political structures and behaviours. In particular, Plato's criticism of sophism and demagoguery was part of an attempt to reestablish the connection between politics and virtue. The consequences of divorcing politics from virtue could be seen in the instability, moral dissolution and political unscrupulousness that Plato thought disfigured contemporary politics. In many of his political works, most notably in the *Republic*, Plato painted a vivid picture of a corrupt state. Drawing an analogy between a grossly self-indulgent individual and a *polis* that has become obsessed with material luxuries, he portrayed this state as bloated and unhealthy (Plato, 1970, p. 107). It cannot rest content with a particular level of overindulgence, but is driven by forces that parallel the psychological restlessness of the greedy individual to seek ever new and often contradictory means of gratification. In the luxurious state these tensions manifest themselves in ruthless competition between self-interested individuals. Attempts to resolve these tensions by expanding the search for means of gratification beyond the boundaries of the state, merely generate conflict with other states. It is important to note, however, that although Plato believed that the weaknesses of the luxurious state have a *moral* source (they reflect a lack of internal regulation or self-constraint) he stipulated that they can only be cured by a radical course of *political* treatment.

That virtue is the end of politics is an axiom, a fundamental principle of Plato's political thought: the *polis* was a cooperative order directed towards the realisation of goodness and the attainment of human perfection. Moral rules subjected the appetitive and irrational aspects of human nature to its rational elements in such a way that the virtuous individual could be said to possess a well-balanced soul. To some degree this conception reflected Plato's attachment to a traditional ideal of the *polis*, but the implications of Plato's views were far from conventional. To the contrary, they necessitated a radical restructuring of political institutions and rejection of the democratic values of Athenian political culture.

The *Republic* opens with a discussion of the nature of justice (or right), a value that both Plato and the other participants in the dialogue took to be central to political life and the defining characteristic of the state. Having refuted definitions of justice as 'telling the truth and paying one's debts' (on the ground that these practices may actually be harmful), and 'giving every person their due' (because this would imply that it is just to harm evil doers and thus lower them further in the scale of human excellence), Plato addressed variations on the theme that justice is merely a cover for the pursuit of self-interest. The first book of the *Republic* closes with refined versions of the self-interest argument. It is claimed that justice is merely a way of dealing with problems produced by the unrestrained pursuit of a natural inclination to self-interest. According to this view, justice is a general term describing systems of regulation that are enforced by coercion, and are necessary to counteract individuals' natural tendency to pursue the benefits that accrue from unpunished wrongdoing.

Neither these arguments nor the question of how justice should be defined are confronted in the first book of the *Republic*. Instead Plato concluded this part of the work with a challenge:

Prove to us ... not only that justice is superior to injustice, but that, irrespective of whether gods or men know it or not, one is good and the other evil because of what it inevitably does to its possessor (ibid., p. 99).

In order to respond to this challenge Plato had first to arrive at a clear and adequate definition of 'justice'; he then had to show its superiority to injustice, and finally he had to explain why its practice is intrinsically beneficial to humanity. In the course of developing these arguments, he made it clear that justice is the key value in politics. To be a just member of a just state is the highest form of virtue to which human beings can aspire; it is so high in fact that politics becomes identified with the pursuit of perfection.

The close link between politics and human virtue is signalled in the opening passages of the second book of the *Republic*. Plato argued that since justice in the individual is so difficult to determine, he will begin by trying to identify it on a large scale, that is, in the state. This approach is presented as a way of compensating for cognitive myopia – we shall be able to see justice more clearly in the state because it appears there writ large – but it also foreshadows the outcome of Plato's analysis where justice in the state and justice in the soul are treated as analogues. Before arriving at this conclusion, Plato traversed an extensive terrain. He developed an account of the growth and corruption of a political community; he then identified the structural and behavioural requirements of an ideal city, and specified the personal attributes required by those who can satisfactorily perform the range of functions necessary to sustain a well-ordered and hence just state. It is important to note that the political and social structure of the ideal state is premised on the idea that functions must be matched with and restricted to distinct capacities. While intellectual and moral potentialities can be fostered through education and training, Plato assumed that different human beings possess differing innate capacities; these may be developed, but they cannot be transformed.

Plato subscribed to the conventional idea that individuals achieve fulfilment as members of a *polis*. He argued, however, that human beings have markedly different capacities and he insisted that the structure of the ideal state must reflect this fact. A key requirement is that political power must be placed in the hands of a 'guardian' class that consists of people with highly developed moral and intellectual qualities. This group occupies the supreme place in a fixed and exclusive hierarchy and monopolises political power. The guardians' total control of the state is justified by their superiority over the rest of the population in terms of the key attribute of governors: the knowledge of what is good for the state. This knowledge is a consequence of the guardians' acquaintance with the 'form' of goodness, that is, with goodness itself as an unqualified quality.

In Plato's theory, the form of goodness and other objective qualities is the source of values that are realised to a greater or lesser extent in the world of ordinary thought and experiences (ibid., pp. 236–43). Individuals' capacity to grasp the forms is a consequence of distinct natural capacities that are possessed by only some members of the population. These potentialities have to be nurtured and refined by a rigorous process of education, and verified through selection procedures that are blind to class, parentage or gender.

An unusual feature of Plato's position is that he argued that biological differences between men and women are irrelevant to fitness to rule. The main 'natural' difference between the sexes centres on their role in the reproductive process, and Plato argued that it is not possible to infer from this that women are necessarily unfit for membership of the guardian class: some women may thus become full members of the guardian class. Plato reiterated this argument in his later account of a second-best state in the *Laws*. (ibid., pp. 201–10). In light of the deepseated misogyny embedded in Athenian life, and the practice and political theory of subsequent societies, Plato's focus on *relevant* differences in settling questions of membership of the state has rightly been described as 'extraordinary' (Okin, 1992,. pp. 36–8).

Since Plato considered the inferior capacities of women to be a consequence of education and social conditioning, it is understandable that his treatment of the political role of women in the ideal state is introduced by refering to the sort of educational regime to which they should be subjected. The fact that women are eligible for membership of the guardian class makes it imperative for them to be exposed to the same system of education and testing as men. This regime is both intellectual and moral: it is designed to endow the guardians with a knowledge of ultimate goodness, and with the fortitude and strength of character necessary to draw the human world into closer correspondence with it. The effectiveness of the educational and selective processes are reinforced by strict specifications concerning the guardians' way of life. They should not possess private property, nor should they enter into familial or marital relationships that will distract them from the single-minded pursuit of virtue (Plato, 1970, pp. 161–5; 211–23). This last stipulation means that women are freed from their traditional roles within the family and are thus able to take their full place within the state (Okin, 1992).

The state that Plato described in the *Republic* is ideal in a double sense: it existed in his imagination, and it is perfect. It is based upon fundamental human needs and its organisation takes account of natural attributes; it is harmonious, orderly and stable. Plato's ideal state is distinguished by its courage (the distinctive virtue of the auxiliaries), its wisdom (embodied in the guardians) and its discipline (which is infused throughout the whole). A society that manages to uphold these virtues and assign corresponding duties to the appropriately qualified people can be said to possess justice. A just state is one in which each element or class performs only the function for which it is fitted by nature; the principle of justice consists in individuals 'keeping to what belongs' to them 'and doing [their] own job' (Plato, 1970, p. 182). The same principle applies to the just individual. The just individual's soul will be well-ordered; its elements will perform their proper function, and they will also exhibit a sense of due proportion. The elements in question are 'spirit', which produces bravery, and 'reason', which produces both wisdom and discipline when it subordinates appetite and spirit to it. The soul is just when these three elements work in harmony to produce a condition of overall balance that parallels that which characterises the just state. In contrast, injustice in the soul is analogous to injustice in the state. In both cases the constituent elements encroach on each other's functions and in so doing they produce confusion, disorder and disharmony (ibid., p. 197).

The order that Plato thought necessary for an ideal state is justified on the grounds that it is perfect in itself and makes it possible for its members to be morally good. Because Plato thought that individuals have differing levels of natural capacities, the practice of virtue will take on a number of forms: some will rule, others will fulfil necessary but subordinate roles within the state. Despite these differences however, the relationship between politics and virtue depends on satisfaction of a single general condition: namely that appetite – the cause of disorder in the luxurious state – must be subject to the governance of reason.

The analogy that Plato drew between the unjust soul, the unjust state and an unhealthy organism signals his response to the question of why justice should be preferred to injustice. The unjust person is racked by contradictory tensions. In contrast the just person enjoys a psychic harmony that is a consequence of the healthy, natural balance of his or her soul. This outcome exemplifies Plato's belief that moral goodness is closely related to beauty. Beauty conveys images of harmony, due proportion and satisfying order. These values played an important role in Plato's political thought and by identifying them with beauty he drew attention to his belief that moral rules reflect absolute values. Like beauty, moral goodness (or the practice of virtue) is infinitely satisfying to those who contemplate it because it reflects a disposition that is marked by a harmonious interrelationship of parts. It thus stands in stark contrast to the driven and discordant condition of those who seek satisfaction in bodily pleasures or immoral aspirations. As Plato put it, 'Virtue is a kind of mental health or beauty or fitness, and vice a kind of illness or deformity or weakness' (ibid., p. 198) To Plato and the other participants in the dialogue, the attractions of virtue make preference for justice over injustice self-evident.

Since virtue (or the attainment of justice) is the goal of human life, one that brings satisfaction to individuals because it reflects a natural ordering of the soul, it must necessarily play a central role in politics. One reason for this is that for Plato, as for other Greeks, the state is the all-embracing focus of human life. However, Plato's belief that there is a direct parallel between justice in the state and justice in the individual adds a distinctive element to this conventional view, one that makes a particular form of politics integral to the pursuit of virtue. Platonic politics are a precondition for the perfection of human nature through the exercise of the highest virtue and their practice must reflect this requirement. Justice in the state and justice in the individual are mutually reinforcing.

Central aspects of Plato's account of the relationship between politics and virtue were challenged by his pupil Aristotle. Aristotle considered a life of contemplation to be the pathway to the highest virtue, but he qualified the rigour of this observation with the comment that such a way of life is unattainable for most human beings. Consequently he offered an account of the ends of politics that relate it to the pursuit of a significant, if less than complete, ideal of human well-being. The *polis* is a focus of human virtue, but in Aristotle's theory this entails a view of the individual and the state that differs markedly from that prescribed for the members of Plato's ideal state.

In *Nicomachean Ethics* Aristotle identified political science – the science of the *polis* – with the realisation of 'human good' (Aristotle, 1975, p. 1094a). Since the *polis* is the most all-embracing of human communities, one that is directed to the good of all the members of the community, Aristotle claimed that it exists for the sake of the 'good life' of its members. For Aristotle the good life is the main end of human life and he adopted a 'teleological' approach to politics that considers it in relation to the ends to which it is directed. In the case of human beings, the pursuit of their end necessitates the cultivation and exercise of two types of virtue, the 'intellectual' and the 'ethical'. The first of these embraces both 'practical wisdom' (which directs humans to ethical ends and the means appropriate to achieve them), and 'wisdom' as such, which involves the contemplation of unchanging objects. While a life of pure contemplation is 'too high' for human beings, Aristotle believed that 'wisdom' plays an important but not complete role in the good life. Such a life is, however, closely related to the pursuit of ethical virtues, and politics is central to their cultivation.

The virtues in question are courage, justice (honesty in business matters), magnificence (generosity to one's friends and one's city), magnanimity (ambition based on an accurate estimation of one's value to the community), good temper, friendliness and temperance (self-control of physical desires). Aristotle's list of ethical virtues has a clubbish air that contrasts sharply with the austerity of Plato's conception of virtue, and reflects the values of the well-educated, well-established members of the Athenian upper middle class with which Aristotle identified (Wood and Wood, 1978, pp. 214–23). One should bear in mind, however, that these virtues are related to the type of political community familiar to Greeks. Seen from this point of view, the practice of ethical virtue is inseparable from membership of the *polis*.

The close relationship between politics and the good life is underlined by Aristotle's account of the *polis* as a 'community', that is, a way of life in which the members of the *polis* have important things in common. In the first book of his *Politics* Aristotle distinguished between three forms of association: the family, the neighbourhood or village and the *polis*. The first two of these associations differ from the *polis*: life in them is limited or incomplete, and these and all other human groupings are embraced by the *polis*. Although these other associations make important contributions to the 'good life', this end can only be realised in a complete, self-sufficient community. The *polis* is

> an association which may be said to have reached the height of full self-sufficiency; or rather ... we may say that while it *grows* for the sake of mere life, ... it *exists* ... for the sake of a good life (Aristotle, 1958, pp. 4–5).

The *polis* is the supreme form of association; it regulates the others and its end is the supreme end for its members. The *polis* is so fundamental to human well-being that it could be described as 'natural'. Aristotle believed that 'natural' things are endowed with supreme value because they have realised their innate potentialities and have thereby attained their end. For human beings, the end is the perfection of their capacity for virtue and since the state is central to this process it is not merely a matter of convention, as the sophists claimed. It follows that the *polis* is natural and man is, as Aristotle said, by nature a political animal (ibid., p. 6). For Aristotle therefore, the state comprises a cooperative order through which its members practice virtue and thus enjoy the 'good life'.

In Aristotle's theory, friendship and 'justice' are central features of the state. The first of these qualities relates to a broad conception of what it means to be a member of a community and encapsulates the idea of a shared existence. In addition to referring to financial honesty, the term 'justice' summarises all the moral values contained within the state. However Aristotle combined ideas of 'what is due to one' with those concerning desserts (or what one deserves), a judgement that is determined by his idea of 'distributive justice'. This principle relates one's shares in and one's contribution to a community to one's attributes and capacity; it specifies that 'equals should be treated equally', and this of course requires the determination of relevant capacities. When this principle is applied to the *polis* it raises questions about how the range of capacities possessed by its different members relate to the pursuit of the ethical goals that constitute the end of the community. Because the *polis* is a form of common existence there are limits to the differences that can exist between its members. A crucial consideration is that they must have enough in common to be able to share in the life of the community.

One important consequence of this stipulation is that the proportion of a given population who can be full members of a *polis* (or 'citizens' as Aristotle calls them) will depend on a variety of factors that bear on its composition. Where all are literally equal, then all may be citizens, but where there are significant differences in wealth, education, function or outlook, distributive justice requires that citizenship is limited to duly qualified sections of the population. Aristotle's analysis of 'constitutions', a term that he used to identify the citizen body, will be discussed more fully in later chapters. At this stage it may be noted that he believed that the principle of distributive justice invariably prevents both women and slaves from being citizens. Aristotle's views on the status of women were far more conventional than those of Plato since he endorsed the Athenian practice of treating them as inferior members of the household, not citizens of the state. Aristotle justified the low status ascribed to women and slaves by pointing to their 'natural inferiority'. He argued that neither of these groups can stand in a position of equality with free males, and consequently they cannot be members of the state. As functionally important members of the family, slaves and women contribute to the good life, but they do so under the direction of their putative superiors. They are 'instruments', as Aristotle put it, and do not, strictly speaking, *share* in the good life. Nor can they aspire to the high levels of virtue that membership of the *polis* makes possible. However Aristotle suggested that by contributing to the good life members of the family partake of it to some degree; presumably they may attain that degree of virtue that their natural inferiority makes possible. Perhaps another way of putting this is to say that incorporation within the state allows women and slaves to perfect their natures, although their natures were regarded by Aristotle as 'lower' than those whose attributes entitle them to full membership of the *polis* (ibid., pp. 36–8). For the most part, however, Aristotle focused on the functions that women perform within a political and social culture that is directed towards the realisation of a citizen body that is never seen as extending beyond the free-born male members of the community (Okin, 1992, pp. 78–9).

If one accepts Aristotle's conception of distributive justice and also his claims about the capacities of different sections of the population, then his assumption that citizenship should be limited conforms to the requirements of justice. Where this is the case, however, it is important to recognise that the positive relationship between politics and virtue applies only to those who are full members of the state: the rest of the population contribute to the life of the state without partaking of it. A corollary of this is that virtue only characterises those states where citizenship is restricted to those who really are equals. Aristotle made this point when he contrasted a 'true' state with a political association that is really no more than a 'mere alliance' to provide mutual defence and promote economic activity (Aristotle, 1958, pp. 118–19).

It should be noted, however, that elsewhere in the *Politics* Aristotle appears to have taken a less extreme position. By recognising that most societies have a mixed socioeconomic, intellectual and moral composition, and in allowing varying types and levels of political participation to those who are not equals in the strict sense, it seems that Aristotle was recognising the limited but significant capacity for virtue possessed, if not by all the adult population, at least by free-born males. Without attaining the status of a true state, some political associations may transcend a 'mere alliance' and assume at least some of the characteristics of a *polis*; that is, they become associations devoted 'to the end of encouraging goodness' (ibid., p. 118).

Of course, if one can identify the basis for a fundamental form of equality that encompasses all human beings, then it becomes possible to see a properly ordered political community as a means of promoting the moral goodness of *all* its members. It was a long time before this consideration was applied to women's political status, but in some medieval political theory ideas derived from Christianity played a significant role in undermining the moral, if not the political, implications of the distinctions upon which Aristotle depended.

Virtue, Politics and Christianity: Aquinas, Machiavelli, Luther, Calvin and Radical Protestantism

Although there are significant differences between Plato's and Aristotle's understanding of the nature and implications of virtue, they both believed it to be intimately related to politics. This general belief was central to the Greco-Romano conception of politics that was restated in the first century BC by the Roman lawyer and statesman Cicero. In *Of the Republic* Cicero defined a commonwealth or state as 'a multitude joined together by one consent of law and their common good' (see p. 207), and identified the common good with the practice of justice; without justice states are, to a greater or lesser extent, no more than large robber bands. This view may be contrasted with Judeo-Christian suspicions of humanly created institutions, with its reliance upon God to produce a truly just society, and its tendency to regard life in the state as at best a form of exile from the promised land. Augustine's rejection of Greco-Roman conceptions of the naturalness of the state, and the divorce between politics and the pursuit of ultimate values that was implied by it, represented an attitude towards politics that was common in early medieval European thought (see p. 25). This view probably related to a general problem (faced both by the Jewish people and by Christians in the Roman Empire) of how the faithful should respond to demands placed upon them by theologically questionable, or at least diverse, political units. It was thus no accident that when the Augustinian position was challenged in the late medieval period, the Christian state had become the predominant form of political organisation in Western Europe. (Copleston, 1975, p. 238). This challenge was made by Christian thinkers who attempted to redefine the relationship between their faith and the recently rediscovered original formulations of the political ideas of a number of 'pagan' Greek thinkers. Important statements of the political implications of this process were produced in the late twelfth and early thirteenth centuries by St Thomas Aquinas (see p. 29).

Although he thought that Greek philosophy could not be regarded as an adequate statement of the human condition because it was not informed by the fruits of Christian revelation, Aquinas insisted that the relationship between Greek and Christian thought was not antagonistic or mutually exclusive. To the contrary, he held that Christianity was in harmony with the high point of philosophy found in Greek writings, and that it completed the understanding of the human condition for which the Greeks had strived. An important consequence of this view was that Aquinas was able to restore the close connection between virtue and politics that had been a feature of Greco-Roman thought. Indeed Aquinas was able to extend the idea of membership of a political community to include virtually the whole of the population.

Unlike Aristotle, Aquinas did not think that a genuine political community needs to be made up of equal beings. In his view inequality is natural to humanity, as is the need for regulation by the 'more wise'. But neither inequality nor subordination detract from the dignity of human beings: all are God's creatures and even the wisest of men are subject to God's direction and control (Aquinas, 1959, p. 103). Aquinas distinguished between political subordination and servile subjection, a penal condition resulting from sin. He argued that only the latter excludes individuals from membership of the state, or from participation in the 'good life'. Political subordination is essential to the pursuit of this good: it entails full membership of the community and involves ideas of sharing and responsibility that elevate ordinary members of society and women above the instrumental status to which Aristotle assigned them (Coole, 1988, pp. 65–9; Gilby, 1958, pp. 154, 193).

In *Summa Theologica* and other writings that bear on politics, Aquinas identified the state with the pursuit of the 'good life' and accorded this goal an important place in the realisation of virtue. Of course, as a Christian thinker Aquinas did not regard the good life as an ultimate end for humanity; this consists in the reconciliation of God and man through the latter's attainment of the 'beatific vision of God in heaven' (Coplestone, 1975, p. 200). However, he argued that political life is natural, and consequently that politics can make a significant and positive contribution to the realisation of ultimate values. By linking the 'good life' to humanity's infinite end, Aquinas elevated the status of politics and closely related it to the practice of virtue and the pursuit of perfection. This point was made quite clear in his discussion of the duties of a king: 'because the aim of a good life on this earth is blessedness in heaven, it is the king's duty to promote the welfare of the community in such a way that it leads fittingly to the happiness of heaven' (Aquinas, 1959, p. 79).

Aquinas insisted that the state is not merely a damage-limitation mechanism made necessary by man's fall from grace. Even if human beings were free from sin, sociability would be necessary to direct and guide them in their pursuit of the common good, which it alone makes possible. (ibid., p. 105). Political institutions maintain peace, ensure an adequate supply and distribution of the material necessities of the good life, and promote 'good action' (ibid., pp. 3–9). Good actions are those that conform to the particular requirements of natural law that bear on the life of a political community. Individuals who promote good action are virtuous because they are taking positive steps to perfect their natures. Aquinas maintained that social and political life is a significant stage in a continuum of human perfectibility: the 'beatific vision' forms *the* end, but it incorporates the goals attainable though political means rather than displacing them.

Thus for Aquinas political authority was an important aspect of a system of cosmic order and guidance that was understood in relation to Christian values. This approach was typical of late medieval and early modern political thought, but it did not go completely unquestioned. The most historically significant challenge to the identification of politics with Christian virtue was produced by Niccoló Machiavelli, a citizen and servant of the republic of Florence. A brief reference to Machiavelli's work will highlight the distinctive presuppositions of the medieval views he rejected.

Machiavelli's understanding of politics was underwritten by a distinction between *virtú*, a morally neutral concept embracing the qualities necessary to preserve states, and the conventional or 'classical' 'virtues'. On the basis of this distinction he developed a conception of political morality that did not incorporate classical virtues, and was in many respects overtly antagonistic to the influence of Christianity in politics. The first of these intentions was signalled in chapters of *The Prince*, where Machiavelli argued that rulers who are guided by the classical virtues will jeopardise their chances of retaining power. The second is apparent in Machiavelli's unfavourable treatment of Christianity in his *Discourses*, and in his attachment to the civic and pagan view of religion, which he identified with the glories of the Roman Republic.

Niccoló Machiavelli (1469–1527)

A citizen of Florence, Machiavelli served the city in a number of administrative and diplomatic positions. He was ousted from office in 1512 when the republican government of Florence was overthrown by the powerful Medici family, whose influence extended throughout Italy and into the papacy. Machiavelli's most important political works are *The Prince* (1513) and *The Discourses* (1513–19), both of which played an important part in early modern political thinking in Europe and North America.

The focus of these two works differs in significant respects: *The Prince* deals with the security of a single ruler, while the *Discourses* are concerned with the practice and maintenance of popular republican regimes that take liberty as their primary aim. However, both works are premised on the general belief that politics is a sphere of human endeavour with distinctive standards of its own. 'Good' princes must adopt values that are appropriate to public persons whose opportunity to practise princely *virtú* depends in the first place upon remaining in office. The inappropriateness of applying conventional notions of virtue is nicely illustrated by Machiavelli's suggestion that it is impossible for a prince to practice the virtue of generosity. Giving to others is only a virtue when it is done for its own sake, and since what the prince does must relate to the security of his kingdom, he cannot be truly generous. Moreover if he indulges in ostentatious liberality he will offend his subjects rather than win their gratitude:

> if generosity is practised in such a way that you will be considered generous, it will harm you. If it is practised virtuously, and as it should be, it will not be known about, and you will not avoid acquiring a bad reputation for the opposite vice. Therefore, if one wants to keep up a reputation for being generous, one must spend lavishly and ostentatiously. The inevitable outcome of acting in such ways is that the ruler will consume all his resources … and if he wants to continue to be thought generous, he will eventually be compelled to become rapacious, to tax the people very heavily, and raise money by all possible means. Thus, he will begin to be hated by his subjects and, because he

is impoverished, he will be held in little regard (Machiavelli, 1988, p. 56).

Important aspects of Machiavelli's political thought will be dealt with more fully in a later chapter. At this point it should be noted that his reaction against attempts to use politics to realise Christian conceptions of virtue, added a new element to political thinking in early modern Europe rather than displacing the older view. Indeed in some respects the link between politics and virtue received a new lease of life at the hands of various thinkers who were important in the Reformation.

Martin Luther, the 'father of the Reformation', identified politics with magistracy, and restricted its scope to maintaining public order and supporting a church based on scriptural principles (see p. 28). Like Augustine, Luther justified coercive authority by refering to the depravity of most human beings, and he ascribed a negative rather than a positive status to the political framework in which this was set. In *On Governmental Authority* (1523) Luther distinguished between those who belong to the 'kingdom of God' and those who belong to the 'kingdom of the world'. He argued that since all human beings are naturally 'sinful and wicked, God through the law puts them all under restraint so that they dare not wilfully implement their wickedness in actual deeds'. Among the few who are true Christians, the government of Christ produces righteousness, but the rest of humanity must be subjected to earthly government in order to bring about 'external peace and [to] prevent evil deeds' (Hillerbrand, 1968, pp. 47, 48). A broadening of this view can be seen in the ideas of Luther's German contemporary, Philip Melanchthon. In Melanchthon's *Philosophical and Moral Epistle* (1530) the state is identified not merely with the good life, but with the 'eternal good'. This end is fostered positively through the efforts of government to 'maintain, cherish and organize the religious life of the community' (Allen, 1951, p. 33). Although Melanchthon's statement of this position was undeveloped, it foreshadowed the fuller account of the relationship between politics and virtue produced by the great French Protestant reformer Jean Calvin.

The chapter in Calvin's *Institutes* that deals explicitly with the nature of politics makes it clear that he was advancing an alternative to what he regarded as two erroneous positions. One of these critiques may reflect Calvin's reading of Machiavelli's account of the separation between the *virtú* of a prince and the virtues of a Christian. The second position refers to anarchic tendencies within contemporary radical Protestantism and particularly to claims that those in receipt of the divine spirit have no need to subject themselves to political authorities (Calvin, 1950, vol. 2, pp. 1485–6). Although Calvin was as much concerned with maintaining order as Luther, he offered a more positive account of the role of political institutions. In response to claims that princes are morally autonomous or that government is unnecessary for true Christians, Calvin argued that although human beings are subject to two forms of government – the 'spiritual' and the political or 'civil' – these are not at variance with one another. God's kingdom 'yet to come' does not deprive political authorities of their moral significance. To the contrary, since it is God's will that humans live as 'pilgrims' on earth, and since political institutions play an essential role in their journey, they are of great moral importance (ibid., p. 1487). For Calvin, no less than for Augustine, these institutions perform important controlling functions, particularly in the case of the ungodly mass of humanity. However he argued that even the 'children of God' required the preparatory discipline of human law in order to ensure that they will be 'partially broken in by bearing the yoke of righteousness' (ibid., vol. 1, p. 359). The fact that Calvin described law by reference to 'righteousness' points to a positive connection between politics and Christian virtue. Thus while government prevents 'tumults', it also establishes and maintains conditions in which humans may live 'holily, honourably, and temperately' (ibid., p. 847). For Calvin, therefore, politics is directly connected to the pursuit of virtue. All political authority comes from God because it is necessary to train humanity in those parts of an all-embracing system of virtue that relate to life on earth. Government exists for the sake of Christian virtue and would be necessary even in a community made up of the 'godly'.

Jean Calvin (1509–64)

A native of France, Calvin was a leader of the Protestant Reformation in Geneva, which city he sought to turn into a model reformed community, a 'Protestant Rome'. His political ideas were presented in *Institutes of the Christian Religion* (1536). His influence was particularly marked among his Protestant compatriots, known as the 'Huguenots'.

Because Calvin's ideas were formulated with the backsliding and 'ungodly' population of contemporary Geneva in mind, he laid great stress upon the corrective and disciplinary role of political institutions. These concerns played an important role in subsequent accounts of politics formulated by writers in the Protestant tradition. Some Protestant thinkers looked to conventional political institutions to provide Christian leadership, but others wished political authority to be replaced by forms of religious leadership. For example the early-sixteenth-century German writer Michael Sattler urged contemporaries to form communities under the guidance of 'shepherds' charged with ensuring that 'the name of God is praised and honoured among us, and the mouths of blasphemers are stopped'. Regulation of this kind differs from conventional politics in both its aim and its method of enforcement: it aims at the direct pursuit of Christian virtue, and it operates by maintaining the spiritual integrity of the community. Sattler argued that the most appropriate form of discipline to be employed within a Christian community is the threat of expulsion from it, and he distinguished this form of enforcement from those employed by the existing government: 'Worldly people are armed with spikes and iron, but Christians are armed with the armour of God – with truth, with justice, with peace, faith, and salvation, and with the word of God' (Sattler, 1991, p. 178).

In the post-Reformation period Christian conceptions of virtue were sometimes given a radical political bearing. Thus the English republican writer Algernon Sidney defined virtue as 'the dictate of reason, or the remains of divine light, by which men are made benevolent and beneficial to each other', and he argued that those who possess reason should not be subject to laws to which they have not given their consent. However those who lack virtue have no claim to political liberty and should be subject to regulation by those who are rational and virtuous (Scott, 1988, p. 39). On occasion heightened expectation of a millenarian transformation of the human condition led radical Protestant writers to hold out the hope that regenerated human beings could form political communities that both embodied and were legitimated by the pursuit of Christian virtue. This view of the relationship between politics and virtue prevailed in mid-seventeenth-century England. The overthrow of a religiously unacceptable monarchy and the military successes of the godly were taken as signs that God had ordained that his 'saints' would have a special and privileged role to play in the process of salvation. At that time a number of writers formulated a conception of the potentialities of a 'godly commonwealth' in which the 'chosen' would create systems of political authority to ensure that the aspirations and duties of members of the state would correspond to radicalised Christian perceptions of perfection. In short, the godly commonwealth would fuse virtue and the requirements of political life to such an extent that it would realise the ultimate expectation of the reign of God upon earth (Wootton, 1994, p. 436). Ideas of a godly commonwealth must be distinguished from various seventeenth-century manifestations of utopian thinking that argued for the need for strict forms of regulation designed to impose godly standards on recalcitrant and weak human beings. The purpose of these arrangements was not so much the promotion of virtue as the elimination of wickedness through institutional constraints and mechanisms such as communism that would eliminate sources of temptation (Davis, 1994, p. 343).

The belief that politics could, and indeed should, be made to correspond to the complete realisation of Christian notions of human perfectibility was a product of the distinctive combination of radicalised
theological doctrines and the breakdown of established patterns of political and social authority in parts of early modern Europe. The experience
of the dangerously disruptive implications of 'virtue politics' in the mid
seventeenth century was to have a significant impact on other, contrary,
ideas about the ends of politics in Western political thought (see pp 283–
4). But while the seventeenth century saw the end of significant attempts
to implement godly commonwealths, it did not mark the termination of
the tradition of virtue politics. This perspective continued to be espoused
by those radical Protestants who were the ideological and theological
descendants of early modern sectarians, and its specifically Christian elements were restated in a morally if not politically radical form by Christian socialists in the nineteenth and twentieth centuries. However the
most theoretically sophisticated modern formulations of virtue politics
appeared in the late-eighteenth-century writings of Immanuel Kant, as
well as in those of some important political thinkers in late nineteenth-
century Britain.

Virtue, Perfection and Freedom: Kant and the British Idealists

While the thinkers discussed in this section did not divorce themselves
from Christianity, they developed a conception of virtue that stresses the
human dimensions of virtue and perfection. These theories uphold the
importance of order – as Kant put it, law is necessary to curtail 'wild
freedom' – but they adhered to a conception of virtue and perfection that
emphasises the role that rational freedom plays in the pursuit of moral
goodness. However, while freedom plays an important role in these
theories, the writers discussed here did not treat it as a primary value.
Rather they regarded freedom as important because it is instrumental to
the pursuit of virtue.

An influential account of the relationship between virtue, perfection
and freedom appears in the writings of the eighteenth-century German
philosopher Immanuel Kant. Kant's understanding of the value of politics
relates closely to his belief that the only thing that is unconditionally
good is a 'good will', a *'will* which is *good*, not as a means to some further
end, but *in itself'* (Kant, 1972, p. 62). The implications that Kant derived
from this view of goodness are that motivation is central to morality, and
that the distinguishing characteristic of moral actions is that they spring
from a 'reverence' for moral law (ibid., p. 65). Moral action conforms to
what Kant called a 'single categorical imperative': *'Act only on the maxim*

through which you can at the same time will that it should become a universal law' (ibid., p. 84). Action of this kind is characteristically human because it is under the direction of reason rather than instinct. Humans thus comprise a 'kingdom of ends', a 'systematic union of different rational beings under common law'. This entails that 'rational beings all stand under the *law* that each of them should treat himself and all others, *never merely as a means*, but always *at the same time as an end in himself* ' (ibid., p. 95). The idea that humans should be treated as *ends* not *means* implies a respect for their humanity, which precludes them from being regarded as mere instruments for the attainment of other ends. This view of morality makes freedom a condition for the pursuit of virtue: if people are to act morally, they must will the good for its own sake, not because of any benefit it will bring them, or in reaction to the coercive influence of other human beings or institutions.

Immanuel Kant (1724–1804)

Born in Konigsberg in East Prussia, where he remained all his life, Kant was an academic philosopher whose work spanned a wide variety of fields. The most renowned philosopher of his day, Kant's emphasis on individual moral autonomy laid the basis for a conception of politics that, because it required a break with the past, was in general accord with the revolutionary events that occurred in North America and Europe in the latter part of his life. Kant's political works include *The Metaphysical Elements of Justice* (1797) and *Perpetual Peace: A Philosophical Sketch* (1796).

But while freedom is central to Kant's conception of right action, he did not regard it as a sufficient condition for morality or for the pursuit of perfection. The goal of human action, the 'essential end', is the development of humanity's distinctive moral and physical capacities. This end provides a means of distinguishing between particular exercises of freedom, and thus forms the basis of the universal law stipulated in the categorical imperative. (Murphy, 1970, pp. 98–101). For Kant, the development of humanity is marked by a progression from 'bondage to instinct to rational control – in a word, from the tutelage of nature to the state of freedom.... This consists in nothing less than progress towards perfection' (Kant, 1975, p. 60). Virtue is thus to be understood in relation to perfection; freedom is valuable because of the role it plays in the practice and development of people's capacity for virtue. Kant's state facilitates good action rather than trying to force people to act morally. (Rosen, 1993, pp. 188–9).

This conditional understanding of the value of freedom provided the basis of Kant's conception of the relationship between politics and virtue. At first sight, the fact that political authority imposes rules upon individuals seems to make it antagonistic to the growth of virtue. Although Kant acknowledged the force of this objection, he resisted the conclusion that virtue and politics are antithetical. Thus while he distinguished 'juridical' from 'ethical' legislation, and argued that only the latter is strictly moral because it operates 'internally' upon conscience rather than externally upon behaviour, Kant argued that government may make important contributions to human perfection. Provided that juridical legislation is a product of a political system based upon the consent of subjects and directed towards their common interests, it can create conditions that foster moral action. Government constrains instinctive behaviour and makes it easier for reason and morality to become the basis of human conduct.

Thus while politics is a matter of practical necessity, it is also conducive to the pursuit of perfection. Kant stressed that its benefits are not merely derived from the constraint imposed upon 'wild freedom'. To the contrary, he argued that the 'veneer of morality' produced by juridical legislation fosters the growth of true morality:

> each individual believes of himself that he would by all means maintain the sanctity of the concept of right and obey it faithfully, if only he could be certain that all the others would do likewise, and the government in part guarantees this for him; thus a great step is taken *towards* morality (although this is still not the same as a moral step), towards a state where the concept of duty is recognised for its own sake, irrespective of any possible gain in return (Kant, 1971, p. 121, note).

From this perspective, the coercive capacities of the state inhibit obstructions to rational freedom and hence also to the practice of virtue and the pursuit of perfection (Murphy 1970, p. 94).

Kant's political thought is connected directly to that of the final group of exponents of virtue politics to be discussed in this chapter. The writers in question are conventionally referred to as the 'British idealists', a label that signals their attachment to ideas that were current in late-eighteenth- and early-nineteenth-century German idealism. The most important thinker in this group was T. H. Green, a highly influential figure at Oxford University in the 1870s and early 1880s. The political affiliations of the British idealists were largely liberal, but they sought to reformulate liberalism into a 'positive' rather than a 'negative' doctrine. In the past liberals had successfully attacked institutions and practices that protected the exclusive interests of privileged sections of the community, but the idealists thought that the time had come to give liberal ideas a more positive aspect. Traditional liberal notions of freedom must be refined to take account of the social context of human action, and to recognise that liberty requires a capacity to act, and not merely the absence of constraints. These modifications would allow liberals to promote an active state that would use its power to enforce acceptable standards of industrial and municipal safety and hygiene, to eliminate misuses of property and promote the education of the population. These measures are justified on the ground that a deprived, unhealthy and ignorant population is not free in any meaningful sense, not free, that is, to act as moral, autonomous beings (Green, 1986, pp. 196–212).

Although autonomy was important for the British idealists, they stressed that liberty itself is not an absolute value. Particular liberties have to be related to what the idealists called the 'common good', that is, a non-exclusive, moral good that individuals share with all other members of the community (Bosanquet, 1899, pp. 118–54; Green, 1986, pp. 25–6). A community that recognises the common good and seeks to attain it through the action of individuals, social groups and the state is pursuing the 'good life'. The idealists derived this notion from Aristotle's writings, but they imbued it with Platonic overtones of perfection. Green stressed, for example, that the state and other social and political institutions exist for the sake of goodness and he related this directly to the perfection of the individuals who comprise it: 'To speak of any progress or improvement or development of a nation or society or mankind, except as relative to some greater worth of persons, is to use words without meaning' (Green 1986, p. 256).

This stipulation drew attention to the idealists' belief that virtue is a personal quality. They insisted, however, that political institutions can play an important role in promoting human perfection. Of course, since this end involves the self-willed pursuit of goodness, the state's role is indirect rather than direct. In idealist political thought the relationship between the state and virtue has a number of dimensions. First, as the experience of 'classical' liberalism shows, political authority can be exercised in an essentially 'negative' way; that is, it can be used to destroy class privilege where this is buttressed by the misapplication of political power. In short, a state that reflects the aspirations of the community as a whole can use its power and influence to ensure that institutionalised impediments to the realisation of the common good are eliminated. Secondly, as indicated above, the state can act in a more positive fashion, extending opportunities for the development and practice of virtue to all its members. In addition, however, there is an important further sense in which the idealist perception of politics is intimately and necessarily linked to virtue. For these writers, the perfection of individuals is brought about by their active and conscious realisation of the 'common good', one that is shared by all members of the community, and provides the ultimate rationale for the regulatory ideas and institutions that make up the state. In other words, provided the state embodies the common consciousness of its members – something the idealists thought became far more probable and less haphazard when it took on a democratic character – then politics is central to the practice of virtue.

Kant's theory applies to 'all rational beings', but in keeping with a tradition that can be traced back to Aristotle he excluded women from this category (Okin, 1992, p. 6). Green implicitly rejected this assumption, arguing that while there are significant differences between men and woman these relate to their functions and not to rationality or moral worth. In the course of a discussion that made direct reference to the shortcomings of the moral ideas of the ancient Greeks, Green argued that all human beings must be recognised as having an equal right to develop their moral personalities. He insisted that modern society must recognise 'the proper and equal sacredness of all women as self-determining and self-respecting persons' (Green, 1986, p. 281), a sentiment that was carried through to his practical involvement in educational initiatives directed at the needs of women (Anderson, 1991).

Conclusion

Many historically significant writers regarded membership of a political community as essential to the pursuit of moral objectives that are fundamental to human well-being. This idea lay behind Plato's and Aristotle's conception of the importance of the *polis*, and played a central role in Christian political thinking. The most developed statement of the last of these views, one that was directly connected to aspects of ancient political thought, was presented by Aquinas, but it also played an important role in the political thinking of Calvin and other Protestant thinkers in the early modern period.

Claims about the positive relationship between politics and virtue gave rise to specifications of institutional forms that foster virtue. These specifications concern the structure of government, the allocation of political power and the conduct of officeholders. Many of the theorists discussed in this chapter assumed the need for systems of regulation that place the more rational and virtuous members of the population in positions of authority. This requirement is reflected in a long tradition of political thinking that promoted various forms of hierarchy, but it is important to note that the thinkers who made these claims justified political hierarchy on the ground that it is necessary to promote virtuous conduct on the part of all, or in some case most, members of the community. Government exists for the good of the governed, and the major task for political thinkers is to identify forms of rule that will facilitate the attainment of this goal. Since the realisation of this objective will be threatened by rulers who use power for corrupt purposes, it is important to establish barriers to misrule. As we shall see, this issue gave rise to a range of ideas about the institutional and normative regulation of political authority (see pp. 297ff).

Although all theories that relate virtue to politics rest on a unified conception of goodness, they do not always give rise to hierarchical conceptions of politics. Indeed, as the cases of both Kant and Green show, there is an important tradition in the history of political thought that makes freedom a necessary condition for moral action. Since these theories relate freedom to moral goodness they must be distinguished from those discussed in the following chapter. In these theories freedom is a primary value that determines issues such as who should rule and how political power should be exercised.

CHAPTER 3

Politics and Freedom

Although a number of historically significant political thinkers regard freedom as a primary political value, treatments of this topic vary. One set of differences hinges on the status of freedom: in some cases it is seen as being a good in itself, while in others it appears as a necessary condition for the realisation of other values relating to human well-being. Discussions of the political implications of freedom are also affected by different understandings of its context. Thus while some thinkers regard freedom as a social attribute, others see it in individualistic terms. These differences are apparent in the theories dealt with in this chapter, but they all share the assumption that the nature, scope and purpose of political authority must be understood in relation to the priority to be accorded to particular conceptions of human freedom.

The theories discussed here are drawn from the early modern and modern world because it was only in these periods that arguments about freedom assumed a central place in the history of political thought. For ancient and medieval thinkers freedom was a secondary value relating to conceptions of the good life, or to the requirements of religious notions of virtue. This chapter begins with a consideration of the strongly political notion of freedom that was central to the classical republican tradition of renaissance Italy. Classical republicans, the most important of whom was Machiavelli, considered freedom in relation to needs of the state, rather than seeing it as an attribute that belonged to individuals and determined the basis of a legitimate political order. Machiavelli's understanding of freedom differed from that of both John Locke and Thomas Paine because both of these writers regarded individual freedom as 'natural': it is a right possessed by individuals that sets limits to the exercise of political authority. A similar idea was advanced in John Stuart Mill's *On Liberty*, but he also insisted that both individuals and society possess interests that may need to be protected. These two approaches to liberty have been challenged by a rival tradition that treats freedom as a product of sociability. The origins of this tradition can be seen in the writings of J.-J. Rousseau and developed versions of it were presented by G. W. F. Hegel and T. H. Green. These writers argued that the modern constitutional state provided new and significant opportunities for human freedom. This line of argument was rejected by anarchists and revolutionary socialists working within the Marxist tradition. Although their positions differed in many other respects, Marx's argument that the relationship between freedom and sociability was fatally compromised by conventional political institutions was similar in its general form to the line taken by anarchist theorists. These writers regarded all forms of political authority as imposing illegitimate and unnecessary restrictions on human freedom, and they sought to develop alternative modes of social organisation.

Freedom and Politics in the Classical Republican Tradition: Marsilius, Bartolus and Machiavelli

Although classical republicanism grew out of the political experiences of the late-medieval and early-modern city states of Italy, its influence was also felt in seventeenth- and eighteenth-century Anglo-American political thought. While it reached forward into the new world, this tradition had close links with antiquity and especially with republican Rome. The reasons for this affinity with the past were geographical, cultural and political: the Italian city states occupied the seat of ancient Rome; they adopted republican forms of government and thus endowed the history of Rome with contemporary relevance. Moreover, their intellectual cultures were the locus of the renaissance of classical learning in the fourteenth and fifteenth centuries. Since the early sixteenth century classical republicanism has been identified most closely with Niccoló Machiavelli, but his treatment of the political significance of liberty must be seen in relation to statements advanced by Marsilius of Padua and Bartolus of Sassaferrato in the first half of the fourteenth century.

The classical republican understanding of the idea of political freedom is similar in its general bearing to that of the Romans. Unlike theorists who focus on the liberty of the individual, classical republicans treated individual freedom in relation to the freedom of the state. A state can be said to be free when two conditions are satisfied: it must be independent of external control by other states or rulers, and it must be ruled by its citizens, not by a single person or 'prince' (Skinner, 1978, vol. i, pp. 157–8). Liberty, in other words, is the distinguishing characteristic of an independent republic. This connection, and its application to the city states of Italy, is clear in the writings of both Marsilius and Bartolus.

These writers rejected Aquinas' claim that monarchy is a generally applicable ideal (see p. 132) and argued that small, self-contained entities are best served by republican forms of government founded, as Bartolus put it, 'on the body of the people' (ibid., p. 53). The rationale for making freedom the basis of the state is that it produces a form of government that rests on the people as a whole and cannot therefore be captured by mutually hostile groups. A free state will thus avoid factionalism and the threat that this poses to peace and tranquillity. Marsilius followed Aristotle in describing the state as a community of freemen: 'every citizen must be free and not undergo another's despotism, that is, slavish dominion' (Marsilius, 1956, vol. ii, p. 47). However, while these writers gave freedom a prominent place in their accounts of politics, their ultimate justification of popular government reflected the belief that peace and tranquillity are preconditions for the realisation of a Christian conception of virtue.

The connection between political freedom and Christian aspirations was rejected by Machiavelli. Moreover, while this writer endorsed some of the central features of the classical republican tradition, his work marked a departure from important aspects of it. Like his predecessors, Machiavelli identified liberty with independence and self-government, and he stressed the role that free citizens play in maintaining the external and internal integrity of the state. However, he denied that peace and tranquillity are hallmarks of a good state, and rejected the idea that a unified citizen body is desirable.

The key to Machiavelli's conception of political freedom lies in his use of the idea of *virtú*. This term has a range of meanings, but it refers in general to those qualities that are necessary for the maintenance of a state. In free states, or republics, citizens must possess the capacity to defend the state, and they must also be willing and able to play an active and wary role in its internal affairs. In other words, the kind of *virtú* that is appropriate to republican government preserves both its external freedom and its internal system of self-government. *Virtú* and liberty have a symbiotic relationship: freedom engenders *virtú*, and *virtú* ensures that the liberty of the state will be preserved.

An important consequence of Machiavelli's understanding of the implications of republican *virtú* was that he thought it made a degree of disorder (or 'tumult') both unavoidable and beneficial. *Virtú* requires *active* dedication to the good of the state, and since different sections of the community will take differing views of this, republics must necessarily be in a condition of tense equilibrium, one that is produced by the clash of different conceptions of how the public good might best be served. The tumultuous condition of popular republics is a sign of health. It indicates that citizens are practising the *virtú* upon which the liberty of the state depends (Machiavelli, 1975, vol. I, p. 218).

This argument, which Machiavelli illustrated with glowing references to the productive tensions that marked the heyday of the Roman Republic (ibid., pp. 218–73), signalled a break with the view that liberty is conducive to internal peace. It also meant that Machiavelli had abandoned the instrumental view of liberty that appeared in the writings of Bartolus and Marsilius: liberty, republicanism and *virtú* are so inseparably entwined that one can hardly say that one value is subsidiary to the others. This feature of Machiavelli's theory is related to his explicit rejection of the conventional idea that *virtú* and virtue are synonymous, and to his reservations about the political value of Christian, as opposed to pagan, religion (ibid., pp. 240–50).

Lying behind these detailed arguments and illustrations is a search for a distinctive standard of *political* morality, for rules of conduct that relate to the requirements of different kinds of state. In his book on principalities Machiavelli urged princes to ignore the dictates of conventional morality and to do whatever was necessary to keep the populace under control (Machiavelli, 1988, pp. 55–71). In republics, however, political morality requires the cultivation of *virtús* that are closely related to liberty; only a free and active population can maintain a free state. Since republican regimes require human beings actively to maintain both their common political life and the distinctive morality that is integral to it, Machiavelli thought that they were glorious *human* achievements.

Politics and 'Natural' Liberty: Locke, Paine, J. S. Mill

For the classical republicans, liberty was an inherently political concept; it related to the needs of the state and its implications for individuals were discussed in these terms. This perspective on freedom is quite distinct from that which attributes liberty to prepolitical or 'natural' human beings, and then seeks to understand what happens when they come together to form political societies or states. One approach to this problem has been considered in an earlier discussion of aspects of Hobbes' political thought. For Hobbes the creation of political society requires the renunciation of natural liberty and the establishment of a sovereign whom all should obey (see pp. 258ff).

An obvious objection to Hobbes' view is that the sovereign may so oppress the subject that membership of political society becomes more burdensome than the state of nature it replaces. Hobbes would not accept this objection because he thought that nothing could be worse than the state of nature. Hobbes' theory was questioned by many of his contemporaries and successors. For example Samuel Pufendorf thought that human beings could create forms of government that would save them from the hazards of the state of nature without requiring submission to an absolute sovereign (see pp. 263ff). The same general point may be made about the position advanced by the late-seventeenth-century English writer John Locke. While many of the central features of his political thought – particularly his understanding of the state of nature and of the factors that would both motivate people to leave this condition and justify their doing so – had been current in European political thought for more than a century before Locke wrote about it, his position was novel in the sense that he made freedom a necessary feature of political relationships. Before Locke, natural liberty was discussed in terms of the creation of political authority, but he insisted that individuals retain some rights even in a political or 'civil' condition (Tuck, 1979).

John Locke (1632–1704)

A philosopher and physician, Locke was a fellow of Christ Church, Oxford, and a close associate of the Earl of Shaftesbury. Shaftesbury's involvement in political manoeuvres and plots against Charles II and his brother (later James II) forced Locke into exile in Holland in the 1680s. Locke's most famous political work, *Two Treatise of Government*, was written some time during the early 1680s in opposition to what he saw as the absolutist pretensions of Charles and James. It was subsequently revised and published in 1689 to justify James' ejection from the throne as a result of the 'Glorious Revolution' of 1688–89.

Although Locke's position may be usefully contrasted with that of Hobbes, the target of his major political work, *The Two Treatise of Government* (1689), was Sir Robert Filmer, the author of *Patriarcha*. Central to Filmer's argument is an emphatic denial of natural liberty. He argued that political power is derived directly from the patriarchal (or fatherly) supremacy conferred by God upon Adam, the first father. From the time of God's grant to Adam there has been no 'state of nature' because all who come into the world are subject to their natural Fathers and to the derivative but supreme power of patriarchal monarchs (see pp. 266ff).

Locke's *First Treatise* presents a detailed refutation of Filmer's universal patriarchalism and a defence of the natural liberty of humankind; the *Second Treatise* explores the political implications of this. Like many of his contemporaries, Locke used the idea of a state of nature to identify fundamental human attributes, to establish a rationale for the state, and to specify the features of legitimate political authority. He argued that human beings in the state of nature are endowed by God with natural liberty so that they can take responsibility for themselves and thus act in conformity with God's wishes. These wishes are embodied in the 'laws of nature', and this means that while natural individuals are free from subjection to other human beings they are in a condition of 'liberty not licence': 'The natural liberty of man is to be free from any superior power on earth, and not to be under the will or legislative authority of man, but to have only the Law of Nature for his rule' (Locke, 1967, p. 301). The laws of nature specify human obligations to God: they must preserve themselves; assist in the preservation of others and must uphold the laws of nature by exercising powers of judgement and punishment over those who breach them (ibid., p. 289). However, while Locke denied there is such a thing as patriarchal authority even within the family – children are subject to 'parental' power, exercised equally by both parents – he subsequently restored the dominion of men over women by claiming the superior strength and ability of the former and restricted the possession of political rights to them (Okin, 1992, pp. 200–1).

Locke's understanding of the conditions under which natural liberty is exercised means that his conception of the state of nature is far less grim than that of Hobbes. He argued that any violence suffered by individuals is likely to be less damaging to them (and far less inhibiting in relation to their fulfilment of their obligations to God) than the dangers posed by a Leviathan or by an all-powerful Filmerian patriarch. However, while a state of natural liberty is far from being a dire one, Locke acknowledged that this condition entails certain 'inconveniences', due more to ignorance and partiality than to ill-will. Whatever their source, these failings are particularly significant in an environment where each individual is responsible for interpreting, applying and enforcing natural law. Consequently Locke argued that the state of nature will be marred by accidental injustice. Moreover he implied that since human beings are under a general injunction to understand the law of nature and to uphold it to the greatest possible extent, they must improve upon the state of nature if they can find a way of doing so. Membership of the state fulfils this requirement because it opens up the possibility of establishing certain and impartial systems of judgement and enforcement in place of the precarious arrangements that exist in the state of nature.

Since human beings are naturally free, any curtailment of their liberty must involve *consent*; in other words they must *agree* to forgo their natural liberty and place themselves under the control of a politically superior human: 'Men being ... by nature, all free, equal and independent, no one can be put out of this estate, and subjected to the political power of another, without his own *consent*' (ibid., p. 348). This process is relatively straightforward in a situation where people actually come together to form a political society, but it becomes problematic if applied to a pre-existing state. Locke addressed this problem formally by means of the idea of 'tacit consent', which involves identification of conditions that, if satisfied, signify consent.

Consent is important to Locke both because it is necessary to explain how free individuals can legitimately come to be under the control of other human beings, and because it means that subjection to political authority must be seen as a *voluntary* act. For Hobbes, there is a sharp qualitative difference between the state of nature and political society, but in Locke's theory natural liberty casts a permanent shadow over political society. Individuals in the state of nature are under an obligation to adhere to the laws of nature; their natural liberty is designed to make them responsible for fulfilling this obligation. In political society this obligation persists; by consenting to obey legitimate political authorities individuals are, in effect, voluntarily assuming responsibility to uphold the laws of nature and live by them. In so doing they are making a conscientious attempt to fulfil the ends for which God created them. Moreover, since humans' fundamental obligation under the law of nature persist within the state, according to Locke they have a responsibility not to tolerate forms of government or exercises of political power that seriously compromise this obligation. This feature of Locke's theory provides the basis for stipulations concerning the institutional requirements of legitimate government, and for a theory of justified resistance to flagrantly unjust sovereigns (see pp. 318ff). It also means, however, that renunciation of natural liberty cannot be unconditional. Membership of political society *suspends* natural liberty rather than *abolishing* it; it always remains in the background. If the purposes for which it exists and the purposes for which it is suspended are not satisfied, human beings must take up their natural liberty and resume responsibility for identifying and maintaining the laws of nature.

For Locke, therefore, the legitimacy of government depends on its willingness to give effective legal form to the implications of the law of nature and to avoid acting in ways that threaten the 'life, liberty and estates' of those who are subject to it. Locke believed that while these requirements are incompatible with the type of arbitrary rule that he associated with Hobbes' Leviathan or with a Filmerian patriarch, they can be satisfied by monarchical, aristocratic or democratic systems of government. Towards the close of the eighteenth century, however, arguments concerning natural liberty were used to promote republican government and to delegitimate monarchy and aristocracy on the ground that they were incompatible with individuals' natural right to liberty. The most notorious and long-remembered statement of this position was advanced by the Anglo-American writer Thomas Paine.

Thomas Paine (1737–1809)

Born and raised in England, Paine emigrated to Philadelphia and made a name for himself as a radical supporter of the American cause during the revolutionary war. He held a number of political appointments in America before returning to Europe in 1787 to promote an iron bridge that he had designed. Paine wrote a number of controversial political pamphlets, including *The Rights of Man* (published in two parts in 1790 and 1791). The radically antimonarchical argument advanced in this work made it necessary for Paine to flee to France to avoid prosecution. While in exile (and before his return to the United State) Paine was active in French politics. He was imprisoned during the Terror and narrowly escaped execution.

Paine's conception of republican government is based on a particular understanding of the relationship between natural liberty and political society. In the first part of his *Rights of Man*, Paine distinguished 'natural' from 'civil' rights. The former 'appertain to man in right of his existence' while the latter 'appertain to man in right of his being a member of society' (Paine, 1976, p. 90). Paine's natural individuals possess a range of rights whose free exercise is subject only to the condition that it does not injure the natural rights of others; these rights include an individual's right to prevent interference in the exercise of their other rights. For Paine the state is a means by which individuals can more effectively protect their rights. He therefore insisted that all individuals retain the right to exercise and protect those rights that are not lodged in the state. In this view, the creation of government involves a pooling of a limited range of rights of judgement and enforcement in order to ensure that these functions are better performed; these tasks thus become matters of 'civil right', subject to public control.

These arguments were designed both to show that civil rights are founded on preexisting natural rights, and to uphold claims for the free exercise of those natural rights that have not been, and need not be, exchanged for civil rights. It should be noted that Paine's account of these matters points to a fundamental continuity between the natural liberty enjoyed by individuals and their condition within a legitimate political society. For Paine, as for Locke, freedom is a central issue in politics because it is the business of government to act in ways that take account of natural liberty.

Although natural freedom is a central value for writers such as Locke and Paine its political implications are not straightforward. At one level, political institutions ensure that liberty, which is necessary for the well-being of individuals, is made secure from infringement by other individuals. At the same time, however, both Locke and Paine argued that individual freedom places constraints upon the exercise of political authority. Seen from this point of view, freedom is not so much an end of politics as something that determines its scope.

A similar element of ambiguity surrounds the account of the relationship between politics and freedom that was advanced by the mid-nineteenth-century writer John Stuart Mill. Aspects of Mill's political thought will be discussed in other chapters of this book, but it should be noted here that Mill's essay *On Liberty* (1859) is often regarded as a seminal discussion of this topic. In this work Mill offered a strong defence of individual liberty and laid down a principle that specified

> the dealings of society with the individual in the way of compulsion and control, whether the means used be physical force in the form of legal penalties, or the moral coercion of public opinion. That principle is, that the sole end for which mankind are warranted, individually or collectively, in interfering with the liberty of action of any of their number, is self-protection. That the only purpose for which power can be rightfully exercised over any member of a civilised community, against his will, is to prevent harm to others (Mill, 1983, pp. 72–3).

Mill thought that freedom is a good in itself, but more consistently and significantly he argued that it is necessary both for the development of the moral and intellectual character of individuals and the progressive advancement of civilised communities. Although Mill insisted that the principle of liberty applies to all adult members of reasonably civilised communities, his interest in freedom was closely related to his belief that genius and originality, qualities found in only some members of the population, are of crucial importance to the progress of humanity. He was thus concerned to protect those who were capable of identifying new and potentially valuable ideas and modes of life from the conformist tendencies that were gaining strength in emerging democratic cultures: freedom was necessary to ensure experimentation and to make it possible for exceptional individuals to 'point the way forward' to their fellows (Thomas, 1985, p. 108).

Mill identified a sphere of liberty that fences off an area where an individual's freedom of action is protected from legally sanctioned and socially endorsed interference. It is important to note, however, that the principle of liberty is not a warrant for indifference towards one's fellows, nor does it reduce government to an agency that merely protects individuals. To the contrary, Mill applied the notion of 'harm' to society as well as to individuals, and he allowed that government may use its regulatory capacities to ensure that individuals do not harm social interests through their actions, or by failing to contribute to the fulfilment of social functions (Collini, 1977, p. 345). As Mill put it in his discussion of what is 'due to society':

> living in society makes it indispensable that each should be bound to observe a certain line of conduct towards the rest. This conduct consists, first, in not injuring the interests of one another; or rather certain interests, which, either by express legal provision or by tacit understanding ought to be considered as rights; and secondly, in each person's bearing his share ... of the labours and sacrifices incurred for defending the society or its members from injury and molestation (Mill, 1983, p. 132).

John Stuart Mill (1806–73)

The most important British political thinker since Hobbes, John Stuart Mill was the son of James Mill. He is credited with having shorn 'Benthamism' of much of its crassness, but he remained committed to a utilitarian approach to politics. He also expressed reservations about the desirability of introducing democratic forms of government into contemporary society. Mill's essay *On Liberty* (1859) has been seen as an important source of modern liberal ideas, and in *The Subjection of Women* (1869) he offered an important early liberal statement of positions that have been subsequently developed by feminist thinkers. His other major political work was *Considerations on Representative Government* (1861).

A number of features of Mill's doctrine of liberty are particularly significant in relation to the idea of freedom as an end of politics. In the first place, Mill argued that freedom places limits on the action of government: it may not impose upon the sphere of liberty. Secondly, the preservation of liberty requires the existence of mechanisms of legal constraint that will protect individuals in the exercise of their individual liberty. Thirdly, since Mill related individual freedom to human progress, there is a sense in which he treated liberty as an instrumental value. Fourthly, Mill insisted that liberty must be enjoyed by *all* sections of the adult population. In a marked departure from the traditional position, Mill argued that the things that make liberty valuable mean that the right to equal freedom should be extended to women as well as to men. This position was advanced in Mill's essay *The Subjection of Women* (1869). In this work he argued that since liberty is important in relation both to self-development and to human progression, there are no grounds for denying equal liberty to women. As Mill put it, the 'moral regeneration of mankind will only really commence, when the most fundamental of the social relations is placed under the rule of equal justice, and when human beings learn to cultivate their strongest sympathy with an equal in rights and in cultivation' (Mill, 1989, p. 211). Even if women were inferior to men – and Mill thought that any inferiority is due largely to social expectations and environmental conditions – this is no reason for maintaining systems of social and political subordination that prevent women from developing their characters and contributing to the 'moral regeneration' of humanity.

Finally, Mill's attempt to promote recognition of a 'sphere of liberty' for individuals was accompanied by identification of a social sphere, an area where the exercise of individual liberty might cause harm to social interests. But while Mill did not deny the claims of society over the individual, he treated what was due to the individual and what was due to society as falling within separate spheres. In this respect his conception of liberty differed significantly from those developed by an important group of modern political theorists who claimed that freedom must be seen as the product of the interaction between individual and social impulses. These thinkers treated freedom as a direct end of politics, and they did so in such a way as to transform liberty from a right possessed by individuals into a quality embedded in social existence and realised within particular political structures.

Freedom, Sociability and the State: Rousseau, Hegel and Green

The beginnings of a distinctly social conception of freedom can be seen in the writings of the mid-eighteenth-century philosopher Jean-Jacques Rousseau. Although Rousseau used the language of natural rights and treated the natural condition as one of complete freedom, he laid the groundwork for later accounts of the relationship between freedom, sociability and the political characteristics of the modern state. For Rousseau and the other writers discussed in this section, freedom is most emphatically the end of politics, but they insisted that an adequate conception of freedom must take account of its social dimensions.

In his *Discourse on the Inequality of Mankind* Rousseau traced the impact of the growth of sociability and related improvements in agriculture and technology to natural liberty. These developments have made possible an existence that is culturally, materially and psychologically richer than that enjoyed by natural human beings. Rousseau warned, however, that these putative benefits may be purchased at a terrible cost: the *Discourse* concludes with an account of a contractual process by which the rich, powerful but insecure members of the population trick their fellows into establishing a state that reinforces existing inequalities and better equips the rich to oppress the poor. In the final analysis, servitude becomes universal: the rich give power into the hands of a despot in order to secure their property and to ensure the continued subjection of the mass of the population.

> Here is the final stage of inequality, and the extreme point that closes the circle and touches the point from which we started. Here all private individuals become equals again, because they are nothing. And since subjects no longer have any law other than the master's will, nor the master any rule other than his own passions, the notions of good and the principles of justice vanish (Rousseau, 1987, p. 79).

This outcome is tragic because it epitomises the corruption of a process that may, in other circumstances, be generally beneficial. Sociability erodes the radical independence of natural human beings, but it may replace this either with domination and servility, or with a form of interdependence that preserves the physical, intellectual and moral integrity of individuals. The second of these possibilities holds out the hope that the natural freedom of humankind may be transformed into a qualitatively different kind of liberty that allows human beings to reap the benefits of sociability while avoiding its pitfalls. This form of liberty is 'civil' or political, and it can exist only in a state that avoids bad faith, delusion and the reinforcement of prepolitical inequalities.

This state is the subject of Rousseau's most important political work, *The Social Contract*. The problem addressed in this book is signalled at the outset:

> Man is born free, and everywhere he is in chains. He who believes himself the master of the others does not escape being more of a slave than they. How did this change take place? I have no idea. What can render it legitimate? I believe I can answer this question (ibid., p. 141).

In common with the theorists discussed earlier in this chapter, Rousseau used the idea of a contract as a device for explaining the process through which individuals agree to curtail their natural liberty and place themselves under the command of a political superior. In Rousseau's account, this process necessitates the complete renunciation of claims based upon natural rights and their recreation as rights recognised and protected by the state. At the point of renunciation, individuals return to the equality of the initial stages of the state of nature; the recreation of rights signals that they are now in a new environment where claims must be considered in relation to the 'common interest' they have created by forming political society. As members of the state, they exchange their *natural* liberty for *political* freedom, for a form of liberty that both reflects and facilitates their interdependence.

> At once, in place of the individual person of each contracting party, this act of association produces a moral and collective body composed of as many members as there are voices in the assembly, which receives from this same act its unity, its common *self*, its life and its will (ibid., p. 148).

The range of individuals' interests has been enlarged by the common concerns they share with their fellow citizens; these provide the focus of their existence as political beings, an existence that is based on freedom and equality and is not (with the notable, but predictable, exception of women) affected by any natural inequalities that may have existed in a prepolitical condition. For Rousseau, the transformative implications of the social contract do not apply to women, who thus remain in a condition of 'natural' subservience that is not overcome by the recognised right to political freedom that men enjoy (Okin, 1992, pp. 144–5).

When thinking of the common or general interest, citizens express what Rousseau called the 'general will'; that is, a will directed towards those shared interests that are different from (but do not necessarily preclude) private interests. When Rousseau stipulated that people in the state are as 'free' as they were before, he does not mean they are free in the same way. To the contrary, political freedom has to do with people's capacity to pursue the shared aspirations that are the focus of their common life. This requirement has important implications for the structure of the state and for the ways in which power is exercised. However the point to note here is that, in Rousseau's view, politics involves a distinctive conception of freedom. Members of the state abandon natural liberty and independence, but they have the opportunity to take on the morally and intellectually challenging mantle of interdependence and political freedom. Thus while Rousseau started with a consideration of natural liberty, he concluded by identifying a new form of freedom that is qualitatively different from that enjoyed by individuals in a natural condition. This view of freedom played an important role in subsequent political thought.

One of the most important of these accounts of the relationship between politics and freedom was produced by G. W. F. Hegel. Because Hegel's *Elements of the Philosophy of Right* contains statements such as 'the real is the rational' and the 'state is the realisation of freedom', it has been easy for his critics to dismiss him as an apologist for absolute, despotic government. The fact that Hegel was (by virtue of his professorial position) an employee of the Prussian government has sometimes been used to underline this interpretation. In fact, however, Hegel was a firm supporter of the constitutional and legal reforms undertaken in Prussia in the second decade of the nineteenth century (Wood, 1991, pp. ix–x). He believed that only a liberalised, constitutional state can be identified with freedom. In other words, only a *modern* (as opposed to an ancient, feudal, absolute or indeed revolutionary) state is capable of embodying freedom in a way that corresponds to a plausible understanding of this term. It was the purpose of Hegel's political philosophy to show what freedom means in the modern world, and to identify the political implications of this idea. Only in this special sense can the 'state' be described as the realisation of freedom.

Georg Wilhelm Friedrich Hegel (1770–1831)

Hegel, who was a German academic philosopher, synthesised important but 'one-sided' conceptions of a range of reflections on human experience embodied in the history of Western philosophy from the ancient Greek world to the present time. Hegel wrote on aesthetics, logic and the philosophies of mind and science, as well as on political philosophy. His major political work, *The Elements of the Philosophy of Right* (1821), is usually known in English simply but somewhat misleadingly as *The Philosophy of Right*. Hegel's understanding of modern political and social life was based on a close study of political and economic developments in the most advanced states of the period: France and Great Britain.

Hegel used the expression the 'idea of freedom' to refer to an aspiration that had developed during the course of human history. Incomplete aspects of this conception had been expressed in various ways and had given rise to a variety of political ideas and institutions that embodied them. Since he believed human thought to be a reflection of human consciousness upon human experience, Hegel maintained that philosophy cannot leap ahead of its time. Because its role is to understand what *is*, the question 'what is the idea of freedom?' must focus on what the term 'freedom' entails in the modern world. However, Hegel did not merely reproduce ordinary accounts of freedom. Rather he sought to identify a conception of 'rational freedom' based upon a philosophical analysis of human aspirations and their institutional manifestations.

Rational freedom harmonises limited or 'abstract' beliefs that freedom consists of the unimpeded pursuit of individual preferences, with the demands and possibilities of social and political life. People are not free when they isolate themselves from others and follow their own arbitrary impulses. To the contrary, individuals act freely when they consciously integrate what is external to them so that these things and people become part of their aspirations and actions (ibid., pp. xiv–xvii). They are only truly free when they act 'universally', that is, in a way that – because it is integrated with what is beyond their bare self – eliminates dependence on the external world. 'Only in this freedom is the will completely *with itself* . . . because it has reference to nothing but itself, so that every relationship of *dependence* on something *other* than itself is thereby eliminated.' Universality thus removes limitations on human action and opens up possibilities that do not exist in the necessarily restricted condition of isolated, non-integrated individuals: the will 'is *universal*, because all limitation and particular individuality . . . are superseded within it' (Hegel, 1991, p. 54). An important implication of this position is that social life, or as Hegel's German contemporaries described it, the 'sphere of duties', is far from being a barrier to human freedom. Freedom will be more complete when people's perceptions of social life and the institutions that embody them contribute to individuality rather than being seen as, and to some degree actually constituting, a barrier to the full exercise of individual liberty.

Human life must constitute what Hegel called a 'concrete universal'. It must provide for the subjective freedom of the individual (thus eliminating 'abstract ' or one-sided universality, which sees the individual only as a member of a collectivity, as in Plato's *Republic*), and it must also recognise and embody collective needs. A concrete universal avoids 'abstract particularity', a perspective that views individuals as atoms that can be brought together (as in Hobbes' *Leviathan*) in mechanical, and to some degree mutually frustrating, combinations. Concrete universality is central to Hegel's notion of rational freedom. It provides the opportunity to formulate and pursue individual goals (thus recognising individuals' particularity) while at the same time providing scope for cooperative social action. In short, the 'concrete universal' abolishes neither the individual nor society but beneficially combines them.

In the *Philosophy of Right* Hegel presented an account of the modern state as a concrete universal. This does not imply that the modern state cannot be improved upon, merely that it marked the most complete embodiment of rational freedom known to Hegel. In this state, freedom is 'actual'; that is, there is scope for individual liberty, but its exercise is harmonised with a collective good that is both genuine and capable of being recognised by individuals within society (ibid., pp. 288–9). In the modern world freedom has three dimensions: abstract or personal freedom; conscience or subjective morality; and 'ethical' or social life. In the first case, individuals think of themselves as *'persons*, indeterminate choosers' (Wood, 1991, p. xiv), who see the world as a place in which they can exercise freedom in the simple arbitrary sense. Hegel described this conception as the basis of 'abstract right', which protects rights through legal institutions regardless of the use to which they are put. However, adult human beings also evaluate their conduct by reference to universal standards. This aspiration forms the sphere of conscience or 'subjective morality', which focuses on conformity to an inwardly valid standard. In order to be effective however, this standard must be recognised and protected by the social institutions that collectively form what Hegel called 'ethical life'. Ethical life is the third dimension of freedom, one that is necessary because of the incompleteness and instability of both abstract right and morality:

> The sphere of right and that of morality cannot exist independently ...; they must have the ethical as their support and foundation. For right lacks the moment of subjectivity, which in turn belongs solely to morality, so that neither of the two moments has any independent actuality (Hegel, 1991, p. 186).

Ethical life contributes to freedom by maintaining institutions whose value is recognised by individuals. Hegel grouped these institutions under three headings: the family, 'civil society', and the 'police and the corporation'. The family meets needs that arise from ties of blood; it is based on love. This aspect of human life contributes to rational freedom, but its basis is *natural* rather than *rational*. Individuals do not choose their families, and while family membership may be a necessary condition of rational freedom, it is not a sufficient one. The reason for this is that the identity of individual family members merges with that of their respective families, and over time particular families disintegrate into a plurality of families. Family life thus fails to recognise fully the particularity of its members, and it is also an unstable condition.

Hegel identified one significant exception to his general claim about the limitations of family life. He argued that the 'vocation' of females 'consists essentially only in the marital relationship', and justified this position by refering to what he took to be the distinctive cast of the female mind. He thus claimed that although 'women may have insights,... taste, and delicacy,... they do not possess the ideal' of freedom. Consequently, 'when women are in charge of government, the state is in danger, for their actions are based not on the demands of universality but on contingent inclination and opinion' (ibid., p. 207). The implications of the political limitations of what are taken to be distinctive female capacities are closely related to Hegel's attempt to restrict female fulfilment to the family sphere because he maintained that citizenship is mediated through 'civil society', a sphere from which females appear to be excluded.

Hegel argued that individual identity is recovered in 'civil society'. In part this terms refers to a modern 'market' society that recognises and protects a realm of private activity where individuals pursue their own conception of their interests. Unlike many modern writers, however,

Hegel did not think that civil society is reducible to self-interest. To the contrary, he insisted that it has social dimensions that are not merely accidental consequences of the working of the 'invisible hand' of market exchanges (Wood, 1991, p. xx). Civil society has a duty to educate potential members; it has a collective responsibility to prevent pauperism because this is incompatible with the ethos of civil society. Moreover Hegel argued that since individuals within civil society identify with trade and professional associations, they are not purely free-floating and isolated. These institutions give a social dimension to economic pursuits, but they will not prevent occasional yet damaging economic crises. For this reason the play of market forces must be set in a framework of general regulation carried out by public authorities performing what Hegel termed 'police functions' (Hegel, 1991, pp. 260–70).

Thus while civil society provides invaluable scope for some expressions of freedom, it is not a final, self-contained model for rational freedom. Modern society requires a political state to resolve the tensions produced in civil society and also to provide a focus of identification that is inherently and completely, rather than partially and to some degree accidentally, social. In his account of the political dimensions of the modern state, Hegel sought to identify the rational dimensions of a constitutional monarchy that incorporates professional administrators and representative assemblies. In a state of this kind, the monarch personifies subjective freedom and the estates represent distinct groups within civil society. Moreover, since they are elected by their constituent members, estates provide a vehicle for the expression of their free subjectivity. Finally, the modern state must have a professional civil service dedicated to the universal or common interests of the community (ibid., pp. 282–359). These details relate closely to Hegel's interest in the reform movement in contemporary Prussia. It is important to recall, however, that this 'political state' (essentially the machinery of government) is only one aspect of the modern state. This entity embraces the whole community and is thus a complex web of ideas, individuals and institutions that together constitute rational freedom and make it possible.

Writers who approach politics from the perspective of natural liberty treat the state as an important but limited agency that reconciles aspects of natural freedom with the requirements of social life. This view played a role in Rousseau's theory, and Hegel was thus critical of Rousseau's attempt to derive the general will from individual wills, and to deduce the state from a contractual arrangement that must necessarily be based on the 'arbitrary will and opinions' of natural individuals (ibid., p. 277). In response to the limitations of Rousseau's theory, Hegel argued that rational freedom can only incorporate viable aspects of the concern with individual freedom if politics is understood in relation to a particular type of society. This society needs government, but its distinctive features cannot be explained solely by reference to the implications of coercive social coordination for natural liberty. Hegel's multilayered conception of freedom underwrote a political theory that encapsulated all the salient features of the modern state and produced a theory of community rather than just a theory of government.

Hegel's political theory has had a mixed reception. Originally rejected for its extreme, even reactionary conservatism, these alleged features of Hegel's conception of the state later provided the basis for admiration of it (Wood, 1991, p. viii). Both these responses rest on a misunderstanding of Hegel's position, a point that has been at least implicitly acknowledged by other critics. As we shall see, these critics included the revolutionary socialist Karl Marx. However it is important not to allow twentieth-century Marxism to obscure the impact of liberal interpretations of Hegel in the nineteenth century. This was largely due to the revival of interest in late-eighteenth-and early-nineteenth-century German political philosophy that took place in England from about 1870. The key figure in this revival was T. H. Green. Green's political thought was centrally concerned with virtue, but he maintained that virtue and freedom are closely linked (see p. 71). In this respect his position echoes aspects of Kant's political theory. However, unlike Kant, Green and his followers placed a great deal of weight on the positive relationship between freedom and the modern state, a feature of their perception of politics that owed much to their reading of Hegel.

Like Hegel, Green thought that freedom involves the integration of individuality and sociability, and also like Hegel he drew attention to the embodiment of these values in the ideas and institutions of modern, constitutional states. Green thought that virtuous conduct has to be *self*-willed or free, but he maintained that state actions can contribute to freedom by protecting rights, or claims to free action; by laying down rules whose infringement is a punishable offence, but which can be treated as a guide to be followed freely; and by removing obstacles to free action that spring from the improper use of economic, social or political power or are a consequence of ignorance, poor environmental conditions or historically ingrained subservience. These measures contribute to what Green called a 'positive' conception of freedom – 'a positive power or capacity of doing or enjoying something worth doing or enjoying, and that, too, something we do or enjoy in common with others' (Green, 1986, p. 199) – which is compatible with the underlying thrust of liberal politics.

Social Freedom and the Critique of State Theory: Marx

While Hegel's political theory did not have a marked impact on the English-speaking world until almost half a century after his death, it generated a far more immediate response in Germany. A number of radical writers treated Hegel as a theorist of the modern constitutional state and gave serious consideration to his attempt to reconcile free individuality with sociability. However, these critics condemned Hegel's attachment to constitutional and liberal values. In terms of the subsequent history of political thought, the most significant response to Hegel was produced by the revolutionary socialist Karl Marx and his associate Friedrich Engels.

Karl Marx (1818–83)

Marx was the founder (along with his collaborator Friedrich Engels) of the school of political thinking that bears his name. He was born and educated in Germany, but spent the second half of his life in exile in London. There he wrote extensively on economics and politics and played a vigorous part in the internal politics of European socialism. Marx's political writings include *The German Ideology* and the *Communist Manifesto*, both of which were written with Engels. Marx was the sole author of the major (but incomplete) statement of the basis of Marxist communism, *Capital*. His theory was developed in critical reaction to those of Hegel, classical political economists, bourgeois liberals, and a variety of anarchist and non-Marxist socialists.

Like Hegel, Marx rejected the political significance of natural liberty, and stressed the extent to which a complete conception of freedom must take account of the social dimensions of the human personality. In Marx's view, however, the philosopher of right failed to understand the true basis of human consciousness, individuality and sociability. Marx argued that an adequate understanding of the state must start from a clear conception of the basis of human existence, namely the social conditions under which human beings produce the material necessities of life. In particular he claimed that human beings cannot be free unless they produce freely; that is, under circumstances in which their activities are directed to fulfilling fundamental human needs through cooperative interactions that reflect their intrinsically social nature.

Although Marx's presentation of this argument is exceedingly complex (and contentious), the implications he drew from it are relatively clear. These implications relate in the first instance to the necessarily oppressive nature of private property. Since production is a fundamental human activity, control of the process of labour and its product by property owners takes away what are really human and social attributes and bestows these on limited sections of the population. This process of 'alienation', as Marx called it, involves a loss of humanity and a consequent diminution of the capacity to exercise all human attributes, including free will: 'the activity of the worker is not his own spontaneous activity. It belongs to another, it is a loss of self' (Marx, 1975, p. 327). Modern society is divided along class lines, reflecting an imbalance of social and economic power between property holders and the propertyless, and therefore it cannot form the focus of a genuinely social existence. Moreover this imbalance makes freedom impossible: those who possess significant amounts of property oppress the rest of the population.

As we have seen, Hegel was aware of the potentially damaging implications of economic inequality and looked to the state to overcome these. Marx argued, however, that the state cannot achieve this worthy end because its structure and ethos are products of, and reflect the inequalities attendant upon, the intrusion of *private* property into the realm of *social* production. For Marx, the state reflects and upholds inequality. Inequalities give rise to class antagonisms, and there can be no genuine sense of community, no universal or general interest in a society divided along class lines. Nor can the state be seen as a disinterested force valiantly struggling to resolve class tensions or limit their impact on freedom. To the contrary, the modern state, like all the states that preceded it, is merely a reflection of the interests of the dominant class. Although it may present itself as an embodiment of the general interest, the state's conduct reflects (in a more or less subtle form) the oppressive tendencies embedded in what Marx called the 'social relations of production'. The state, Marx wrote, 'is nothing more than the form of organization which the bourgeois necessarily adopt for internal and external purposes' (Marx and Engels, 1968, p. 59).

Marx's conclusion was that the realisation of freedom must await the overthrow of political institutions and of the systems of economic inequality that underpin them. True and universal freedom requires a social system that is both communistic (meaning that productive resources are collectively rather than privately held) and stateless. Freedom is the goal of Marxian communism, but it can only be attained when private property and the state have been destroyed.

This conclusion was endorsed by a number of revolutionary socialists who were part of a tradition of nineteenth- and early-twentieth-century anarchist thinking. For these writers, however, the sort of theory advanced by Marx and Engels posed at least as much of a threat to the realisation of human freedom as that promoted by Hegel and his followers. In the late nineteenth and early twentieth centuries anarchism was thus an important source for critiques of Marxism from a socialist perspective, but this strand represented only one part of a tradition that also had a strongly individualistic orientation.

Freedom and Anarchy: Godwin, Proudhon, Bakunin, Kropotkin, Stirner, Warren and Tucker

If one thinks of the state as a core aspect of politics, then anarchism points to the termination of politics as this is usually understood. Even so, the anarchist critique of the state forms an important tradition in the history of political thought. Anarchist thinking is especially germane to any consideration of political theories that take freedom as their starting point because its rejection of the state hinges on a belief in its necessarily harmful effect on human liberty. Although all anarchists regard freedom as a fundamental value, they take differing views on the implications that should be drawn from this insight. While one important strand in anarchist thinking adopts a social conception of freedom that seeks to avoid the authoritarian implications of Marxist forms of revolutionary socialism, other anarchists have focused on the autonomy of the individual and regarded the demands of society as a threat to it.

This line of argument was first formulated systematically in William Godwin's *Enquiry Concerning Political Justice* (1794). Godwin's political ideas are marked by a concern with rational independence, and a suspicion of many of the features of the political and religious establishment in England. Political justice depends on people's capacity to take an impartial view of their interests and those of their fellows, and to act in ways that maximise human happiness: 'by justice I understand that impartial treatment of every man in matters that relate to his happiness, which is measured solely by a consideration of the properties of the receiver, and the capacity of him that bestows' (Godwin, 1769, vol. i, p. 126). Political justice, in other words, is a product of 'rational benevolence', of a reason-guided intention to take account of the happiness of others. Godwin argued that freedom is crucial to benevolence because resort to coercion displaces rational deliberation and rational assent with calculations based on fear. Consequently he rejected a wide variety of attitudes, practices and institutions that he regarded as hostile to the exercise and development of rational humans' faculties. Many of these coercive influences can be identified closely with the monarchical and aristocratic culture of eighteenth-century Europe, but Godwin's critique of the state is a general one. States work through systems of law that blindly predetermine how actions should be evaluated and responded to. Moreover, since the final sanction of law is coercion not reason, Godwin argued that governments can neither respect reason nor – however good their intentions – create an environment where reason becomes the basis of human conduct.

Godwin's political prescriptions are very cautious. For example, although he admitted that revolutions may be necessary to free society from tyranny, he was not sanguine about their capacity to promote human and social progression: they rely upon violence and create situations where rational deliberation is virtually impossible (ibid., pp. 272–3). Since Godwin believed that benevolence can flourish only when individual freedom is restrained by reason alone, he looked forward to the replacement of the state by a large number of small and intimate communities where individuals would be subjected only to the rational and non-coercive influences of their neighbour's arguments (Godwin, 1969, vol. ii, pp. 191– 212).

The stress Godwin laid on non-coercive human interaction and the rejection of the legitimacy of the state became a feature of subsequent anarchist writings. Nineteenth-century anarchists often treated Godwin as an important figure in the development of anarchist thought, but those who regarded anarchism as a form of revolutionary socialism abandoned his practical caution and rejected his tendency to treat social influences as a threat to the autonomy of individuals.

The most important accounts of social anarchism were produced by the French writer P.-J. Proudhon and two Russian thinkers, Michael Bakunin and Peter Kropotkin. Proudhon maintained that since authority and liberty are inescapable, mutually dependent facts of human existence, it is necessary to identify forms of social and political organisation that balance authority by liberty so as to maximise the scope of the latter. He argued that only anarchy, a system in which 'social order arises from nothing but transactions and exchanges', can satisfy this requirement (Proudhon, 1979, pp. 6–7,11). Anarchy was to be created through a contractual process recognising the autonomy of the participants and giving rise to a 'federation' rather than a centralised state:

What is essential to and characteristic of the federal contract ... is that in this system the contracting parties ... not only undertake bilateral and communicative obligations, but in making the pact reserve for themselves more rights, more liberty, more authority, more property than they abandon (ibid., p. 39).

Central government would be replaced by an agency responsible for creating legislative machinery, which would remain under the direction of local authorities and of citizens themselves. Federation 'consists in ruling every people, at any given movement, by decreasing the sway of authority and central power to the point permitted by the level of consciousness and morality' (ibid., p. 49). Proudhon contrasted the order created through anarchy with the liberty-sapping chaos of a centralised state: 'what you call unity and centralisation is nothing but perpetual chaos, serving as a basis for endless tyranny; it is the advancing of the chaotic condition of social forces as an argument for despotism – a despotism which is really the cause of chaos' (Proudhon, 1923, p. 246).

Pierre-Joseph Proudhon (1809–65)

Brought up in humble circumstances in the Jura region of south-central France, Proudhon began his adult life in the printing trade. While working as a printer he continued his education, and by the 1840s had gained a reputation as an important radical thinker. At first his ideas were admired by Marx, but Proudhon's subsequent development of an anarchist position made him a target of Marxist criticism. His most important political writings are *What is Property?* (1840), *Philosophy of Poverty* (1846), *The Idea of the Revolution of the Nineteenth Century* (1851) and *Federation* (1863).

For Proudhon, as for many other anarchists, the preservation of liberty required economic as well as political change. Proudhon regarded the principle of federation as a key element in this process. He described capitalism as a system of 'financial feudalism' and argued that it must be replaced by an 'agro-industrial federation' that would organise public services and regulate the economic condition of the individuals and associations that were contractual members of it (Proudhon, 1979, pp. 70–1). Large-scale industrial enterprises would be controlled by working men's associations made up of those involved in them, but these organisations must resist the temptation to infringe on the autonomy of their members: 'the best association is one into which, thanks to a better organisation, liberty enters most and devotion least' (Proudhon, 1923, p. 98).

In Proudhon's account of anarchism, federation is the key to forms of social solidarity that do not undermine individual freedom. A stress upon combining liberty and solidarity is a central theme in social conceptions of anarchism. In Bakunin's case this point was made by reference to the conditions of human consciousness. Bakunin maintained that people's consciousness of themselves is a product of their interrelationship with others. Consequently he thought that *individual freedom* can only be understood in the context of a *free society*:

> Being free ... means being acknowledged, considered and treated as such by [another person] and by all [others] around him.... [T]he liberty of any individual is nothing more or less than the reflection of his humanity and his human rights in the awareness of all free men – his brothers, his equals (Bakunin, 1973, p. 147).

This doctrine combined two of the slogans of the French revolutionaries – 'liberty' and 'fraternity' – and implied the third: 'equality'. Like other social anarchists, Bakunin considered the inequalities produced by capitalism to be incompatible with both freedom and fraternity. Social control of resources reflects the inherently cooperative nature of human life and ensures that they do not become the means through which some individuals deprive their fellows of liberty. Authority of any kind is incompatible with human freedom and also with free sociability.

Michael Bakunin (1814–76)

The son of a member of the Russian gentry, Bakunin spent the greater part of his adult life in various European countries propagating anarchism and engaging in fruitless revolutionary conspiracies. His view of the revolutionary potential of the peasantry was influential in parts of Italy and Spain. Bakunin engaged in a bitter dispute with Marx on revolutionary tactics and struggled with him for control of the First International, an organisation of European socialists. Bakunin's political ideas were presented in a range of pamphlets, and his most developed statement, *Statism and Anarchy* (1873), an extended critique of Marxism, was published a year after his expulsion from the International.

Bakunin conceived of anarchy as a new social order where the only restrictions on human freedom come from moral and intellectual influences. In a true society people are

> *compelled not by the will or oppression of other men, nor by the repression of the State and legislation, which are necessarily represented and implemented by men* and would make them slaves in their turn, *but by the actual*

organization of the social environment, so constituted that while leaving each man to enjoy the utmost possible liberty it gives no one the power to set himself above others or to dominate them, except through the natural influence of his own intellectual or moral qualities, which must never be allowed either to convert itself into a right or to be backed by any kind of political institution (ibid., pp. 152–3).

These conditions can be satisfied if human life is focused on small-scale organisations, reflecting the natural sociability of limited sections of the population. Autonomous communities should be linked by a system of federation that facilitates cooperative activity. Federalism thus produces the same benefits for communities as anarchism does for individuals. Externally imposed authorities are to be swept away and replaced by the self- recognised, self-imposed authority of science and of the natural laws that underlie human interaction. The authority of the state and of its religious handmaidens is counter productive; it produces conflicts and injustices that would not exist in a stateless, free environment.

This rejection of the state rests upon the idea that social life is natural and does not have to be sustained by the intrusive oversight of government. For anarchists, the state's unnecessary curtailment of freedom damages sociability. This line of argument is clearly at odds with mainstream political thinking. Although the history of political thought presents a range of accounts of the ends of politics, there is general agreement that the state is an unavoidable and important feature of human existence. Towards the end of the nineteenth century this belief was reaffirmed by writers who reflected on the political implications of theories of natural selection. Thus T. H. Huxley (who thought of himself as a follower of Charles Darwin) argued that the state ensures that the 'struggle for existence' is directed towards the benefit of the community (Huxley, n.d., pp. 339–40). Huxley's argument implies a challenge to anarchism because it makes the state essential and justifies it by reference to a fashionable scientific theory. This challenge was taken up by Peter Kropotkin, a leading late-nineteenth-century exponent of social anarchism.

Peter Kropotkin (1842–1921)

Born into a well-connected and noble family, Kropotkin served in the Russian imperial college of pages and in the army. He subsequently acquired a reputation as an important geographer and a mild-mannered but effective theorist of revolutionary anarchism. His conception of the scientific basis of this doctrine was expressed most completely in a series of articles that were published in book form as *Mutual Aid* in 1897.

In *Mutual Aid* Kropotkin surveyed a wide range of historical and scientific data that he thought lent support to an anarchist conception of the cooperative and social basis of human life. An examination of both the natural and human world led Kropotkin to reject the idea of a struggle for existence. He argued that successful species, that is, those that survive and develop, are distinguished by their capacity for 'mutual aid'. Kropotkin acknowledged that struggle plays a role in this process, but he claimed that it takes place *against* external forces, not *between* members of the same species. Species and human groupings that survive and flourish do so through processes of natural selection that reinforce cooperative behaviour and eliminate antisocial tendencies. Consequently the course of evolutionary development is marked by a growth of mutual aid and a decline in competition within groups and species. In human history this process has produced systems of social ethics that give priority to cooperation and discourage conflict.

Kropotkin's explanation of the mechanics of human and social development leaves no room for the state. Human beings are naturally sociable and any progress they have made has followed an evolutionary pattern that can be explained by the principle of mutual aid. For Kropotkin, the state is an aberration in human history, one that appeared relatively late in the day (Kropotkin, n.d., pp. 216–22). In making this point, Kropotkin extolled the virtues of the guild system of medieval Europe, arguing that it provided a sophisticated exemplification of the principle of mutual aid. Significantly, the rise of the modern state has involved the destruction of guild society. In place of cooperative self-regulation, the state has imposed a system of direction from the top, and has sought to justify its position by a range of theories that make the existence of political authority a precondition of social life (ibid., pp. 226–7). Kropotkin argued that the state is a standing contradiction of the mutual aid principle and is fundamentally antisocial. It is based on sectional and class domination, and despite its elaborate ideological trappings, it has been unable to deliver what it promised. In place of harmony, justice, peace and progress it has generated conflict, injustice and stagnation. For Kropotkin, the regressive effects of political authority are epitomised by the state's reliance on law – a system of imposed, insensitive and impersonal regulation – and by the brutality of penal practices that are a logical consequence of its reliance on repression as a tool of social control (Kropotkin, 1971, pp. 338–72).

In common with other revolutionary anarchists, Kropotkin believed that the breakdown of the modern capitalist state would provide an opportunity for reconstituting a genuine society based on natural principles. He also endorsed the common anarchist view that the revolutionary process must not be perverted by the institution of other forms of authority, least of all by systems of revolutionary government or

'state socialism'. For Kropotkin, anarchism should be based on a federation of decentralised territorial 'communes', or voluntary associations,
which would embody *all* social interests. However, unlike Proudhon and
Bakunin, Kropotkin thought that the organisational principle of
these communes should be 'collectivism' rather than 'mutualism'. That is,
the commune itself should own all productive resources, rather than
these being under the mutual control of those engaged in particular
forms of production. The community would be responsible for allocating
goods on the basis of *need* rather than *contribution*. Kropotkin maintained
that these arrangements would most accurately reflect the natural principle of mutual aid: voluntary association means that all members
of the community can exercise and develop their capacities for 'free
initiative, free action, free association'. Collectivism recognises the fundamentally mutual and integrated·character of social existence. The goal is
to foster 'the most complete development of *individuality* combined
with the highest development of voluntary association in all aspects, in
all possible degrees, for all imaginable aims' (Kropotkin, 1970, pp.
127, 123).

During the last years of his life Kropotkin witnessed the early stages of
a nightmare that had haunted the imaginations of nineteenth-
century revolutionary anarchists. Under the influence of the Marxist leader V. I. Lenin, the revolution in Russia proved to be the harbinger of an
extreme form of state collectivism instituted by a minute section of the
population that was divorced from both the peasantry and industrial
workers (see p. 335). An important step in the consolidation of Lenin's
revolutionary elite was the elimination of the anarchists, a process that
was to be repeated in the course of the civil war in Spain in the late
1930s.

These events were part of the history of revolutionary socialism in
Europe, but more or less from its inception social anarchism had been
subject to powerful challenges by other, individualist anarchists. The
potential for conflict between social and individualistic anarchism was
clearly signalled by Max Stirner in *The Ego and Its Own*. Like Marx,
Stirner was a radical critic of Hegel, but he also rejected revolutionary
socialism. In *The Ego and Its Own* Stirner drew a distinction between 'political liberalism', a theory that upholds personal equality as a goal and
promotes a 'rational' democratic state, and 'social liberalism' or communism. Political liberalism subjects individuals to a rational state, while social
liberalism subjects them to society: according to the latter '*no one* must
have, as according to political liberalism *no one was to give orders*; as in
that case the *State* alone obtained the command, so now *society* alone
obtains the possessions' and will make individuals work for it (Stirner,
1995, p. 105).

> **Max Stirner (1806–56)**
>
> Born Johann Caspar Schmidt in Bayreuth, Stirner had an undistinguished career as a student at the universities of Berlin, Erlangen and Konigsberg. While working as a teacher in Berlin in the early 1840s, Stirner was associated with 'the free', a group of radical Hegelians whose meetings were attended by Friedrich Engels. His major political work, *The Ego and Its Own*, was published in 1844 to widespread critical comment.

This line of criticism was a consequence of Stirner's wish to uphold the integrity of what he called the 'ego', understood not as a set of desires or a conventionally selfish individual, but as an empty potentiality that fills itself by taking whatever the world offers. Stirner shared his radical contemporaries' distaste for religion, monarchy and fatherland, but he went far beyond them and rejected all ideals on the grounds that they impose external standards upon the ego and seek to recruit it for alien causes. In Stirner's account, the ego is ensnared by moral, religious and political ideas that are merely devious and self-serving representations of other people's aspirations. The effect of social conditioning is such that these impositions are to some degree self-inflicted. Originally external creations, they are adopted by individuals as *their* cause, and thereby become especially tenacious. Like the 'spooks' that haunt the minds of those 'possessed' by supernatural spirits, these ideas are products of the imagination that return to control and terrify their creators. As Stirner put it:

> Man your head is haunted; you have wheels in your head! You imagine great things, and depict to yourself a whole world of gods that has an existence for you, a spirit realm to which you suppose yourself to be called, an ideal that beckons to you. You have a fixed idea! ... [a]n idea that has subjected the man to itself (ibid., p. 43).

Since Stirner wrote in a context that was influenced by Hegel's account of the state and by radical extensions of this general position, it is not surprising that one of the spooks he wished to lay to rest was the state. However his anarchism was unusual in that he rejected not only political authority, but *all* ideas and practices that claim the individual's allegiance and respect. Community, 'humanity', love, property and religion are all hostile to the ego. Once people understand this, these 'spooks' will be banished; the ego will regain its purity and can set about realising its self-formulated purposes. These purposes often require interaction with other egos, but Stirner wished to distinguish this from both conventional and radical conceptions of sociability. When egos cooperate with one another they do so from their own points of view, and on the basis of their own conception of their own interest; they *do not* act on the belief that they are contributing to causes that are not their own. The interaction of egos creates no 'common interests'.

Having rejected all bases for human action that rest on extra-individual claims, Stirner was left with an environment made up of morally and psychologically self-contained beings. His theory thus embodies a radically individualistic form of anarchism. Paradoxically, however, it does not preclude certain forms of domination. To the contrary, Stirner thought that some individuals may choose to place themselves under the absolute control of others. In doing so, however, they yield to superior power or attraction, but not because they believe that other individuals have a claim upon their loyalty (ibid., p. 150). In this case, as in that of cooperation between egos, nothing new is produced by interaction: it is merely a matter of one ego subjecting itself to another and making use of it. In this, as in other Stirnerian relationships, there is no meeting of minds: each party relates to the other from its own point of view. Even if large-scale cooperation or subjection appears in a Stirnerian world they cannot provide the basis for the state because they lack any of the psychological and moral features that distinguish social and political relationships.

This outcome reflects a belief that even liberty can acquire the status of an idol to which the ego is sacrificed. Stirner's extremism is unusual, but the sorts of reservation that he expressed about the damaging implications of social integration are a feature of individualistic anarchism. For example the mid-nineteenth-century American writer Josiah Warren defined liberty as the 'sovereignty of the individual', and argued that this is incompatible with social arrangements that imply anything more than a trivial degree of combination: 'The only ground upon which man can know liberty, is that of DISCONNECTION, DISUNION, INDIVIDUAL-ITY' (Warren, 1970, p. 322). The state is necessary only because human beings become interdependent and develop 'united' interests. Warren's solution to this problem was to make government unnecessary by urging individuals to be self-subsistent and independent:

If governments originate in combined interests, and if government and liberty cannot exist together, then the solution to our problem demands that there be NO COMBINED INTERESTS TO MANAGE.... [A]LL INTEREST AND RESPONSIBILITIES MUST BE ENTIRELY INDIVI-DUALIZED, before the legitimate liberty of mankind can be restored – before each can be sovereign of his own without violating the sovereignty of others (ibid., pp. 325, 329).

Warren's views on the tension between liberty and sociability, and his attempt to dissolve this by reducing interdependence, are echoed in the writings of his American follower, Benjamin Tucker. Tucker contrasted the benefits that result from competitive exchanges between free individuals with the tendency for collective action to become enshrined in monopolies that favour some sections of the population over others (Tucker, 1970, p. 175). Anarchism undercuts the basis of monopolies in land, capital and professional services because it withdraws from them the support of the state and throws these areas of life open to the invigorating breezes of individualised competition. This principle can also be applied to individual protection: there is no need for this function to be monopolised by the state and indeed many dangers result from such an arrangement. Tucker therefore looked to voluntary associations for self-defence, or to commercial agencies to provide protection for individuals without requiring the creation of authoritative institutions that undermine individual freedom (ibid., p. 181).

Conclusion

Both individual and social anarchists argued that the nature of freedom is such that it rules out all types of political authority. In contrast, while the other writers considered here regard some forms of political organisation and practice as incompatible with human freedom, they nevertheless thought it possible to identify political conditions that promote it. Machiavelli related individual freedom to the requirements of a particular form of government; he thought that membership of a popular republic provides unique opportunities for the realisation of distinctly human potentialities. Machiavelli's position may be contrasted with Locke's and Paine's focus on individual entitlements as specified by natural rights. These writers argued that political power should be organised and regulated in ways that take account of the role that freedom plays in enabling individuals to exercise their rights. This requirement plays a central role in Locke's and Paine's evaluation of systems of government, and of the ways in which political power is exercised.

John Stuart Mill rejected natural rights theory, but he thought individual liberty to be so important that it would set intractable limits on the restrictions that either government or society could place upon individuals. While he wished to protect individuals from society, Mill also thought it necessary to protect social interests from improper individual conduct. Unlike social proponents of liberty such as Rousseau, Hegel and Green, however, Mill did not regard significant forms of freedom as products of social membership. For these writers, freedom was only possible for members of political and social groups. They thus sought to identify systems of government that would allow socially embedded individuals to realise the potentialities of social membership. Since theories of this kind set individual freedom within a social context, they imply that the scope for and the benefits of free action will be constrained by the way in which freedom is understood, and by provision of the political and social institutions that are necessary to sustain it. The social conceptions of freedom advanced by these writers are similar in some respects to those that underwrite both social anarchism and Marxism. However, Rousseau and his successors regarded political institutions, and particularly the state, as a way of sustaining free action, not as an insuperable hindrance to it.

CHAPTER 4

Politics, Happiness and Welfare

This chapter discusses a number of political theories that start from the assumption that the primary purpose of politics is to promote human interests, happiness or welfare. In particular they regard government as an agency with a distinctive and general responsibility for ensuring that those who are subject to it enjoy as many of life's advantages as possible. While some of these theorists argue that this responsibility entails an active and positive role for government in, for example, distributing material goods, this is not a necessary feature of this perspective on politics. As we shall see, in some cases it is thought that the most important contribution that government can make to general welfare is to guarantee a framework of human interaction in which individuals can pursue their own conception of their own best interests.

At first sight it may appear that the claim that happiness or welfare are the ends of politics is self-evident and cannot provide the basis for a distinctive approach to the subject. This judgement is however inadequate. While we may accept unquestioningly the close and direct relationship between the legitimate activities of government and the advancement of the welfare of the general population, we must be aware that many significant traditions in the history of political thought rest on other views of the ends of politics. Moreover, with a few notable exceptions this approach to politics is a largely modern phenomenon. These points are obscured by the fact that virtually all accounts of politics place considerable stress on a government's role in promoting, or at least facilitating, the material and general welfare of its subjects. Even if one leaves aside those theories that subjugate any plausible conception of individual and social welfare to impersonal ends such as the good of the race, or the attainment of a distant goal such as that held out by Marxists, it is apparent that many political thinkers relate happiness or welfare to other, more fundamental values and understand them in terms of these.

Plato, for example, argued that the virtuous will be happy, and medieval injunctions concerning the welfare of subjects are set within a framework that makes well-being dependent upon the realisation of Christian values. Hobbes' account of the rationale of the state gains much of its force from his grim depiction of the miseries of the state of nature. But since Hobbes thought that any political condition is preferable to this, and since he stressed the relationship between sovereign power and order, it is plausible to think of him primarily as a theorist of order. He assumed, however, that it is only in the context of an order (as he understood this term) that human beings have any prospect of avoiding extreme misery. Theorists of natural liberty take for granted that the exercise of freedom is conducive to the realisation of human happiness.

The accounts of the ends of politics discussed in this chapter are distinctive because they make human well-being the starting point of political analysis. In the theories discussed here, human interests, human happiness or general welfare are regarded as *primary* political values, ones that provide criteria for evaluating political institutions and political action. Since this perspective on politics is a distinctly modern one, this chapter will focus largely on eighteenth- and nineteenth-century writers. It will begin with a brief sketch of the form of Christian utilitarianism developed by the late-eighteenth-century English philosopher William Paley.

Other early European proponents of utilitarian theories, such as the Abbé Saint-Pierre, also discussed ideas of human happiness in relation to Christian belief, but in its developed forms the doctrine became a fundamentally secular one based on a 'scientific' approach to politics. This development will be traced from the writings of the French writer Claude Helvetius and his Italian contemporary Cesare Beccaria to those of Jeremy Bentham, who is usually regarded as the most significant exponent of utilitarianism. Bentham's position was modified by his English successors, John Stuart Mill and Henry Sidgwick. Mill and Sidgwick accepted the general premise of utilitarianism – that political institutions must promote the 'greatest happiness of the greatest number' – but they subjected Bentham's account of this doctrine to significant revisions. The chapter will conclude with a brief discussion of the diffusion of a utilitarian perspective on politics in late-nineteenth- and early-twentieth-century political theory.

Although this chapter focuses on eighteenth- and nineteenth-century thinkers, it is important to note that elements of a utilitarian position can be found in earlier periods. For example the opening book of Plato's *Republic* includes accounts of justice that identify it either with the subjective interests of individuals or with the needs of the community, rather than with the pursuit of Platonic virtue. In roughly the same period, the Chinese thinker Mo Tzu formulated an account of the ends of politics in terms that have been compared to modern European theories of utilitarianism (Hsiao, 1979, pp. 234–5; Rubin, 1979, pp. 33–54).

Mo Tzu promoted the idea of 'universal love' as a solution to the conflict-ridden condition of contemporary society, and stressed the importance of adopting an impartial concern for human welfare rather than focusing on the particular interests of a ruler, a family or an individual (Tzu, 1963, pp. 39–40). In contrast to the emphasis on individual feeling and virtue that appeared in Confucian thought, Tzu argued that universal love forms an objective standard that focuses attention on the consequences of action rather than on the character of the actor. 'Every doctrine, discipline, and standard of benevolence and righteousness is intended on a larger scale to be used in governing men, and on a smaller scale to fit one for holding office' (Hsiao, 1979, p. 234; Mo Tzu, 1963, p. 130). This standard should be maintained by a just superior who forms part of an elaborate hierarchy that is similar in some respects to the feudal system that emerged in medieval Europe. Tzu argued that government should play a central role in identifying the general interest and in ensuring that the actions of individuals contribute to it. Human beings' tendency to selfish conduct has to be overcome by establishing a system of regulation that rewards those who serve the general interest and punishes those who undermine it. These rewards and penalties should be maintained by government, and Tzu made it clear that the purpose of such a system is to promote appropriate behaviour: 'To place ... honours upon the virtuous is not so much to reward virtue, as to bring about the success ... of government' (Mo Tzu, 1973, p. 33).

Tzu's insistence that politics should be directed to furthering the welfare of the population by promoting benevolent behaviour, his identification of the role played by rewards and punishments in this process, and his lack of interest in using government to promote personal virtue, were echoed by the thinkers discussed below. It is important to note, however, that there is a significant difference between his utilitarianism and that of many later Western writers. For Tzu, the ideal of universal benevolence rests upon the conventional religious ideas of the time. Benevolence is ordained by the spiritual forces that are the ultimate rulers of the universe:

> the interests of the magnanimous lies in procuring benefits for the world and eliminating its calamities.... When we try to develop and procure benefits for the world with universal love as our standard, then attentive ears and keen eyes will respond in service to one another, then limbs will be strengthened to work for one another (Tzu, 1973, p. 89).

Early Utilitarianism: Paley, Saint-Pierre, Hume, Helvetius and Beccaria

William Paley (1743–1805)

Paley taught at Cambridge University and was Archdeacon of Carlisle. He was the author of *Principles of Moral and Political Philosophy* (1785), a standard late-eighteenth- and early-nineteenth-century political text.

In the late eighteenth and early nineteenth centuries some versions of utilitarianism were set within a Christian framework. One of the most influential figures in this tradition was William Paley, the author of a widely read work entitled *The Principles of Moral and Political Philosophy*. Paley maintained that God's intentions for humanity could be identified by the tendency of actions to 'promote or diminish general happiness.' (Paley, 1803, vol. i, p. 69). He defined happiness as a condition in which the 'aggregate of pleasure exceeds that of pain' (ibid., p. 22) and argued that individuals and governments can act in conformity to God's will by identifying actions that tend to promote general happiness, and by aligning human conduct with this standard. But while Paley thought that *actions* should be judged by their tendency, he maintained that *actors* (or 'agents') should be judged by their 'design' or intention in acting. Paley's identification of a utilitarian standard of judgement is thus part of a theory of virtue, although he believed that God promotes virtue through utilitarian means. He thus defined virtue as *'the doing good* to mankind, in obedience to the will of God, and for the sake of everlasting happiness':

> It seems most agreeable to our conceptions of justice, and is constant enough to the language of scripture, to suppose, that there are prepared for us rewards and punishments of all possible degrees, from the most exalted happiness down to extreme misery (ibid., pp. 50–1).

Rewards or sanctions applied by God thus reinforce the influence of human agencies to encourage individuals to act with a view to maximising the happiness of their fellows.

The Abbé Saint-Pierre identified rationality with 'the diminution or cessation of evils and of sorrows, and the multiplication and augmentation of goods and pleasures', and stressed the role played by supernatural sanctions in encouraging individuals to overcome their narrowly selfish aspirations, and to act in ways that contribute to the happiness of their fellows (Keohane, 1980, p. 365). In addition, however, he urged governors to educate their subjects so that they may acquire a true understanding of their interests and learn to regulate their passions by reason. The educational role of the state should be supplemented by a machine-like system of government that encourages actions that contribute to the public happiness and discourages those that harm it. Saint-Pierre argued that

> it is necessary to assume that in society the interests of individuals will incessantly and strongly conflict with the public interest and often come to dominate and ruin society unless the Legislator arranges laws and regulations so that particular individuals cannot advance their selfish interest except by procuring the interests of others at the same time.... [T]he penalty necessarily attached to the infringement of the law ... [must be] sufficiently inevitable that no citizen is ever tempted to resist the law (ibid., p. 372).

The regulatory influence of the law is crucial to Saint-Pierre's scheme. Individual freedom should only be allowed when it can be shown to advance the general happiness of the population: 'Liberty should be augmented when it makes for good, license repressed when it leads to evil' (ibid., p. 365).

David Hume (1711–76)

Hume was a leading figure in the eighteenth-century Scottish Enlightenment. He served briefly in administrative roles in the British Army before returning to his historical and philosophical studies. A sceptic in matters of religion, Hume produced a variety of works on this subject and wrote extensively on English history, philosophy and politics. His most important political writings are contained in *Essays, Moral and Political*, first published in 1741.

Although Christian versions of utilitarianism continued to be important in the late eighteenth and early nineteenth centuries, this period witnessed the development of a quite distinctive tradition of utilitarianism. This tradition was marked by growing scepticism about the role of religion in political theory and by a desire to arrive at a scientific understanding of politics. An important impetus to this development was provided by David Hume. According to Hume, accounts of politics that are premised on Christianity are conceptually incoherent and empirically untenable. He argued that politics should focus on the satisfaction of interests valued by members of a particular community, and he described justice as an 'artificial' virtue that specifies modes of conduct that are conducive to the realisation of human interests (see pp. 284–5). In making this case, Hume maintained that the purpose of government is to promote the 'utility of the public' and he argued that the best way of doing so is for it to formulate and uphold rules of justice that reflect a community's experience of how its interests can best be realised.

Hume's approach to politics was endorsed by a number of his contemporaries and successors, but while they accepted his argument that the ends of politics could be described by reference to the realisation of interests, they thought that *all* actions and institutions should be subject to continual scrutiny using means–end calculations to gauge their consequences. These writers rejected Hume's argument that the most useful practices and institutions emerge as a consequence of human experience, and are upheld by habit and authority (Miller, 1981, p. 191). An important consequence of this move was that while Hume stressed the role of justice in giving stability to human interaction and depreciated rapid change, other utilitarians promoted radical political reform as a means of ensuring that political power is consciously used to maximise utility.

Jeremy Bentham (1748–1832)

After undergoing legal training, Bentham's private fortune enabled him to devote his life to projects aimed at legal, penal and political reform. Recognised as the founder of the English school of utilitarian political and moral philosophy, Bentham's political ideas were expounded in *A Fragment on Government* (1776), *An Introduction to the Principles of Morals and Legislation* (1789) and a range of other works, many of which remained incomplete and unpublished on his death. In the early decades of the nineteenth century Bentham was at the centre of a group of radical political reformers known as the 'Benthamites'. This group included James and John Stuart Mill, and John Austin.

Jeremy Bentham does not seem to have been aware of Saint-Pierre's writings, but he acknowledged a direct debt to both Hume and Claude Helvetius, the author of *De l'Esprit* (1758). Helvetius equated moral order with an underlying structure of rationality that enables humans to identify scientifically valid notions of right and wrong. The moral order focuses on *this* world, not on the world to come; it legitimates immediate enjoyment, and it integrates individual and social needs in such a way that the maximisation of individual pleasure promotes social utility. For

Helvetius, morality consisted not merely in adherence to the rules of justice, as it had for Hume, but in the *direct* pursuit of what he called 'the interest of the public, that is, 'of the greatest number'. Justice entails the performance of 'actions useful to the greatest number' (Halevy, 1972, p. 19). Since Helvetius believed human action to be governed by self-interest, the interests of the public have to be brought into harmony with those of individuals. The identification of interests can be brought about by social and educational influences, including those supplied by government.

> Moralists declaim continuously against the badness of men, but this shows how little they understand of the matter. Men are not bad; they are merely subject to their own interests. The lamentations of the moralists will certainly not change this motive power of human nature. The thing to complain of is not the badness of men but the ignorance of legislators, who have always put the interest of individuals into opposition with the general interest (Horowitz, 1954, p. 77).

Helvetius was no less insistent than Saint-Pierre that the main role of government is to identify and maintain systems of law that cause the interests of individuals and those of the public to correspond. The interests of the public are those of the *general* population, not particular classes or groups. Good governments are those that promote the interests of all members of the community.

Ideas that could be brought to bear on the application of this doctrine were developed by the Italian philosopher Cesare Beccaria. Beccaria's *On Crimes and Punishments* was first published in the author's native language in 1764 and was quickly translated into both English and French. In this work Beccaria attempted to solve the problem of the identification of interests by a minute analysis of the motivational requirements of a utility-maximising system of penal law. While he did not deny the importance of Christianity, Beccaria restricted his analysis to the province of political thought and action:

> It is for theologians to chart the boundaries of the just and the unjust, insofar as the intrinsic good or evil of an action is concerned; but it is for the student of law and the state to establish the relationship between political justice and injustice, that is to say, between what is socially useful and what is harmful (Beccaria, 1995, p. 5).

From this point of view, the definition of what is 'criminal' depends on a consideration of 'harm to society', and the purpose of punishment is to prevent such harm and deter future offending (ibid., p. 24).

Beccaria's influence on later developments in utilitarian thinking are most apparent in his impact on Bentham. Bentham adopted Beccaria's critical or 'censorious' stance towards existing legal codes and practices, and sought to reduce legal prescriptions to a series of clear and unequivocal statements that would allow individuals to understand their obligations. Bentham also followed Beccaria in rejecting the dangerous practice of allowing judges to interpret law. Judge-made law undermines the function of legal codes because it means that specification of criminal action took place *after* the fact. Proper systems of law should identify prohibited actions and should specify an appropriate penalty so that those who are subject to them can take these considerations into account when deciding how they should act. In such a system the role of the judge is merely to determine when the law has been broken and to apply the appropriate penalty or 'sanction' (ibid., pp. 14–15).

Benthamite Utilitarianism: Bentham, J. S. Mill and Sidgwick

Despite the fact that Bentham was impressed with Beccaria's account of law and its implications for systems of punishment, aspects of his theory differ significantly from those of his predecessor. Unlike Beccaria, Bentham rejected conventional ideas such as natural law and the contractual basis of government. He also ignored Beccaria's attempts to limit the pursuit of utility by refering to implications derived from assumptions about the dignity of humankind (Hart, 1982, pp. 49–51). For Bentham utility was an unqualified end of politics. Moreover, while Beccaria defined the notion of utility by refering to the *equal* maximisation of the happiness of each person within a given society, Bentham understood it in aggregative terms: the principle of utility stipulates that human action should be evaluated by reference to the 'greatest happiness of the great number'.

Bentham's career as a philosopher grew out of his concern with the deficiencies of the English legal system and legal thought. This interest continued throughout his life and gave rise to a staggeringly large body of writings on the topic; it also led, naturally enough, to a consideration of political thinking and political practice. Since law operates within and on the basis of a framework that is established and maintained by government and specified in legislation, the two areas are closely related, and from early in his career Bentham argued that both government and the legal system should be evaluated by direct reference to the standard of 'utility'.

Seized by the belief that he had a genius for 'legislation' and being in receipt of a legal education, Bentham first applied himself to what he regarded as the dangerous absurdities of the English Common Law. His initial target was Sir William Blackstone, a noted jurist and author of the widely read *Commentaries on the Common Law of England* (1765–9). Blackstone epitomised the deafness to the 'voice of reason and utility' that

Bentham thought characterised those who were wedded to the English system of law. In *A Fragment on Government* Bentham attacked the methodological and verbal obscurities of English law, rejected its penchant for conflating description and justification, and deplored its reliance on ideas such as 'precedence', which endow the past with unquestioned authority. *A Fragment* invited Bentham's contemporaries to 'break loose from the trammels of authority and ancestor worship in the field of law' and to ground legal reasoning and legal practice on the principle of utility (Bentham, 1967, p. 103).

In *An Introduction to the Principles of Morals and Legislation* (1789) Bentham wrote that 'utility' is best described as

> *that principle* which states the greatest happiness of all those whose interest is in question, as being the right and proper, and only right and proper and universally desirable, end of human action: of human action in every situation, and in particular in that of a functionary or set of functionaries exercising the powers of Government (ibid., p. 125, n.1).

In order to give precise content to this formula, Bentham insisted that the idea of happiness should be specified in terms of maximisation of pleasure and minimisation of pain so that it is linked directly to the 'springs' or originating impulses of human action: 'Nature', Bentham wrote, 'has placed mankind under the governance of two sovereign masters, *pain* and *pleasure*. It is for them alone to point out what we ought to do, as well as to determine what we shall do' (ibid., p. 125). Bentham thought that by characterising happiness in this way he had identified a simple, empirically quantifiable reference point for private individuals and legislators (Lyons, 1973, pp. 32–4). This reference point was completely devoid of any theological trappings and was not dependent upon supernatural sanctions. Moreover, since it made no attempt to distinguish pleasures except in terms of quantitative standards relating to intensity and duration, it was inherently non-elitist in its implications: pleasures and pains are sensations experienced by *all* human beings and are not dependent upon intellectual enlightenment or the example or leadership of elites.

Bentham's theory of human behaviour was based on a general assumption concerning egotism, but he regarded the principle of utility as a basis for both individual and social life. At times he pointed towards a natural harmony of interests. More often however, he argued that the purpose of government is to harmonise, or at least to integrate, the personal interests of individuals with those of their fellows. In short, government should use its coercive capacities to maximise happiness in the society over which it rules, or over those whose interests are 'in question'. It is significant that the title of one of Bentham's most important published works linked 'morals' and 'legislation'. Utility is seen as both a moral and a political principle: it is intended to guide private individuals and those who exercise power over others.

In his treatment of the 'greatest happiness principle' Bentham at times suggested that it provides a standard to which people *ought* to conform (as in the above quotation), but he also thought that it is a standard to which all other systems of morals actually conform or aspire (Plamenatz, 1949, p. 8). These positions are quite different – the first is prescriptive, the second essentially descriptive – but they both reflect Bentham's desire to establish a clear, incontrovertible standard by which to evaluate the conduct of governors, and the institutional mechanisms through which they operate. This standard relates to the identifiable interests of the individuals who make up the community, not to the requirements of an omnipotent God or to particular individuals or classes. Consequently one of Bentham's primary political concerns was to discredit systems of government that pursue 'sinister' interests in disregard to those of the community as a whole. He maintained that happiness is the end that all individuals can be expected to value above all others, and that the purpose of politics is to give reality to this aspiration by ensuring that the maximisation of happiness is pursued in the most effective manner possible:

> An action...may be said to be conformable to the principle of utility...when the tendency it has to augment the happiness of the community is greater than any it has to diminish it.... A measure of government...may be said to be conformable ... to the principle of utility, when in like manner the tendency it has to augment the happiness of the community is greater than any which it has to diminish it (Bentham, 1967, p. 127).

Of course the fact that pains and pleasures are 'real' in the sense that they are, as Bentham thought, the 'springs' of human conduct, does not mean that their determination and quantification is straightforward. For example Bentham acknowledged that the same stimuli may have differing effects on different individuals. However, he did not think that these variations impose an insuperable barrier to the application of the principle of utility. He argued that since it is relatively easy to determine what causes pain to most human beings, government can specify actions that should be prohibited in order to protect the innocent, and to ensure the effective punishment of those who inflict pain on their fellows. Although pain is to be minimised, it may be necessary to employ it in order to deter potential wrong-doers from causing a greater amount of pain through their disregard of the principle of utility.

In the *Introduction*, Bentham presented a detailed analysis of the relationship between modes of punishment and the maximisation of utility.

This aspect of his work was related to his long-standing interest in penal reform, an interest that gave rise to concrete proposals for constructing and regulating penal institutions so that they would serve utilitarian purposes. However, while Bentham believed that an effective penal system is necessary to discourage individuals from causing pain to their fellows, he believed that the role of government is far more limited when it comes to the promotion of pleasure. He argued that since individuals are the best judges of what gives them pleasure, it is incumbent upon government to leave them as much freedom as is consistent with the avoidance of harm to others. Individuals can then maximise their pleasures, and hence maximise the total amount of pleasure experienced by their community. On the one hand, then, by means of its protective and penal activities the government should prevent people causing pain to others, while on the other hand it should leave people to identify those things that give them pleasure and allow them to pursue these provided that they do not do so in ways that inflict pain on others. Bentham was a stern critic of theories of natural rights, partly because they are inconsistent, but also because they embody claims that are not derived from the principle of utility and might be hostile to its realisation (see p. 224). However, both protection from interference by others and individual freedom can be justified by reference to general happiness.

While Bentham stressed the negative and protective role of government, he did not think that the relationship between politics and happiness could be dealt with solely in these terms. In an unpublished statement he wrote that in order to 'produce pleasure ... the Legislator has but one course to take, which is to lay in a man's way some instruments of pleasure, and leave the application of it to himself' (Parekh, 1973, p. 118). This statement reflects the role of individuals in pursuing happiness, but it also suggests a positive role for government. Just what this might involve is apparent in Bentham's identification of four goals that should be secured by a sound, utility-sensitive constitution: the provision of subsistence, abundance, security and equality (ibid., p. 196).

Bentham thought that to a considerable degree the first three of these objectives could be satisfied by the maintenance of conditions favourable to the operation of a free market. In most circumstances the market provides an effective mechanism for encouraging individuals to undertake productive labour, and it allows them to benefit from their efforts. The fact that free markets recognise the right to private property ensures that people will be secure in their possessions. Bentham warned, however, that any attempt to impose equality will limit the effectiveness of the market, and if it is achieved by periodic redistribution it will threaten security of property and thus produce uncertainty, which is a form of pain. For these reasons, Bentham did not promote thoroughgoing equality. He insisted, however, that extreme inequality inhibits the maximisation of happiness because the increase of pleasure derived by the rich for a given increase in income is far lower than that experienced by the poor. Great inequality is also objectionable because it augments the power of the rich over the poor. This consideration was an important one for Bentham, for while he believed that government *can* serve the cause of utility, he argued that it will not do so if it is under the control of particular classes or individuals. Bentham was thus left with the problem of balancing the benefits derived from a system of free exchange with those produced by the very different principle of equality. For the most part, he was prepared to leave the market to produce a generally beneficial balance, but he also identified a role for government in this process. Government can help ensure subsistence by establishing a maximum price for the basic subsistence provision, namely bread, and can assist the attainment of subsistence and the pursuit of abundance by boosting the money supply so as to stimulate growth and hence employment. Since these measures help to reduce indigency, they also make a modest contribution to softening the grossest inequalities without undermining the generally beneficial role of a free market (Bentham, 1952–4, vol. iii, pp. 257–8).

These applications of the principle of utility were formulated in writings that were not published until long after Bentham's death, therefore they could not have a significant public impact. Indeed those of his friends who knew of Bentham's thoughts on these matters disagreed with them. However, these comments provide a valuable way of illustrating Bentham's approach to political thinking. Having identified human happiness as the starting point of political analysis, and having specified this in terms of maximisation of pleasure and minimisation of pain, Bentham was able to take an instrumental view of other ideas and values. He thus rejected natural right theory, and what he regarded as the mischievous and confusing formulations of the Common Law. These doctrines lack the clarity of the principle of utility and tend, if anything, to buttress claims that will impede its realisation. He also refused to be tied down by the dogmas of *laissez-faire*, or the idea that it is desirable for government to restrict itself to performing a narrow range of regulatory and protective functions. Bentham rejected a dogmatic attachment to this doctrine: 'I have never', he wrote,

> nor ever shall have, any horror ... of the hand of government in economic matters.... The interference of government, as often as ... any the smallest balance on the side of advantage is the result, is an event I witness with altogether as much satisfaction as I should its forbearance, and with much more than I should its negligence (ibid., pp. 257–8).

At the same time, however, he argued that personal freedom is generally conducive to human happiness, and he gave both the political and the economic dimensions of this an important but derivative and secondary role in his theory. Equality is treated in a similarly flexible but far more restricted way. Freedom and equality were thus important for Bentham, but he believed their role has to be determined by reference to the master principle of politics, the idea of the greatest happiness of the greatest number. These values could serve the cause of utility; they are not themselves of ultimate value and politics cannot be explained by reference to them.

The implications that Bentham derived from his understanding of the principle of utility were far reaching. In addition to his long-standing interest in legal and penal reform, he also developed complex specifications concerning the distribution and exercise of political power. In the latter part of his life Bentham looked to systems of democratic representation to provide a check upon the actions of legislators. He also argued that strict accountability should be built into the structure of public bureaucracy, and that the operation of government should be subjected to the checking influence of public opinion and a free press. The purpose of all these measures was to ensure that the exercise of political power would be directed towards the greatest happiness of the greatest number, not to the private 'sinister' interests of elites (Hume, 1993; Rosen, 1993; Schofield, 1993).

Bentham's statement of the principle of utility enjoyed a wide circulation in a number of European countries and also made an impact on newly independent states in South America (Dinwiddy, 1993). It has also been claimed that his ideas had a significant effect on various aspects of nineteenth-century political and administrative reform. This issue is a matter for contention, but it seems clear that Bentham's account of the relationship between happiness and politics was of great significance for nineteenth- century political thinking. Some responses were hostile. A number of writers objected to the radically secular nature of Bentham's theory (ibid). Others, for example Samuel Taylor Coleridge and Thomas Carlyle, criticised Bentham for producing a mechanical, degraded and despiritualised conception of human nature and social relationships. Carlyle in fact rejected happiness as a goal for human beings, but even some of those who subscribed to this idea were uneasy about the way in which Bentham had formulated his case. The most important sympathetic statement of this view was advanced by John Stuart Mill in an essay that he thought of as a defence of utilitarianism.

Mill's father, James, was a close associate of Bentham (see p. 83), and in his early life the younger Mill was an ardent proponent of 'Benthamism'. While Mill's general admiration for Bentham never waned, he came to the view that aspects of his political philosophy needed to be restated in a way that took some account of the sorts of criticism levelled by Carlyle and others. In particular Mill argued in *Utilitarianism* (1861) that while

Bentham had performed a valuable service by pushing human happiness to the forefront of the political agenda, the idea of what happiness meant, and what it implied, needed further refinement. In place of Bentham's essentially quantitative understanding of pleasure, Mill argued that an account of the greatest happiness needed to recognise the existence of 'higher' and 'lower' pleasures:

> It is quite compatible with the principle of utility to recognise the fact, that some *kinds* of pleasure are more desirable and more valuable than others. It would be absurd that while, in estimating all other things, quality is considered as well as quantity, the estimation of pleasures should be supposed to depend on quality alone (Mill, 1983, p. 7).

Mill placed particular emphasis on a *qualitative* notion of pleasure, and he claimed that the superiority of higher pleasures can only be determined by those who are exposed to a range of pleasures (ibid., p. 10). An important consequence of this view was that it tended to erode the universally objective features of Bentham's theory. Mill's views on what constituted a source of higher pleasure also had important implications for his reformulation of utilitarianism. Mill included among the higher pleasures those connected to 'altruism', or a disinterested concern with the well-being of others, and thus displaced Bentham's assumption concerning egotism. He also attached great weight to pleasures derived from the cultivation of aesthetic sensibilities and intellectual faculties. These modifications to classical utilitarianism have the effect of elevating the role of elite judgement in determining questions of utility. If elites are exposed to a wider range of pleasures than others, and if they are particularly well-placed to appreciate the pleasures derived from artistic and intellectual experiences, there are good grounds for allowing them to determine the implications of the principle of utility.

In addition to introducing a qualitative dimension to calculations of 'greatest happiness', Mill made other significant additions to classical utilitarianism. In a review of an essay by James Mill, T. B. Macaulay chastised him for building a theory of government without reference to its history: 'We have here an elaborate treatise on Government, from which, but for two or three passing allusions, it would not appear that the author was aware that any governments actually existed among men' (Macaulay, 1984, p. 101). John Stuart Mill responded to Macaulay's criticisms by relating the idea of utility to the particular circumstances of a given society. He argued that the pursuit of happiness can not, and ought not be, divorced from considerations that will promote human progress within a particular social and political context. This stipulation means that the question of utility has to take account of the prospects of future happiness that progress will produce, and it implies that the long-term prospects of improvement might often take priority over short-term considerations, particularly in cases where the latter is based largely on lower pleasures. Thus while Mill still regarded happiness as the goal of politics, he insisted that political issues should be discussed in relation to the role that progress plays in extending the scope and the quality of human happiness.

One consequence of this view was that Mill developed a complex response to demands for 'popular' or democratic forms of government (see p. 186). It also led him to argue that it is improper for society to interfere with individual liberty except in cases where it interferes with the liberty of others. This principle is spelt out in one of Mill's most famous works, *On Liberty*: 'the only purpose for which power can be rightfully exercised over any member of a civilised community, against his will, is to prevent harm to others' (Mill, 1983, p. 73). Mill's argument in this work is related to his reformulation of utilitarianism because liberty is held to be essential to the progress of human kind: it is upon such progress that the increase in human happiness (as Mill understood it) depends.

During the latter part of the nineteenth century the process of revising Benthamite utilitarianism was continued by Henry Sidgwick. In terms of the themes discussed in early chapters, it is significant that Sidgwick's political thought was developed in quite conscious opposition to the ideas of virtue and perfection that appeared in T. H. Green's political philosophy (see pp. 45–6). Green and his followers admired Mill's attempt to refine utilitarianism, and they were encouraged to see that he had moved away from the merely quantitative idea of pleasure that they identified with Bentham (Green, 1986, pp. 24, 313, 360–1). At the same time, however, they thought that the fact that aspects of Mill's arguments were not compatible with Bentham's formulations pointed to fatal weaknesses in utilitarian moral and political philosophy. In addition to confronting Green's criticisms, Sidgwick also tackled other contemporaries who held that liberty is the primary focus of political thinking.

Henry Sidgwick (1838–1900)

An academic philosopher who taught at Cambridge University, Sidgwick defended utilitarianism against T. H. Green's critique, but presented a version of it that eschewed many of the radical implications drawn from Benthamite formulations of the doctrine. His most important political work was *Elements of Politics* (1891).

Sidgwick argued that utilitarianism is the 'only scientifically complete and systematically reflective form of that regulation of conduct, which through the whole course of human history has always tended substantially in the same direction' (Sidgwick, 1874, p. 396). He rejected Green's claim that perfection is the goal of human endeavour and the end of government, on the grounds that this notion is dogmatic and philosophically incoherent. In Sidgwick's view, utilitarianism embodies the common sense of humanity in a rational form and he claimed a

> general – if not universal – assent for the principle that the true standard and criterion by which right legislation is to be distinguished from wrong is conduciveness to the general 'good' or 'welfare'. And probably the majority of persons would agree to interpret the 'good' or 'welfare' of the community to mean, in the last analysis, the happiness of the individual human beings who compose the community; provided that we take into account not only the human beings who are actually living but those who are to live hereafter (Sidgwick, 1891, p. 34).

However, while Sidgwick shared Bentham's interest in determining the extent to which governments satisfy the requirements of utility, he linked these to common opinion, and argued that the prevailing conceptions of government and its actual structure reflected a general endorsement of utilitarian aspirations and values. For this reason Sidgwick was far less critical of existing institutions than Bentham had been. Consequently much of his political writing focused on the relationship between utilitarianism and the structure and practice of contemporary British government.

In his treatment of these issues Sidgwick dealt with claims that contemporary government was paying insufficient attention to individual freedom. It was argued, for example, that liberty is sacred and that the action of government should be restricted to preventing individuals harming one another. These claims are more extreme than those of J. S. Mill because his principle of liberty does not preclude government action in pursuit of public objectives. In response to this line of argument, Sidgwick contended that both 'paternalistic' and 'socialistic' interferences with liberty might be justified. These two forms of interference may be necessary on occasion because the psychological and sociological assumptions upon which a utilitarian defence of individual liberty rests are not always soundly based. Paternalistic legislation, that is, government action directed towards the good of the individual whose liberty is interfered with, may be necessary because individuals are not always the best judges of their own interests. This is clearly so with respect to children, but it might also apply to people's capacity to judge the services offered by, for example, professional practitioners. Sidgwick was wary of this form of interference, insisting that the central principle to be kept in mind is that paternalism can only be justified where there is empirical proof that individuals can not be trusted to look after their own interests (ibid., pp. 40–61).

'Socialistic' interference – for the good of society – deals with cases where the pursuit of individual interests does not maximise general welfare (ibid., pp. 137–40). In presenting an example of this type of interference Sidgwick echoed Hume's argument that government is necessary to provide services ('public goods') that can not be reliably produced through individual effort; he also discussed the right of the state to control property when the public good requires it (ibid., pp. 144–7). Sidgwick insisted however, that these measures are not 'collectivistic'; that is, they are not related to doctrines promoting the redistribution of wealth within society. Although such measures may be justified in some circumstances, Sidgwick argued that under the existing conditions they would be detrimental to the pursuit of utility because they would undermine the benefits produced by individual liberty (ibid., pp. 151–60).

The Diffusion of Utilitarianism: Socialism and Welfare

Sidgwick's writings mark the effective conclusion of nineteenth-century attempts to use Bentham's formulation of utilitarianism as the basis for large-scale, systematic political theorising. As we have seen, some of his contemporaries questioned the underlying basis of utilitarian philosophy and sought to reestablish a tradition that made virtue the core of politics. However, while idealism was an important current in late-nineteenth-century political thought, the termination of the full Benthamite project was not due to its critique of attempts to define politics according to the principle of greatest happiness. Rather than being overcome by other accounts of the ends of politics, utilitarianism was diffused into a number of different political theories. This tendency was apparent to some degree in Sidgwick's generally conservative, *status-quo*-oriented reformulation of what had begun as an overtly provocative challenge to existing thought and practice. It also reflected the extent to which a secular, human-centred, want-regarding approach had come to form the mainstream of Western political thinking. Henceforth theories that took virtue, order or freedom as their starting point had to present themselves as more plausible alternatives to an approach towards politics that had received its most systematic and influential formulation in the tortured prose of Jeremy Bentham.

While Sidgwick reconciled utilitarianism with conservative politics, other late-nineteenth- and early-twentieth-century writers adapted it to causes that sustained its radical credentials. In this period non-Marxist socialists were among the most important absorbers of at least the spirit of Benthamite political thinking. From its origins in the early nineteenth century, socialist thinkers had sharply contrasted the misery produced in a competitive capitalist society with the potentialities for general well-being that existed in those social and political structures that fulfilled the promise held out by the revolutionary ideal of 'liberty, equality and fraternity'. Since socialists supposed that humans possessed an inherent tendency for sociability, their understanding of happiness went beyond the minimalist, hedonistic formulation favoured by Bentham. They tended to adopt the position on the integration of individual and social values that lay at the heart of Helvetius' theory (Horowitz, 1954, p. 192).

In addition, many socialists adhered to a qualitative conception of utility that resembled aspects of J. S. Mill's reformulation of Bentham's doctrine. For example Beatrice Webb described Bentham as the 'intellectual god-father' of her husband Sidney, an important figure in the history of British socialism. She argued, however, that while she and her husband thought that action should be judged in terms of its utilitarian consequences, they took a broad view of what this involved:

> There is no other sanction we care to accept but results, though we should be inclined to give, perhaps, a wider meaning to results. For instance, the formation of a noble character, the increase of intellectual faculty, stimulus to sense of beauty, sense of conduct, even sense of humour, are all ends that we should regard as 'sanctioning' action; quite apart from whether they produce happiness of one or all, or none (Webb, 1948, p. 210).

But while socialist thinkers adhered to a strongly qualitative conception of happiness and endowed this with social requirements, they shared with other writers discussed in this chapter the view that the end of politics is to enhance human well-being. Socialist views on how this goal can be achieved vary considerably, but they generally tend to place particular emphasis on the role of government in eliminating poverty and eroding those degrees of social and economic inequality that are inconsistent with human happiness. As the English socialist G. D. H. Cole put it, 'The reason – the only valid reason – for being a Socialist is the desire, the impassioned will, to seek the greatest happiness and well-being of the greatest number' (Cole, 1935, p. 16).

Conclusion

The absorption of a utilitarian perspective into socialism meant that at least some expressions of this conception of the ends of politics retained the radical bearing that had been the hallmark of early versions of the doctrine. Both Helvetius and the early Benthamites regarded the principle of utility as the key element in programmes of radical political reform. Politics was seen in largely secular terms and was related to the satisfaction of the interests of ordinary human beings. To some degree, John Stuart Mill's attempt to introduce qualitative distinctions into utilitarian thinking weakened the egalitarian assumptions of classical formulations of utility. This tendency is apparent also in the ideas of at least some late-nineteenth-century socialists. However, these thinkers continued to think of utilitarianism as a *public* doctrine that served as a guide for deciding between various policy options. As will be noted in the concluding chapter, this conception of utility has given way to discussions that concentrate upon the moral implications of the idea of utility. Rather than being applied to problems of public policy, utilitarianism has been used as a means of determining how individuals should respond to various moral dilemmas (see p. 374).

PART II

The Location of Political Authority: Who Should Rule?

The first part of this book discussed a number of historically important accounts of the purpose of government. In this part we shall examine a range of responses to the question: 'Who should rule?' Consideration of this problem leads to questions about the structure of political authority and the qualities required by those who exercise it. Since political authority carries with it the capacity to coerce human beings, to specify goals and the means of their attainment, to maintain systems of order, and to infringe individual liberty, it is understandable that many political thinkers have given considerable thought to determining how such authority should be allocated. It should be noted that views of *who* should hold political authority are distinct from questions about *how far* that authority should extend. It is important, for example, to guard against the tendency to suppose that monarchy must be absolute while democracy is necessarily limited in what it can demand. The fact that a particular person or persons hold political power does not necessarily imply anything about the way in which it is used, although, as we shall see, some theorists identify particular forms of government with the advancement of particular interests.

The tenacity of the theme of this part of the book is reflected in the framework adopted for it. Aristotle classified types of government by reference to the location of political authority, and distinguished between the rule of the 'one', the 'few' and the 'many'. This framework is similar in some respects to that which distinguishes between 'monarchic', 'aristocratic' and 'democratic' forms of government, but it has the advantage of extending the discussion of single-person rule beyond the range of types that are usually associated with monarchy, aristocracy and democracy. The first two of these forms of rule carry connotations that are peculiar to distinct political cultures and do not apply to all conceptions of rule by a single person or by a select and limited group within a given population. In the chapters that follow, these conventional forms of government will be treated as special types of rule by the one, the few and the many.

CHAPTER 5

Rule by a Single Person

The claim that political authority should be located in the hands of a single person has appeared in a variety of forms. The prevalence of democracy in the modern world should not blind us to the fact that the idea of single-person rule has had a dominant place in the history of Western political thought. Indeed the modern preference for popular government is an exception to a pattern of political thinking that has generally been hostile to democracy. While this hostility has been a common feature of defences of monarchy – that is, rule by a single person who is endowed with the sanctity and trappings of 'kingship', it has been shared to some degree by those promoting non-monarchical conceptions of rule by 'the one'. In particular, proponents of single-person rule share a common belief in the need for a ruler to provide a sense of unity in the state and to give direction to its activities. They also assume that it is possible to identify a person who possesses the distinct and relevant attributes that are necessary to attain these ends. This chapter will discuss ancient, early modern and modern accounts of government by 'the one', some of which present defences of monarchy. It will also examine modern, non-monarchical accounts of single-person rule. Some of these theories regard the ruler as the only really significant political actor in the state, but others focus on the need for a supreme ruler within systems where other actors also play important political roles.

Single-Person Rule in the Ancient World: Plato, Aristotle and Cicero

Plato's republic was to be governed by a class of rulers whose claim to supreme authority rested on their capacity to maintain a state that had virtue as its supreme end. However, the *Republic* also contains brief but significant references to single-person rule. Plato's account of this theme deals with both pure and corrupt rule by 'the one' and represents an early, historically important, treatment of the subject.

In his discussion of the forceful objection that, whatever its merits, his ideal state could never be brought into existence, Plato suggested that single-person rule would provide a solution to this problem. Given the qualities required by Plato's guardians, the problem of creating an ideal state is especially taxing. Guardians must be *philosophers*, that is, lovers of 'eternal and immutable truth', the object of 'knowledge'. Plato contrasted knowledge with 'opinion', or the ideas held by those who are attached to the shifting world of 'appearances', which at best reflects partial and unstable elements of absolute goodness (Plato, 1970, p. 244). This way of thinking is prevalent in all non-ideal states, but Plato maintained that it had reached its apotheosis in contemporary Athenian society. The weight placed upon 'knowledge' in the ideal state and the steps taken there to foster a philosophical class are seriously at odds with the ethos and experiences that confront most individuals in democratic cultures. As a consequence it is most unlikely that the ideal state can emerge out of democracy, a system that marginalises and despises true philosophers, or corrupts those who are endowed with a 'philosophic' nature. In order to succeed in democracy these individuals must adopt the ethos of the masses and forsake the world of reality in their quest to satisfy the debased and illusory aspirations of ordinary democratic citizens (ibid., pp. 248–58).

In the *Republic* Plato identified two escapes from the dilemma confronting those who wish to promote an ideal state. One option is for philosophic recluses to take advantage of some chance occurrence in order to take control of the state and compel the community to listen to them. Another possibility is that an existing head of government, or his heir, may be inspired by philosophy to embark upon a programme of radical reconstruction. In short, philosophers must become kings, or a king must become a philosopher (ibid., pp. 259–65).

In addition to providing a positive account of the relationship between monarchy and the ideal state, Plato also discussed a corrupt and harmful form of single-person rule – or 'tyranny'. Plato thought that tyranny grows out of the excessive desire for complete liberty that characterises democratic regimes. In democracy, the freedom of the common people produces an air of lawlessness in the state, one that is exacerbated by the poor's determination to use their political influence to plunder the rich. In response the rich plot to overthrow democracy and thereby drive the poor into the hands of popular champions, who often end up controlling those they once served. The tyrant is thus the direct product of a corrupt society. At first he and the population are in a relationship of symbiotic debasement – he flatters and indulges them, they admire and reward him

– but once he gains a position of dominance the state is gripped by a new kind of lawlessness. Rather than being subjected to the whims of a fickle and debauched population, government is now under the control of an arbitrary and cruel individual. Plato characterised tyranny as a form of 'patricide' – the offspring of the populace, the tyrant, ends up using violence against his 'parents' – and portrayed the tyrannical character as a criminal type. While philosophers prepare themselves for rule by remaining detached from the intellectually and morally debasing influences of a corrupt society, the tyrant climbs to a position of unregulated supremacy by first immersing himself in this society and then outdoing the population in baseness. The servant of a corrupt master turns the latter into his slave by the consistent and single-minded cultivation and exercise of many of the same character traits (ibid., pp. 324–49).

The contrast between a corrupt and a good form of single-person rule reappears in Aristotle's writings. In *Politics* Aristotle defined kingship as a form of rule that is directed to the common good. In contrast tyrants govern in their own interest, ignoring any legal constraints on their conduct (Aristotle, 1958, pp. 131, 160–80). This point is important because, like Plato, Aristotle considered rule according to law to be preferable to personal rule by *ordinary* human beings because it avoids the caprice and partiality to which all such people are naturally inclined (ibib. pp. 171–2; Mulgan, 1977, pp. 83–5; see p. 278). However the corollary of this argument is that completely enlightened people can rule without law. There is no danger of them acting corruptly, and since they are not bound by law they can react sensitively and appropriately to the requirements of a particular situation.

Aristotle's views on the appropriateness of rule by the one rest on his belief that the distribution of political power should reflect the relative merits of different sections of the population (see p. 171). Where people are unequal in relevant respects, political equality is actually unjust. This stipulation means that single-person rule is just if a particular individual is morally superior to the rest of the population. However Aristotle was vague about how this justification of monarchy relates to the conditions he laid down in his discussion of the relationship between law and enlightenment. In general, he took the view that even where one person is entitled to rule, he should do so by reference to a fixed scheme of law (see p. 277). Aristotle's discussion of single-person rule is also overshadowed by a certain scepticism about such a marked degree of superiority, and by doubts over whether it would gain general acceptance among the population. The first point is reflected in his observation that those who deserve supremacy will be like gods among men, while the second is apparent in his treatment of revolutions. One consequence of a lack of virtue is an inability to appreciate this failing and a marked reluctance to acknowledge the virtues possessed by others (Aristotle, 1958, pp. 135–59, 204, 237–41).

Like Plato and Aristotle, the Roman writer Cicero distinguished between corrupt and good forms of single-person rule and expressed a guarded preference for kingship as the best type of simple constitution (Wood, 1988, p. 146). However, he thought that the benefits of monarchy – understood as a system that provides a sense of unity and direction and acknowledges the marked superiority of an individual – can be reaped without its dangers if it comprises merely one element of a 'mixed' constitution. Cicero's model for this type of government was derived from the political experience of pre-imperial Rome. Monarchy was embodied in the office of consul while aristocratic and democratic elements were represented in the special status of the Senate and in the political role ascribed to the people (ibid., pp. 165–6). The idea of mixed government has played an important role in the history of political thought, but since it places the monarchical element within a larger and more expansive framework, it *embodies* the principle of single-person rule rather than *being* a form of such rule (see pp. 227ff). Elements of this approach to allocating political power are apparent in medieval political thought, but they are generally secondary to a quite distinctive conception of kingship.

Medieval Ideas of Monarchy – Early Theories of Kingship: Thomas Aquinas and Christine de Pizan

In the medieval period theories of single-person rule rested upon ideas of kingship. While these theories were given a distinctive character by the requirements of Christianity, they cannot be divorced from other traditions. Early Christian accounts of monarchy (dating from the sixth century), developed in a context where imperial power had begun to lapse and the Roman Empire had begun to fragment into a number of largely autonomous political units, built upon earlier 'Barbarian' (non-Roman and non-Christian) ideas. Moreover towards the end of the medieval period – that is, from the thirteenth century – accounts of rule by the one were often framed within the context of Aristotle's writings on this topic. For example medieval writers repeated observations that had appeared in classical statements on the evils of tyranny and also endorsed Aristotle's views on the relationship between monarchy and the personal virtues of the monarch.

Early examples of a Christian idea of kingship appeared in the legal code issued under the authority of the Emperor Justinian in the first half of the sixth century. The key point of this theory, one that distinguishes it from earlier Barbarian accounts which had made kingship a matter of election or choice, is that the powers of rulers are held to be divinely instituted and divinely ordained; the power and authority of kings is a gift of God, and the source of their powers is symbolised by anointment (Ullmann, 1975, p. 48; Nelson, 1991, p. 218). This conception of 'descending' power has a number of important implications. In the first place, while it means that kings have no *right* to their power – one cannot have the right to receive a gift – it gives them a unique standing in relation to the conduct of human affairs, and can thus be used to discredit claims that monarchs are subordinate to religious authorities: their power comes directly from God. Moreover, while the power of single rulers was thought to be independent of choices made by their subjects, this theory made it clear that kings have distinctive, divinely ordained responsibilities for them. In many medieval writings the various sections of the population are presented as members of the king's household, a point that reinforces the idea that monarchy embodies a paternal or 'patrimonial' conception of government. This image of kingship is captured in a poem written by Archbishop Wulfstan of York in the tenth century:

> For the Christian king
> It is very fitting
> That he be in the place of a father
> For the Christian people.
> And in watching over and warding them
> Be Christ's representative... (Nelson, 1991, p. 240).

Monarchical power is not only paternal, it is also intensely personal: the king keeps 'faith' with his leading subjects and they with him. Moreover, while kingship is seen as a direct grant from God, this model of rule stresses consensus and 'faithfulness' rather than coercion.

Medieval conceptions of kingship place great stress on the distinctive personal qualities of rulers, particularly their responsibility to be both the model for and sustainer of virtue. This feature of medieval political thought, and the characterisation of the relationship between the monarch and his subjects in paternal terms, unwittingly echoes far earlier conceptions of kingship that were current in China from the fourth century BC. Chinese ideas of paternal monarchy (identified particularly with the philosopher Confucius (551–479 BC) were produced in reaction to the tendency for semifeudal princes to adopt conceptions of rule that focused on their self-interest. When this principle was applied to a ruler's relationship with other princes and with his subjects, it gave rise to widespread conflict and social dislocation. Confucius' response to these developments was to promote a patriarchal conception of the state, one that stressed the protective role of rulers, the need for them to retain the confidence of their subjects and their special responsibility to adhere to *li*, a term used to designate all the institutions and relationships that made for a harmonious life by reflecting the fundamental principles of human nature. This idea to some degree paralleled Western conceptions of natural law (see pp. 203ff), not least in its stress on the ruler's responsibility to uphold peace, and in the link that it forged between this goal and the benevolence and righteousness of the monarch (Hsu, 1932, pp. 35–40, 106–16; Bodde and Morris, 1967, pp. 19–20).

Both ancient Chinese and medieval European accounts of kingship reflect the fact that the primary role of the ruler is to ensure peace, and that he is endowed with supreme moral authority. The latter of these ideas was rejected by medieval proponents of papal power because they wished to secure ultimate moral authority for the Church. The conflict between these views on the ultimate human source of moral authority gave rise to a number of important lines of medieval political argument. From the late thirteenth century, however, those who upheld the moral supremacy of temporal rulers were able to fortify their position by drawing on the recently rediscovered political works of Aristotle.

Aquinas, for example, accepted Aristotle's arguments about the naturalness of political life on the ground that government is necessary if human beings are to reap the benefits of sociability. God made human beings dependent upon their fellows and tied their perfection to the cultivation of a range of virtues that are intrinsically social. It is clear, however, that social life will only be a source of benefit if human action is directed by a 'general ruling force' that harmonises the relationships of a multiplicity of human beings so that they can live together in the 'unity of peace'. This requirement is satisfied to some degree by all legitimate forms of government, but Aquinas (following Aristotle) argued that rule by a single person is capable of producing the greatest benefit for those subject to it (Aquinas, 1959, pp. 11, 107). Because monarchy places power in one person's hands it can provide a unified direction for society; it thus avoids the internal dissension and factionalism that often occurs in collective forms of rule. Moreover Aquinas argued that government by a single person corresponds to a 'natural principle'. In the same way as the heart rules the body, reason rules the soul, bees are ruled by a single bee, and the whole universe is ruled by one God:

> So, since the product of art is but an imitation of the work of nature, and since a work of art is the better for being a faithful representation of its natural pattern, it follows of necessity that the best form of government in human society is that which is exercised by one person.

This argument by analogy is buttressed by the fruits of human experience. Properly conducted monarchies are stable and generally beneficial, but where power is shared, society is frequently torn with dissension (ibid., pp. 13, 17–19).

Aquinas' reference to the quality of monarchical rule reflects the widely held ancient and medieval distinction between kingship and tyranny. Earlier medieval thinkers stressed that tyrannical conduct impugns the moral authority of a ruler. As we shall see in a later chapter, this point could provide the grounds for disobeying, or even resisting, rulers who have become tyrannical (see pp. 301ff). In his treatment of tyranny Aquinas endorsed the conventional view that good rulers serve the common good while tyrants ignore the interests of the community and look to their own private interest. However Aquinas claimed that the impact of the improper exercise of monarchical power is unlikely to be as harmful as the corruption of an aristocratic form of government. Aristocratic corruption is invariably accompanied by violent factionalism, which, because of the number of parties or families involved, destroys social peace. Except in very extreme cases however, the corruption of monarchy tends to bear on particular individuals, not on the entire community. Aquinas deployed this line of argument to support his general preference for monarchy, but he did not attempt to conceal the evil involved in the tyrannical exercise of monarchical power. To the contrary, he adopted Aristotle's views on the incompatibility of tyranny and virtue. Lacking virtue themselves, tyrants are jealous of the virtue of any of their subjects; they try to prevent the virtuous combining with one another since this will pose a threat to their continued dominance. Moreover tyrants often sew discord among their subjects so that, fearing one another, they cannot unite against the tyrant. The result of this characteristic of tyranny is that it undermines the very idea of government. Instead of preserving peace and fostering virtue, it generates strife and debases the population (ibid., p. 19).

Aquinas' treatment of the evils of tyranny – it essentially involves exercises of power in ways that are incompatible with the true function of government – gives a special weight to the virtue of the ruler. The importance that medieval writers ascribed to princely virtue appears very clearly in an extensive body of literature presented as 'mirrors of princes'. Works in this genre contain accounts of ideal princely qualities and seek to develop the appropriate virtues in the particular prince to whom they are addressed. Thus in *The Book of the Body Politic* (1406), Christine de Pizan laid great stress on the duties that princes owe to both God and their subjects, and urged them to follow the biblical example of the good shepherd (Pizan, 1994, p. 16). Princes should exemplify the virtues of love, generosity, human pity, mercy and good nature and should eschew the vices of lechery, bad temper and cruelty (ibid., pp. 23–30, 53–4). Christine likened the sovereign to the 'head' of the political community (the body politic) and treated princely virtue as a precondition for a virtuous state: 'in order to govern the body of the public polity well, it is necessary for the head to be healthy, that is virtuous. Because if it is ill, the whole body will feel it' (ibid., p. 5). Although virtues are universal in the sense that they should be cultivated by all members of the community, Christine made it clear that the distinctive position occupied by the prince means that the way in which he practises virtue differs from that which is appropriate to people occupying other positions within the body politic: 'the thing that is appropriate for the prince is not appropriate for the simple knight or the noble, and likewise the opposite' (ibid., p. 58).

Christine de Pizan (c. 1364–c. 1430)

Born in Venice but brought up in France where her father was a court physician, Christine de Pizan is regarded as France's first woman of letters. She wrote a number of works, the best known of which were intended to further the education of women. Her major political work, *The Book of the Body Politic* (c. 1404), was written during a time of crisis in French politics to guide the fourteen-year-old heir to the throne, Louis of Guyenne.

In the medieval period the stress upon the virtue of the monarch underwrote theories of government that gave rulers extensive, indeed virtually unlimited power (Dunbabin, 1991, pp. 483–92). It should be noted, however, that this was set in a context in which the ruler was expected to consult with his subjects, to maintain faith with them and to be ever mindful that while human law might be in his hands, he would always be subject to natural law and to the control of God, the direct source of the power of legitimate rulers.

Monarchy in Early Modern Political Theory: Bodin, Hobbes, Filmer and Bossuet

In the later medieval period, the conception of kingship sketched above was combined with ideas that modified the impact of royal supremacy. Increasing weight was given to customary law and to the idea of counsel, especially when this was applied to the law-making process. The implications of claims concerning 'natural rights' to property, and the need for these to be recognised in a cooperative approach to taxation, strengthened the representative role of estates. These developments were reinforced by the idea that since government relates to the needs of the governed, it could be said to reflect their consent. They thus provided seeds that later grew into theories that challenged the ideas of descending power and monarchical supremacy (ibid. pp. 501–19).

One response to these developments was the formulation of early modern sovereignty theory. In its essential assumptions, sovereignty theory does not concern itself with who rules. What matters is that there is a sovereign capable of imposing order in human society (see pp. 252ff). This point emerges very clearly in Hobbes' writings. While expressing a weak preference for single-person rule on the (not very plausible) ground that a ruler's appetite for rapacity is likely to be less damaging than the demands of a collective sovereign, Hobbes took a generally cool and detached attitude to the question of whether the one, the few, or the many should rule.

Hobbes' French predecessor, Jean Bodin, also gave a relatively even-handed account of various forms of government, stressing (in line with medieval precedents) that sovereigns are subject to the laws of nature and are charged with furthering the common good. [Bodin, n.d., pp. 51–2). Bodin maintained, however, that monarchy is likely to be more stable than either aristocratic or democratic forms of government; the former has a tendency for factionalism, while the latter, because it incorporates the entire population, suffers from their ignorance, passion and gullibility (ibid., pp. 190–200). Indeed when Bodin talked of the 'sovereign' he almost always had a monarch in mind. In light of his concern with French affairs this focus on monarchy is understandable. In any case, Bodin's treatment of sovereignty often echoed medieval theories of kingship. An example of this aspect of Bodin's argument appeared in his attempt to connect sovereignty with the rule of fathers over their families, a strategy that played a central role in Sir Robert Filmer's account of patriarchal monarchy (ibid., pp. 6–17). Between 1630 and 1652 this otherwise obscure English country gentleman produced a trenchant and single-minded defence of monarchy that played an important role in subsequent early-modern thinking on this form of government.

Filmer's political writings were produced in the context of the challenges to single-person rule that occurred before and during the English Civil War. However in *Patriarcha* (a work significantly subtitled 'A Defence of the Natural Power of Kings Against the Unnatural Liberty of the People') Filmer made it clear that his arguments were directed not only against proponents of popular government in his own society, but also at a recent European tradition in political thought that ascribed natural liberty to human beings and claimed that this entitled them to choose their own form of government (Filmer, 1949, p. 53). In response to this 'plausible and dangerous opinion', Filmer made a case for absolute monarchy. He argued that only this form of government conforms to God's expressed will as conveyed through the Scriptures and reflected in the history of human society. A consideration of Filmer's theory of absolute government will be reserved for a later chapter (see pp. 266ff); here the discussion will focus on his conception of monarchy.

Sir Robert Filmer (1588–1653)

Filmer, a country gentleman from Kent, upheld the absolute power of the English crown and was a virulent critic of the pretension of the crown's opponents before and during the English Civil War. During the war he was briefly imprisoned by the parliamentarians and suffered financially as a result of his adherence to the royalist cause. Filmer's principal political work, *Patriarchia* (1636–42), was written before the Civil War but was not published until 1680, when it was brought into service during the crisis provoked by attempts to exclude the Catholic Duke of York (subsequently James II) from the succession. It is a measure of the significance of this work that it prompted a lengthy response from John Locke.

Although he rejected natural liberty, Filmer offered a naturalistic defence of single-person rule. Filmer took the biblical account of the creation as the bench-mark of what is natural because it is the clearest statement of God's intentions for humanity. He argued that when God granted the whole world to Adam, he pointed to a divinely ordained model of human government. Adam's dominion over his offspring showed that God intended human beings to be subject to a single ruler. From this starting point, Filmer argued that patriarchal rule, the rule of the eldest male over his family and the rule of descendants of the first father over multitudes of families, is the only legitimate form of political authority. By dividing the world between his sons, Noah created a number of kingdoms in place of the single one that he had inherited from the descendants of Adam, but these states were themselves governed in conformity with the patriarchal principle. In a detailed analysis of post-biblical history, Filmer sought to establish that this principle lies behind *all* legitimate and beneficial systems of government in the ancient and modern worlds (ibid., pp. 53–60).

For Filmer, the Scriptures provided proof-positive of the rightness of monarchy: God has taught us 'by natural instinct, signified to us by the Creation and confirmed by His own example, the excellency of monarchy'. This conclusion is confirmed by the fruits of human experience: 'the best order, the greatest strength, the most stability and easiest government are to be found in monarchy, and in no other form of government'. It is also buttressed by the lack of any convincing evidence of alternatives, either in relation to God's expressed intentions or in the experience of humankind. Indeed much of the burden of Filmer's case for monarchy rests on arguments concerning the biblical illegitimacy, conceptual incoherence and practical dangers of all other forms of rule. Thus in his discussion of the period when the ancient Hebrews lacked a king, Filmer commented that, 'where every man doth what he pleaseth, it may be truly said, there is no government'. Similarly, in his examination of Aristotle's account of types of government, Filmer focused critically on Aristotle's classifications of aristocracy and democracy. He claimed that monarchy is the only good form of government of which a coherent account can be given, and summoned up the past to confirm his judgement: if 'godliness and honesty' are taken to be the ends of government, then the histories of ancient Rome, Venice and the Low Countries show that these ends can be fulfilled only where political authority is placed in one person's hands (ibid., pp. 84, 86, 189, 196–99).

The Scriptures, history and philosophy therefore concurred in identifying monarchy as *the* form of government; they also established that rule by a single person must conform to a hereditary pattern of transmission. This feature of legitimate government rests upon Filmer's claim that authority descends through the line of the eldest male, a stricture that not only identifies female subordination as God-ordained, but also means that their general inferiority to patriarchs in the family and the state is perpetual. All humankind is born into natural subordination, and while some exercise patriarchal authority as heads of families, only a few assume complete superiority by inheriting political authority from their fathers. This conception of familial and political power strikes a discordant note in modern Western ears, but to Filmer's contemporaries it corresponded with much of the imagery, language and legal forms of their society (Schochet, 1975). Moreover Filmer's strictures on popular government, and his jeremiads on aristocratic interference with monarchical power, and the hazards of mixed government go a long way towards explaining why his theory found a receptive audience among those who had experienced the turmoil of the Civil War.

Filmer's use of a literal interpretation of the Bible to justify absolute monarchy found an independent parallel in Jaques Bossuet's *Politics drawn from the Very Words of Holy Scripture*. This work, which was commenced before the publication of Filmer's *Patriarcha* but was not published until 1709, was part of a tradition of French political thinking that went back to Bodin. Bossuet utilised the Bible in support of paternal forms of government and claimed that these conform to a divinely ordained model. Unlike Filmer, however, Bossuet allowed that legitimate governments of this sort can be formed either on the basis of the consent of subjects, or by conquest; the latter being subsequently legitimised by gaining the approval of the conquered subjects. In both cases the mechanism of consent merely confirms the natural pattern of paternal government:

> Men ... saw the image of a kingdom in the union of several families under the leadership of a common father, and ... having found gentleness in that life, brought themselves easily to create societies of families under kings who took the place of fathers.

Bossuet argued that monarchy is the most ancient, common and hence the most natural form of government and he identified it with a number of distinct and unique advantages. It is least likely to suffer from divisions and most conducive to unity, and it is also particularly appropriate when it comes to satisfying the military requirements of the state. Moreover, hereditary (as opposed to elective) monarchy reinforces these advantages. It establishes a natural pattern of perpetuation, encourages the king to care for his state as a patrimony to be transmitted to his male heir, and endows rulers with the dignity that derives from an office that is beyond the reach of contention (Bossuet, 1990, pp. 44, 47–8, 49–51).

As we shall see, the absolutist aspects of Filmer's and Bossuet's positions parallel Hobbes' theory in important respects, but their emphatic and exclusive preference for monarchy harks back to medieval political thinking (see pp. 130ff). In this respect it is significant that in the opening chapter of *Patriarcha*, Filmer portrayed the idea of natural liberty as a 'new' opinion, one that had acquired currency only within the last century. Like medieval thinkers, Filmer identified a divine source for monarchy, and like them he endowed it with paternal images. He also related monarchy to the good of the community, understood, as we have seen, in terms of 'holiness and peace' (Filmer, 1949, pp. 53, 103). However these aspects of Filmer's thought must be placed alongside others that mark a departure from medieval patterns. In the first place, Filmer's patriarchal imagery has more to do with power and constraint than with fatherly affection. When the eighth-century-ruler Alfred the Great of England wished to identify the common strand in his relationship with his subjects, he referred to the love he felt for them all (Nelson, 1991, p. 239). In contrast the subjects of Filmer's patriarchal ruler are more likely to be identified by the fact that they all owe unquestioning obedience to the king's commands. Secondly, in Filmer's theory, medieval ideas of royal supremacy as a partnership give way to a stress on the unrestrained and all-embracing power of the monarch. Finally, medieval thinkers had regarded the power of kings as a direct, unmediated *gift* from God. Filmer, however, thought that kings possess supreme power as a *right* derived from the natural law of patriarchal inheritance; power comes originally from God, but its transmission is mediated through human generation and rulers have a right to it. As we shall see in a subsequent chapter, this point has important implications for subjects' capacity to respond to bad government (see pp. 300ff).

Monarchy in Eighteenth- and Nineteenth-Century Political Thought: Absolutists, Romantics, Maistre and Maurras

Following the Glorious Revolution of 1688–89 the British monarchy developed in a mixed rather than an absolutist direction, and so in some ways Filmer's arguments were overtaken by events. However aspects of his theory had an impact in the modern period. Echoes of Filmer's patriarchalism can be discerned in late eighteenth-century accounts of monarchy. They can also be seen in the political attitudes of romantically inclined young aristocrats in the 1840s (Gunn, 1983, p. 171; Francis and Morrow, 1994, p. 175). For the most part however, these Filmerian survivals were peripheral to mainstream political thinking in England. This point can be illustrated by reference to two of the most significant British political thinkers of the eighteenth century; David Hume and Edmund Burke. While the former allowed that monarchy could be an admirable form of government, he rested this judgement on the assumption that the king would govern in a regular and law-bound manner rather than arbitrarily. Provided these conditions were satisfied, Hume thought there was little in principle wrong with absolute monarchy (Hume, 1987, pp. 51–3, 94; Miller, 1981, pp. 145–8). Burke, in contrast, treated monarchy as an aspect of a broadly based aristocratic political culture. Burke's monarch infused warmth and civility into politics, but except in symbolic terms, or as part of a representative structure in which the aristocratic and wealthy have a dominant influence, did not stand at the centre of politics (see pp. 155–7).

On the Continent, ideas of monarchy were closely connected to absolute conceptions of sovereignty. In eighteenth-century France, monarchy was sometimes presented in neo-Filmerian hues, but it was also discussed in terms that he would have deplored. Thus while Denis Diderot (a key figure in the French Enlightenment) allowed that kingly authority was a 'gift of heaven', he traced its legitimate origins to the consent of the governed expressed through a contractual arrangement, and criticised the hereditary transmission of political offices (Diderot, 1992, pp. 7–11, 90–1, 200–1; Rowen, 1980, pp. 133–4). In the German states, some accounts of monarchy utilised notions of natural liberty against which Filmer had railed. It was claimed that having once possessed natural freedom, individuals seek to protect their interests by exchanging freedom for the benefits provided by an enlightened, absolute ruler (Krieger, 1972, pp. 50–71).

In the wake of the French Revolution a number of French and German writers produced accounts of monarchy in response to both popular republican government and to the enlightened despotism of the eighteenth century. For example in the late eighteenth and early nineteenth centuries some German Romantics reacted to the French Revolution by attempting to refurbish monarchical government so as to provide an alternative to both despotic and popular regimes. The romantic regeneration of monarchy rested upon a critique of eighteenth-century theories of absolute monarchy. This critique identified a connection between the underlying basis of absolutist rule and the system of popular government that had displaced it during the 1790s. It also focused on the spiritually impoverished character of eighteenth- century conceptions of monarchy. The Romantics claimed that eighteenth-century political thinkers presented a mechanical conception of the state. Having based their theory on isolated individuals who possessed natural liberty, these writers adopted a narrowly instrumental account of the relationship between rulers and their subjects. Theories of absolute monarchy thus shared common ground with revolutionary doctrines, and could not offer an effective alternative to them because they had deprived monarchy of the aesthetic and poetic qualities that were necessary if it was to appeal to the affection and loyalty of its subjects (Beiser, 1992, pp. 236–9; Müller, 1955, p. 153). In place of these dangerous and uninspiring doctrines, the German Romantics sought to reaffirm ideas of community and interdependence and to identify a distinctive role for monarchy that recaptured many of the images of medieval kingship. They thus stressed that political authority should be endowed with an aura of aesthetically satisfying, psychologically reassuring familial warmth, and they argued that a paternal conception of monarchy would best satisfy these requirements. This feature of romantic political thought is particularly marked in the writings of Novalis, but it appears also in those of Frederick Schlegel and Adam Müller. For example Novalis pictured an idealised royal family made up of a young, pure and devoted couple as the symbol of true monarchy based on faith and love (Novalis, 1996; Beiser, 1992, pp. 264, 272). Schlegel also maintained that monarchs can only be effective if they are presented as objects of veneration (Schlegel, 1964, pp. 122–4). Much of the substance of German political Romanticism dealt with the aura of monarchy. But these writers claimed that this must be underwritten by political arrangements that endow the monarch with a distinctive and supreme set of political functions. He must be the symbolic and effective centre of a cohesive, organic community, not merely the most powerful actor in what Novalis tellingly described as the 'factory state' of eighteenth-century absolutism (Novalis, 1996, p. 45).

One of the key points of romantic conceptions of monarchy is the demand that it must conform to deep-seated human needs. In this respect, romantic political thought has a naturalistic frame of reference, but it relates this to the historical experiences of a community rather than to the original creative power of God. The idea that monarchy is natural to certain political communities also played an important role in the writings of Joseph de Maistre, a contemporary of the German Romantics.

Maistre, however, buttressed his account of monarchy with a general defence of the need for authority in human relationships that was similar in some respects to the position advanced by Filmer. Like Filmer, Maistre argued that hereditary monarchy produces a range of practical benefits that count in its favour and tell against alternatives, particularly those that involve popular rule. For example, in an echo of Bossuet's position, he claimed that hereditary monarchy settles questions of succession and thus puts supreme power beyond the reach of ambition. Single-person rule also provides unity and stability by concentrating power in one pair of hands. Moreover, since Maistre endorsed commonly held assumptions about the partiality and wilfulness of the mass of the population, he thought it important for power to be placed in the hands of a person whose upbringing and lack of private interests will minimise the risks involved in any form of human rule. Finally, Maistre argued that the unquestioned supremacy of a single person allows his subjects to feel a degree of relative equality; none could aspire to supremacy and none could feel slighted by or envious of the relatively minor distinctions that exist between subjects (Maistre, 1965, p. 27).

Joseph de Maistre (1753–1821)

Born into a noble family in the Kingdom of Sardinia, Maistre served as a legal official and later as ambassador of the government-in-exile at the Russian imperial court in St Petersburg. In 1817 Maistre returned to Europe, but rapidly became disillusioned with the monarchs whose restoration he had long awaited. Maistre's standing as a critic of the revolution and its ideological basis matches, if it does not surpass, that of Edmund Burke. His major political writings are *Considerations on France* (1796) and *Study of Sovereignty* (first published in 1884).

While there is no indication that Maistre was ever well-disposed to the changes that occurred in France from 1789, his defence of monarchy was based on experiences of a republican system of government that had become internally authoritarian and externally aggressive. Maistre was a shrewd observer of the bloody course of political events in France, and as a subject of the King of Savoy he suffered great personal hardship when the revolutionary armies invaded his native country. One effect of this experience was that Maistre emphasised that monarchy produces real benefits for those who are subject to it. He argued that since monarchy is a system of rule that recognises a natural principle of subordination, it is able to make the exercise of supreme power relatively benign and generally beneficial. In contrast, those who attempt to put the unnatural idea of natural liberty into effect are necessarily driven to adopt forms of government that allow self-interested and rapacious elites to wield unbridled and cruelly exercised power from behind a facade of popular government legitimated by Rousseau's idea of the 'general will' (see p. 86). Against this view, Maistre argued that the corporate and communal aspects of human existence derive from the ruler, and that this must be recognised by ascribing power and legitimacy to a single, preferably monarchical, head of state (ibid., pp. 68–9, pp. 113–19). Once this principle is established there will be no need for government to go to cruel and unnatural lengths to maintain a system of rule that must be oppressive precisely because it ignores natural principles of social and political organisation.

Although Maistre's defence of monarchy reflected his wish to see the Bourbons restored to the French throne, his conception of monarchy was not that of the enlightened absolutism of the eighteenth century. The same general point may be made of the last significant defence of monarchy in Western political thought. This account was produced by Charles Maurras, a prominent figure in French right-wing politics in the late nineteenth and early twentieth centuries (see p. 40). Like Maistre, Maurras argued that a properly constituted monarchy is far less oppressive than republican forms of government, and like Maistre also, his views on this issue were closely related to the historical tradition and recent experiences of France. Maurras did not presume to make universally applicable statements about forms of government, but he thought that sociability and hierarchy are prevailing features of *all* forms of human life.

Maurras' motto was 'Authority at the top, liberty below'. He argued that these two conditions can be satisfied by monarchy because it takes a national focus and only utilises supreme power directly for national purposes. In this respect it is quite different from republicanism, a system of government in which electoral processes and the demands of parliamentary government necessarily bring local and private interests within the orbit of national government, and thus the power of central government is felt directly throughout society (Maurras, 1971a, pp. 220–1). Paradoxically, a free republic is more harmful to liberty than other forms of government. 'Liberty is a right under the republic, but only a right: under the sovereignty of the royal throne, liberties will relate to actual practice – certain, real, tangible, matters of fact.' In democratic regimes the state is the temporary but all-effective slave of those who control a majority in parliament; under monarchy it becomes a disinterested source of authority and control. A monarchical state thus protects liberties in general rather than being under the control of sectional interests who attain their freedom at the expense of the rest of the population (ibid., pp. 230, 220–1, 231, 225).

These advantages could presumably be produced by any form of single-person rule, but Maurras identified them particularly with the French monarchy. The benefits of rule by a single person were compounded by the long-established ties that bound the French people to their historical royal family. Like Edmund Burke, Maurras regarded historical experience as a form of 'second nature'; it is so ingrained in the psyche of members of the community that it forms the mental and emotional furniture of their minds. From this perspective, the connection between the French people and their royal family reinforced the natural character of the traditional social and political hierarchy (ibid., pp. 235–6). When writing of the French royal family (known in modern times as the 'House of Bourbon'), Maurras referred to them by their ancient designation, the 'House of Capet' (ibid., p. 237). This archaic language reflects his tendency to think of monarchy in medieval rather than modern terms, a point that is underlined by the contrast he drew between the leniency of traditional royal rule and the intrusively centralising aspirations of late seventeenth- and early eighteenth-century monarchs.

Despite Maurras' close self-identification with the exiled Bourbons, his ideas were not endorsed by the royalist mainstream. In the later stages of his life, Maurras supported Marshall Pétain, the head of the 'Vichy' regime established in the southern part of France by the triumphant ruler of the German Reich. At that time Pétain seemed the only hope of saving the historical and authoritarian France to which Maurras was committed. This shift in allegiance was spurred by desperation, but in some respects it was a fitting end to what was the swan song of monarchical thinking in the Western tradition. Monarchy persists in a number of European countries and lingers fitfully in some former colonies. However, while crowned heads play symbolic roles within these states, they can hardly be said to rule. The mantle of single-person rule has passed from monarchs to a new type of personal dictator.

Presidents and Dictators in Modern Political Theory: Weber, Hitler

In the twentieth century, when monarchs can be said to 'reign' rather than 'rule', government by a single person has largely been the prerogative of dictators. Unlike the dictators of republican Rome, who were installed in power in order to stave off crises, most modern dictators aim for lifetime tenure of office and seek to determine who will succeed them. While these rulers have supremacy in the state, they are often identified with a movement and/or mass party, or with a segment of an existing elite, most commonly the military. Historically, the most important example of this form of rule occurred in Germany between 1932 and 1945 under Adolf Hitler, head of state and leader of the National Socialist Party. This case is particularly significant because, while many effective dictators have had to operate within and justify themselves by reference to systems of government that are nominally based on a non-dictatorial principle, Hitler's domination of German politics was set in a state that was overtly based on personal leadership. In contrast Hitler's Italian contemporary, Benito Mussolini, held the title of chief of government in Italy, but the fascist regime over which he presided was set within the framework of a constitutional monarchy. Similarly, many South American dictators have been presidents of their republics, or have headed supposedly stop-gap administrations dominated by the military, but loosely connected to republican constitutions by incorporating a few non-military figures.

Adolf Hitler (1889–1945)

Hitler, the leader of the National Socialist movement in Germany, wielded complete power as *Fuehrer* from 1933 until the collapse of his regime at the end of the Second World War. His political ideas (Hitler can hardly be said to have advanced a political philosophy) were propagated in *Mein Kampf* (My Struggle) (1925).

Hitler originally came to power through a legitimate electoral process, one that had its origins in the events following the collapse of the German monarchy at the end of the First World War. At that time Germany adopted a federal system of government based on democratic principles, a move that prompted Max Weber, an eminent economist and sociologist, to argue for an element of single-person rule within the constitutional structure of the Weimar Republic. In 'The President of the Reich' (1919), Weber made a case for a popularly elected president in order to counteract the fragmentation that would result from a constitutional structure in which state governments played an important role, and the national assembly was elected upon the basis of proportional representation. He argued that in the immediate past under an authoritarian system of monarchy, democrats had looked to the majority in parliament to provide a popular input into the political process. Under the existing constitutional arrangements parliament alone was not a sufficient guarantee for democratic rule: 'today … all constitutional proposals have succumbed to crude blind faith in the infallibility and omnipotence of the majority – of the majority in parliament, that is, not the majority of the people' (Weber, 1994, p. 307).

Max Weber (1864–1920)

Weber, a German academic economist and sociologist, made important contributions to theories of authority, drawing a distinction between traditional,
charismatic and legal–rational forms. These ideas were applied in a number
of articles discussing the formulation of a constitution for the German
Republic in the wake of the First World War.

In order to forge unity and avoid the fragmentation that would result
from a parliament made up of representatives of diverse particular interests, it was necessary for the will of the people to be embodied in a
president who was elected by them, rather than being chosen by the
majority in parliament. It was, Weber argued, *'essential for us to create a
head of state resting unquestionably on the will of the whole people*, without
the intercession of intermediaries' (ibid., p. 304). He claimed that:

A popularly elected president, as the head of the executive, of official
patronage, and as the possessor of a delaying veto and the power to
dissolve parliament and to consult the people, is the palladium of genuine democracy, which does not mean impotent self-abandonment to
cliques but subordination to leaders one has chosen for oneself (ibid.,
p. 308).

While Weber saw a leader chosen by the people as essential to the maintenance of democratic government, the conception of single-person rule
that emerged in Germany in the early 1930s was premised upon the
intractable difficulties produced by parliamentary democracy. Of course
some theories of monarchy rely heavily on judgements concerning the ills
of popular government, but the case of modern dictatorship is rather
different. These regimes invariably developed in reaction to practical
experience of modern, parliamentary democracy, and their rationale is
closely bound up with this experience. In particular, theories of modern
dictatorship involve a two-pronged attack on democratic government, one
directed at parliamentarianism, the other reflecting a general contempt for
ordinary citizens. These themes are clearly apparent in Hitler's *Mein
Kampf*. In this work, written before Hitler came to power, observations of
the decadence of parliamentary politics and the insipid, self-interested
character of conventional politicians are invariably coupled with references to what Hitler called the 'unshakeable stupidity of the voting citizenry'. These criticisms are directed particularly at the politics of the
prewar Austro-Hungarian constitutional monarchy and the postwar Ger-

man Republic, whose failings were held to be due to a departure from a general principle (Hitler, 1969, pp. 339–40).

The 'leadership principle' (*fuehrerprinzip*) makes parliamentary democracy untenable. In its place, Hitler promoted a conception of government based on the personal responsibility of the leader and the total obedience of the rest of the community. The *fuehrerprinzip* determines how supreme power should be located, but it is also applied as a general principle of social and political organisation. All levels of society should be subject to the oversight of responsible leaders who regulate the activities of dutiful subordinates in particular spheres of political, social or economic activity (Brooker, 1985, p. 60). Neither the supreme leader nor his subordinates owe their position to success in conventional electoral competitions. In response to the question 'Does anyone believe that the progress of this world springs from the mind of majorities and not from the brains of individuals?' Hitler stressed the primacy of struggle in elite selection and depreciated the bravery and sagacity of ordinary citizens (Hitler, 1969, pp. 465–6, 78–81). Much the same point is made in Mussolini's account of Fascism. Rejecting the ideals of conventional parliamentary democracy, he identified Fascism with a new conception of the state that, under its leader, incorporates the population into a system of 'organised, centralized, authoritarian democracy' (Mussolini, 1935, p. 27). Mussolini's and Hitler's goals differed significantly – the former wished to recover the glories of Rome, while the latter sought to protect the German race – but they shared a belief that the sort of organisation and commitment needed to attain these goals would not be produced through parliamentary democracy.

An implication of the *fuehrerprinzip* is a commitment to a radical elitism that makes the position of the *Fuehrer* a consequence of proven capacity to further the interests of the German race. This aspect of Nazi ideology was a result of Hitler's identification of a new goal for the state; it also reflects a lurking animus towards the existing upper classes and the intelligentsia. Elitism of this kind signalled the non- traditional nature of Hitler's conception of single-person rule, a feature of his political thinking that was also apparent in his understanding of the relationship between the leader and the masses. Although he rejected conventional notions of democratic representation, Hitler claimed to have identified a 'truly Germanic democracy' in which the leader is elected by the masses but then assumes full, personal responsibility for the state. He insisted however, that the genius of the leader is not discovered through the electoral process. To the contrary, those capable of assuming supreme power establish a direct relationship with the population through the force of their personality conveyed through public performances. As a result of his interaction with the masses at public meetings, the putative leader transforms 'philosophy' into a 'tightly organised political community of faith and struggle, unified in spirit and will'. This transformation can only be brought about by the spoken word, 'the power which has always started rolling the greatest religious and political avalanches in history' (Hitler, 1969, pp. 392, 83, 346, 98).

This account of the process through which the leader is first identified and then formally elevated to a position of supremacy points to one of the distinctive features of modern dictatorship. Although this form of rule is a product of the reaction against the experience of modern parliamentary democracy, it nevertheless incorporates aspects of modern political culture. While the relationship between the leader and the people is held to be a 'Germanic' one based on 'faith, honour and care' (Neumann, 1944, p. 342; Brooker, 1985, p. 56), these echoes of medieval kingship do not bridge the gap between monarchical and dictatorial conceptions of single-person rule. The leader's legitimacy springs from his role in relation to 'the race', or in Mussolini's case the state, not to universal values. Moreover he elevates himself to a dominant position in the minds of the population and is then elevated to a position of unquestioned and unquestionable supremacy through the modern (but self-terminating) mechanism of mass election.

Conclusion

While it would be misleading to equate monarchical, theocratic and dictatorial theories of government, these accounts of the way in which power should be allocated share certain common and distinctive features. In the first place, they all assume that ability and/or virtue of a kind required by rulers is found only in a few individuals. A corollary of this claim is an underlying assumption of the general political incapacity of the vast bulk of humanity. Furthermore, proponents of single-person rule assume that the unity of a community must be created by and symbolised in a single, personal head of state. An organic conception of the state is not the sole preserve of those who endorse rule by a single person, but theories of this kind give the organic analogy a peculiarly literal interpretation. Like the human organism, the state must have a head who controls and directs the actions of its members. Finally, it seems clear that these conceptions of government are more usually related to a belief that the state exists for the purposes of virtue or order, rather than having freedom or individual happiness as its end.

CHAPTER 6

The Rule of the Few

In the previous chapter it was noted that some accounts of monarchy set that form of single-person rule in the context of a system of social and political authority in which the 'aristocracy' plays an important role. Theorists of 'mixed government' argue that a combination of monarchic, aristocratic and democratic elements provides a way of ensuring that political power is exercised properly (see pp. 227ff). In both these cases the 'aristocracy' – or to use Aristotle's phrase, 'the rule of the few who are the best' – does not possess supreme power. A consideration of the role of the aristocracy in a mixed government will be presented later in this book, but since a more restricted conception of 'aristocracy' as a central aspect of monarchy has occupied an important place in the history of Western political thought, it will be considered in some detail in the present chapter. It is important to note, however, that Aristotle's definition indicates that the idea of rule by the select few can, and indeed has, been given a more literal interpretation; that is, one can identify a number of significant statements about the desirability of rule by the few that are not related to monarchical conceptions of government and do not mean rule by those of 'noble' birth. These ideas played an important role in ancient political thought, and they have also had currency in the nineteenth and twentieth centuries.

Arguments in favour of allocating exclusive or supreme power to the few generally rest on assumptions about the limited moral and/or intellectual capacity of ordinary members of the population. It is claimed that the attributes necessary to ensure that political power is exercised in ways that will be conducive to realising the ends of politics are restricted to relatively narrow sections of the population, and they should therefore play a leading role in government. The attributes in question are moral and intellectual, although in some cases they also relate to cultural values that are acquired through membership of a class whose claim to political supremacy has been recognised in customary or legally legitimated processes of hereditary transmission. The existence of a hereditary ruling class is the hallmark of conventional conceptions of aristocracy, a system of rule by the few that can be contrasted with theories of elite rule that rest upon demonstrated ability and, in some cases, claims to moral and intellectual preeminence. In all cases, rule by the few is held to be to the benefit of the community as a whole, not the exclusive benefit of the rulers themselves.

This chapter will present accounts of the more or less pure forms of elite rule promoted by Plato and Aristotle. In these theories the stress is upon moral and intellectual excellence, although in Aristotle's case notions of cultural superiority also play a role. Classical accounts of rule by the few can be contrasted with the more conventional accounts of aristocracy developed by medieval, early modern and modern theorists. Although these theorists often refered to classical sources, many of them emphasised the hereditary basis of beneficial forms of aristocratic government. The chapter will conclude with a discussion of modern, non-aristocratic ideas produced by writers who promoted rule by cultural, intellectual and/or party elites.

The Rule of the Few in Ancient Political Theory: Plato and Aristotle

Plato's guardians clearly exemplify rule by the few: even though they comprise a small section of the total population of the state, they exercise complete control over the ideal republic. Members of this class are distinguished by their knowledge of and their attachment to ultimate goodness. In the exercise of their political functions they are assisted by the auxiliaries. Taken together these groups give an essentially aristocratic cast to Plato's ideal state. The system of selection and training to which the population are exposed, and the intensive process of education that is specified for those who appear to have the natural aptitude to become guardians, are designed to ensure that the state is ruled by its 'best' citizens. The guardians are held to possess the intellectual, moral and temperamental qualities necessary to determine and single-mindedly pursue the good. Plato regarded a state ruled by the best as just in a double sense. It is right and just that the most rational element rules the less rational. Moreover, where this happens, the outcome will be just; that is, political power will be exercised for the good of the whole community. These advantages of rule by the few are highlighted by Plato's frequent pejorative references to popular rule. Democracies are dominated by the least rational members of the population, and they are disfigured by their tendency to produce a narrowly selfish form of class rule that ends up in chaos or tyranny (see pp. 128–9).

In the *Republic* Plato did not offer an overt defence of his conception of rule by the few against the claims of 'the one', but a number of aspects of his account of the guardians point to the advantages of collective rather than single-person rule. One of the problems lurking below the surface of the ideal state is the corruption of those who wield supreme power. If the guardians really possess the qualities that Plato ascribed to them then corruption would seem to be impossible. However, he was not overly sanguine about this outcome. One sign of his lack of certainty is that the details of Plato's account suggest that collective elite rule is a way of establishing a series of checks carried out *by* members of the guardian class *upon* each other. Perhaps as a way of lessening the potentially insidious features of this system, Plato stressed that the guardians form a 'family', something that is made easier by their lack of natural familial relationships and their communal way of life (Plato, 1970, pp. 220–2). An advantage of this family feeling among the guardians is that Plato thought that it would encourage a unified commitment to the ethos of this class, a means of assurance and support that would not be available to the single ruler, however wise and good he might be. Indeed, as Aristotle pointed out, justifiable single-person rule necessarily means that the person in question is qualitatively different from the rest of the population, a 'man among gods', and will be isolated from people who are only nominally 'fellow' human beings.

Although Plato's guardians form an 'aristocracy' in Aristotle's sense of the term, 'meritocracy' is perhaps a more appropriate designation for the system of rule in the ideal republic. While the guardians and auxiliaries are the few and the best, their right to rule is stripped of any of the conventional connotations of aristocracy. Their status is strictly 'achieved' rather than 'ascribed'. Plato was vague about many of the details, but the general thrust of his argument implies that the ruling class should be drawn from all classes, and that their children must be expelled from that class if they fail to come up to scratch. Moreover rulers enjoy no mundane privileges as a consequence of their position in the state. To the contrary, they neither possess property nor enjoy conventional family life. In response to a criticism that rulers living under these conditions will not be happy, Plato upholds his ascetic ideal by retorting that the state does not exist for the benefit of its rulers; their way of life is justified by the need to avoid private interests that may corrupt them or distract their attention from the pursuit of goodness. In any case, goodness entails a degree of ultimate satisfaction that cannot to be equated with the alluring but, according to Plato, debasing creature comforts that are usually associated with 'happiness' (ibid., pp. 163–5).

The strict asceticism that Plato saw as part of rule by the few in the *Republic* is modified in *The Laws*, where he dealt with a second-best state designed to cope with a lack of supreme virtue among rulers. This state is to be structured and regulated by a system of law that will compensate for the deficiencies of its members. However, in order to apply these laws and ensure that they are subject to periodic revision, Plato set up an elaborate system of judicial and reviewing councils. Some of these bodies are to be filled by members of the ordinary population; others will be staffed by the more virtuous members of the community. Plato thought that the political structure laid down in *The Laws* would avoid the dangers of democracy on the one hand and monarchy on the other; it would achieve this goal by combining aristocratic and democratic elements. The former would result from a system of election, the latter from the use of a mechanism known as the 'lot'. The Greeks' understanding of the implications of selection through election differed significantly from that associated with modern systems of democratic government. For the Greeks, election favoured the upper classes because it meant that judgements of worth and social prestige could play a role in selection procedures. In contrast the lot, essentially a draw, or lottery, identified officeholders through a process of chance. This process was blind to the particular qualities of candidates, and the laws of probability would ensure that the numerically superior lower classes would dominate assemblies or offices selected by lot. The fact that Plato included a system of election within his second-best state provided for the incorporation of an aristocratic element in the constitution. However, since all citizens would be eligible for office, the system was based upon a meritocratic, rather than a hereditary, conception of aristocracy (Plato, 1980, pp. 223–45; Klosko, 1986, pp. 211–25).

Aristotle's *Politics* presents an account of rule by the few that embraces some of the features conventionally associated with 'aristocracy'. However it also describes an ideal form of collective rule by the best in a state where the entire citizen body is virtuous. Aristocracy exists where the best men rule in the common interest, but Aristotle assumed that in other than ideal states the best will be only a small section of the population. These types of regime, dubbed 'so-called aristocracies', are distinguished by the fact that, while 'the best' play a prominent role in politics, their claims are based on relative rather than absolute virtue. These aristocrats, or 'nobles' as Aristotle often called them, are markedly superior to other members of the community but have not attained true virtue. One consequence of their imperfect virtue is that while they play a central role in the state, their power is not absolute and is placed within a variety of mixed constitutions. These arrangements combine virtue with wealth, numbers, free status or some combination of these, thus acknowledging the limited degree of virtue among even 'the best', and the consequent need to recognise the weight of other claims derived from wealth, freedom or numbers. In addition, since 'the best' are only relatively so, it is important to guard against the corrupt use of power and the appearance of 'oligarchy', a system of rule in which the few, usually economically dominant, rule in their own interest rather than in the common interest (Aristotle, 1958, pp. 117, 131–2, 204–5).

Setting a pattern that was to be common in subsequent treatments of aristocracy, Aristotle assumed that the virtues of 'so-called' aristocrats are related to their unobsessive possession of wealth, to their education and cultural and intellectual milieu. This assumption corresponds to the treatment of virtue in Aristotle's *Ethics*. Although he identified the contemplative life with true virtue, he made it clear that this end is too exalted for most human beings, and concentrated on a range of virtues that are more appropriate to ordinary social and political life. The moral virtues include 'courage' (especially as applied to military action), 'justice' (honesty in business dealings), 'liberality' (manifesting itself in generosity to one's friends and the *polis*), 'magnanimity' (a proper sense of one's worth), 'good temper' and 'temperance' (Aristotle, 1975, pp. 115aff; Mulgan, 1977, p. 4). These qualities are of a kind that is commonly identified with aristocratic culture.

In addition to the imperfect but nevertheless beneficial form of 'so-called' aristocracy, Aristotle discussed an ideal form. His treatment of this topic is incomplete and inconsistent, but it is clear in its general outlines. In a genuine aristocracy, political power is assigned to the truly virtuous, who rule in the common interest. However, since Aristotle treated this form of rule in the context of an ideal state, he tended to focus on an aristocratic community rather than on the narrow question of aristocratic rule. That is, he equated the citizen body with those who are both absolutely and relatively fit to rule – they are both virtuous and equal in virtue with their fellow citizens – and he consigned those whose birth (slaves), gender (women) or occupations (agricultural, commercial, unskilled) preclude the attainment and practice of virtue to an underclass who are necessary for the realisation of the ends of the state but are not members of it. By dividing the aristocratic citizen body into those who fight (the young) and those who rule, Aristotle effectively undermined his own stipulation that the state is ideally a union of equals, sharing the function of ruling and being ruled. Whatever the coherence of this distinction, it means that within the context of an aristocratic community Aristotle's conception of an ideal state is in fact a system of rule by all full members of the community. As in his account of so-called aristocracy, his treatment of its ideal form incorporates the prejudices based on age, birth, gender and class that are conventionally associated with aristocratic rule (Aristotle, 1958, pp. 279–306).

Medieval and Early Modern Conceptions of Aristocracy: Aquinas, Machiavelli and Harrington

Aristotle's discussion of an aristocratic element in mixed government had an important influence on subsequent political thought. For example the Roman thinker Cicero identified an aristocratic component within the republican constitution of Rome, assigning this role to a senatorial class to whom he ascribed many of the cultural and intellectual qualities that Aristotle associated with 'so-called' aristocracies. For medieval writers, however, government by the few was one of the elements in a broader conception of rule that was essentially monarchical (see pp. 130–4). In early medieval Europe, kings were held to have been endowed with supreme power by God, but this power formed the basis of a complex web of interactions and responsibilities, the most immediately important of which were those embodying the 'faith' that bound a king to his closest and most important subjects. These people were the king's servants, and their proximity to the throne, together with their economic, cultural and military importance, gave them a distinctive role in the state. They formed what was, in effect, an aristocratic class within a mixed government.

In practical terms the relationship between the king and his most powerful subjects was a consequence of the tendency towards feudalism in emerging European states, but with the rediscovery of Aristotle's writings in the thirteenth century these relationships could be described in ways that consciously echoed the political theory of the ancients. Thus Aquinas argued that the danger of tyranny is greater in pure aristocracy than in monarchy because, when a number of people rule, conflict is more likely, and this often tempts members of the ruling group to subvert political power for their own purposes. He credited mixed government with the ability to forestall this threat and the less immediate one presented by monarchy. This solution echoes Aristotle's writings, but it fuses monarchy, aristocracy and democracy rather than democracy and oligarchy. The role of aristocracy – that is, 'government by the best elements, in which a few hold office according to virtue' – is justified by their power, wealth and moral attributes. Like the monarch, the members of the aristocracy derive their legitimacy from their virtues, and while these are not as exalted as those expected of good kings, they are nevertheless significant. 'The best form of constitution ... results from a judicious admixture of the *kingdom*, in that there is one person at the head of it; of *aristocracy* in that many participate in government according to virtue; and of *democracy* or popular rule, in that rulers may be elected from the people and the whole population has the right of electing its rulers' (Aquinas, 1959, p. 149). The fact that members of the aristocracy are usually wealthy and that their position is based on birth provides a further link between medieval conceptions of the role of the few and that found in Aristotle's writings.

The claim that aristocracy should be set within the framework of monarchy to produce a mixed system of government persisted into the early modern period. During that time, however, there appeared a republican conception of aristocracy in a mixed government. This perspective on the political role of the virtuous few is most closely identified with the city states of renaissance Italy, but it produced echoes in political thinking in seventeenth-century England and eighteenth-century America. In the second half of the fifteenth century a number of Florentine writers drew upon an idealised, indeed in some ways mythical, picture of the popular *and* aristocratic constitution of Venice in order to assert claims to influence by wealthy Florentines who resented the dominant power wielded by the semi-princely house of Medici. Harking back to classical discussions, they ascribed to 'the few' the role of guardians of the state, who would fill important offices on behalf of the population and thus use their virtues in the service of the common good (Pocock, 1975, pp. 100–3, 185–6). In this case the 'few' are closely integrated with the life of the city state. Machiavelli emphasised this point by observing that while aristocracies of this kind are consistent with long-lived but territorially non-aggressive republics, the existence of landed aristocracies or 'gentry' is generally fatal to all republican forms of government, (Machiavelli, 1975, vol. i, pp. 220–2, 335).

James Harrington (1611–77)

Harrington, an attendant to Charles I in 1647, is best known for his subsequent involvement in republican politics in the years of the Cromwellian protectorate. His major political work, *Oceana* (1656), has been seen as an important contribution to the anglicisation of notions of civic republicanism derived from renaissance Italy.

Partly as a result of the influence of Italian models, ideas of aristocratic republicanism were used in seventeenth-century England and eighteenth-century America when alternatives were being sought for discredited conceptions of monarchical government. Both of these environments produced accounts of what have been called 'natural' aristocracy; that is, claims to rule based on a general recognition of natural superiority. Since monarchy is no longer acceptable, neither is the hereditary determination of elite status. Leaders are still required, but these should be selected by the people, whose role is to recognise the capacities of 'natural aristocrats' and to defer to them. These leaders possess extensive property, education and leisure, but such attributes are not qualifications for office; to the contrary, they are entitled to aristocratic standing because of their 'natural superiority of talent' (Pocock, 1975, pp. 414, 515–17). As the mid-seventeenth-century English writer James Harrington said of his ideal state 'Oceana', 'our' nobility:

> have nothing else but their education and their leisure for the public, furnished by their ease and competent riches, and their intrinsic value which, according as it comes to hold weight in the judgement or suffrage of the people, is their only way to honour and preferment (Harrington, 1992, p. 141).

Hereditary Aristocracy in Modern Political Theory: Burke, Coleridge, Chateaubriand and Constant

While 'the few' played a central role in early modern conceptions of republican government, they were also important in late-eighteenth- and early-nineteenth-century accounts of constitutional monarchy. This form of government is not 'aristocratic' in any strict sense because sovereignty is lodged either in the monarch or in the 'king in parliament', that is, in the king in association with representative bodies. The distinctive character of the positions outlined in this chapter is highlighted by Edmund Burke's strictures on the 'despotism of aristocracy' (Burke, 1834, vol. i, p. 130). Like some other late-eighteenth- and early-nineteenth-century writers, Burke treated aristocracy as a necessary feature of constitutional monarchy, not as a form of pure government.

Edmund Burke (1729–97)

Burke, a native of Ireland, made a career in English politics as an intellectual man-of-business for a leading faction of the Whig Party. He played an important role in parliament and in a number of administrations from the mid 1760s until the 1790s. Burke was a famous orator and published many of his speeches. He also wrote a number of important political pamphlets, including *Reflections on the Revolution in France* (1791), a work that attacked French revolutionaries and their English sympathisers and resulted in a breach between Burke and leading members of his party.

The aristocracy has made two distinct but related contributions to constitutional monarchy. In the first place, because the members of hereditary aristocracies have been among the wealthiest members of their society and particularly well-endowed with landed wealth, they have exerted an important influence in societies where wealth and political power have been closely correlated. In both England and post-revolutionary France, hereditary aristocrats had their own chamber in parliament, and by virtue of their economic and social influence they exerted both direct and indirect influence on elections to the lower house. Secondly, and more importantly in relation to the distinctive status of an aristocracy within a constitutional monarchy, it was claimed that the influence ascribed to members of this class was justified because they formed the central element in a generally beneficial social and political culture. The hierarchical structure of this culture was conducive to general benefit, at least in the long-established, inegalitarian and historically derived conditions that were the norm in late-eighteenth- and early-nineteenth-century Europe. Before they were disrupted by the French Revolution, these governments had ensured stability, provided general security of property and encouraged commerce and material progression. It was argued that they could play a similar role in the post-revolutionary world when monarchies were reestablished in a number of European states.

Burke's response to the revolution indicates that he included among the advantages of an aristocratic political culture its capacity to insulate the process of government from the direct influence of an invariably ignorant and often blindly and destructively self-interested populace. Aristocracy also ensured that equally dangerous adventurers from other social classes could not seize control of the state. However, in addition to these merely negative advantages Burke ascribed a number of important positive attributes to aristocracy. To some extent these have to do with ability and probity, with what might be called 'political virtue', but Burke's defence of the predominant social and political influence of 'the few' extended beyond an exclusively meritocratic standpoint.

The breadth of Burke's conception of the benefits of aristocratic government is apparent in his treatment of the hereditary basis of European aristocracy. The fact that influence and wealth are transmitted through a process that mirrors the transmission of biological characteristics, endows the social and political structure with a 'natural' aspect. Moreover, by giving society a historical dimension, a sense of location in the past that is also connected to the future, this principle provides members of society with a sense of belonging. Human beings are not alone in the world but can face its adversities clothed in a reassuring 'cloak of custom'. In addition to these symbolic but psychologically valuable consequences of a society patterned on hereditary aristocracy, Burke claimed that the connection between aristocracy and large, stable landholdings encourages respect for property of all kinds. The property of the aristocracy provides 'ramparts' that protect other forms of property within the state (Burke, 1969, p. 140). Finally, Burke associated aristocracy with 'manners', that is, with ideas of 'civility', a system of cultural ethics that modifies the generally beneficial but potentially disruptive pursuit of economic self-interest. Aristocratic influence, resulting from its insulation from pressing material necessity and from its educational and cultural experiences, complements that of religion. Both religion and aristocracy embody values that safeguard society without preventing progression built on the inheritance of the past (Pocock, 1985, pp. 193–212). At the same time, however, the cultural ethics of aristocracy provides society with less immediately practical but nevertheless significant benefits. In Burke's writings, as in those of the German Romantics, monarchs are endowed with an aura of warmth and grace that underwrites their political position (see p. 139). This concern with tone is also applied to the aristocracy. As Burke put it, 'nobility is a graceful ornament to the civil society. It is the Corinthian capital of polished society' (Burke, 1969, p. 245).

While Burke treated the influence of aristocracy and religion as parts of the same political and social culture, an alternative position was developed by his near contemporary, the poet and philosopher Samuel Taylor Coleridge. Like Burke, Coleridge placed weight upon the moderating influences of the non-material aspects of aristocracy – the 'delicate superstition of ancestry' may to some degree 'counteract the grosser superstition of wealth' – but he argued that in a well-balanced state the political influence derived from both ancestry and wealth must be subjected to humanising influences embodied in philosophical and clerical elites, or a 'clerisy'. The 'clerisy' are an independent section of society charged with the responsibility of conveying intellectual and moral values and ensuring that these are brought to bear on the practice of politics (Coleridge, 1990, pp. 62, 172–95).

The basis of Coleridge's conception of 'clerisy' lay in his distinctive understanding of the intellectual requirements of Christianity, but this approach to politics has appeared in a number of forms in the history of political thought. As we shall see, J. S. Mill stressed the importance of secular elites in democratic societies (see p. 186). The idea of the clerisy also has a parallel in Islamic political thought. For example in the reform of the Iranian state, which was embodied in the constitution of 1906–7, religious leaders were assigned a corrective and monitorial role over those who held political office. In light of Coleridge's insistence that a clerisy is necessary to infuse human values into the political system, it is interesting to note that in Iran those who derived their moral authority from their knowledge of divine law (*sharía*) were seen as having a special responsibility for the matters of social justice specified in that body of law (Akhavi, 1980, pp. 15–16).

Burke's account of the role of aristocracy was produced in response to what he saw as the desecration of aristocratic monarchy by the French revolutionaries. Similar accounts of the role of the aristocracy appeared in the works of post-revolutionary writers in France. These theorists accepted many of the consequences of the revolution and attempted to forge a new image of constitutional monarchy for the post-revolutionary age. Thus both François Chateaubriand, a conservative but non-reactionary figure in restoration politics, and the liberal writer Benjamin Constant justified the retention of an aristocratic element in the social and political structure of the restored monarchy after 1815. Chateaubriand was intensely critical of the pseudo-aristocracy created by the Emperor Napoleon and argued that the restoration of the Bourbons required the restoration of a genuine aristocracy in France. It was necessary, he argued, to reestablish *'aristocratic families'* as 'barriers and safeguards of the throne'. Such families would provide a setting in which to place a monarch who symbolised

> that tradition of ancient honour, that delicacy of sentiment, that contempt of fortune, that generous spirit, that faith, that fidelity which we so much need, and which are the most distinctive virtues of a *gentleman*, and the most necessary ornaments of a state (Chateaubriand, 1816, p. 231)

In addition, however, Chateaubriand stressed that the influence and wealth of an aristocracy must be embodied in the chamber of peers if it is to balance the democratic influences represented in the elected chamber of deputies (ibid., p. 30). For Chateaubriand, therefore, aristocracy was an essential part of a new form of constitutional monarchy, a view that was endorsed by Constant. The latter argued that a hereditary aristocracy with its own chamber in parliament is necessary to sustain a constitutional monarchy. An aristocracy of this kind makes *hereditary* monarchy less extraordinary. Moreover, since it is independent of both the crown and the people, it forms an intermediary between the monarch and a popularly elected assembly, one that is capable of safeguarding the interests and rights of these other elements in the constitution (Constant, 1988, pp. 198–9). Hereditary preeminence ensures that a restricted group within the population occupies the social position and possesses the qualities of wisdom and virtue, which are necessary to ensure the beneficial operation of a system of government that combines traditional notions of hereditary rule with the modern demand that the state be based on the principle of popular sovereignty.

These justifications of aristocracy, like those of Burke and contemporary English writers such as Coleridge, mark the effective termination of conventional aristocracy as an important theme in Western political thought. Indeed, even in Burke's statements there are discordant elements that point forward to other conceptions of rule by the few. For example, in a pamphlet defending his acceptance of a pension from the crown in the face of criticism from the Duke of Bedford, the aged and ailing Burke emphasised the importance of meritocracy as a basis for high office. He remarked that able men of business like himself were responsible for maintaining the structure 'which alone' made Bedford 'his superior'. Elsewhere Burke included within a 'true natural aristocracy' not only the nobility, but also leading judges, intellectuals and the most successful and respectable members of the business community. People with these qualifications 'form in nature, as she operates in the common modification of society, the leading, guiding, and government part' (Burke, 1833, vol. ii. p. 265, vol. i, p. 525). Neither of these remarks are enough to detach Burke from conventional aristocratic conceptions of politics, but the lurking animus implied by the first, and the generalised meritocracy conveyed by the second, point towards a non-aristocratic view of government by the few. Since the middle of the nineteenth century important statements of this position have been advanced by writers who have sought to justify the political superiority of non-aristocratic, non-hereditary elites.

Non-Hereditary Elites in Modern Political Thought: J. S. Mill, Nietzsche, Mosca, Pareto, Blanqui and Lenin

Conventional aristocracy has persisted in parts of the modern world, but like monarchy it has long ceased to an object of interest for political theorists. The main reason for this is that since about the middle of the nineteenth century the general tendency of Western political development has been towards representative democracy, or the rule of 'the many'. Although this development has given the mass of the population an important *formal* role in politics, it has not always been accompanied by an abandonment of arguments concerning the effective dominance of the few. To the contrary, the spread of democratic government has seen the development of a distinctive body of political thinking that deals with the role of elites *within* systems that are ostensibly democratic. These arguments must be distinguished from conventional accounts of aristocracy that are set in a monarchical context, and place a great deal of emphasis on ideas of heredity and tradition. In contrast elite theory stresses merit and demonstrable political ability rather than the inherited social qualities that are ascribed to conventional aristocracies.

One important account of the relationship between elite rule and emerging democracy appeared in John Stuart Mill's writings. Mill's understanding of human progression led him to adopt a wary attitude towards democratic rule; he thought that under the prevailing conditions, systems of mass politics would accentuate the conformist tendencies that were already apparent in modern society. At its most extreme, these tendencies would produce a 'tyranny of the majority', but even their more restrained manifestations would discourage the intellectual and moral experimentation to which Mill attributed the progress of civilisation. In response to these threats to progression, Mill assigned a general educational role to an intellectual elite within society. Its purpose was to equip the masses for intellectual and moral development. In addition, however, he insisted that the administration of the state must be left in the hands of the enlightened and expert few, and he promoted an electoral system that would ensure that the checking and regulatory institutions of representative government would have an elite bias. This last goal was to be achieved by a franchise that gave all sane adults at least one vote, while endowing those who satisfied certain educational, professional and occupational qualifications with a number of votes. The purpose of this allocation was to allow the mass of the population to gain experience in fulfilling a political role while ensuring that they were unable to bring the weight of numbers of bear in a way that undermined Mill's educational and progressive conception of the state (Mill, 1983, pp. 284–6).

Since the elites' influence and political experience were held to have an educational role, Mill's unequal distribution of electoral influence was to be a long-term, but still temporary, feature of modern politics. Provided that the bulk of the population were sufficiently enlightened, Mill thought that representative democracy was the ideally best form of government. It would allow for the most efficient protection of individual interests, and it would also provide scope for self-development by allowing people to practice what was, in effect, self-regulation.

> Human beings are only secure from evil at the hands of others in proportion as they have the power of being, and are, self-*protecting*; and they only achieve a high degree of success in their struggle with Nature in proportion as they are self-*dependent*, relying on what they themselves can do, either separately or in concert, rather than on what others do for them (ibid., p. 208).

Mill's position was a somewhat uneasy one. On the one hand he thought that democracy was inevitable, but on the other his concern with human progression led him to place emphasis on the need for elite, intellectual leadership in the foreseeable future to curb the impact of democratic politics. The fact remains, however, that Mill conceived of circumstances in which elite rule should give way to democracy. In this respect his position differed from that advanced by the late-nineteenth-century philosopher Friedrich Nietzsche, who regarded democracy as an unmitigated disaster that could at best serve to prepare the ground for a new and quite distinctive political system based on the preeminence of an elite group that was seen in essentially aristocratic terms.

Nietzsche's conception of aristocracy emerged out of a wide-ranging assault on values such as pity and the depreciation of individual self-affirmation that he identified with Christian morality and humanism, liberalism and socialism. These movements were modern surrogates for ossified religious faiths, sharing with them ideas of fundamental equality framed in terms of universal moral laws that Nietzsche took to be embodiments of the 'herd instinct' of ordinary human beings. In place of these corrupt, self-serving and dehabilitating ideas, Nietzsche promoted an alternative morality that would direct human beings to take personal responsibility for realising their wills. Nietzsche's conception of 'will' is essentially active: it is a personal force directed to the single-minded pursuit of the satisfaction of its own desires for pleasure or joy, a process that necessarily involves attempts to mould the world to its purposes. 'It is *not* the satisfaction of the will that causes pleasure ... but rather the will's forward thrust and again and again becoming master over that which stands in its way' (Nietzsche, 1968, p. 370). These aspects of Nietzsche's theory resemble parts of Stirner's work, with which he may have been familiar (Carrol, 1974; Leopold, 1995, pp. xi–xii). However, Nietzsche thought that only *some* human beings are capable of conforming to a conception of morality that he identified with realisation of the *Ubermensch*, the superman who transcends the ordinary human condition and whose life constitutes a supreme form of cultural existence.

Wilhelm Friedrich Nieztsche (1844–1900)

Born in the Prussian province of Saxony, Nietzsche was an academic philosopher whose work was devoted to a critique of the moral basis of modern Western cultures. His ideas on elite leadership and the 'will to power' proved amenable to adoption by later fascist and national socialist thinkers. Of his works, *Beyond Good and Evil* (1886) and *The Genealogy of Morals* (1887) have the closest bearing on political theory.

The only positive prospect that Nietzsche associated with liberal democracy was the possibility that its levelling and enervating tendencies would clear the ground for the emergence of a new aristocratic class of supermen who would seize control and subject the population (Detwiler, 1990, pp. 173–4). In all other respects, Nietzsche's position entailed a radical aristocratic critique of the cultural, moral and political structures of both democratic and more authoritarian forms of mass state (Ansell-Pearson, 1994, pp. 151–2). 'Every heightening of the type "man" ... has been the work of an aristocratic society – and thus it always will be; a society which believes in a long ladder of rank order and value differences in men, which needs slavery in some sense' (Nietzsche, 1967, p. 199). This is not just a matter of conventional subservience since Nietzsche stressed the need for what he called 'the pathos of distance'; that is, he believed that the length of the social hierarchy encourages 'that other more mysterious pathos, that longing for ever greater distances within the soul itself, the evolving of ever higher, rarer, more spacious, more widely arched, more comprehensive states – in short: the heightening of the type "man," the continued "self-mastery of man"' (ibid., p. 199). Essential to this 'mysterious pathos', however, is the complete subordination of the masses. The population is effectively sacrificed to the interests of an aristocratic cast that is free of the humanitarian delusions of service that has sapped the will of conventional European aristocracy:

> the essential nature of a good and healthy aristocracy is that it does *not* feel it is a function (whether of royalty or of the community) but its meaning, its highest justification. Therefore, it accepts with a clear conscience the sacrifice of an enormous number of men who must *for the sake of the aristocracy* be suppressed and reduced to incomplete human beings, to slaves, to tools (ibid., p. 200).

For Nietzsche, therefore, aristocracy is a mutually exclusive alternative to other forms of government because it necessitates rule by an elite in their own interest. This position not only contrasts with Mill's views on the guiding and enlightening function of elite rule, but is also radically at odds with other contemporary strands of European political thinking that regarded elitism as an inevitable and persistent feature of democratic politics.

In the late nineteenth and early twentieth centuries the Italians Gaetano Mosca and Vifredo Pareto, and the former's German disciple, Robert Michels, developed supposedly descriptive, 'scientific' accounts showing that all systems of social and political regulation are elitist (Parry, 1970, pp. 30–63). As Mosca put it,

> In all societies ... two classes of people appear – a class that rules and a class that is ruled. The first class, always the less numerous, performs all political functions, monopolises power and enjoys the advantages that power brings, whereas the second, the more numerous class, is directed and controlled by the first (Mosca, 1939, p. 50).

The experience of representative democracy in late-nineteenth- and early-twentieth-century Europe, and their desire to prove their general case by showing that even these regimes conformed to the general elitist pattern, led Mosca, Pareto and Michels to pay a great deal of attention to the rule of the few in putatively democratic environments. They thought that their theory of elite rule was an empirical one reflecting the fact that, whatever the constitutional formalities of a society, elites always *do* rule. As Pareto put it, an elite 'exists in all societies and governs them even in cases where the regime in appearances is highly democratic' (Pareto, 1966, p. 155). This position differs from many of those discussed earlier because these writers stressed the normative claim that elites *should* rule.

Democratic societies, even the most self-consciously democratic organisations such as working-class parties (the object of Michels' attention), are effectively subject to the rule of the few. Elites are not seen as uniform cohesive entities; indeed both Mosca and Pareto identified elite strata (Bottomore, 1966, pp. 9–10). They are, however, thought to possess a number of common qualities that explain their controlling position, and they are endowed with organisational capacities, political skills and a clear sense of purpose. Moreover their power is cumulative – its sources are strengthened by the possession of power – and self-perpetuating. Mosca and Michels stressed the organisational capacity of the elite and observed that their restricted size and frequent interaction makes effective organisation easier for them to achieve than for the masses. Pareto's account focuses on the distribution of psychological character traits within a given population. In democratic systems these organisational or psychological characteristics allows members of the elite to manipulate a supposedly all-powerful mass made up of a large and diverse number of unimaginative, poorly organised and not clearly directed individuals (Mosca, 1939, pp. 247, 411–12).

These judgements on the relative superiority of elites provided the basis for the preferences for particular forms of elite rule that lurk behind the scientific form of both Mosca's and Pareto's theories. Thus Pareto was dismayed at the decadent and corrupting effects of rule by those with highly developed political intelligence but little grasp of large moral aspirations or ideas. Writing in the wake of the First World War, Pareto identified an increasing tendency for newly rich members of society (the 'plutocracy') to enter into manipulative alliances with the masses to produce a form of 'demagogic plutocracy'. This alliance, directed against the well-established propertied classes, was the predominant feature of modern parliamentary government:

> The modern parliamentary system, to all intents and purposes, is the effective instrument of demagogic plutocracy. Through elections and through political transactions in parliament, considerable scope is given

to the activities of individuals who are well endowed with instincts of combination. Indeed it now seems clear that the modern parliamentary system is to a great extent bound up with the fate of plutocracy (Pareto, 1966, p. 315).

Subsequently Pareto looked to the Italian dictator Mussolini as a heroic representative of solidarity, order and discipline who would renovate the moral basis of Italian society. In contrast Mosca's preferences were those of a liberal-conservative (Parry, 1970, pp. 41, 47). In his later writings he bemoaned the tendency for the political elites who had emerged under democracy to manipulate the population by pandering to tawdry moral standards. However, as universal suffrage had now become irreversible, it was too late to restrict the vote to the middle classes, who could have provided an intellectually and morally sound source of stimulation for and replenishment of the elite. As an alternative to this more desirable state of affairs, Mosca redefined the idea of the ruling class. He appealed to what was, in effect, an extra-political elite, to restore the moral tone of social and political life by assuming an educational rather than a degenerative role in their interaction with the masses. Writing in the years of political and moral crisis that followed the conclusion of the First World War, Mosca urged the ruling class to 'gain a clear conception of its rights and duties. . . . Then only will it learn to appraise the conduct of its leaders soundly, and so gradually regain in the eyes of the masses the prestige that it has in large part lost'. He appealed to enlightened members of the middle class to 'make up a small moral and intellectual aristocracy, which keeps humanity from rotting in the slough of selfishness and material appetites' (Mosca, 1939, p. 493). In this formulation, Mosca's ruling class has become an intermediary body that stands between political leaders and masses: its influence is exercised through moral and cultural means rather than through its possession of political office. Democratic politics involves the masses on the one hand and political leaders on the other, but since the latter are unable to provide moral and intellectual leadership this will have to be supplied through an elite whose impact on politics is indirect.

Assertions of mass incapability reflect a salient general feature of arguments that ascribe a dominant political role to 'the few'. The few must rule because the many are either incapable of exercising political authority, or they do so in a morally reprehensible manner. A different version of this view of the relationship between elites and masses has played an important role in theories of revolutionary politics.

These theories have been used to justify the role of an elite or 'vanguard' party in galvanising the masses into effective revolutionary action (Parry, 1970, pp. 55–6). The idea of a conspiratorial elite party can be found in the writings of a number of nineteenth-century French writers and is associated in this period particularly with Auguste Blanqui (1805–81). Although Blanqui thought that 'the people' would play a crucial role in the revolutionary process, he maintained that their oppressed and listless condition meant that they would have to be galvanised into action by a group of intellectuals whose revolutionary commitments removed them from the class structure of contemporary society. This elite would forge an alliance with the masses, but Blanqui insisted that it would have to be based upon a strict division of labour. The elite would form a closed, conspiratorial body that would be safe from infiltration by the authorities and would organise the masses and direct their action. They would not consult the people, and nor would they take them into their confidence: like the general staff of an army they would direct their troops, not be directed by them. Blanqui adhered to a vision of a radically libertarian and egalitarian future, but he insisted that the pursuit of this goal necessitated the temporary subjugation of those who would finally enjoy the fruits of social and political transformation (Bernstein, 1971, pp. 62–4).

In the relatively brief periods of his adult life when he was not in prison, Blanqui operated on the revolutionary fringes of nineteenth-century French politics, but his idea of a revolutionary elite came to fruition in the history of twentieth-century revolutionary Marxism. The key thinker in this tradition was not Marx himself, but his Russian follower V. I. Lenin, the leading figure of revolutionary communism in early twentieth-century Russia. In *What is to be Done*? Lenin argued against spontaneous mass action on the ground that it would produce riots rather than concerted and effective revolutionary action. Lenin maintained that under prerevolutionary conditions, and especially within the context of an autocratic police state, the masses lack the unity and informed sense of direction that will make them an effective revolutionary force. Even under more favourable circumstances, the most that could be hoped for is the growth of a 'trade union consciousness', which will organise the masses in such a way as to curb their revolutionary capacities. These capacities are latent within the bulk of the population, but they need to be fostered and channelled by a trained, politically conscious, tightly knit and centrally directed elite organisation (see p. 335).

In Lenin's version of revolutionary elitism, the members of the vanguard are distinguished by their attachment to and knowledge of a theory of revolutionary transformation. However, the basic assumptions of his theory – the formlessness of the masses and the need for them to be given shape, unity and a sense of direction by an elite – is common to all forms of elitism. It is true, of course, that Lenin's conception of elite rule is directed to the attainment of an end that will make it redundant, but as in Mill's case, of this is a distant goal. For Lenin and his successors the overthrow of autocracy marks only the first stage; it is also necessary to create the economic, political and social conditions necessary for the transition to a communistic society.

Vladimir Ilyich Lenin (1870–1924)

Lenin was leader of the Bolshevik Party at the time of the (second) Russian Revolution in October 1917. His revolutionary tactics played an important part in that event and in the subsequent development of the Soviet Union. Lenin's application of Marxist ideas to the Russian situation laid the basis for a form of state socialism that was built upon the dominance of the Communist Party, and justified its position by reference to the tenets of 'Marxist-Leninism'. *What is to be Done?* (1905) and *The State and Revolution* (1917) are among the most important works in Lenin's vast output.

The transition to communism requires the abandonment of forms of elite rule and the creation of a genuinely democratic system of government. In common with other Marxists, Lenin adopted a view of the democratic credentials of modern society that endorsed Mosca's and Pareto's observations about their elitist character. Unlike these writers, however, Lenin did not regard elitism as inevitable. In formulating his conception of democracy Lenin thought he had produced a theory that rested on a full understanding of the requirements of democratic government and the implications of it. As we shall see, his position built upon a long tradition of democratic thinking, but Lenin tailored this to his understanding of the prospects for human liberation held out by Marxism. This tradition will provide the focus of the next chapter.

Conclusion

Since modern elite theorists based claims to rule upon the personal qualities possessed by certain members of the community, they shared some common ground with Plato and Aristotle. However, significant variations existed within this general pattern. For Lenin the qualities in question were largely intellectual and ideological. In this respect at least, his position was similar to that of Plato, Mill and Nietzsche. While other elite theorists tended to relate elite status to membership of a particular class, they did not argue for forms of class rule. Rather they assumed that people occupying certain positions in the social structure enjoy the educational advantages and way of life that will make it possible for them to play a prominent role in politics. Elite status is personal, but it is accepted that elites usually come from particular classes.

In contrast, theories of hereditary aristocracy involve a notion of class rule. Although only particular members of the aristocracy occupy leading state offices, the class itself is given a privileged political and social position. It also provides forms of leadership that are social and cultural as well as political. This class is hereditary, membership of it is legally defined and entry to it is strictly controlled. While hereditary aristocracies have sometimes existed within republics (as, for example, in Rome and Venice) they have more usually formed part of systems of government that possess hereditary monarchs. In these cases, aristocracy is one reflection of ideas about the location of political power that rest upon the claim that appropriate ability and status should be determined according to the principle of hereditary transmission.

The Rule of the Many

Because democracy of one kind or another is a feature of the modern world, it is easy to overlook the fact that arguments about the positive political significance of 'the many' have had a chequered career. Aristotle used the term 'democracy' to refer to a form of government that is necessarily unjust because it involves the exercise of political power by ordinary members of the population in their own, exclusive interests. Both he and Plato associated democracy with lawless and unstable rule and many of the unfavourable connotations that they attached to this form of government were accepted by their successors. Despite this persistent hostility, the history of political thought has been punctuated by the appearance of arguments that have sought to show that democratic (or 'popular') government is both just and beneficial. In arguing their case, proponents of rule by the many have had to show that exclusive claims made on behalf of the 'one' and the 'few' are incompatible with the effective pursuit of the ends of politics. It should be noted, however, that arguments in favour of popular rule have often made a case for giving the many a significant formal role in politics, but not exclusive control of the state.

This chapter opens with a consideration of the arguments presented by Protagoras, Democritus and Aristotle about democracy in the Greek world. Although some medieval theorists stressed that rulers should hold office with the consent of their subjects, and others thought that 'the many' should have a political role in the state, fully developed statements of this argument did not appear until the early modern period. The second section of this chapter will therefore examine a tradition of popular republicanism in renaissance Italy that built upon insights derived from ancient political theory. The third and fourth sections of this chapter will discuss theories of popular government that were produced during periods of revolutionary activity in England in the seventeenth century and in the United States and France in the late eighteenth and early nineteenth centuries. The rise of democracy as a political aspiration in the nineteenth century produced wide-ranging discussions of its merits, possibilities and dangers. These arguments provide the focus for the fifth and sixth sections of this chapter. It will conclude with an examination of modern critiques of aspects of Western democracy produced by thinkers in the Marxist tradition, and by those promoting the independence and development of Third World states.

'The Many' in Ancient Greek Political Theory: Protagoras, Democritus and Aristotle

Although democratic government in Athens was occasionally challenged by those who wished to introduce government by 'the few', its longevity suggests that it was generally accepted by most of the population. Indeed evidence from Greek drama – produced for popular rather than elite consumption – and from documents such as the funeral speech given by the popular leader Pericles during the war with Sparta, convey a sense of pride in Athenian democracy (see p. 51). Unfortunately, however, the most developed statements of Greek political ideas available to us were written by people such as Plato and Aristotle, whose attitude towards Athenian democracy was either openly hostile or at best extremely sceptical. (Jones, 1957, pp. 41–2; Sinclair, 1988, pp. 202–3). Positive accounts of democracy in Athens have survived only in fragmentary and/or second-hand statements of the ideas of Protagoras and Democritus.

These writers' political ideas embody their reflections on the practice of democratic politics in Athens and point to the capacity of this system of government to combine the free pursuit of collective goals with respect for the autonomy of the individual (Farrar, 1992, p. 22). Protagoras and Democritus believed that the Athenian way of government satisfied both communal and individual aspirations. It produced a harmonious form of political life that was buttressed by respect for traditional values, and set popular participation within the context of elite leadership. This feature of Athenian democracy was emphasised by Democritus in his account of the formation of the democratic *polis* under the guidance of Solon (594–593 BC). At that time, according to Democritus, the dominant nobility showed 'compassion' for the many by giving them a political role. He argued that this gift created consensus within the community, and laid the basis for Athens' subsequent prosperity by ensuring that it avoided the interfactional and interclass strife that plagued many of its neighbours. However Democritus did not rest his case for the democratic state on this basis alone. He also identified democracy with freedom and argued that by participating in the state individuals are able to reconcile their personal aspirations with those they share with other members of their community. Citizens are thus full members of an institution that is widely recognised as the focal point of a truly human existence (Havelock, 1964, pp. 142–3).

Protagoras' conception of democracy also rests on the idea that this form of government is intrinsically beneficial to human beings. He argued that *all* human beings (or at least, all male adults) are endowed with 'respect' and a sense of justice, and that this entitles them to play a role in the *polis*:

> when there is a question about how to do well in carpentry or any other expertise, everyone, including the Athenians thinks it right that only a few should give advice, and won't put up with advice from anyone else ... but when it comes to consideration of how to do well in running the city, which must proceed entirely through justice and soundness of mind, they are right to accept advice from anyone, since it is incumbent on everyone to share in that sort of excellence, or else there can be no city at all (Plato, 1991, p. 15).

Citizens' participation in the political life of the state reinforces their original endowment and enhances these distinctly human attributes: excellence is not restricted to aristocrats, but is generalised (Farrar, 1992, p. 24). It should be noted, however, that Protagoras and Democritus still left a place for aristocrats within the democratic *polis*. Like the natural aristocracy of early modern political thought, these figures provide leadership by assuming the burden of important offices. They are however, chosen by the people and are subject to periodic scrutiny by them (Havelock, 1964, pp. 146–53).

The claim that a democratic *polis* integrates collective and personal interests was questioned by a number of Greek writers of the late fifth century. One line of criticism came from those who produced accounts of politics that questioned the possibility of reconciling self-interest and collective aspirations. Arguments along these lines were advanced by some of Plato's opponents in the first book of the *Republic*. Elsewhere in this work Plato himself portrayed democracy as a system of rule in which the irrational many use the democratic *polis* as a vehicle for the rapacious and ultimately self-defeating pursuit of their own, narrowly conceived interests (Plato, 1970, pp. 62–99, 327–31). The *Republic* embodies Plato's response to this state of affairs. His ideal state is premised on radical differences between human beings and is based on an order that is structured in such a way that it restricts humans to fulfilling the narrow range of activities that correspond to their natures (see p. 23). Since the many are held to be deficient in reason and self-control, they have no political role in the state (Farrar, 1992, pp. 30–1).

Despite his reservations about Plato's ideal republic, Aristotle's account of an ideal aristocracy bears important similarities to it. He effectively banishes all but the truly virtuous from this state, thereby creating a system of government that is not significantly different from the elite egalitarianism of Plato's guardians (see pp. 149–50). However, while this state represents Aristotle's ideal, his *Politics* contains extensive discussions of worthy but less than ideal states, including those with a democratic element.

In his formal classification of constitutions, Aristotle identified two types of rule by the many. One of these, 'polity', is a good constitution because the many rule in the common interest; the second is a corrupt variant, 'democracy', in which they rule in their own interest. He later pointed out that 'rule by the many' usually means rule by the poor (Aristotle, 1958, pp. 110–16). Given Aristotle's understanding of the political implications of distributive justice, and given that the populations of most societies are unlikely to be strictly equal, there is a sense in which rule by the many will always be suspect: democrats wrongly believe that 'equality in one respect – for instance, that of free birth – means equality all round' (ibid., p. 136). This claim is unjust because it rests on a single criterion and ignores other relevant and significant inequalities. The implications of this line of argument is that 'polity' will only be just when all are equal in a number of significant respects.

Aristotle's detailed treatment of democracy identifies five sub-types. The least unjust gives some recognition to the claims of wealth and refinement. From here we descend through three increasingly unjust types to an extremely unjust form. Each stage in the descent is marked by the abandonment of moderating influences – property, the law, and a mixture of rural and urban populations – leaving a state in which the urban poor, supported through taxes imposed on other classes, exercise direct control in a system of grossly self-interested, unrestrained rule that is analogous in its arbitrary, lawless characteristics to the worst form of tyranny (ibid., pp. 167–9; Mulgan, 1977, p. 74).

This dire picture of mass indulgence matches that of Plato, but Aristotle was prepared to allow that 'the many' may have *some* claim to a political role. While ordinary people are individually inferior to 'the few', they may *collectively* possess a degree of wisdom that is greater than that found in a few superior individuals. In support of this argument Aristotle used the analogy of a shared feast to which many contribute, and he also referred to the role ascribed to the general public in Athens in judging theatrical performances. In addition he argued most plausibly, that there is a difference between the expertise required to *produce* something, and the practical experience needed to *judge* whether the object in question works well (Aristotle, 1958, pp. 123–7; Mulgan, 1977, p. 105). In other words, those who feel the effect of political actions may well be the most appropriate judges of them. Unlike Protagoras, who ascribed important and relevant moral attributes to humanity in general, Aristotle took a mundane view of the capacities of the many. However, he allowed that they may be endowed collectively with limited but politically significant qualities.

These concessions to democracy relate to Aristotle's later suggestion that in many circumstances 'polity' will be the most practicable form of government. In this formulation the term 'polity' no longer refers to a good form of rule by the many, but is applied to systems that successfully mix 'democratic' and 'oligarchic' elements so as to moderate their vices. The many are thus given a judging role (as in Democritus' theory and also to some degree in Athenian practice), but executive functions are left in the hands of the more able, subject of course to the scrutiny of the population at large. Another possibility is that while some offices are filled by 'lot', others are filled by election (Aristotle, 1958, pp. 176–8, 180–4), an arrangement that allows considerations of capacity and prestige to play a role in selecting key officers of the state (Jones, 1957, p. 49). These procedures contrast with the exclusion of the populace from the political institutions of Plato's ideal state, but they are similar in important respects to the 'second best' state sketched in *The Laws*. The laws of this state provide for popular elections, but arrange the electoral system in such a way as to ensure that the distinctive attributes of 'the few' are recognised (see p. 230).

An important benefit of giving limited recognition to the claims of the many is that it satisfies the idea of distributive justice: it acknowledges that they have *some* worth and make a significant contribution to the state. In addition, 'polity' also tempers the dangers of democratic and oligarchic domination of the state. It should be noted, however, that because Aristotle regarded 'polity' as a merely practicable rather than a desirable state, his account of the political significance of 'the many' has an instrumental air. It thus differs from the positions taken by both Protagoras and Democritus. These thinkers based the claims of the many on generalised moral attributes and argued that democracy generates not only safety, but a distinctly human way of life. Respect and justice in Protagoras' account, and compassion and consensus in that of Democritus, harmonise individual and collective aspirations and make the democratic *polis* an admirable form of government.

'The Many' in Early Modern Political Theory: Classical Republicans, Radical Protestants and Levellers

Many of the themes that appeared in ancient accounts of the rule of the many resurfaced in the first half of the thirteenth century. At that time a number of Italian city states began to incorporate male householders within political systems formerly dominated by nobles. At first these states looked to Roman models, but following the appearance of a Latin translation of Aristotle's *Politics* in the middle of the thirteenth century, Greek ideas came to play an important role in justifying systems of popular government (Skinner, 1992, p. 59).

Defenders of the Italian republics emphasised independence from external control and the need for the state to be governed by free citizens as a whole, rather than by restricted groups or individuals. The second of these goals would be achieved by a variety of measures that would subject officials to the scrutiny of 'the many', and through a conception of active, participatory citizenship that would ensure the state was directed towards common rather than to particular ends. In Machiavelli's political writings these two forms of freedom are related by his claim that the external liberty of the state is most likely to be maintained by a militia made up of free citizens (Machiavelli, 1975, vol. i, pp. 266–7, 310–11, 361–7). Internally, the free citizens ensure that the republic is not corrupted by the self-interest of particular classes; externally, they bring the same sense of general commitment to defending the state from foreign enemies.

Given the hostile monarchical and imperial environment in which they were placed, it is not surprising that the political thinking of the classical republicans focused on questions with a bearing on survival. In addition, however, classical republicans associated other important goals with the maintenance of independent popular republics. Political freedom, and the institutions through which it is expressed and maintained, is conducive to glory as well as safety; it also provides opportunities to develop and exercise the talents of the many. Service in the militia and participation in the political life of the republic thus serve to reconcile communal and personal aspirations. The active citizen develops his capacities through participation in the life of the state, and in so doing he contributes to the maintenance and glory of the community with which he is identified. Ordinary citizens can thus attain fame, honour and glory – by serving the state's interests the individual can enhance his own capacities.

One of the central assumptions of popular republicanism is that the loyalty of the many can be relied upon because they have the largest stake in the common interest and will thus seek to protect and advance it. However, popular government is also justified on other grounds. For example Marsilius of Padua argued that loyalty and obedience are relatively easy to secure in popular republics because citizens think of the law as something they have created and imposed upon themselves. In an echo of an argument common in classical political theory, he also claimed that ordinary members of the population are best equipped to evaluate officeholders' attachment to the common good, and can be relied on to see through the self-interested proposals advanced in the cause of a faction (Marsilius, 1956, vol. ii, pp. 46–7).

The most significant seventeenth-century developments in democratic political thought took place within 'Leveller' circles in the late 1640s during the English Revolution. The term 'Leveller' is used by historians to describe a group of publicists and activists who were connected with elements within the victorious parliamentary army. Following the defeat of the Royalist forces in 1647, members of the army debated the conduct of the parliamentary leadership and the basis upon which the state should be 'settled'. Many of the Levellers' demands raised matters of particular concern to the rank and file of the army, but their interests also included questions of economic, legal and religious policy. In addition, some Levellers took up the question of parliamentary representation. They often addressed the issue of electoral corruption, but at times they also raised fundamental issues concerning the basis, distribution and use of political power (Wootton, 1994).

The idea that government is authorised by the people plays an important role in Richard Overton's *An Appeal from the Commons to the Free People* (1647). As the title of this work suggests, Overton believed that individuals retain a residual right to free action, even within a civil condition. Overton grounded this right upon 'reason', a faculty that is only fully developed in God, but which is possessed to a significant degree by all sane adults. 'Right reason' is 'the firm and sure foundation of all just laws and governments'. Governments are just when they act in accordance with reason, and when their actions are of a kind to which rational human beings will consent: 'all just human powers are but betrusted, conferred, and conveyed by joint and common consent; for to every individual in nature is given an individual propriety by nature, not to be invaded or usurped by any' (Woodhouse, 1951, pp. 324, 327).

In the *Appeal*, Overton was largely concerned with establishing the grounds for challenging unjust government and with urging rulers and elected officials to recognise that they derived their authority from the consent of rational beings. At times however, some of the Levellers utilised the idea of a fundamental (rather than a conventional or historical) basis for government to argue for the inclusion of the adult male population within the electoral process. The most well-known example of this line of argument occurred in a debate held at Putney on 28–29 October 1647 in the 'General Council of the Army', a body that included the commanding officers and regimental representatives of the parliamentary army. The council was convened to consider a printed paper, *The Case of the Army Stated*, but when it met this document was superseded by another subsequently published as *An Agreement of the People*. Among a variety of demands, the *Agreement* stipulated that the right to elect parliamentary representatives should be vested in every adult male (Tuck,

1993, p. 247). This demand alarmed some senior officers, and their objections to it provoked a defence of the electoral role of 'the many'. A system of popular election was justified by referring to the 'birthright' of every Englishman and the sacrifices made by the common people in the Parliamentary cause. In addition one of the participants in the debate, Colonel Rainborough, identified a relationship between human reason, consent and just government that was similar to that advanced by Overton. Unlike Overton, however, Rainborough extended the idea of consent to include participation in the process through which law is created, and he buttressed this by a reference, designed to refute arguments that connect electoral rights with 'fixed' (material) possessions, to a universal interest in good government. All have an interest in the law since all must be regulated by it; all are endowed with reason, and therefore all should elect those who make the law (Woodhouse, 1951, pp. 53, 61, 56).

At a later stage in the debate Rainborough argued that recognition of the electoral claims of the many is necessary to avoid 'enslavement' of the population, (ibid., p. 67). It is not clear, however, whether he thought that their exclusion would produce unjust laws, or whether the mere fact that the many lack political rights entails enslavement. In a subsequent discussion of the franchise, the Levellers' demands were modified to exclude those who receive poor relief, or who are servants under the exclusive control of a particular employer. This concession, a response to the hostility aroused by the more radical position advanced by Rainborough, was in keeping with a central presupposition of early modern political thinking. The franchise will not protect the freedom of servants and paupers whose lives are constrained by economic dependence; to the contrary, it will extend the influence of those upon whom they depend. Even allowing for this concession, however, it seems clear that at times the Levellers produced arguments that point to a significant electoral role for the many. While there is no question that the many will *rule*, they are to be assigned an important role in the process through which legislators are chosen and their actions scrutinised. Some formulations of the Leveller position thus rest on ideas of popular sovereignty, consent and the significance of human reason, and these came to play an important role in subsequent accounts of the location of political power.

Popular Government in the Age of the American and French Revolutions: Madison, Sièyes, Condorcet, Wollstonecraft, Thompson and Wheeler, Paine

In seventeenth-century England the demand for universal male suffrage was a radical proposal, but it did not entail a departure from the conventional idea that 'the many' were only one part of a political system in which elites played a central role. This way of thinking persisted in the eighteenth century. It was common among English writers who extolled the virtues of a mixed constitution containing 'monarchic', 'aristocratic' and 'democratic' elements, and it also attracted the admiring attention of foreign writers such as Baron Montesquieu of France (Montesquieu, 1949, vol. ii, pp. 151–62). In the last third of the eighteenth century, however, a series of political crises, the first occurring in Britain's North American colonies in the late 1770s and early 1780s, the second in France and a number of other European countries from 1789, produced challenges to this conventional picture of government. These challenges involved the formulation of new and historically significant restatements of the political importance of 'the many'.

Britain's North American colonies rejected hereditary monarchy and aristocracy and established republican forms of government. The most striking feature of this process was an extension of the idea of popular participation to include significant elements of popular *rule*, particularly at the local level. These developments involved a clear rejection of the view that 'the many' were 'virtually' represented by a restricted section of the population who possessed electoral rights, and an even smaller proportion of the community who sat in representative assemblies and filled important public offices. Although some white males were excluded from the franchise, the political nation was, by contemporary standards at least, very extensive. Moreover the range of positions filled by election and the practical eligibility for office was very wide (Wood, 1992, pp. 91–2). In the years following the war with Britain, and particularly in 1787 when a new constitution was being discussed, the implications of popular government were the subject of extensive debate.

'Anti-federalist' writers (those who opposed the introduction of a federal structure and promoted a confederation that located power within the states themselves rather than in a central institution representing them) claimed that voting and office holding are necessary to promote the distinctive and private interests of the variety of individuals within the political community. People enter political society to promote their *own* good, and the only way to ensure this is to endow them with political rights. These rights give them the opportunity to choose representatives and office holders whose interests are the same as theirs. An important feature of this position is that it abandons the idea of unitary public interest, which was central to classical republicanism, and adopts a pluralistic conception of government: since electors have a variety of interests they need to be represented by a range of different individuals who constitute a representative cross-section of the population. Thus while 'the many' are entitled to have their interests reflected in the distribution of legislative and other offices, their diversity means they have ceased to exist as a coherent, unified political grouping. From this point

of view, it is significant that one of the most important of the anti-federalist writers talked not of 'the many', but of a range of narrowly defined
sectional interests: 'professional men, merchants, traders, farmers,
mechanics etc' (ibid., p. 101). Since 'the many' do not exist, popular government does not pose a threat to particular sections of society.

The extent and consequences of this fragmentation of the political community, and the related denial of the political significance of a 'common
interest', were questioned by those who wished to promote a federal constitution. Contributors to the *Federalist Papers* argued that despite the frag-
menting effect of 'interest' politics, 'the many' share an interest in
undermining the property rights of the few. Consequently they argued
for a federal system of government on the grounds that its extended scale
would weaken the immediate political influence of the ordinary members
of the population. A leading 'federalist', James Madison, argued that it is
necessary to 'filter' the narrow interests of local communities and interest
groups through a more extensive electoral process so that the better educated will tend to be elected to federal offices. These people possess 'a
knowledge of the interests and feelings of the people'; they do not merely
reflect the aspirations of a range of narrowly self-interested groups
(Hamilton *et al.*, 1942, pp. 45–6, 169).

James Madison (1751–1817)

Madison, a leading figure in revolutionary politics in America, was later
Secretary of State and President of the United States (1809–17). Together with
Alexander Hamilton and John Jay, he was author of *The Federalist* (1787–88).

Madison made it clear that he believed there *was* a public interest, not
merely a variety of individual or sectional interests: 'the public good, the
real welfare of the great body of the people is the supreme object to be
pursued' (ibid., p. 234). In its general bearing, Madison's position echoed
earlier ideas concerning 'natural aristocracy' within a system of popular
government (see p. 154). However he relied less upon the capacity of the
many to pursue the common good by recognising the *virtú* of their natural superiors, than on the effect of socio-political mechanisms that avoid
narrow sectionalism. Despite the self-interest of the bulk of the population, Madison thought it possible to produce a disinterested and informed
elite at the federal level.

While most of those involved in the early stages of the French Revolution aimed to establish a constitutional monarchy rather than a republic,

the series of events that began with the calling of the Estates General in Paris in the summer of 1789 had important implications for the development and spread of ideas of popular government. The revolution itself involved a degree of popular participation in public affairs that was quite foreign to large, long-established European states (Fontana, 1992, pp. 107–10). As in the United States, abolition of hereditary aristocracy and adoption of the idea of fundamental human equality eroded formal class distinctions and merged 'the many' into 'the people'. As the Abbé Sièyes put it, 'There was once a time when the Third Estate was in bondage and the nobility was everything. Now the Third Estate is everything and nobility is only a word' (Sièyes, 1963, p. 145).

This change was signalled quite clearly in a declaration issued by the National Assembly in Paris. The *Declaration of the Rights of Man and of Citizens* treats 'men' and 'citizens' as virtually synonymous: 'Men are born, and always continue, free and equal in respect of their rights .... The end of all political associations, is the preservation of the natural and imprescribable rights of man.' The *Declaration* identifies law with the 'will of the community', and stipulates that the rights that individuals possess in a political condition include 'a right to concur, either personally, or by their representatives, in its formation' (Ritchie, 1894, pp. 291, 292). In the formulation advanced by the Marquis de Condorcet, a leading philosopher of the period, this right derives from people's natural liberty: 'no citizen can be obliged to obey laws to which he has not contributed as much as any other citizen, either directly, or by an equal right to elect representatives and to be elected' (Baker, 1975, p. 268). Contemporary understandings of the qualification for citizenship varied. For example when Sièyes spoke of the 'Third Estate' he meant the propertied classes rather than to the entire population (Sièyes, 1963, pp. 13–14). Drawing a distinction between 'active' and 'passive' citizenship, he argued that only those who satisfy a tax-based qualification should vote, and that eligibility for election should be determined by a property qualification. In contrast Condorcet moved towards a position that entails universal male suffrage. Significantly, both he and Sièyes could see no reason in principle for women to be excluded from the active exercise of political rights, provided they satisfy other appropriate qualifications. Since women are, moral and rational beings they have the same claim to political rights as men, and this claim cannot be undermined by pointing to differences between men and women. These are either irrelevant to the allocation of political rights or are accidental, and avoidable, consequences of educational and environmental influences.

This qualified acknowledgement that women are part of 'the many' was given more forceful expression among some political activists in the 1790s, and in the thinking of some nineteenth-century English and French socialists. Mary Wollstonecraft's *A Vindication of the Rights of Women*

(1792) challenged constitutional reformers in France and England to extend the logic of the rights of man to the rest of humanity:

> If the abstract rights of man will bear discussion and explanation, those of women, by a parity of reasoning, will not shrink from the same test.... Consider ... whether, when men contend for their freedom, and to be allowed to judge for themselves respecting their own happiness, it be not inconsistent and unjust to subjugate women, even though you firmly believe that you are acting in the manner best calculated to promote their happiness? Who made man the exclusive judge, if woman partake with him the gift of reason? (Wollstonecraft, 1995, pp. 68–9).

Later in the same work Wollstonecraft suggested that 'women ought to have representatives, instead of being arbitrarily governed without having any direct share allowed them in the deliberations of government' (ibid., p. 237).

***

Mary Wollstonecraft (1759–1797)

Wollstonecraft was the author of a wide range of educational, literary, religious and political works, and was associated with the dissenting Protestants who played an important role in the intellectual life of late-eighteenth-century England. During the last two years of her life Wollstonecraft was companion to William Godwin, whom she married in 1797. Wollstonecraft's first major political work, *A Vindication of the Rights of Men* (1790) was written in response to Edmund Burke's *Reflections on the Revolution in France*. Her *A Vindication of the Rights of Women* (1792) had a broader cultural focus, but it nonetheless included the claim that women should have political and civil rights and elected representatives of their own.

***

In some cases feminist writers advanced notions of equality based on a recognition of 'difference'. These theories gave rise to ideas of 'moral' rather than political authority that would allow women to fill leadership roles in certain spheres of social life (Grogan, 1992). However other socialist thinkers, for example the English Owenites William Thompson and Anna Wheeler, extended this analysis to apply to political functions (Coole, 1988, pp. 154–78; Okin, 1992, p. 205). In their *Appeal of One Half of the Human Race, Women, Against the Pretensions of the Other Half, Men, to Retain Them in Political, and thence in Civil and Domestic, Slavery* (1825), a reply to James Mill's arguments in his *Essay on Government* (see p. 183),

Thompson and Wheeler pointed out that 'If the conduct of men possessing exclusive political powers has been unjust to their fellow-men, has it not been atrocious every where, even in what are called the most civilised countries, towards women' (Thompson and Wheeler, 1993, p. 170). They argued that the possession of equal political rights by women is essential to their happiness, both because it provides the only security for equal civil and criminal laws, and because it contributes to 'the expansion of the mind, of the intellectual powers, and of the sympathies of benevolence' (ibid., p. 169).

Like the proponents of popular government in the United States, their counterparts in France had to confront the possibility that incorporation of 'the many' within the political system might unleash the rapacious tendencies that had been associated with democracy since ancient times. Thus despite his support for universal suffrage, Condorcet remained apprehensive about the ignorance and capacity for destruction that he thought characterised the urban masses in Paris. Consequently he insisted that public instruction to produce general enlightenment was necessary if the potentialities opened up by the Revolution were to be realised (Baker, 1975, p. 269). Sièyes' views on the extent of the 'political nation' were more limited than those of Condorcet. However he still thought it necessary to filter the influence of ordinary voters through a system of indirect election. Sièyes also envisaged an elaborate range of additional precautions against the empowerment of what might be merely a transient, self-interested and reckless majority, including annual replacement of parts of the assembly and division of this body into separate sections that would consider legislation independently (Sièyes, 1963, pp. 20–1).

The quality of the majority produced through a process of popular election was of crucial importance to Sièyes because he thought it should express the 'general will' of the community, one that was directed towards its common interests. If this was achieved, the majority could thus be regarded as 'the *nation*' (ibid., pp. 151, 154, 163–4). Sièyes understood the general will as an aggregate of individual wills, but his strictures against transitory, and in a sense unrepresentative, majorities implied that popular participation in the electoral process would not necessarily produce a true expression of the common interest that defined the nation. This point became perfectly clear in Saint-Just's attitude towards 'the many'. Louis-Antoine Saint-Just, a leading member of the Committee of Public Safety during the Terror, looked to popular elections to produce an 'elective aristocracy'. Once in power, this body should give the people what was good for them rather than what they seemed to want (Hampson, 1991, pp. 42–6, 105–6). As we shall see, this conception of the relationship between popular politics, the 'general will' and elite domination came to play a central role in the vision of modern democracy developed by twentieth-century Marxist revolutionaries (see p. 194).

Perplexity about the perils of popular politics and the relationship between leaders and followers in a new, representative environment does not appear to have played a significant role in the thinking of Thomas Paine (see p. 81). One reason for this is that Paine regarded the American Revolution as an exemplar of non-destructive but radical political change. Moreover Paine discounted the excesses of the French Revolution as a regrettable but understandable consequence of previous repression, and of the tensions created by the reactionary stance adopted by the upper classes in France and other European countries. He believed that 'society' possesses a natural cohesion and that the main threat to beneficial social interaction comes from oppressive and unjust government, particularly monarchy and hereditary aristocracy (Paine, 1976, pp. 193–206).

Paine maintained that natural and beneficial interdependence, reciprocal interests and a natural tendency to social living, create bonds between human beings that will survive the destruction of the state. In support of this claim, Paine referred to the experience of the American colonies during the period between the rejection of the authority of the British crown and the creation of a 'new' republican form of government. The term 'new' refers to a distinctive form of popular representative government that first appeared in North America. Unlike classical democracy, which involves *direct* rule by the people and is only viable in geographically limited city states, representative government is suitable for large and populous states. The key to this form of government is the idea of 'delegation of power for the common benefit of society'; it 'takes society and civilization for its basis; nature, reason, and experience for its guide'. Since representative government grows out of society, it avoids the imposition and frustration of the social purposes that Paine thought were necessary features of 'old' monarchical and aristocratic forms of government (ibid., pp. 185–7, 193, 197).

Paine's understanding of the benefits of representative government emerged from a series of trenchant contrasts between 'new' and 'old' governments. He identified the former with rationality, sensitivity to the real interests of society and a diffusion of knowledge throughout the community. In contrast hereditary forms of government are established by usurpation or conquest; they are associated with ignorance, a disregard for social interests and the suppression of human intelligence. The hereditary principle gives supreme power to those who have no proven capacity for ruling, and who lack knowledge of or sympathy for the interests of the general population. This unjust and irrational superiority can only be maintained by coercion, and by promoting the ignorance and incredulity of the ordinary people. In contrast representative government draws upon *all* the talents of the community; it 'concentrates knowledge necessary to the interest of the parts, and of the whole'. By banishing the mystery in which monarchy is shrouded it 'diffuses such a body of knowledge throughout a nation, on the subject of government, as to explode ignorance and preclude imposition'. For Paine, inclusion of the whole population in the political system was thus a matter of both justice and great practical benefit: it would make government the *servant* of society; it would prevent imposition, and it would create a climate of openness and informed sensitivity that would promote the interests of individuals and of the society to which they belonged (ibid., pp. 198–206, 203, 206).

Democracy in Nineteenth-Century Political Theory: James Mill, Constant, Tocqueville, J. S. Mill, Taylor, Green and Hobhouse

The practical impulse given to popular government by the French Revolution was initially short-lived. By the close of the 1790s France had adopted a constitution in which representative institutions served as a facade for military dictatorship. After 1815 the restoration of monarchical regimes throughout Europe signalled a widespread reaction against the political claims of 'the many'. Despite these setbacks, the nineteenth century witnessed the creation of representative regimes in many European states. By the middle of the century a number of important writers had begun to argue that the advent of 'democracy' (a term that was beginning to lose the unfavourable connotations that had attached to the rule of the many since ancient times) was inevitable. There was a feeling that deep-seated socioeconomic changes were producing tendencies within modern society that meant that while the establishment of democratic government could be delayed, it could not be postponed indefinitely (Maier, 1992, pp. 126–7). Although these developments were seen as inevitable, they did not meet with universal approval. As we have seen, some theorists identified a tendency for the few to dominate even within the context of ostensibly popular systems of government (see p. 162). However, it remains true that in the nineteenth century arguments about the merits of popular government assumed a volume and importance not previously attained in the history of political thought.

In the early decades of the nineteenth century the adoption of 'universal' male suffrage was frequently seen as an antidote to the deficiencies and injustices of aristocratic politics. This perspective loomed large in the writings of Thomas Paine, but it continued to have currency among those who survived the revolutionary period and lived to see (and to deplore) the restorations of 1815. In England, for example, William Cobbett, the self-proclaimed 'People's Friend', argued for an extension of voting rights on the ground that the corruption of traditional elites meant that it was necessary for the people to protect their own rights and defend their own interests (Cobbett, n.d., pp. 5, 12–13). His contemporary, William Hazlitt, took a similar line, but also stressed that a system of popular representation was necessary to ensure that government would embody the 'wisdom of the community' rather than the narrow, self-seeking attitudes of the aristocratic classes (Hazlitt, 1819, p. 318). However the most trenchant early-nineteenth-century justification of democracy was presented by the utilitarian writer James Mill in his *Essay On Government*, a work that was endorsed by his patron Jeremy Bentham.

James Mill (1773–1836)

Born in Scotland, Mill embarked on a literary career in England, where he enjoyed the friendship and patronage of Jeremy Bentham. His *Essay on Government* (1820) was widely regarded as a Benthamite blueprint.

Mill took it for granted that in large and populous states the people cannot exercise power themselves; they can, however, effectively safeguard their interests by choosing representatives who will 'check' the actions of government. Popular representation provides 'security' against 'bad government', that is, one in which privileged minorities use political power to further their own 'sinister' interests at the cost of the interests of the rest of the community. Since government exists to protect individuals, it is inconsistent with the ends of government to leave power in the hands of individuals or classes whose interests are contrary to those of other members of the community (Mill, 1984, pp. 72–3). However, Mill argued that effective representation, and hence effective security against 'bad government', does not necessarily require a full-blown system of representative democracy. Those whose interests are 'included in', or covered by, the interests of other people – children, women with husbands or fathers, and young adult males – will be adequately protected even if they do not have the right to vote (ibid., pp. 78–80). The same happy outcome will result from a property-based franchise that embraces the majority of the population. Mill simple-mindedly assumed that the majority's interest in exploiting the minority would not be sufficiently strong to overbalance the general benefits of 'good government' (ibid., pp. 81–2). In countries such as England, this arrangement would produce the further benefit of curbing the irrationality of those in the lower classes who were qualified to vote: the majority would be dominated by the middle classes whose moderation and rational good sense would provide guidance for them (ibid., pp. 93–5).

These arguments allowed Mill to restrict popular participation but still ensure that government would not be biased by 'sinister interests'. A similar position was advanced by his French contemporary, Benjamin Constant (Constant, 1988, pp. 206–9). However, Constant produced a sophisticated view of government that incorporates a bedrock concern with justice and the rights of individuals, and stresses the importance of general limitations on the exercise of power. Constant thought that the need for limited government must become a widely accepted belief that is enshrined in 'public opinion' and supported by a balance of powers lodged in distinctive constitutional bodies (ibid., pp. 183–5). As individual liberty is a fundamental requirement of modern society, Constant was worried that popular sovereignty would be converted into the idea that the government could do anything.

Constant's reservations on this issue resurfaced in a sharper and more developed form in the writings of Alexis de Tocqueville and John Stuart Mill. These thinkers challenged what they saw as James Mill's and Jeremy Bentham's complacent endorsement of majority rule and they also expressed doubts about the sort of 'public opinion' that was beginning to emerge within the democratic, egalitarian societies of the modern world. Tocqueville's views on democracy were presented in an account of the social and political life of the United States following his visit to that country in the early 1830s. These observations were published as *Democracy in America* (1835, 1840) with an eye to developments within European states.

Alexis de Tocqueville (1805–59)

Tocqueville was a French politician and historian, and his place in the history of political thought is largely a consequence of *Democracy in America* (1835–40), a work that resulted from his tour of the United States. Tocqueville's observations and arguments had an important impact on John Stuart Mill's understanding of democracy in modern societies.

According to Tocqueville, the adoption of popular forms of government is an inevitable consequence of the growing democratisation of modern societies. These developments are admirable in many ways: democratic government promotes the welfare of the mass of the population and it also engenders a spirit of self-reliance, and respect for what are, in effect, self-made and self-imposed laws. However, the benefits of democracy are offset to some degree by undesirable features: systems of popular election provide no guarantee that capable people will attain public office; and the pressure upon government exerted by the relatively poor members of society, who form the majority, result in marked increases in public expenditure. For Tocqueville, Paine's claim that representative government was just, rational and cheap had proved to be overly sanguine. Furthermore Tocqueville had serious doubts about the quality of popular opinion in a political system based on the principle of majority rule. These doubts were underwritten by his belief that *political* democracy is affected by tendencies inherent in democratic society (Tocqueville, 1945, vol. i, pp. 48–56; 206–58).

The basic feature of such a society is widespread acceptance of the idea of equality. Egalitarianism is beneficial in some respects, but Tocqueville argued that it can have an injurious effect on intellectual standards and the cohesion of society. For example, in the United States people had given priority to the individual reason of ordinary members of the population, and rejected ideas of intellectual authority or leadership by enlightened elites. Social egalitarianism had reinforced these fragmentary tendencies by producing a strident individualism that had isolated people from one another. Tocqueville argued that such features of democratic society produce some peculiar and undesirable results. The absence of social or intellectual authorities creates a vacuum that is filled by a generally ill-informed public opinion. All are equal, but since they are mentally isolated from their fellows, they cannot (indeed they often see no need to) withstand the force of a body of public opinion that reflects the combined prejudices of a majority of their equals (Tocqueville, 1945, vol. II, pp. 104–7; Lively, 1965, pp. 87–8). Democratic citizens have shaken off traditional yokes, but they have assumed new, self-imposed ones that sap intellectual vigour and impede moral and cultural progression. These tendencies are apparent in democratic attitudes towards government. Behind the apparently anarchic impulses of modern democracy are social forces for conformity and dependence that encourage the growth of a centralised and paternalistic state. In eighteenth-century Europe a state of this kind had been imposed upon a population who were bereft of political rights; in democratic America it had been imposed by the majority upon the rest of the community (Tocqueville, 1945, vol. i, pp. 267–78; vol. ii, pp. 99–104, 304–48).

Tocqueville's depiction of democracy in America had a salutary effect on English attitudes towards popular government and the democratisation of social relationships. For example, in *On Liberty* the younger Mill alluded to the United States when warning his readers that the end of aristocracy does not necessarily mean the end of tyranny (Mill, 1983, pp. 67–8). 'Popular government' invariably means majority rule and there is no reason why this body should be any more sensitive to individual liberty than traditional rulers have been (ibid., p. 75).

Some of the more strictly political implications of the concerns raised in *On Liberty* were addressed by Mill in *On Representative Government*. In this work Mill described representative democracy as the 'ideally best' form of government: it allows for both the most effective form of protection for individuals – 'self-protection' – and for the exercise and development of a range of capacities that will make individuals dignified, self-reliant, yet self-consciously and freely attached to the interests of other members of the community (ibid., pp. 208–18). However, Mill denied that inclusion in the franchise is a matter of right: voting involves the exercise of power over others and no one can claim the right to this. Rather, political rights are a privilege that should be extended only to those who will use them properly. Mill believed that most ordinary members of the population in Europe and North America at that time lacked the rationality and self-control needed to resist the temptation to use their power tyrannically. Consequently, he proposed a modified form of representative democracy that would yield practical and educational benefits while avoiding the dangers inherent in trying to establish an ideal form of government in less than ideal circumstances. In his subsequent consideration of a form of representative government that would be appropriate to the condition of mid-nineteenth-century England, Mill suggested that the conduct of a professional governing elite should be subject to the scrutiny of an elected chamber chosen through a system of 'plural voting': every one would have one vote, but those fulfilling academic, professional and property qualifications should be given additional votes. This system would allow the least developed members of the community to protect themselves, and to experience the developmental benefits of political participation without allowing them to impose their generally unenlightened and self-serving demands on the rest of the population (ibid., pp. 284–90).

Mill's argument that there were no grounds for withholding the vote from women that did not apply with equal force to men (see p. 84), echoed the position taken by his partner Harriet Taylor. In an essay published in 1850 Taylor applauded the female emancipation movement in the United States because it involved a plea *by* women for political rights as well a plea *for* these rights. Drawing a parallel with the position of slaves, Taylor argued that exclusion of women from the franchise was inconsistent with the fundamental principles of US government. It also ran counter to the arguments employed in contemporary movements for a 'universal' manhood suffrage in Britain (Taylor, 1850, pp. 4–6). Political distinctions between the sexes were contrary to political justice because they ignored the well-established connection between taxation and political representation, and, since government had long since ceased to be a matter of superior force, they could not be justified by reference to relative physical strength (ibid., pp. 7–10). Taylor also rejected arguments based upon the need to maintain a distinction between a private (female) sphere and a public (male) one. This distinction imposed an arbitrary and improper limitation on women's range of action and on their capacity to utilise their abilities fully: 'The proper sphere for all human beings is the largest and highest which they are able to attain to. What that is, cannot be ascertained, without complete liberty of choice' (ibid., p. 11).

Harriet Taylor (1807–58)

Harriet Taylor was first the companion and later the wife of John Stuart Mill, and she is thought to have had a marked influence on a number of aspects of Mill's thinking. Taylor went beyond Mill in arguing for the economic independence of women, and she is credited with encouraging Mill to adopt a generally radical view of women's legal, social and political rights.

In the latter part of the nineteenth century Mill's idea that the exercise of political rights would serve the dual function of protecting the individual and facilitating the development of admirable character traits was incorporated within a framework where sociability was a primary value. Democracy became an important component of the new conception of political community that was developed by the British Idealists (see p. 45). T. H. Green, for example, regarded popular government as a way of eliminating 'bias by private interests' and making the state the vehicle of the common good. In addition he argued that the idea that law reflects the conscious pursuit of the common good is strengthened if the population has a direct or even an indirect, role in the processes through which laws are made (Green, 1986, pp. 93, 96–7).

The importance of democracy for the Idealist conception of the state was stressed by Green's successors. Bernard Bosanquet regarded democracy as an important modern development that provides a way of canvassing and expressing conceptions of the common good that spring from the experiences of members of the community. These conceptions need to be interpreted and put into effect by elected officials and by professional public servants, but democracy prevents expert rule from developing into elite domination; it ensures that experts are ultimately responsible to the citizenry at large (Nicholson, 1990, pp. 214–15). It is a central contention of political idealism that the state should be seen as an expression of the moral aspirations of the community of which it forms a part, not as a coercive institution that stands *above* society. The growth of democracy has facilitated this process of reorientation. It means, as D. G. Ritchie pointed out, that the state should no longer be seen as an object of suspicion. It is natural that citizens are wary of government when it is in the hands of particular classes, but once a state becomes democratic these suspicions become groundless because the government can now reflect the aspirations for the realisation of the common good that are embedded in the ideas and practices of the whole community (Ritchie, 1902, p. 74).

L. T. Hobhouse (1864–1929)

Educated at Oxford, Hobhouse taught at that university and was later the first professor of sociology at the University of London. In addition to his academic work, Hobhouse was a prominent journalist and was closely associated with the liberal *Manchester Guardian*. Like T. H. Green, by whom he was influenced, Hobhouse sought to formulate a new but still liberal conception of an active democratic state. His principal statement of this position was *Liberalism* (1911).

This conception of democracy was endorsed by a range of influential late-nineteenth- and early-twentieth-century political thinkers, but some of these writers felt a sense of unease about the practice of democratic politics. L. T. Hobhouse, a late-nineteenth-century proponent of the new liberalism inaugurated by Green, considered representative democracy to be both unique and valuable: it provides a way of giving 'recognition of the duties of government and the rights of the people'; it protects 'personal freedom and (the) equal consideration of all classes' and expresses 'a growing sense of social solidarity', upon which the modern state rests' (Hobhouse, 1990, pp. 188–9). However Hobhouse noted that although Britain had become increasingly democratic in its internal politics it continued to impose its will on a large empire. Hobhouse was opposed to imperialism, and he was also perturbed at the impact of the imperialistic control of other communities upon the ideals lying behind democracy, and upon the practices of democratic politics. Moreover the resurgence of imperialist sentiment had been accompanied by the manipulation of public discussion by those who controlled the popular press, and this, together with the demagogic tendencies of modern political leaders, seemed to Hobhouse to be depriving popular government of its moral standing.

Socialism and Democracy: Babeuf, Owen, Marx, Webb and Bernstein

While democracy became increasingly important for liberal thinkers in the nineteenth century, it also formed a key aspect of socialist political theory in that period. Many of the themes of nineteenth-century socialism – liberty, the end of class government and the revival of a true sense of community – were similar to advanced liberal ideas, but the socialists' understanding of the economic dimensions of oppression led them to use the term 'democracy' to refer to a system of general equality, and to regard popular government as an instrument for reconstituting social and economic relationships. An important consequence of this view was that many socialists were critical of what they saw as the formal, restricted and purely political understanding of democracy to which liberals subscribed.

This line of argument can be seen in the speech made by Francois-Noel ('Gracchus') Babeuf when he and his fellow conspirators were on trial before the High Court of Vendome in 1796. This conspiracy has been described as 'the last episode of the French Revolution' (Bax, 1911); it was also, however, the first act in the development of modern socialism. Babeuf was sharply critical of the narrowing of the franchise by the new constitution of 1795. He also attacked the restoration of privilege under the Directory, the group of five legislators who were, Babeuf held, responsible for rolling back the imperfect but significant gains of the revolution. These developments undermined the principles of liberty and equality that encapsulated the central idea of the revolution, namely that 'the aim of society is the welfare of its members' (Babeuf, 1972, p. 44). This goal was not achieved in the early stages of the revolution and had now been virtually abandoned. 'The Revolution is not yet at an end, since the wealthy have diverted its fruits, including political power, to their own exclusive use, while the poor in their toil and misery lead a life of actual slavery and count for nothing in the State' (ibid., p. 47). Babeuf's conspiracy was meant to remedy these defects by creating a 'republic of equals' in which political authority would be vested in the hands of the people and used to satisfy what he regarded as the just and egalitarian social and economic demands of the mass of the population.

Babeuf's ideas attracted the sympathetic attention of Bronterre O'Brien, a leading figure in English socialism in the early nineteenth century (Plummer, 1971, p. 60). O'Brien, together with followers of Robert Owen and others associated with the Chartist campaign for universal male suffrage in the 1830s and 1840s, developed a social and economic conception of democracy that rests on a belief that equality and justice in a legal and political sense are worthless unless economic and social forms of oppression are ended (Claeys, 1989, p. 83). This goal necessitates a general democratisation of human relations that extends beyond, and cannot be adequately reflected in, parliamentary institutions. The socialists stressed the importance of popular participation in a range of small-scale political and social institutions (community councils, cooperatives and trades unions), they were hostile to conceptions of politics that embodied competition, selfishness and the representation of sectional interests, and they promoted moral improvement as a way of developing people's social capacities and sympathies (ibid., p. 321). One expression of the early socialist conception of government was presented in Owen's scheme to place power in the hands of councils made up of all those members of a community in a particular age cohort. The aim was to

> *prevent* divisions, oppositions of interests, jealousies, or any of the common and vulgar passions which a contention for power is certain to generate. . . . By this equitable and natural arrangement all the numberless evils of elections and electioneering will be avoided (Owen, 1991, p. 296).

Owen's socialism focused on small communities as the basic unit of government, and thus contrasted with the position taken by other social- ists who wished to democratise and socialise the state. For example in the 1840s the French social democrat Louis Blanc argued that state capital should be used to fund autonomous enterprises, which were to be con- trolled neither by capitalists nor by the state, but by directors elected by the workers themselves. A system of 'workers' democracy' was to be inaugurated by a popularly elected government committed to the inter- ests of all the members of the community rather than particular classes. A similar aspiration motivated Blanc's contemporary Auguste Blanqui, but he developed a conception of revolutionary politics that harked back to Babeuf. Having set the revolution in train, a conspiratorial elite would institute a 'dictatorship of true republicans' (Lichtheim, 1968, p. 67), which would be responsible for dispossessing the rich and creating an egalitarian society. For Blanqui this dictatorship was a necessary, albeit temporary means of realising the goals that lay at the heart of the tradi- tion of radical democracy that had been inherited from the French Revo- lution (see p. 165).

The Blanquist conception of dictatorship was revived by Lenin when he sought to create a rationale for a 'people's democracy', a form of govern- ment that would bridge the gap between the revolutionary overthrow of the Tsarist state and the emergence of a state-less condition to which Marx had given the name 'communism'(see p. 100). The fact that a 'peo- ple's democracy' could be presented as a legitimate development of Marx's political ideas reflected the ambiguities of his treatment of popular government. One the one hand, Marx made it clear that without a fundamental transformation of the socioeconomic structure, the liberating claims made for conventional representative democracy are purely formal. If human beings are not freed from the deepseated oppression that is integral to capitalism, popular participation in politics cannot seriously change the character of the state. Marx saw 'bourgeois government' as merely the latest expression of a state that furthers the interests of the dominant class within society. Democratic representation does not alter the character of the state; it merely conceals its true nature: universal suffrage is a mechanism for determining 'once in three or six years what members of the ruling class should misrepresent the people in Parliament' (Marx and Engels, 1973, vol. ii, p. 221). Since the state is a class instrument, the advent of communism will see the end of politics. In the meantime, political democracy could be harnessed to the pursuit of this goal.

In the *Manifesto of the Communist Party* (1848) Marx and Engels claimed that a successful proletarian revolution would raise 'the proletariat to the position of ruling class', a measure they identified with triumph in 'the battle of democracy' (Marx, 1973, p. 86). Later, in his reflections on the Paris Commune of 1870–71, Marx presented the 'commune' – government by relatively small, locally based committees of popularly elected representatives – as a valuable alternative to the sham democracy of 'bourgeois' systems of representative government. The commune would give back to the community 'the State power which claimed to be the embodiment of that unity independent of, and superior to, the nation itself, from which it was but a parasitic excrescence' (Marx and Engels, 1973, vol. ii, p. 221). Marx believed that communal government based on universal suffrage would provide a way for the people to direct their collective action towards the transformation of economic and social relationships. However the peculiar context of the Paris Commune – a revolutionary civil war – severely limited its general applicability as a model for immediate socialist politics. In other situations, Marx regarded conventional democracy as a way of developing the consciousness and organisational capacities of the working class so that they could become a revolutionary force that would take over the state and inaugurate a 'dictatorship of the proletariat'.

This dictatorship would be like other forms of government in that it would act in the interests of a particular class, but it would differ from them in that the class in question would represent the interests of humanity. Having overthrown the bourgeoisie, it would use state power to destroy the social, economic and political vestiges of bourgeois rule, thus preparing the ground for its own demise and for the end of class government. Since the state was a class instrument, the attainment of full equality and freedom under communism would make it redundant; the state would 'wither away', leaving a genuine community of cooperating human beings who would collectively organise the administration of their own affairs.

The limited scope of Marx's political (as opposed to his historical, economic and social) theory posed problems for his successors (Dunn, 1984, p. 21). In the late nineteenth century a number of socialists adopted more conventional conceptions of democracy than that proposed by Marx. For example many important English socialists reformulated conventional justifications for popular representation, and presented socialism as an extension of what they saw as a tradition of democratic reform. Thus Sidney Webb, a leading member of the reformist Fabian Socialist Society, described socialism as the 'economic side of the democratic ideal' that had emerged as the dominant feature of the nineteenth-century political developments (Webb, 1889, p. 35). The advent of democracy meant that the state was no longer under the control of what the Benthamites had called 'sinister interests'; it was now a conscious agent of the common good and could be used to harness the economic resources of society to the requirements of the community. While Webb thought that efficient government would only be possible if administration was placed in the hands of expert elites, he insisted that representative institutions were necessary to guard against 'sinister interests'. This principle was applied to both central and local government.

Eduard Bernstein (1850–1932)

Bernstein was an early member of the Marxist German Social Democratic Party and subsequently developed a theory of gradual, non-revolutionary political and social transformation that orthodox Marxists branded as 'revisionist'. Bernstein had first-hand experience of late-nineteenth-century British socialism and drew upon this to present an alternative path to socialism that did not require class war or violent revolution. This position was advanced in *Evolutionary Socialism* (1898), a work that has been seen as an important influence in the development of contemporary European social democracy.

Webb also applauded the appearance of a combination of expertise and popular responsibility in organisations such as trades unions. His description of these developments in terms of 'industrial democracy' (ibid., pp. 30–6) attracted the favourable attention of the German social democratic writer Eduard Bernstein. Bernstein described trades unions as 'the democratic element in industry. Their tendency is to destroy the absolutism of capital, and to procure for the worker a direct influence in the management of an industry' (Bernstein, 1972, p. 139). However, unlike Webb, who was largely untouched by the influence of Marx, Bernstein developed a theory of 'social democracy' in response to what he saw as the inadequacies of the Marxist understanding of the nature of socialism and of how this condition could be achieved.

According to Marx, the 'political sovereignty' of the 'class party of the workers' was an essential condition for the attainment of socialism. Bernstein observed however, that even in advanced capitalist societies the workers did not form a homogenous mass. Consequently if government 'by the people' was to be anything other than a temporary outburst of aimless and destructive terror like that which appeared in the French Revolution, it would be necessary to avoid class government and identify a system that would be capable of embracing the interests of the whole community. Democracy and socialism would come together as different manifestations of a desire to place the interests of the community above those of classes who monopolised the economic and political resources of society.

Bernstein defined democracy as 'an absence of class government, as the indication of a social condition where a political privilege belongs to no one class as opposed to the whole community'. In both its political and economic manifestations, socialism involved an idea of 'universal citizenship' not class dictatorship; it should really be seen as an extension of the concern for 'free personality' that had inspired but had only been partially understood by liberals. Conventional democratic institutions embodied the political aspects of this tradition. Socialists should build upon the assumption of political power by the community, utilising the state as a vehicle for pursuing the material and social interests of the community. Socialism was based upon the 'principle of association' and the democratic state was a way of expressing the political aspects of this principle and realising its social and economic dimensions (ibid., pp. 96, 142).

Non-Liberal Theories of Democracy in the Twentieth Century: 'People's' and 'Third World' Democracy

In the twentieth century the prevailing patterns of democratic thinking in Western societies have been 'liberal-democratic'. Modern systems of popular representation have been justified on the grounds that they combine liberal concerns with individual freedom with the protective, developmental and social benefits that are held to flow from rule for and by the many. In the twentieth century, however, liberal conceptions of democracy have been challenged by two rival traditions. The first of these theories, variously known as people's, proletarian or communist democracy grew out of an attempt to fill the gaps left by Marx in his account of post-revolutionary politics; the second, Third World or developmental democracy has been important in a number of newly independent former colonies.

People's democracy built upon aspects of the Blanquist and Marxist traditions, but was a direct consequence of Lenin's understanding of what was necessary to further the revolutionary process after the collapse of Tsarist autocracy and the coup that allowed the Bolsheviks to seize power in 1917 (Harding, 1992, pp. 161–77). As we have seen, Marx's theory of 'true democracy' was extremely sketchy; in addition, however, the situation confronting Lenin was problematic in Marxist terms. Having seized control of the state, Lenin's conspiratorial elite was faced with the problem of pursuing the elusive goal of communism in a society that lacked the economic, social and political characteristics that Marx identified with an appropriately advanced state of capitalist development. Imperial Russia was autocratic rather than bourgeois, and possessed neither a developed economy nor an extensive class-conscious proletariat.

In response to these difficulties, Lenin formulated a new conception of democracy that would enable a class-conscious party elite to use the power of the state to create the conditions necessary for true communism. The party must assume responsibility for eliminating internal opposition, for developing an economic basis that would match the technical and productive achievements of advanced capitalism, and for creating a class-conscious proletariat that would carry the revolution to its end. These herculean labours were to be directed by a unified elite party that was able, by virtue of its knowledge of Marxism and a ruthless commitment to the true interests of the proletariat, to discern and implement the 'real will' of the people (Lenin, 1971, pp. 303, 322–3, 326–32, 371, 534–8).

In the hands of Joseph Stalin, Lenin's successor at the head of the Communist Party, this model was transformed from a dictatorship of the class-conscious proletariat into the virtual dictatorship of an individual, a step that many commentators see as an inevitable consequence of an authoritarian theory of leadership. It is important to note, however, that at least in its formal structures and in its rationale, Lenin's conception of a people's democracy incorporated ideas that are only explicable in relation to less contentious accounts of popular government. In the first place, although party membership was far from universal, the party itself operated on the basis of 'intraparty democracy'. That is, party positions were formulated after full and free discussions among all its members, and once they had been adopted by the party they were binding on all its members. Secondly, while people's democracy did not allow for competition *between* parties, the policy of the party and the appointment of those holding representative and other positions was carried out through and legitimated by electoral processes based on universal suffrage. Given the

'revolutionary vanguard' role that Lenin ascribed to elites, it is not surprising that these examples of democratic practice were set in a framework where party elites played a central role (see p. 166). For example
intraparty democracy took place within a party that also adhered to
the principle of 'democratic centralism', according to which leadership
flowed downwards and responsibility flowed upwards; in addition, candidates for election were nominated by the party (White *et al.*, 1982, pp.
222–5).

It is clear that features of people's democracy have facilitated elite
manipulation and, given a certain combination of circumstances, the most
oppressive tyranny. However it is at least arguable that while people's
democracy is incompatible with the values enshrined in liberal democracy, its distinctive features reflect an attempt to operationalise a conception of popular politics that rests on values that have played a role in the
history of democratic thinking. People's democracy takes a strongly collectivist rather than an individualistic focus; it adopts an 'objective' rather
than a 'subjective' conception of interests, and it incorporates a strongly
positive understanding of freedom. None of these considerations justify
people's democracy, but they may explain why it must be regarded as
incorporating at least some aspects of democratic conceptions of rule. Just
because people's democracy is democratic, we do not have to approve of
it; by the same token it should not be divorced from democracy because
it has been shown to be morally reprehensible.

Much the same point may be made about Third World democracy.
During the colonial period democratic ideas played an important role in
independence movements. They provided the basis for appeals to liberal
elites within colonising powers, and to indigenous populations. However
leading figures in anticolonial movements argued that 'liberal' Western
notions of democracy could not be adopted by their societies. These theories clashed with indigenous values and could not address the developmental imperatives (in education, public health, economics and nation
building) facing countries emerging from long periods of colonial domination. Third World democracy was presented as a system of democratic
rule that embodied values appropriate to non-Western societies and also
matched their needs.

Third World democracy has a number of components. First, it rests
upon the recovery of indigenous values. An important example of this
approach grew out of the 'Negritude Movement', a name given to a
group of African writers who were active in the period immediately
before and after the Second World War. In conscious opposition to the
derogatory stereotypes that were prevalent in colonial culture, these writers promoted a pride in blackness and upheld the continued relevance of
traditional practices and ideas derived from precolonial village and tribal
cultures. An idealised image of the past was to serve as the basis for

reconstructing *post*-colonial society; the years of colonisation were seen as a period of slumber that had no positive bearing on the liberated state (Nursey-Bray, 1983, p. 97).

In theories of Third World democracy, traditional values provided the basis for a new conception of a democratic society, of which a democratic state was only one element. They also promoted economic structures that spurned the individualistic ethos of free market capitalism. They sought to develop community resources for community purposes and stressed the importance of social relationships that reflected ideas of harmonious community, which they identified with the precolonial village. These societies lacked class divisions. Interaction was structured only by kinship and age, and was marked by cooperation based upon and reinforced by traditional values. In these circumstances there was no place for either the individualism of Western capitalism, or the class-structured society that provided the focus of Marxist analysis and practice (Macpherson, 1965, p. 30).

The political counterpart to this social pattern is the 'consensual community', held together and directed by decision-making processes that involve consultation and agreement rather than the imposition of majority views on the minority. However, because villages and tribes in the modern world are grouped together in extensive and often artificial nation-states, post-colonial societies have had to establish systems of central coordination and decision making that were not part of the precolonial condition. In Third World democracy a national consensus is forged and expressed through a single ruling party, whose position is endorsed through mass election. The party becomes a focus of unity, one that cuts across ethnic, religious and tribal lines (Nursey-Bray, 1983, pp. 104–6).

Like people's democracy, this distinctive form of post-colonial rule has often descended into single-person or tribal tyranny, but it retains theoretical justifications and institutional features that connect it to aspects of the democratic tradition. Third World democracy is collectivist rather than individualistic; it rests on a positive rather than a negative conception of liberty – promoting liberation and development among the oppressed and deprived – and it advances a substantive rather than a purely formal notion of equality: it presupposes that a democratic community is a community of economic, social and political equals (Macpherson, 1965, p. 33). Moreover it is premised, like people's democracy, on the idea that the community has a single, unified, true interest: only when this exists can the 'real will' of the community be embodied in a single party.

The recent history of post-colonial societies forms fertile ground for deep scepticism about the legitimacy and viability of Third World democracy. However, the system has worked tolerably well in some countries at some times. In any case the attempt to create a political role for the many in societies that lack the cultural, economic and social values found in long-established Western states reflects a more widespread concern about the appropriateness of Western democracy in non-Western countries. This issue plays an important role in the political practice of states such as Singapore, and it also lies behind assessments of the authenticity of democracy in large and relatively long-established post-colonial states such as India (Khilnani, 1992, p. 205).

Conclusion

Having long been regarded as a marginal and generally unsatisfactory alternative to monarchy and aristocracy, democracy now occupies the centre of the political stage. The reasons for this development are complex, but an important clue to its theoretical significance can be found in the connection that both Tocqueville and John Stuart Mill made between the democratisation of nineteenth-century society and the spread of democratic forms of government. The first of these developments eroded ideas of natural superiority and subordination, prompted the disappearance of legally enshrined status distinctions, and thus created conditions that made democracy more likely. An earlier, although less overt, statement of this position is implied in Paine's arguments about the need for government to correspond to a social structure made up of individuals who possess equal claims to consideration and protection. In Paine's case these claims were based upon natural rights, but this alone is not sufficient to justify claims to political equality. It is possible to assume, as earlier writers had done, that these rights would be adequately protected by non-democratic forms of government. For this reason an important part of the historical case for democracy has involved attempts to show that the interests of individuals will not be satisfactorily served unless they are endowed with political rights. Many arguments in favour of democracy thus focus on the inadequacy of monarchical and aristocratic alternatives.

The Exercise of Political Authority

Having considered a number of historically significant accounts of the ends of politics and the location of political power, we will now examine statements about how such power should be exercised. Conceptions of the ends of politics imply general specifications of the purposes to which political authority should be directed, but detailed statements about their implications vary considerably. We have already seen, for example, that the pursuit of virtue has given rise to a defence of both monarchical and democratic systems of rule. A similar degree of variation is apparent if one considers views about the exercise of political authority, particularly those concerning the means used to determine the propriety of rulers' conduct, and the extent to which their actions should be subject to either *normative* or *institutional* constraints. Normative constraints specify standards to which rulers should conform and to which subjects may appeal, while institutional constraints are formed by mechanisms that regulate the way in which power is exercised. These issues play an important role in accounts of legitimate political practice; they also provide the basis for challenges to political authority, which will be dealt with in the final part of this book.

Part III opens with a chapter examining theories of natural law and natural rights. These theories reflect a common belief that the exercise of political power should conform to objective standards that are beyond the reach of those whose behaviour is regulated by them. The second chapter in this section will examine a number of theories of 'mixed government'. These theories stipulate that power should be distributed between a number of institutions in order to ensure that rulers do not abuse their position and that they act in the interests of the community as a whole. The

viability of mixed government has been questioned by a number of thinkers, who have argued that order can only be attained in states presided
over by an all-powerful, unquestionable ruler, an absolute sovereign. This
approach has given rise to the absolutist theories of government that will
be discussed in Chapter 11.

Part III concludes with an examination of claims about the need for
those who hold political power to be subject to legal constraints. In addition to dealing with a range of arguments concerning the rule of law,
Chapter 11 outlines an important strand within this tradition that claims
the exercise of political power must be set within a framework of rules
that conform to the requirements of justice. These theories imply that the
approaches taken by all the thinkers discussed in earlier chapters are
inadequate, but they focus particularly on the dangers posed by theories
of absolute government and the related idea that laws are commands.

CHAPTER 8

The Sanctions of 'Nature'

The idea that it is possible to identify standards that correspond to fundamental facts about human beings and may thus be described as 'natural',
has played an important role in a range of theories that have implications
for the regulation of political authority. In order to understand the regulatory role of an appeal to 'nature', it is necessary to distinguish theories
that rely on the idea of 'natural law' or 'the law(s) of nature' from those
that focus on 'natural rights'. Theories of natural law identify a structure
of expectations and norms that are not themselves the product of human
intention or human will. These norms serve to legitimate human action
and to justify the exercise of political authority (Finnis, 1980, p. 23). Natural law is held to be 'natural' in two related senses. In the first place, it
is so fundamental to human life that its binding force is a matter of moral
necessity rather than choice: to recognise that there is such a thing as a
'law of nature' and to fail to abide by it is to fly in the face of a standard
that is intrinsic to humanity. Secondly, and as a consequence of this, it is
claimed that adherence to natural law is supremely appropriate for
human beings.

Natural law theories often depend on a particular understanding of
God's authoritative role in human life. Natural law is a system of
rules that tell human beings how they must act if they are to achieve the
ends for which God created them and towards which he directs
them. These laws are said to be 'rational' because they are appropriate
means to attain specified ends; they are also rational in the sense that
human beings discover them by the use of their reason. However, some
writers also relate the rationality of natural law to its role in meeting
fundamental human needs. This point can be illustrated by a comment
made by the Dutch writer Hugo Grotius (1583–1645). Grotius was a
devout Christian, but he thought that natural law would be binding even
if 'there is no God, or he takes no care of human affairs', because it

embodies rational precepts that are necessary for social existence (Grotius, 1738, p. xix).

Whatever view they took on the source of natural law, the writers discussed in this chapter believed it to have important implications for evaluating the conduct of rulers, and for determining the fundamental rightness of those humanly contrived rules by which social and political life are regulated. This last point lies behind discussions of the relationship between *natural* and *positive* law, that is, between laws that do not owe their form or their authority to human enactment and those that are laid down (or 'posited') by human beings and enforced through human agency. Human law is necessary because the laws of nature are general rather than specific, and lack the element of physical compulsion that is required to induce selfish human beings to act rationally (Finnis, 1980, pp. 28–9). However, positive law is only legitimate if is compatible with the general purposes specified by natural law.

Whereas natural law is a *framework* within which human actions are lauded or condemned depending on their conformity to the overall teleological design of the creator, 'natural rights' are *entitlements* that individuals can claim against other individuals and governments. These entitlements belong to people by virtue of their humanity and exist in a prepolitical condition. 'Human rights and natural rights are synonymous: they are fundamental and general moral rights' (ibid., p. 198). Unlike legal rights, natural rights are not created by the state; to the contrary, it is the duty of legitimate government to recognise these rights and to take account of them. Since natural rights are ascribed to human beings, they are frequently associated with an individualistic approach to politics; they belong to individuals and embody an 'active' conception of rights. That is, they identify claims to free action by right holders that other human beings (including those who wield political authority) are obliged to respect.

The emphasis on liberty on the one hand and a duty of recognition on the other, may be contrasted with the 'passive' accounts of rights that appear in many versions of natural law theory. In these theories the focus is on the *duties* of others (typically rulers) rather than on the *liberty* of the right holder. Subjects have rights only in the sense that they are entitled to expect rulers to perform their duty towards them. The difference between 'active' and 'passive' rights can be illustrated by comparing property rights with the right to charitable assistance. Claims relating to private property are based on an active conception of rights: they include a recognised and enforceable claim freely to use and dispose of those things to which one has a property right. In contrast the right to charitable assistance is a passive right, one that takes the form of a claim *against* other individuals, and obliges them to act charitably in specific circumstances (Tuck, 1979, pp. 7–15).

The distinction between active and passive rights underlies some important differences between the political implications derived from theories of natural rights and those that focus on natural law. However, the thinkers discussed in this chapter all maintained that an appeal to nature provides criteria for evaluating the conduct of rulers. They argued that if rulers ignore the injunctions of natural law, or if they fail to recognise their subjects' natural rights, they misuse the power vested in them. Since they are not acting in ways that are compatible with the ends of politics, their exercise of authority is inconsistent with the grounds that justify their possession of it. Consequently the legitimacy of their rule is called into question.

In what follows, examples of these approaches to politics will be drawn from a number of influential figures in the history of political thought. We shall begin by examining the role played by the idea of the 'natural' in ancient political theory and then trace the development of natural-law thinking in the ancient, medieval and early modern periods. Aspects of this tradition are closely connected to the emergence of radical theories of natural rights during the revolutionary decades of the late eighteenth century. Subsequently the language of natural rights fell into disuse, but as will be noted in the concluding chapter of this book, it has been revived by some contemporary thinkers (see p. 375).

The 'Natural' in Ancient Political Theory: Plato, Aristotle and Cicero

Plato's and Aristotle's views on the regulatory role of an appeal to nature were framed in opposition to contemporary claims about the purely conventional character of law and the *polis*. In Plato's *Gorgias* this argument is made by Callicles. An even more forcefully stated version of it is advanced in the early stages of the *Republic* by Thrasymachus, who argues that since it is 'natural' for the strong to dominate the weak, the regulative actions of rulers are often merely a cover for the effective pursuit of their self-interest (Plato, 1970, pp. 65–6). If rulers protect the weak from the strong they are acting contrary to nature. Paradoxically the mass of humanity applaud rulers whose behaviour is unnatural and condemn those who use the state in ways that correspond to nature. Since laws that protect the interests of all are not natural, they must be 'conventional', that is, the products of human ingenuity grounded in agreement.

In contrast Plato's ideal state promotes the satisfaction of fundamental human needs and its hierarchical structure reflects the distinctive natural endowments of the various classes within the community. Plato supported his conception of the naturalness of the ideal state by drawing a parallel between the well-ordered state and the well-ordered 'soul':

we agreed that a city was just when its three natural constituents were each doing their job, and it was disciplined and brave and wise in virtue of certain other states and dispositions of those constituents.... Well, then, ... we shall expect the individual to have the same three constituents in his character and to be affected similarly, if we are to be justified in attributing the same virtues to him (ibid., pp. 185–6).

A just state is 'natural' because it corresponds to fundamental human attributes and satisfies basic material, social and psychological needs. Both the structure of the ideal state and the conduct of true rulers (directed towards the creation and maintenance of a just state) satisfy these requirements. In contrast the behaviour of rulers in unjust states reflects a corruption of the soul and produces its dissolution. 'This sort of situation, when the elements of the mind are in confusion, is what produces injustice, indiscipline, cowardice, ignorance and vice of all kinds' (ibid., p. 197).

Plato's account of these distempers is designed to show that the apparent attractions of his opponents' positions conceal the deepest and most destructive illusions. It *is* natural that the strongest rule, but the strength appropriate to just rulers is the strength of reason and character necessary to enable them to identify the true good of the community and to subjugate their own narrowly conceived self-interests to those of the community to which they belong. Political regimes that satisfy this requirement are natural, and because they conform to patterns of orderly interaction that are fundamental to human life and in accordance with divine commands, they will be stable and long lasting.

Like Plato, Aristotle resisted contemporary claims about the purely conventional nature of justice, law and the state. In the *Nicomachean Ethics* he distinguished between the 'natural' – that which 'everywhere has the same force and does not exist by peoples' thinking this or that' – and the purely 'legal', or that which is 'originally indifferent, but when it has been laid down is not indifferent' (Aristotle, 1975, p. 1134b). 'Political justice' is partly 'natural' and partly 'legal' and so some things (adultery, murder and theft) are always wrong and are not subject to the discretion of rulers. In addition to this understanding of nature as a source of universal standards, Aristotle also developed one that relates the natural to the distinctive good or end of an object. According to this view, that which is more fully developed is more 'natural' than that which is not because it has achieved its potential, or realised its 'essential' qualities.

Aristotle's 'teleological' conception of nature (one that is framed in terms of an object's end or *telos*) plays a central role in his account of human development and of the political dimensions of this process. Since Aristotle argued that membership of a *polis* is necessary if the end of human activity (the 'good life') is to be realised, he regarded the *polis* as a natural institution. Although the family and the neighbourhood appear first in human experience, they cannot offer the same scope for virtuous conduct as the state. Consequently Aristotle described these institutions as 'prior' to the state: their contribution to the 'good life' can only be fully realised in the wider, more complete, self-sufficient environment created and maintained by the *polis*. Because humans can only achieve their ends as members of the *polis*, the state itself is natural. Man is, as Aristotle put it, 'by nature a political animal'; that is, a being whose potentialities can only be developed fully within the *polis* (see p. 59).

Aristotle's teleological treatment of the *polis* means that an appeal to nature provides a criterion for the legitimate exercise of power by some individuals over others and for questioning exercises of power that do not satisfy this criterion. For example Aristotle distinguished 'right' from 'wrong' constitutions by examining whether power is exercised for the good of the community, or merely for the good of those who wield it (see p. 129). Right constitutions accord with the requirements of nature because they provide a political framework within which citizens can realise their potentialities. In contrast, unjust forms of government pervert the state from its true and natural role.

Another application of Aristotle's understanding of the requirements of a state that will conform to the requirements of nature can be seen in his critical reaction to the familial and property-holding arrangements that Plato specified for the 'guardian' class in his ideal state. Aristotle considered the family to be an essential component of the process of development that culminated in the state. For this reason he rejected Plato's arguments about the marital communism of ideal rulers. Aristotle thought that these stipulations ignored the role that the family plays in people's pursuit of the good life and deprived Plato's guardians of the opportunity to acquire and practise those virtues which Aristotle associated with domestic life. Much the same can be said of Plato's prohibitions against private property. In each case the guardians are required to dispense with institutions and practices that Aristotle regarded as essential for the pursuit of the good life and therefore central to the natural status of the state, and consequently to the perfection of human nature (Aristotle, 1958, pp. 47–67).

Although the idea of nature played a role in aspects of Plato's and Aristotle's political thinking, they did not present it in the distinctive and systematic form that was to be a marked feature of medieval and early modern political thought. An important stage in this process of development can be seen in the writings of the Roman politician and philosopher Marcus Tullius Cicero, whose account of natural law was built upon a tradition that derived from the stoic school in Athens. Members of this school (originating in about 300 BC) argued that the universe is governed by 'right reason'; this pervades all things and is identical to the supreme god, Zeus. As the stoic writer Chrysippus put it, reason is 'the ruler over all the acts both of gods and men.... For all beings that are social by nature, it directs what must be done and forbids what must not be done' (Sigmund, 1971, p. 21).

Marcus Tullius Cicero (106–43 BC)

Born into a lower division of the Roman nobility, Cicero trained as a lawyer in Rome and Athens. He became a leading figure in Roman legal circles and built a political career upon this success. In 63 BC he served as consul, the most important office in Roman politics. Cicero was deeply committed to the traditional republic, in which the aristocracy had a leading role. The closing years of his life were overshadowed by events that signalled the final collapse of this system. Cicero's major political writings are *The Laws* (c. 50 BC) and *The Republic* (c. 54 BC), titles that reflect his attachment to the tradition of classical political philosophy that originated in Athens.

Like Plato, Cicero's political ideas were formulated against a background of social and political dissolution. A leading figure in the quasi-aristocratic upper echelons of Roman political culture in the first century BC, Cicero utilised a theory of natural law to combat what he saw as rampant and destructive self-interest among his contemporaries, and to defend the traditional structure and practice of Roman politics. Since Cicero thought that many features of the Roman constitution embodied the principles of natural law, he argued that the malign interaction of unscrupulous members of the Roman elite and the propertyless masses was undermining a system of government that conformed admirably to the requirements of nature.

Cicero maintained that 'right reason in agreement with nature', which is 'universal in application, unchanging and everlasting', forms the basis of 'true law' (Cicero, 1970, p. 211). Law is divine in origin and is made accessible to human beings by virtue of their possession of reason: 'just as that divine mind is the supreme Law, so, when [reason] is perfected in man, [that also is Law]' (ibid., p. 383). All human law (whether of a customary or positive kind) is legitimate insofar as it conforms with the fundamental principles of natural law. In an echo of Aristotle's language, Cicero defined justice as a 'mental disposition which gives everyman his desert while preserving the common interest' (Wood, 1988, p. 74). Its 'first principles ... proceed from nature' and serve both right and utility. Since the 'common interest' embraces the legitimate claims of all members of the state, there can be no conflict between the *real* interests of individuals and those of their fellows. The state is 'an association in justice', regulated by objective criteria enshrined in natural law (Cicero, 1970, p. 77). Adherence to natural law is of universal benefit; those who ignore it act unnaturally, unjustly and contrary to their own real interests.

In concrete terms, the law of nature enjoins human beings to refrain from wilfully injuring one another, respect both public and private property, keep their promises, and act generously to one another (Wood, 1988, p. 76). The last of these duties is an essentially private obligation, but the first three all have important and direct implications for the exercise of political authority. Office holders should provide protection for both the persons and the property of those who are subject to their authority, and should enforce promissory obligations. In addition to contributing positively to the common interests of the community, rulers must refrain from abusing their powers. Cicero, in common with both Plato and Aristotle, thus condemned the use of public authority for private purposes: such activity is the hallmark of the tyrant, one who governs through force and fear because his actions have no basis in justice and no hold upon the moral consciousness of his unfortunate subjects. There is, Cicero claimed,

> no creature more vile or horrible than a tyrant, or more hateful to the gods and men ...; for though he bears a human form, yet he surpasses the most monstrous of the wild beasts in the cruelty of his nature. For how could the name of human being rightly be given to a creature who desires no community of justice, no partnership in human life with his fellow-citizens – aye, even with any part of the human race (ibid., p. 156).

This remark refers to Tarquin the Proud, a notoriously bloody despot, but his grossly illegitimate use of political power – epitomised by his disregard of 'partnership' or 'community of justice' with his fellows – is merely an extreme example of a form of rule that is inhuman because it is unnatural. The self-interested use of power by the masses was no more acceptable to Cicero than that of a despot. He was thus highly critical of attempts to institute 'agrarian laws', which deprive the rich of their property. Laws of this kind undoubtedly offended Cicero's pro-aristocratic sensibilities, but he also condemned them because they were contrary to the natural law that obliges rulers to protect the property of their subjects.

Cicero's responses to the injustice of the despotic Tarquin and to the rapacity of the propertyless masses reflect the impact of natural-law thinking upon his understanding of the requirements of political justice. They also explain his reservation about the practical dangers of rule by the 'one' or the 'many', and his preference for the form of mixed government that he identified with the Roman Republic. Since pure forms of government are peculiarly liable to be corrupted by the self-interest of those who control them, adherence to the laws of nature is more likely in regimes that prevent any one section of the community or any single individual from assuming a position of independent supremacy (see pp. 235–7).

Medieval Conceptions of Natural Law: Canon and Civil Law, and Aquinas

During the medieval period Cicero's ideas provided an important point of reference for those political theorists who developed a sophisticated body of natural law theory. In its later stages (that is from the late twelfth century) medieval natural law thinking was also influenced by the rediscovery of Aristotle's writings on this subject. However, in place of the ancients' appeal to gods presided over by a supreme god, medieval thinkers looked to a single source of divine authority. Their understanding of the attributes of God and his relationship with human beings was derived from Christian revelation and from the body of theology that had been deduced from this by the early leaders (or 'fathers') of the Church. Medieval natural law theory involved a series of attempts to work out the implications of divine leadership for the conduct of human affairs in a situation where the focus of attention was shifting from a transnational empire to a multitude of nation states. This development raised questions about the relationship between a variety of systems of humanly created law, and the universal standards of justice implied by Christian doctrine.

Initially the development of Christian theories of natural law was closely bound up with debates on 'canon law', that is, the body of law that regulated the 'temporal' or earthly affairs of the Catholic Church. This system of law was distinguished from 'civil law', which applied within states. Throughout the medieval period, however, the Church was a large and complex international institution, often presided over by popes whose ambitions were not solely directed towards the world to come. The publication in about 1139 AD of Gratian's *Concordantia Discordandium Canonum* (usually referred to as the *Decretum*) marked an important stage in the integration of aspects of natural and canon law. In compiling this work Gratian drew not only upon the Roman tradition of law, but also upon the writings of the Church fathers, particularly those of Ambrose, Augustine and Isidore of Seville (Sigmund, 1971, p. 37).

Since late antiquity, bishops had performed the dual role of spiritual lord and temporal lord within their own territories or sees. That is, they were office holders in two complementary hierarchies, one ecclesiastical, the other secular. Canon law attempted to regulate these sometimes conflicting duties and loyalties. The universal authority claimed by the bishop of Rome, because of his unique position as the vicar of Christ and head of the Church, posed special problems. The 'Investiture Controversy' (1075–1122) – the conflict over who had the authority to appoint bishops and determine their powers – generated much canonical and courtly opinion about the nature and limits of secular authority. However, imperial and papal theorists *did* agree that temporal power was divine in origin. Both sides adhered to the 'Gelasian doctrine' that God had instituted two types of authority: secular and spiritual, through which the world was administered.

In considering medieval views of how political authority should be exercised, it is important to bear in mind that the powers of earthly rulers were attributed to a divine source. This assumption produced a marked reluctance to acknowledge that any one other than God had the right to regulate the way in which this authority was exercised. As was noted above, medieval writers did not think that the ideas of consent conferred any rights of oversight or scrutiny upon subjects: this role was reserved for God who was the ultimate source of political power (see p. 134).

Although this doctrine was endorsed by many medieval thinkers, it did not provide a generally acceptable solution to two difficulties. First, there were sharp differences of opinion over whether the ruler or the law should be given ultimate authority; second, there was the question of whether the law could change, and if so, how this could be done. One response to these questions indicated that rulers could 'dispense' from the law. That is, in cases of necessity, or where the Jewish law of the Old Testament was superseded by the new law, rulers could ignore previously accepted standards. However, writers in the canon law tradition stressed that acknowledgement of the discretionary powers of temporal rulers did not relieve them of their overriding obligations under natural law. Where positive laws were in conflict with natural law, this provided grounds for its annulment. Moreover rulers' deployment of their dispensing powers was hedged around by impediments that were supported by the prescriptive force of natural law.

One significant example of these constraints was the argument that, because property rights were a product of natural law, they lay beyond the bounds of the sovereign authority of secular rulers and must be respected by them (Pennington, 1991, p. 438). In this, and in most other cases, issues of adjudication and enforcement were reserved for God alone. To modern ways of thinking a reliance on divine punishment may seem a precarious way of regulating the exercise of political power, but in a medieval context it was a serious impediment to those who were tempted to use their political power in an obviously wilful, self-serving manner. In this world their moral stature would be diminished; in the next, they could look forward to a regime of punishment that was conventionally pictured in unremittingly fearsome terms.

Among both canonical lawyers and their 'civilian' counterparts, ideas derived from natural law provided a means of specifying the ways in which rulers should use their authority. It is generally acknowledged, however, that the most sophisticated and influential account of natural law in the medieval period was produced by St Thomas Aquinas, a theologian–philosopher rather than a lawyer. Aquinas brought a distinctive orientation to bear on the issue of how natural law relates to the exercise of political power by temporal rulers. An important aspect of this approach was Aquinas' attempt to integrate ideas about the naturalness of the state that were derived from ancient, pre-Christian political thought, with a body of theology that built upon the fruits of Christian revelation.

Aquinas' treatment of natural law begins with a general definition of law as 'a rule or measure of action in virtue of which one is led to perform certain actions and restrained from the performance of others' (Aquinas, 1959, p. 109). Rules of this kind are directed towards the common good of the community to which they are applied, and are framed and enforced by the person or persons responsible for fostering it. Since 'reason' (or more fully, 'right reason') is the faculty that directs action to its appropriate end, one can say that law is 'nothing else than a rational ordering of things which concern the common good; promulgated by whoever is charged with the care of the community' (ibid., p. 113). Ultimately this responsibility lies with God, the creator and governor of his entire creation, but in the human world, and especially in less extensive communities such as the state, it lies with the ruler.

In line with his view of God's position, Aquinas argued that systems of legitimate law derive from 'eternal law', that is, a set of rules formulated by God to direct the actions of *all* of his creation.

> Just as in the mind of every artist there already exists the idea of what he will create by his art, so in the mind of every ruler there must already exist an ideal of order with respect to what shall be done by those subject to his rule.... Accordingly, the eternal law is nothing other than the ideal of divine wisdom considered as directing all actions and movements' (ibid., pp. 119–21).

While eternal law forms the core of all legitimate or true systems of law, those which are specifically formulated for the direction of human beings may be subdivided into distinct types. In his discussion of this topic in *Summa Theologica*, Aquinas identified three such categories of law: divine law, natural law and human law. These terms differentiate between the immediate *sources* of law, not those whom it directs. All these forms of law direct human beings to their 'end', but they are derived from a number of sources, and to some degree at least they focus on different aspects of human experience.

Unlike many earlier Christian exponents of natural law theory, Aquinas went to some pains to differentiate natural law from divine law. While the former relates to the 'natural' qualities of humanity, the latter is necessary because the destiny of human beings lies in their attainment of 'eternal blessedness', a condition that extends far beyond the limitations imposed by their natural faculties. In addition Aquinas argued that these faculties, and hence humans' understanding of the system of law that relates to them, vary and undergo development. They may thus produce erroneous or incomplete specifications arising from ignorance or other natural weaknesses. Since it is necessary for humans to be placed under a system of law that is incapable of error and addresses both the external activities of humankind and those 'hidden interior actions of the soul' that are an important aspect of human perfectibility, they must be subject to divine as well as to natural law. Divine law is necessarily all-encompassing; it supplements the variable products of human reason with the fruits of revelation and the teachings of the Church. In contrast human and natural law are limited in scope, the latter by its very nature, the former because of its unavoidable concern with the external rather than the internal side of human action. If human law were to attempt to prevent *all* evil it would interfere with some parts of human action that are actually good; it thus embraces only those aspects of life that can be known to human beings and regulated effectively by them. Given the unavoidably limited applications of human law and the need to punish all evil if perfection is to be attained, 'it was necessary that there should be a divine law which would prohibit all manner of sin' (ibid., p. 117).

Aquinas argued that natural law is derived from and closely related to humans' natural faculties and inclinations. Rational reflection upon these inclinations enables humans to understand the implications of eternal law for their natural existence. Because humans share in divine reason to some degree, they can acquire both 'a natural inclination to such actions and ends as are fitting' and an understanding of the substance of natural law. Hence 'the natural law is nothing else than the participation of the eternal law in rational creatures' (ibid., p. 115). Aquinas identified three major 'precepts' (or general rules) of natural law, each of which corresponds to a natural inclination. The inclination towards *preservation* gives rise to precepts enjoining the preservation of human life and prohibiting its wilful destruction; the inclination towards *procreation* produces precepts governing sexual relationships and the care of children, while that promoting a positive concern for the *good of humanity* produces an inclination to live in society (since this is necessary to human well-being), as well as precepts ensuring that social life produces the benefits of which it is capable (ibid., p. 123).

When the general precepts of natural law are subjected to a rational reflection that takes account of circumstantial considerations, this forms the basis of legitimate or 'true' human law. 'Human reason' proceeds 'from the precepts of the natural law, as though from certain common and indemonstrable principles, to other more particular dispositions ... [which are] called human laws' (ibid., p. 115). Both the specification of human law and its enforcement are necessary to provide the discipline required for a virtuous life, particularly in respect of those things which are directly dependent upon social life. Although human law is not merely a copy of natural law because legislators exercise creative freedom, Aquinas maintained that the laws they produce are validated by natural law (Finnis, 1980, p. 28). The detailed specifications of legitimate human law relate to natural law in one of two ways. They are either 'conclusions' drawn from its precepts – for example a law against murder is a conclusion drawn from the precept prohibiting harm to other human beings – or they are applications of a general requirement to a particular instance. In the latter case, human laws are what Aquinas calls 'a determination of certain general features'. Human laws thus specify penalties 'in determination of' the natural law requiring that those who transgress should be punished (Aquinas, 1959, p. 129).

These distinctions identify the relationship between human and natural law, and they also address more specific queries concerning the extent to which particular human laws can be derived from natural law. The first of these issues is important if positive law is to be seen as legitimate, while the second deals with problems arising from the variety of human laws. In either case the relationship between human law, natural law and eternal law provides a criterion for distinguishing 'just' from 'unjust' laws.

The fact that true human laws are just, does not preclude the possibility that there will be a variety of such laws. Human laws are formulated to promote the welfare of particular communities: they must differ in their details according both to the circumstances of the community in question and the characteristics of those whose lives they are designed to regulate. The crucial point is that any variations must accord with the general purposes specified by natural law and embodied in its secondary, or derivative, precepts. Laws that benefit only those who hold political office, those that extend beyond the ruler's competence because they cannot usefully regulate other members of the community, and those that narrow the idea of the common good by imposing unfair burdens on some members of the community, are contrary to natural law and must necessarily reflect the illegitimate exercise of political power. The same holds true of laws that fly in the face of divine law, such as those enforcing idolatry. Human law simply cannot address the positive, internal requirements of divine law since these relate to the conscience, but some uses of political authority may be illegitimate because they are clearly contrary to the expressed will of God. (ibid., p. 137).

In the same way that eternal law embodies the will of God, human law is the will of the human lawgiver or ruler. Because rulers create and enforce human law they cannot be subject to its constraining force. However, just rulers will subject themselves to what Aquinas called the 'directive power' of human law because they are under an overriding moral obligation to further the common good: just laws are important means of realising this end. However, because rulers *are* the immediate source of human law, they may amend it when this becomes necessary, and they may also dispense with it in particular cases. But these and all their other legitimate actions are not arbitrary. Rulers must be guided by a sincere and impartial concern for the common good, not by self-interest, and they must act in conformity with the precepts of natural law (ibid., pp. 137–9, 143).

Aquinas' account of the relationship between natural and human laws provides a criterion with which to evaluate the former and specify the general but overriding concerns that determine the ways in which political power should be exercised. For example, in common with a number of his predecessors, Aquinas identified tyrannical rule with a wanton disregard for natural law, one that gives rise to unjust actions on the part of rulers and their agents, and to the maintenance of systems of regulation that are perversions of the very idea of law (ibid., pp. 55–61). He also deployed natural law theory to delegitimate particular uses of political authority. For example Aquinas argued that private property is in accordance with natural law because it is necessary for peaceful and generally productive social interaction. This means that rulers are under an obligation to recognise these rights and consequently, except in emergencies, subjects can only be taxed with their consent, or be obliged to forego their property rights if a general obligation to provide charitable assistance comes into play (ibid., p. 171).

The regulatory force of natural law applies to external as well as internal relations. Aquinas thus argued that it is illegitimate for rulers wilfully to attack other states. This particular application of political authority must be justified by reference to the more extended common good that other states share; it must be the only means of seeking redress; and it must be carried out in line with the general provisions of natural law, the standard of both just rule and just war (ibid., pp. 159–61).

Natural Rights and Unlimited Government in Early Modern Political Theory: Suàrez, Grotius, Hobbes and Pufendorf

'Active' conceptions of rights focus on the liberty of individuals and thus correspond closely to one of the distinctive features of natural right theory (see p. 202). In this tradition, original, prepolitical claims determine the conditions under which political authority can be created and the ways in which it can be exercised. For Aquinas, coercive political authority is necessary for fallen humanity. Political authority existed before the Fall (that is, there is no prepolitical condition for Aquinas and he follows Aristotle on the naturalness of the political), but it is directive not coercive. At the end of time human political authority will become redundant because Christ will assume direct kingship.

Discussions of 'natural freedom' became far more important in early modern political theory, although for some time they were treated in a conventional natural law framework that was similar in most respects to that developed by Aquinas. For example the influential Spanish writer Francesco Suàrez (1547–1617) argued that if humans had not fallen from grace they would not have been subjected to coercive authority. Even in this situation however, they would be directed or guided by other human beings and they were, in any case, subject to divine jurisdiction as specified by both divine and natural law (Suàrez, 1856–78, vol. iii, p. 417).

This change of focus reflected a growing awareness of the diversity of political authorities in post-reformation Europe, as well as a need to address the problems created by Europeans' contact with the indigenous populations of the 'new world'. By considering the political implications of a condition of natural freedom, Suàrez and his contemporaries were able to establish a basis for evaluating the appropriateness and legitimacy of regimes and of rulers who presided over societies that subscribed to a variety of religious faiths. Suàrez was deeply committed to Roman Catholicism, but the approach to natural freedom that appeared in his writings formed the starting point for theories of politics that became increasingly divorced from the theological underpinnings of Christianity. Suàrez's writings show quite clearly the beginnings of a conception of rights that was later to form the basis of natural rights theory. Having distinguished between a right and a law on the ground that a right is what is 'prescribed or measured by law', he specified the true meaning of right as 'a certain moral power which every man has, either over his property or with respect to that which is due to him' (Suàrez, 1944, p. 30).

An important stage in the secularisation of natural rights theory can be discerned in Hugo Grotius' and Samuel Pufendorf's writings. Although Grotius continued to regard natural law as a product of divine wisdom enforced by divine command, he raised the possibility that it could be justified on the grounds of reason alone (see p. 201). Given the absence of human superiors in the state of nature, and given also the dependence of human beings upon the fruits of sociability, there is a logical necessity for effective systems of regulation that will make sociability viable. From this perspective, the 'law of nature' can be understood as a system of regulation that is necessary for social life, rather than one that derives its binding force from its divine source: 'sociability ... or this care in maintaining society in a manner conformable to the light of human understanding, is the foundation of right property so called ... .' For Grotius, the primary requirements of sociability necessitate rights to natural liberty, promise keeping and respect for private property (Grotius, 1738, p. xvii; Haakonssen, 1985; Tuck, 1979, pp. 67–77). For Pufendorf the law of nature stipulates natural equality – 'every man should esteem and treat another man as his equal by nature, or as much a man as himself' – and this facilitates reciprocity, rules out natural servitude and underwrites the impartial adjudication of wrong-doing (Pufendorf, 1934, pp. 330, 336–40).

However, Grotius believed that even when sociability is sustained by the logical force of the laws of nature it is likely to be precarious. The reasons for this unproductive uncertainty are spelt out most graphically in Thomas Hobbes' account of the state of nature, but his is only one of a number of contemporary statements that point to the hazards of a natural condition and identify the state as a solution to them. For example, while Pufendorf traced the evils of the state of nature to depravity, ignorance and weakness, rather than to the implications of the legitimate pursuit of one's rights, the contrast he draws between this condition and civil society is at least as sharp as that of Hobbes: in a natural condition 'there is the rule of passion, war, fear, poverty, ugliness, solitude, barbarism, ignorance, savagery'. In contrast, membership of political society makes it possible for human beings to enjoy 'the rule of reason, peace, security, riches, beauty, society, refinement, knowledge, good will' (Pufendorf, 1927, p. 91).

Since these writers considered natural beings to be free, they insisted that the acquisition of political power must be based on consent (Tuck, 1993, p. 175). However, this condition applies only to the *original* creation of sovereign power. Once sovereignty came into existence, those who had been subject to the paternal power of their fathers assumed the obligations that had been entered into by them. This stipulation weakens the consent requirement, but in any case the fact that government is created by consent does not necessarily impose restraints upon the exercise of political power by sovereigns. The reason for this is that bearers of naturals rights are free to place themselves under an absolute ruler, or even to become slaves.

In a later chapter we will look more closely at theories of absolute government; at this point it is necessary merely to note that this state of affairs has been portrayed as the rational outcome of a condition of natural freedom, one that involves the renunciation of natural rights through processes of agreement, consent, promise and contract, or what early modern writers referred to as 'compact'. This process is compatible with natural freedom, and since it provides a means of making sociability more advantageous, it corresponds to the general rationale of the laws of nature. In addition, of course, the viability of consent is underwritten by the natural law stipulation that people should honour their promises.

The fact that the subjects of Hobbes' sovereign are not obliged to submit to sovereigns who pose a serious threat to their lives, reflects the residual impact of the laws of nature in the state (see p. 261). Moreover, certain of these laws – including the stipulation that individuals should not cause others to regret bestowing the gift of sovereignty upon them – imply some obligation on the part of the sovereign (albeit one that cannot be enforced by his subjects) to act in the interests of the community. However, while Grotius and Pufendorf regarded the creation of an unlimited (even despotic) sovereign as a legitimate outcome of consent, they did not make it a necessary one. Subjects may renounce all their rights, but they can create a useful source of political authority by consenting to something less awesome than Hobbes' Leviathan. This possibility rests upon the principle of 'interpretative charity', whereby subjects retain some rights. The contractual arrangement that creates sovereignty permits the contracting parties to set limits on the way in which sovereign power is exercised (Pufendorf, 1934, p. 1064; 1927, p. 131). These stipulations rely on the obligatory force of promises and are therefore products of the law of nature.

Natural Law, Natural Rights and Limited Government: Locke

Despite Grotius' and Pufendorf's argument that original natural freedom can give rise to absolute sovereignty of a despotic kind, their theories raised the possibility of using ideas of natural rights to produce liberal or even radical statements about the limitation and regulation of political authority. Examples of radical utilisations of natural rights can be seen in the utterances of figures identified with the leveller movement during the English Revolution in the mid seventeenth century. Participants in the Putney Debates of 1647 related demands for an extension of franchise to a 'right of nature' and were criticised by others for doing so. It should be noted, however, that these references to natural rights were often alloyed with claims relating to 'the rights of Englishman', a particular and legal category rather than a universal and natural one (Woodhouse, 1951, pp. 53–9).

The most developed seventeenth-century account of radical natural law and natural right theory was produced by John Locke in the closing decades of the century. As noted above, Locke presented a detailed refutation of Sir Robert Filmer's argument that God had imposed a system of absolute government upon humanity when he granted complete, paternal power to Adam and his male heirs. Locke reinstated the idea of natural freedom that Filmer had rejected, but unlike Grotius, Hobbes and Pufendorf he argued that if the rationale of natural freedom is placed in its proper context of the laws of nature, it conditions what individuals can legitimately consent to (Tuck, 1979, p. 173). Absolute government is illegitimate because this form of political authority is incompatible with the moral grounds of natural freedom.

Locke outlined some crucial distinctions bearing on this line of argument in an early work, the *Essays on the Law of Nature*, dating from 1660: natural rights are 'grounded on the fact that we have the free use of things', natural law 'enjoins or forbids the doing of a thing' (Sigmund, 1971, p. 91). While Locke thought it important to differentiate natural rights from natural law, he insisted that they are closely related: the primary natural right, the right to complete freedom from control by other human beings, is set within the context of the law of nature. As he put it in the *Second Treatise of Government*,

[a]ll men are naturally in ... a *State of perfect Freedom* to order their actions, and dispose of their Possessions, and Persons as they think fit, within the bounds of the Law of Nature, without asking leave, or depending upon the Will of any Man (Locke, 1967, p. 287).

This state of 'perfect freedom' is related negatively to the law of nature. Being a condition of equality no one has the right to assume a position of supremacy without the consent of those who will become their subjects. Locke deployed this argument in refutation of Filmer's claim that subordination is natural because it follows a pattern established by God when he granted Adam absolute power over his wife and children (see p. 266). In addition, however, he offered a positive justification for natural freedom, one that rests on his understanding of human beings' responsibilities to God, their acknowledged creator and master:

For Men being all the Workmanship of one Omnipotent, and infinitely wise Maker; All the Servants of one Sovereign Master, sent into the World by his order and about his business, they are his Property, whose Workmanship they are, made to last during his, not one anothers Pleasure. And being furnished with like Faculties, sharing all in one Community of Nature, there cannot be supposed any such *Subordination* among us, that may Authorize us to destroy one another, as if we were made for one anothers uses, as the inferior ranks of Creatures are made for ours (ibid., p. 289).

This responsibility provides the basis for a prioritised list of obligations. First, human beings should seek to secure their own preservation. Second, they should be actively concerned for the preservation of others when this does not conflict with self-preservation. Third, they must avoid harming others. Finally, they should uphold the law of nature by punishing transgressors and extracting compensation from them (ibid., pp. 289–90).

In the state of nature the fulfilment of these obligations is problematic because of the limited power possessed by natural individuals, and because of their tendency to judge partially and punish harshly (and thus unjustly) in cases that affect themselves. Locke argued that the 'inconveniences' of the state of nature will be compounded if arbitrary, unlimited power is placed in the hands of governors. Those who lay claim to such power put themselves into a state of war with their fellows by posing an active threat to their preservation (ibid., pp. 293–4, 297). In direct contradiction to the position advanced by Grotius, Hobbes and Pufendorf, Locke argued that voluntary submission to an absolute ruler is a breach of the law of nature: it makes self-preservation, and by implication the fulfilment of other obligations to God, dependent upon the will of another:

> *Freedom* from Absolute, Arbitrary Power, is so necessary to, and closely joyned with a Man's Preservation, that he cannot part with it, but by what forfeits his Preservation and Life together. For a Man, not having the Power of his own Life, *cannot*, by Compact, or his own Consent, *enslave himself* to any one, nor put himself under the Absolute, Arbitrary Power of another, to take away his Life, when he pleases. No body can give more Power than he has himself; and he that cannot take away his own Life, cannot give another power over it (ibid., p. 302).

Locke denied that paternal power is absolute, and he would not allow that submission to a parent can provide the basis for subjection to an absolute sovereign. 'Paternal power' (which is more accurately termed 'parental power') is regulated by the laws of nature, and since it concerns the nurturing and education of children, it can only be exercised over those who have not attained adulthood. In any case, Locke drew a sharp distinction between 'paternal' and 'political' power. The latter rests on a right created by the consent of free, rational beings and is directed to the good of the community: 'The great and *chief end* ... of Mens uniting into Commonwealths, and putting themselves under Government, *is the Preservation of their Property*', or 'their Lives, Liberties and Estates.' By providing 'established, settled known laws', 'known and indifferent judges' and power to back their right judgement (ibid., pp. 368–9), government alleviates the problems of determination, adjudication and just and effective punishment that occur in the state of nature; it thus makes an invaluable contribution to human preservation.

However individuals can only forego their natural freedom under conditions that conform to the law of nature and produce systems of human regulation that assist them in fulfilling their obligations under this law. Sovereignty must be created by consent, and must be exercised in ways that are consistent with humans' obligations under the law of nature.

> A Man ... having in the State of Nature no Arbitrary Power over the Life, Liberty, or Possession of another, but only so much as the Law of Nature gave him for the preservation of himself, and the rest of Mankind; this is all he doth, or can give up to the Common-wealth, and by it to the *Legislative Power*, so that the Legislative can have no more than this. Their Power in the utmost Bounds of it, is *limited to the publick good* of the Society' (ibid., p. 375).

When rulers act in defiance of these stipulations, government can be said to have 'dissolved', a phrase that Locke used to show that it has lost its legitimacy. In these circumstances rulers exercise despotic, not *political* power. Consequently they no longer have any claim upon the loyalty and obedience of their subjects. Indeed Locke argued that subject's of unlawful rulers have an obligation to cast off their authority and recreate a legitimate government, one that acts in correspondence with the laws of nature, and uses political power to fulfil the ends that were only partially realised by naturally free beings in a state of nature (see pp. 318–22).

The Radical Application of Natural Rights in Eighteenth-Century Political Theory: Rousseau, Condorcet, Paine, Wollstonecraft and Thelwall

In eighteenth-century Germany, Grotius' and Pufendorf's conception of prepolitical beings consenting to trade their freedom for the security provided by an all-powerful monarch, provided the basis for theories of absolute monarchy. Thus Christian Wolff argued that 'natural freedom' provides a contractual basis for unlimited sovereignty: 'he who exercises the civil power has the right to establish everything that appears to him to serve the public good' (Krieger, 1972, p. 67). Elsewhere, however, a more radical tradition of natural rights theory emerged. One strand of this was formulated by Rousseau, but as we have seen, his attitude towards a condition of natural freedom and equality was ambiguous. The natural condition of humanity is not, strictly speaking, a moral one at all. Moral consciousness develops as a consequence of human interaction, and Rousseau believed that this process will only be beneficial if freedom and equality are transformed into moral attributes. This necessitates a political structure that embodies genuine interdependence, not the radically amoral independence of the natural condition, or the slavish, harmful dependence that reaches its nadir in a grossly inegalitarian and exploitative social condition presided over by a cruel and self-interested despot (see p. 85).

The key features of this state are outlined in Rousseau's *Social Contract*. In this work he argued that the benefits of sociability can only be realised if political power is directed by a 'general will' that reflects the common interests of the community, not 'particular' or private interests. This stipulation mirrors the position taken by earlier natural law thinkers. However, by portraying the state as an institution that makes possible a form of moral existence that is qualitatively different from that possible in other circumstances, Rousseau made it clear that citizenship transforms both human beings and their natural rights. The

> passage from the state of nature to the civil state produces quite a remarkable change in man, for it substitutes justice for instinct in his behaviour and gives his actions a moral quality they previously lacked (Rousseau, 1987, p. 150).

This conception of moral community pointed forward to the theories of both Hegel and Marx, but other eighteenth-century writers produced more conventional statements of the radical implications of natural law and/or natural rights. The *philosophe* Denis Diderot followed Pufendorf in identifying the law of nature with the requirements of sociability (Diderot, 1992, pp. 19–20). Other thinkers of the period developed theories that echoed aspects of Locke's political theory. Thomas Jefferson's 'Declaration of Independence' of 1775–6 appealed to 'inalienable rights' to 'life, liberty and the pursuit of happiness', while at an earlier stage in the contest between Britain and her North American colonies James Otis, in *The Rights of the British Colonies Asserted and Proved* (1764), argued that the law-making powers of the British parliament were conditioned by a higher authority, variously described as 'the laws of nature and of nations, the voice of universal reason, and of God' (Sigmund, 1971, p. 112). However, the most politically far-reaching statements of the radical implications of natural right were produced during the period of European revolutions that began with the collapse of the *ancien régime* in France in 1789.

The 'Declaration of the Rights of Man and Citizens', issued by the French National Assembly in 1789, placed natural rights at the centre of the new system of government. The preamble to this document stated that 'ignorance, neglect, or contempt of human rights, are the sole causes of public misfortunes and corruptions of Government', while its second clause stipulated that 'the end of all political associations, is the preservation of the natural and imprescriptible rights of man; and these rights are liberty, property, security, and resistance to oppression' (Ritchie, 1902, p. 291). This 'Declaration' was prefixed to the French Constitution of 1791. Some writers saw this document as a significant but incomplete embodiment of the political implications of natural rights. For example, in his *Sketch for a Historical Picture of the Progress of the Human Mind* (1793) Antoine-Nicolas De Condorcet looked to future developments to produce a social and political structure that took full account of the expansive possibilities opened up by the recognition of universal human rights. For Condorcet, rights were related to the realisation of the potentialities of all human beings, and he thought this required universal suffrage, full equality between the sexes, the self-determination of colonial societies, freedom of thought and expression, and the assumption of social responsibility for education, welfare insurance and a measure of wealth redistribution (Condorcet, 1955, pp. 171–202).

Condorcet's theory involved a radical application of natural rights doctrine, but even its less far-reaching utilisation by other French and English supporters of the Revolution came in for sharp criticism from its opponents. As we have seen, both Edmund Burke and Joseph de Maistre rejected natural rights theory and argued for natural subordination within a community; rights are derived from historical development and recognised in positive law and customary practice. Far from discouraging appeals to natural rights, however, these conservative responses to the revolution provoked an outburst of radical literature presenting trenchant critiques of the prevailing structure and practice of government in European states. One of the most widely circulated of these arguments appeared in Thomas Paine's *Rights of Man*.

Paine rejected Burke's appeal to historical precedent on the grounds that it was partial and conceptually vacuous – 'The fact is, that portions of antiquity, by proving everything, establish nothing' (Paine, 1976, p. 87) – but he replaced it with a more thoroughgoing regress that took the argument back to the creation. Paine utilised a radical interpretation of biblical history to argue that the creation provided an egalitarian and libertarian model that had binding implications for the regulation of human affairs: 'Every history of the creation, and every traditionary account ... all agree in establishing one point, *the unity of man*; by which I mean, that all men are all of *one degree*, and consequently that all men are born equal, and with equal natural right.' This equality was enjoyed by succeeding generations as well as by the original human inhabitants of the world: 'every child born into the world must be considered as deriving its existence from God. The world is as new to him as it was to the first man that existed, and his natural right in it is of the same kind' (ibid., p. 88). Paine thus identified a direct relationship between each individual and God, and he used this as a basis upon which to claim that all human beings possess inviolable natural rights of an identical kind.

These rights – to intellectual and religious liberty, to pursue one's 'comfort and happiness' in any way that is 'not injurious to the natural rights of others', and to judge and to punish those who breach this condition – 'appertain to man in right of his existence'. They provide what Paine called the 'foundation' of 'civil rights', those rights 'which pertain to man in right of his being a member of society' (ibid., p. 90). When people enter political society they do so in order to exercise their natural rights more effectively. For Paine, as for Locke, problems of jurisdiction and enforcement provided the motivation for creating political authority. As in Locke's theory, the exchange of natural for civil rights created a moral continuity between the natural and political condition:

> The natural rights which are not retained, are all those in which, though the right is perfect in the individual, the power to execute them is defective. They answer not to his purpose. A man, by natural right, has a right to judge in his own cause; and so far as the right of mind is concerned, he never surrenders it: but what availeth it him to judge, if he has not power to redress? He therefore deposits this right in the common stock of society, and takes the arm of society, of which he is a part, in preference and in addition to his own. Society *grants* him nothing. Every man is a proprietor in society, and draws on the capital as a matter of right (ibid., pp. 90–1).

Because no one has a right to subject other human beings to their authority, government must be based on the consent of those who wish to place *some* of their natural rights in a collective agency. Paine insisted that individuals must retain full control over their religious and intellectual rights ('rights of mind') because they can be exercised perfectly well without the assistance of government. These and other retained rights are beyond the control of government and any attempt to interfere with them is illegitimate. In addition to these historically significant limitations on the exercise of political power, Paine's conception of natural rights had other important implications for the way in which rulers should behave. Like Locke's predecessors, Paine employed the idea of 'interpretative charity' to eliminate the possibility of a total surrender of rights to an absolute sovereign: 'Man did not enter into society to become *worse* than he was before, nor to have fewer rights than he had before, but to have those rights better secured' (ibid., p. 90). This stipulation explains why Paine thought that people should not give up their right to religious and intellectual freedom; it also underwrote his claim that as many tasks as possible should be left to voluntary social cooperation (see p. 81).

The idea of interpretative charity plays a particularly important role in Paine's critique of monarchical and aristocratic government. Paine thought that free individuals will never voluntarily place themselves under monarchy because they will then be worse off than they were in a state of nature. Monarchs lack information and expertise – they are selected on the basis of irrational, hereditary processes – and they have no sympathy with the interests of their subjects. In contrast 'new' governments – by which Paine meant representative democracy – are closely attached to the true feelings of the community and utilise its talents. If office holders represent the interests of their constituents and are selected on the basis of proven ability and probity, there will be a close fit between the interests and intelligence of society and the attributes and motivation of office holders. Under these conditions the exercise of political power will really contribute to the good of all the members of the community and will thus ensure that the purpose of civil society – to facilitate individuals' pursuit of their 'comfort and happiness' in accordance with the purposes underlying their endowment with natural rights – will be fulfilled.

Paine's critical deployment of natural rights theory was only one of a number of radical defences of the French Revolution that appealed to this line of argument. In the hands of Paine's contemporary, Mary Wollstonecraft, natural rights provided the basis for a critique of women's servile position in contemporary social and political culture, an argument that involved implicit rejection of Paine's endorsement of the biblical warrant for female subjection (ibid., p. 89). In her *Vindication of the Rights of Men* (1790) Wollstonecraft pointed to the divergence between the structure and practice of British government and what she referred to as the 'rights of humanity' (Wollstonecraft, 1790, p. 2). Two years later, in the *Vindication of the Rights of Women*, she related contemporary claims about the moral and intellectual weakness of women to the inferior yet covertly powerful position in which they were placed. Lacking formal rights, their influence was exerted through corrupt and debasing means that were more appropriate to the mores of a harem than to those of a free and supposedly civilised society. Consequently Wollstonecraft argued for the universal benefits that would result from acknowledging women's claims to a full range of social and political rights: 'let women share the rights, and she will emulate the virtues of man' (Wollstonecraft, 1983, p. 319).

Another of Paine's contemporaries, John Thelwell, developed a sophisticated argument about the relationship between natural and civil rights. In making his case, Thelwell implicitly acknowledged the force of Burke's observation that the development of human society had cast doubts on claims based on a natural condition, but he argued against the implications that Burke derived from this. Thelwell allowed that in the course of social development it had become necessary to abandon the equal natural right to the earth's fruits that had guaranteed the preservation of individuals in the state of nature. However, while recognition of private property rights had contributed to human progression by encouraging the efficient utilisation of material goods, Thelwell argued that this benefit had transformed individuals' natural claims rather than obliterating them. In societies where equal property rights were no longer appropriate, the purpose underlying these rights should be realised by redistributive measures that would ensure that the loss of the natural right in question did not leave ordinary members of the community worse off than they would have been if economic and political development had not taken place (Hampsher-Monk, 1991).

Among radical democrats and socialists, appeals to natural rights continued to be used until well into the nineteenth century (Claeys, 1989), but this period also saw a growing hostility to this way of thinking. As we have seen, a number of conservative thinkers rejected the individualistic focus of revolutionary appeals to natural rights. They argued in favour of the restoration of ideas of historical community on the grounds that they matched the facts of human development and provided the framework for psychologically satisfying and stable social and political systems. Burke and Coleridge in England, and Maistre and Romantic writers in both France and Germany traced the traumas of the revolutionary era to the prevalence of natural right theories in eighteenth-century Europe, arguing that their original deployment by proponents of absolutism had paved the way for the radical applications that had wrought such havoc at the close of the century. However, among other radical thinkers it was not the individualistic cast of natural rights theories that was at issue, but rather their detrimental impact upon favoured programmes of political reform.

A rhetorically powerful example of this approach was presented by the utilitarian writer Jeremy Bentham in his essay 'Anarchical Fallacies' (1824). Bentham claimed that rights are a product of government and that there can be no rights in a natural condition. He dismissed the contrary view as

> mischievous nonsense: immediately a list of these pretended rights is given, and those are so expressed as to present to view legal rights. And of these rights, whatever they are, there is not it seems, any one of which any government *can*, upon any occasion whatever, abrogate the smallest particle (Bentham, 1843a, vol. ii).

Bentham argued that rights should only be recognised in what is 'advantageous to society', a term that refers to the principle of utility. Natural rights are dangerous fictions: they do not conform to the criterion of utility, and they impose inappropriate constraints on the exercise of political power. Claims to natural rights are thus on a par with those malign verbal obstupefications that comprised the Common Law of England, and of which, on some accounts, they formed a part. Neither respect for the

Common Law nor the recognition of natural rights provided appropriate guidance for reforming rulers. Bentham believed that the possession and exercise of political power should be used to foster the 'greatest happiness of the greatest number' (see pp. 112ff).

Bentham and his followers were not the only non-conservative critics of natural law and natural rights. These ideas were rejected by the anarchist William Godwin in the 1790s, and were thought to be incompatible with the social conception of freedom developed by a number of nineteenth-century thinkers. For example the British idealists argued that rights are a product of social recognition that owe their binding force to their embodiment in law. Rights can be said to be 'natural' to the extent that they contribute to the perfection of humanity by advancing the common good, not because they derive from an original, presocial condition (Green, 1986, pp. 16–17). Similarly, although Marx regarded communism as the true and complete fulfilment of human social nature, this condition is, as we have seen, apolitical. As the requirements of nature necessitate the eclipse of politics, they can hardly be said to throw any light on the exercise of political power (see p. 47). Bentham's, Green's and Marx's reaction against natural rights theory was part of a more general tendency for this way of thinking about politics to be pushed to the margins of nineteenth- and early-twentieth-century political thought. As we shall see, however, natural rights theory has enjoyed something of a revival in recent years (see p. 375).

Conclusion

Theories of natural law and natural rights identify normative constraints upon the exercise of political power. Actions that fail to satisfy the requirements of natural law, or encroach upon natural rights, frustrate the purposes for which government exists and are therefore illegitimate. Natural law was used by Aquinas to identify the features of good government. It provides an objective standard that is beyond the control of rulers, and is related to the pursuit of fundamental values. Natural law is framed in general terms that leave rulers free to construct systems of human law that address the particular situation for which they are responsible, but they are under an unavoidable obligation to act in the interests of their subjects.

Although natural law theories frequently involve a 'passive' conception of rights (see p. 202), they give rise to a more positive conception of government than those that rest upon ideas of natural right. In many formulations, natural rights doctrines are strongly defensive. That is, they specify individual claims to free action and they prohibit exercises of political power that infringe natural rights. These features of natural rights theory are reflected in Locke's condemnation of arbitrary government, and in Paine's rejection of hereditary monarchy and aristocracy. However, even where natural rights play an important defensive role they may give rise to positive political outcomes. Thus while Paine insisted that legitimate forms of government must take account of individuals' natural rights, he also argued that these rights can only be adequately defended in systems of popular, representative government.

CHAPTER 9

Mixed Government, Balanced Constitutions and the Separation of Powers

This chapter will examine a number of theories that seek to regulate the exercise of power by constitutional arrangements that ensure those occupying important political offices are constrained from acting wrongly and are encouraged to act rightly. The theorists discussed here almost invariably assume that assigning exclusive power to particular individuals, groups or classes carries with it the risk of tyranny, or the use of power for the benefit of those who hold it rather than in the interests of the community. This concern forms an important part of a range of theories containing very different specifications of the ends of politics and the location of power. However, to the concern about avoiding bad government is often added the problem of how government may be made a more effective force for the realisation of fundamental goals. In other words, mixed government, balanced constitutions and the separation of powers are seen as ways of making the exercise of political power more effective, as well as avoiding its abuse.

The means chosen tend to be *institutional* rather than *normative*. That is, they focus primarily on arranging the mechanisms of government in a particular way, rather than identifying and promoting certain standards of political behaviour. However, this point must not be pushed too far. As we shall see, it is common for theorists of mixed government, balanced constitutions and the separation of powers to connect these institutional arrangements to particular value systems that help make them effective means of regulating the exercise of power.

Although these forms of institutional restraint are frequently combined, it is important to distinguish one from the other because they are sometimes offered as alternatives. In any case, ideas of mixed government, balanced constitutions and the separation of powers entail differing approaches to the exercise of political power. Mixed governments utilise the conventional distinction between rule by the one, the few and the many, placing particular weight on the risk attendant on any of these pure forms of government. It is argued that systems of rule that assign specific, complementary roles and powers to institutions and/or offices that embody monarchical, aristocratic and democratic principles provide a way of maximising the benefits of these pure forms of government while avoiding the danger of tyranny or anarchy. Very often these offices are reserved for the members of different social groups or classes, and are portrayed as appropriate vehicles for utilising the virtues of the one, the few and the many. It is sometimes said that these arrangements involve a 'sharing' of power (Fritz, 1954, p. 84), but it is perhaps more accurate to say that supreme power is created *through* the interaction of the various elements that participate in government. It is produced by the system rather than being located in, or shared by, its constituent elements.

An important feature of mixed government is that the various elements check the use of power by the others in order to produce a balance between the elements charged with performing different functions. Most commonly, legislative (or law-making) functions are performed by the democratic and aristocratic elements, the latter being given a distinctive leadership role in this process; executive (or rule-implementing and governing) functions are reserved for the monarchical element. Taken together, this division of functions gives rise to a balance of power that produces stability in the conduct of government and counterbalances tendencies towards tyranny, self-interested high-handedness or self-interested lawlessness, which lurk beneath the surface of rule by the one, the few and the many, respectively. For these reasons, the idea of mixed government seems inseparable from that of a balanced constitution.

However, systems of checks and balances may also be organised in a way that only indirectly involves ideas that are central to theories of mixed government. The key idea in these systems is the separation of functionally distinct powers (typically of an executive, legislative and judicial kind) so as to ensure that the coercive influence of government can only be brought to bear if these powers act in concert. This arrangement requires neither a mixture of principles nor a mixture of social forces or classes. Consequently, separation of powers may be instituted in a democratic republic such as the United States. In other words, mixed government is an alternative to democracy, while separation of powers may be a feature of a democratic polity.

Finally, it is useful to distinguish between mixed constitutions and those that rely on separation of powers on the one hand, and on the other hand what some ancient philosophers called 'moderate' constitutions, or governments of the 'middle-way'. The latter form of government may be combined with a mixed constitution and/or separation of powers, but it differs from them. Rather than seeking to mix pure elements or to separate functions, moderate government forges a compromise between pure forms of government. Significantly, this compromise does not rely on the interaction of elements or classes. It identifies a middle ground between them, one that may incorporate or acknowledge some democratic, oligarchic or monarchical features but does not derive these from interaction of the one, the few and the many. A particular class is held to embody the virtues of other sections of the population while being free of their vices. A constitution of the 'middle-way' is one in which this class plays a predominant role; it produces moderate government and thus avoids the extremism of pure forms of rule.

The discussion that follows focuses on a number of accounts of these ways of regulating the exercise of power. We shall look first at their treatment by philosophers in ancient Greece and Rome, and will then examine the ways in which these ideas were adapted by early modern writers. The chapter will conclude with a consideration of mixed government and the separation of powers in revolutionary and post-revolutionary America and France.

Mixed Government in Ancient Political Theory: Plato, Aristotle, Polybius and Cicero

Plato's *Republic* presents an argument for the most pure of pure governments. Subsequently, however, Plato acknowledged that the difficulties involved in establishing and maintaining a regime of this kind make it necessary to identify a good, but less than perfect, state in which no single class or individual will be endowed with absolute authority. This argument, put forward in *The Laws*, takes account of the dangers of locating supreme power in the hands of those who do not meet the rigorous standards required of true guardians. His treatment of this issue reflects an awareness of the tendency for power to corrupt the character of those who possess it and to give rise to various forms of tyrannical rule.

In *The Laws* Plato proposed two strategies for eliminating this danger. First, the constitution of Plato's 'practical utopia', 'Magnesia', limits the scope for human corruption by making the laws themselves, rather than office holders, supreme (see pp. 276–7). Magnesia is provided with a complete and elaborate system of 'constitutional' laws defining a range of offices and courts, and regulating the conduct of those who exercise political and judicial authority. These laws provide a fixed framework that promotes good government and prevents the abuse of political power by office holders. The sanctity of the law is reinforced by the symbolism adopted by the new state and is ensured by the 'guardians of the laws', whose primary task is to uphold the law and ensure strict adherence to. These guardians are elected by the population at large, but Plato insisted that the electorate must be divided into four classes based on property holding. The purpose of this arrangement is to allow all to vote, but to give greater weight to the more educated; it therefore conforms to what Plato described as a true understanding of 'equality': 'much' is granted to 'the great' and 'less to the less great' (Plato, 1980, p. 230). It also supports Plato's second strategy, that is, the production of a constitution that is 'a compromise between' monarchy and democracy, one that combines a system of mixed government with devices associated with a 'moderating' approach to the exercise of political power.

In addition to the moderating effect of the electoral system, aspects of mixed government are incorporated into a complex range of other political and judicial offices that have distinctive functions and are filled by different classes and age cohorts. These arrangements produce a mixture of elements and establish processes for checking and balancing particular exercises of power. For the most part, the constitution of Magnesia combines democratic and aristocratic/oligarchic elements, but an important institution, the 'nocturnal council', adds an element of Platonic kingship. This council (so named because it meets before dawn) is made up of priests of high distinction, the ten senior guardians of the laws and the current minister of education. Each of these people are attended by a protegé aged between thirty and forty who undertakes research for the council. The research role of the protegés is important because the nocturnal council is charged with a range of legal, philosophical and didactic functions. It evaluates the soundness of the laws, drawing where necessary on external experiences, suggests amendments to them, and inculcates an understanding of the moral basis of the state among the general population (ibid., pp 502, 512ff). It should be noted that except for the influence exerted by members of the council in their other offices, its role is not, strictly speaking, a governing one: it cannot *change* the laws (this power is reserved for the guardians of the law), nor does it wield executive or judicial power. The nocturnal council provides a monarchical element in the constitution that reflects a functionally restricted version of the guardians or philosopher king of Plato's *Republic*.

Like Plato, Aristotle regarded mixed government as a practical rather than an ideal option. However, if one takes account of his recognition that many states have mixed populations, and his belief that there is something to be said for the claims of the one, the few and the many, there is a sense in which mixed government is not only prudent but just. It is prudent because it avoids the resentment of those excluded from the exercise of power under pure forms of government, and it may be just because it acknowledges the distinctive, but not overriding, merits of various sections of the population and their capacity to contribute to the state.

These considerations have an impact on Aristotle's understanding of how the exercise of power can be regulated effectively. Given the existence of a mixed population, and given also the impracticability of pure forms of government, a properly constructed mixed constitution, or one that ensures moderate rule, will enhance the prospect of good government by curbing the dangers that accompany pure forms of government. It will also harness the beneficial qualities of various elements within society, and thereby minimise the resentment felt by those who believe they have been excluded from political office unjustly.

Aristotle referred to this form of government as 'polity'. Having been used originally to identify a constitution in which the many rightly hold power and exercise it for the common good, 'polity' was subsequently seen either as a form of government that mixes elements of democracy with oligarchy (tinged with aristocracy), or as one whose social composition gives it a moderate cast. Aristotle's version of mixed government adopts various mechanisms that recognise the legitimate but not exclusive claims of the many who are poor and the few who are wealthy. Since the many have some capacity to discern whether power is being exercised properly, they can judge the performance of office holders at the end of their terms and also identify those who seem most likely to govern impartially. These arrangements are premised on a distinction between being qualified as an elector, and being qualified for office. The many elect, but they choose from among members of the population whose wealth and education endows them with the attributes required of office holders (Aristotle, 1958, pp. 123–7). In addition, however, Aristotle also discussed a variety of electoral practices that produce mixed government by ensuring that the poor have a chance to occupy some offices, while other offices are restricted to members of the upper classes. The first of these outcomes can be realised through a 'lot' system, or random selection; the second is produced by election through a ballot. Unlike selection by lot, election through ballot (whether open or secret) allows for merit to be taken into account; it also permits the direct or indirect influence of social factors such as deference to play a role. Similar results can be achieved by attaching a property qualification to some offices, but not to others (ibid., pp. 174–8).

These arrangements produce a form of rule that mixes elements of democracy with those of oligarchy. They may thus satisfy the requirements of distributive justice. This is a good thing in itself, and since power is held justly it may also facilitate its proper exercise. Mixed government prevents one dominant class from abusing its position because it must rely to some extent on the approval of other classes. It also makes good government more likely because it capitalises on the imperfect but valuable merits of the wealthy few and the numerous poor.

Finally, Aristotle suggested that the regulatory effects of mixed government may be enhanced if they are built upon a social structure dominated by the middle orders of society. It should be noted, however, that this 'moderate' form of government seems to be an alternative to conventional forms of mixed government. The fact that such a class is relatively large means that the numerical preponderance of the poor will be reduced, in which case any mixing that does occur involves *principles* rather than elements (ibid., pp. 179–84). One effect of this arrangement is that Aristotle's treatment of 'polity' involves an important shift in focus: its superiority depends on the distinctive attributes of the middle class, not on the superiority of a mixed constitution over other, pure, forms (Mulgan, 1977, p. 106). However, a mixture of principles may be an important addition to this system because it gives some recognition to the claims of other classes and thus avoids the reactive dangers that result from the exclusive possession of power by one class.

Aristotle argued that a large middle class will have a moderating effect on the exercise of political power because of the distinctive attributes of this group. Lacking both the arrogance of the rich and the combination of fecklessness and desperation among the poor, the middle class are more likely to act reasonably than either the rich or the poor. Moreover, since they are comfortably off they are neither obsessed by wealth nor consumed by a greedy desire for power, nor are they forced by hardship and encouraged by envy to see political power as a means of material salvation. Consequently they will not seek to use their political position to enrich themselves at the expense of the public. This attitude towards wealth corresponds to some degree with Aristotle's belief that the virtuous regard property merely as an instrument to the good life, and to his condemnation of great wealth and a high regard for it as unnatural.

In addition to capitalising on the political implications of the middle classes' attitude towards wealth, Aristotle argued that their social position and outlook reenforce their moderating influence on the exercise of political power. The rich, being used to getting their own way, tend to rule despotically, while the poor are habituated to servitude. Both these classes are thus ill-fitted to share rule and being ruled. When the rich have exclusive control of the state it takes on the appearance of a master–slave relationship, interrupted from time to time by outbursts of lawless rebellion by the poor. Such a state is not an association that exists for the good of all its members, and since the rich and the poor are so antagonistic towards one another, there can be no friendship between them. A state dominated by the middle class will exhibit markedly different characteristics. Members of this class are self-assured without being arrogant, and being part of a similarly disposed group, they can form relationships of friendship and are willing to share in rule and being ruled. Moreover the middle class acts as a buffer between the rich and the poor, preventing each group from despoiling and oppressing the other. This class thus forms the basis of a government that, because it acts properly, is able to win the support of most of the population and avoid the instability and injustice that invariably accompanies revolutions. Aristotle thought that turmoils are a consequence of the illegitimate exercise of political power. This danger can be avoided if those who have a disposition and an incentive to rule justly play a central role in the state.

Aristotle's belief that both mixed and moderate constitutions provide a means of preventing bad government and promoting beneficial exercises of political power was shared by the later Greek thinker, Polybius (*c.* 200–118 BC). Polybius was primarily a historian, and rather than analysing the general benefits of mixed government, he sought to use this idea to explain the longevity and success of the Roman Republic. Writing under the shadow of the Roman conquest of Greece in the early part of the second century BC, Polybius sought initially to explain to his compatriots why the Romans had succeeded in gaining control of the Mediterranean region. However, as his work progressed he also offered assurance to the Romans themselves about the prospects and requirements of their continued preeminence.

Polybius (c. 200–118 BC)

Born in Arcadia in Western Greece Polybius played a prominent role in the Achaean League prior to the absorbtion of the Greek city-states by Rome. At the conclusion of the Third Macedonian War in 167, Polybius was among the thousand hostages sent to Italy. During a long period of exile he became closely associated with the politician and general Scipio Africanus. He later acted as an intermediary between the Romans and the Achaean League and took an administrative role when the League was finally dissolved in 144 BC. His most important work was an extensive history of the Roman Republic.

Polybius ascribed the success of the Roman Republic to its system of mixed government. Unlike pure constitutions, which undergo a natural process of growth and decay – from military despotism through kingship, tyranny, aristocracy, oligarchy, democracy and mob rule, ending in despotism (Polybius, 1979, pp. 307–9) – mixed government is able to combine 'all the virtues and distinctive features of the best government, so that no one principle should become preponderant, and thus be perverted into its kindred vices'. It ensures that the 'power of each element should be counterbalanced by the others, so that no one of them inclines or sinks unduly to the other side. In other words, the constitution ... remain[s] for a long time in a state of equilibrium thanks to the principle of reciprocity or counteraction' (ibid., pp. 310–11). This arrangement had been achieved by Lycurgus when he established the Spartan constitution, but it was adopted by the Romans only after a long series of experiments and difficulties.

In Polybius' analysis the constitution of the Roman Republic combines monarchical, aristocratic and democratic elements. The consuls, the senate and the people (both through the tribunes and in the assembly) exercise a considerable but incomplete range of powers. The constitution thus rests on the interdependence of elements that check the pursuit of sectional interests to produce a form of government in which the exercise of political power is directed towards the good of the state (ibid., pp. 313–16). In addition to showing that this system avoided the misuse of power, Polybius also emphasised its effectiveness. The key point in this respect is the capacity to capitalise on the positive virtues of each of the pure forms of government. In Rome, the monarchical, aristocratic and popular elements not only exercised a jealous watch over one another, but they also demonstrated their particular commitment to the good of the state, especially in times of crisis:

> whenever some common external threat compels the three [elements] to unite and work together, the strength which the state then develops becomes quite extraordinary. No requirement is neglected, because all parties vie with one another to find ways of meeting the needs of the hour, and every decision taken is certain to be executed promptly, since all are cooperating in public and in private alike to carry through the business in hand (ibid., p. 317).

The mixed constitution of the Republic thus provided a check on the abuse of power, and also stimulated a sense of corporate spirit that built upon competitive, sectional pride and was regulated by religious and social customs that made honesty a cardinal virtue. In these circumstances, a 'spirit of emulation and the ambition to perform deeds of gallantry' actively promoted the public good. In so doing it endowed Rome with the commitment and power that allowed it to maintain its territorial integrity and establish control over states that were far more extensive and populous (ibid., pp. 348–9; Fritz, 1954, pp. 84–5).

Polybius' treatment of the virtues of the mixed constitution of the Roman Republic focused on elements embodying the principles of monarchy, aristocracy and democracy rather than social classes or forces.

However, his familiarity with conventional Greek modes of constitutional classification, together with his detailed knowledge of Roman history and politics, meant that his account implicitly assumed a link between elements and classes. In Rome the consuls and the senate (drawn from the upper echelons of society) had responsibilities that corresponded to ideas of kingship and aristocracy. Similarly 'the people', the democratic element in the constitution, comprised those who Aristotle had described as 'the many who are poor'.

The connection between ancient conceptions of constitutional elements and classes is a marked feature of the writings of Polybius' Roman successor, Cicero. While Polybius was a well-informed and well-connected outsider in Roman politics, Cicero was a member of the lower division of the senatorial class and served a term as consul. His defence of mixed government focused on what he took to be the ideal state that had existed in Rome before the slide into anarchy and military despotism that began with the Gracchi's assault on the landholdings of the aristocracy in 133 BC.

In his *Republic*, Cicero employed a musical analogy to describe a properly constituted state, that is, one in which the exercise of political power was directed towards the common good:

> as ... perfect agreement and harmony is produced by the proportionate blending of unlike tones, so also is a State made harmonious by agreement among dissimilar elements, brought about by a fair and reasonable blending together of the upper, middle, and lower classes, just as if they were musical tones (Cicero, 1970, p. 183).

Although Cicero actually discussed the mixed constitution in relation to its beneficial effect on the relationship between 'the people' and the upper classes, this analogy is useful because it draws attention to the 'proportionate', 'fair and reasonable' blending of dissimilar elements. Cicero's formulation reflects his belief that if a mixed constitution is to ensure good government, it must take account of the differing weights to be ascribed to different elements, and not merely, as in Polybius' account, of the need to assign different functions to the elements. Cicero argued that the balance achieved by the Roman constitution in its heyday was a consequence of the prominent role ascribed to the senate, and hence also to the upper classes from which its members were drawn. The constitution of Republican Rome established an 'even balance of rights, duties and functions, so that the magistrates have enough power, the counsels of the eminent citizens enough influence, and the people enough liberty' (ibid., p. 169). Under this system

> the government was so administered by the senate that, though the people were free, few political acts were performed by them, practically

everything being done by the authority of the senate and in accordance with its established customs, and that the consuls held a power which, though one of one year's duration, was truly regal in general character and in legal sanction (ibid., p. 167).

While the people were said to possess sovereign power (*potestas*) in the sense that government existed for the common benefit and was sanctioned by the entire population, authority (*auctoritas*), the influence that determined how this was to be exercised, resided with the upper classes: 'liberty has been granted in such a manner that the people were induced by many excellent provisions to yield to the authority of the nobles' (ibid., p. 487).

In the ideal state outlined in Cicero's *Laws*, these 'excellent provisions' reserve the most important offices for those who have been born into, or are acceptable to, the nobility. They also include a system of election that accords great influence to members of the aristocracy. The people vote by a secret ballot (rather than by voice or a show of hands) as a 'safeguard to their liberty', but they are not prohibited, as they were by a number of recent laws, from showing their ballots to members of the upper class if they wish: 'these ballots are to be shown and voluntarily exhibited to any of our best and most eminent citizens, so that the people may enjoy liberty also in this very privilege of honourably winning the favour of the aristocracy' (ibid., p. 505). The last part of this quotation is particularly important because it conveys Cicero's belief that the effectiveness of a mixed constitution depends not only on its formal stipulations, but also on its impact on the informal relationship between the people and the aristocracy. If voters are permitted to show their ballots to members of the nobility, this will foster deferential relationships – based on voluntary submission to the guidance offered by those one respects – between the most important classes in the state.

Given the risk of corruption that is posed by a pure aristocracy and the risks involved in excluding the people from any role in regulating the partnership of which they form a part, a mixed constitution with a strong aristocratic bias not only satisfies the requirements of proportionate justice, but is also relatively stable and conducive to good government. Cicero's statement of this case is reinforced by his belief that the provisions of natural law are closely reflected in the historical practice of the Roman state, being embodied either in its laws or in the 'customs of our ancestors' (ibid., p. 399). Since the nobility contains a large hereditary element (derived from what the early Romans called 'fathers of the state') who are responsible for and knowledgeable about custom, it follows that a constitution that gives aristocrats a leading position will help ensure that political power is exercised through desirable means for appropriate ends. However, because even aristocrats may stray from the path of custom and virtue, it is necessary to integrate them with the people by their joint involvement in elections, and to subject them to the regulative influences of religion (Wood, 1988, p. 174). The very fact that the people have some political influence makes it necessary for the nobility to take their interests into account: deference implies voluntary submission and mutual benefit. Although Cicero considered that the rich have a larger stake in the state than the poor (Cicero, 1970, p. 151), his definition of the state as a partnership and the literal meaning of the word 'republic' (*res publica*, the public thing), mean that legitimate power must be directed to the interests of the entire community. In short, the mixed constitution is a means of ensuring that the exercise of political power conforms to the ends of the state.

Mixed Constitutions in Early Modern Political Theory: Marsilius, Guicciardini, Machiavelli and Harrington

As we have seen, medieval conceptions of government were overwhelmingly monarchical. Even when attention was paid to various elements of government, these were usually treated in relation to a single supreme figure. Thus while Christine de Pizan identified three estates that make up the body politic – the prince and princes, knights and nobles, and the common people – and stressed their interdependence, her theory is not one of mixed government because the prince is the ruling element in the state. Princes rule, nobles play a protective and supporting role, and the common people sustain the whole body (Pizan, 1994, pp. 4, 63–4, 90). When mixed government was discussed by most medieval writers they did little more than reiterate the position taken by Greek and Roman theorists and incorporate this within a monarchical framework. Thus when Aquinas referred to Aristotle's classification of constitutions, he stressed the supremacy of the one, the virtuous conduct of the few who will hold office and the participation of the many:

> the best ordering of power within a kingdom is obtained when there is one virtuous head who commands over all; and who has under him those who govern virtuously; and when, furthermore, all participate in such government, both because all are ·eligible, and because all participate in the election of those who rule (Aquinas, 1959, p. 149).

Despite Aquinas' reference to Aristotle, however, this is not a mixed government in the classical sense. Rather it stipulates that princes should utilise the virtues of their subjects both in ruling and in identifying those fit for office under them.

An important exception to the pattern represented by Aquinas appeared in the writings of the late medieval philosopher Marsilius of Padua. Marsilius subscribed to the conventional medieval idea that the purpose of government is the common good and that this can best be ensured if power is exercised in such a way that it produces peace and unity in the state. However, unlike Aquinas, Marsilius thought that this form of rule is most likely in a popular republic that balances various functions. Although power lies with the people, it is exercised by councils or officials, but the discretion of these groups or individuals is constrained by a system of checks that allows the people to ensure that officeholders act in the common interest (Skinner, 1978, vol. i, p. 64). A very similar position was advanced by Marsilius' contemporary, Bartolus, and a significant and novel variation of it was produced by Juan de Segovia (1393–1458). In an argument that was originally formulated to support the final supremacy of councils of the Church over the pope, but which also applied to secular rulers, Segovia likened rulers to the heads of corporate bodies such as colleges. These figures act as the *agents* for their corporation and their power can be checked by its members if it is not exercised in ways that accord with their understanding of the common good (Black, 1993, pp. 177–8). In all these cases, the fact that those exercising power are dependent on the scrutiny of electors serves as a check upon them.

Such checks as these are aspects of a pure system of government and do not rest upon the claims about the virtues of mixed government that appeared in ancient political theory. These ideas were revived, however, among Marsilius' successors in the city states of Italy. An important feature of renaissance political thought was the tendency to use Venice as a model. Venice was of great interest to other Italians because its enjoyment of a long period of stability and prosperity contrasted markedly with the chequered experiences of many of its neighbours. Venice's success in avoiding the damaging effect of internal dissension was attributed to the fact that its constitution mixed monarchical, aristocratic and democratic elements in a way that exemplified the doctrine laid down by Plato in his *Laws*. The beneficial effects of this arrangement was assisted by an elaborate system of balloting, which minimised the risk that power would be utilised by factions (Skinner, 1978, vol. i, pp. 140–1). By eliminating internal strife the Venetians avoided the dehabilitating weaknesses that made states an easy prey for their better-directed and more united neighbours. For renaissance writers, the liberty of the state was the primary goal of politics, one that was likely to be undermined by factional disputes and by the direction of the powers of government by sectional interests. Good government required power to be exercised with a view to the common good, and the mixed constitution of Venice was held up as an admirable example of how this could be ensured.

In the fifteenth and sixteenth centuries the Venetian example was widely discussed in Florence, a strife-ridden city that had succumbed – with brief periods of respite from 1494–1512 and 1527–30 – to the princely domination of its most powerful family, the Medicis. Ironically, the time when the popular republic in Florence was most precarious was marked by an intense interest in republicanism. Understandably, much of the theorising on this subject focused on the question of how a republic could be constructed so as to allay the threats posed by external enemies and overmighty citizens.

Some writers urged the Florentines to inject a strong aristocratic element into their constitution. Thus Francesco Guicciardini (1438–1540) argued that the Republic of Florence was weakened by a polarisation of the monarchical element – the *gofaloniere*, who was elected for life – and the democratic element, which dominated the popularly elected *Consiglio Grande*. The creation of a senate drawn from the upper classes would provide a means of balancing these two elements: it would act as a 'moderating force between tyranny and popular licence' and it would provide a way of keeping the most able and best qualified citizens happy, because restricting government to such people would not only ensure that things were governed by those capable of it, but it would also satisfy those citizens whom it would be bad to alienate (Guicciardini, 1994, p. 114). Although Guicciardini took Venice as his model, the role he ascribed to the senate and his promotion of an essentially aristocratic or oligarchic constitution as a means of ensuring the legitimate exercise of power, echoed aspects of Cicero's account of the Roman Republic (Pocock, 1975, pp. 122–38).

The experience of the Roman Republic was put to a very different use by Machiavelli in his *Discourses*. In common with many of his contemporaries, Machiavelli identified good government and the proper exercise of political power with the preservation of internal and external liberty. However he thought that both aspects of liberty make it imperative that political rights are extended to the ordinary people and that they should exercise these rights vigorously (see p. 173). These requirements are set within the framework of a mixed rather than a pure constitution. In their prime, monarchy, aristocracy and democracy provide good government, but because they lack effective check and balance arrangements they invariably degenerate into tyranny, oligarchy or anarchy (Machiavelli, 1975, vol. i, pp. 212–14). Like Polybius, Machiavelli presented mixed government as a solution to this problem, one that will slow, if it cannot stop, the corruption that inevitably afflicts both the natural and the human worlds. In part, Machiavelli regarded a mixed constitution as a defensive device – 'if in one and the same state there was principality, aristocracy and democracy each would keep watch over the other' (ibid., p. 215) – but he also thought that it would produce positive benefits. An extensive democratic element provides the state with a powerful citizens' militia that enables it to defend itself and to expand.

Machiavelli discussed this point by comparing the restricted, static polities of ancient Sparta and contemporary Venice with the expansive republic of Rome. Rome's time of glory was short compared with the centuries of stability enjoyed by Sparta and Venice, but it is clear that Machiavelli regarded the former as more worthy of emulation than the latter. An expansionary republic provides scope for *virtú*, both in the commitment it requires of its citizens and because expansion is itself a form of *virtú*: it involves an attempt to bring aspects of a hostile environment under the control of a state and thus provides a way of contending with *fortuna*. For both these reasons, Machiavelli portrayed the expansionary republic as a glorious expression of active humanity (ibid., p. 226).

Unlike many other proponents of the mixed constitution, however, Machiavelli did not regard it as a way of ensuring internal tranquillity. On the contrary, he argued that the class conflict that marked the history of the Roman Republic had actually been beneficial: 'in every republic there are two different dispositions, that of the populace, and that of the upper class and ... all legislation favourable to liberty is brought about by the clash between them' (ibid., p. 218). This clash was productive because the populace had a distinct place in the political structure of the republic and were thus provided with an outlet for their collective energy. It also meant that they possessed a recognised bargaining tool that they could bring to bear if they thought that their interests were being ignored (ibid., p. 219). In sharp contrast to conventional accounts of the dangers of popular republics, Machiavelli did not regard 'the people' as a threat that has merely to be kept in check. To the contrary, the ordinary people are the true friends of liberty. They do not desire power (the aim of the rich), but freedom from oppression; they lack the sense of insecurity felt by those in a privileged but not impregnable position, and being poor they are less able to effect a rapid change even if they wish to (ibid., pp. 220–2). Unlike Cicero and other defenders of an aristocratic republic, Machiavelli regarded the rich as the most significant threat to the liberty of the state because of their own ambitions and their capacity to corrupt the poor. Aristocratic ambition either spurs the poor to seek vengeance for slights and oppression, or it encourages them to collaborate in the corruption of the state in order to win their share of the spoils of bad government (ibid., p. 222).

These dangers can be avoided if a strong and independent popular element is maintained in the constitution, one that counters the pretensions of the rich and prevents them from subverting government from its proper concern with the common good. Popular government is not incompatible with a degree of elite direction, but this must come from a natural aristocracy rather than one distinguished solely by birth or riches.

Since Machiavelli thought that the many are amenable to honest direction – although ignorant, the populace is 'capable of grasping the truth and readily yields when a man, worthy of confidence, lays the truth before it' (ibid., p. 219) – his position implies that prolonged mass discontent is a sign of elite corruption and/or ineptitude.

For Machiavelli, therefore, a mixed constitution ensures that political power is exercised for the good of the entire community; it is thus essential if a republic is to be preserved from corruption. Except in static and geographically secluded republics such as Venice, these goals can only be realised if the state has a strong and politically active popular basis. The people are not merely a threatening force that have to be bought off and controlled; to the contrary, they form an essential component of the state, one that possesses distinctive capacities that help ensure the proper exercise of power by those who hold office.

Guicciardini's admiration for the Venetian constitution was echoed by the English republican writer James Harrington in the mid-seventeenth century. In response to the collapse of monarchical government in England, Harrington argued for a return to the lessons of 'ancient prudence', that is, the approach to government exhibited in the uncorrupted form of the Roman Republic and surviving in the modern world in the constitution of Venice. Like his Italian predecessors, Harrington equated just government with the pursuit of the common good, and he stressed that this end could only be achieved by a system of rule that did not merely counteract self-interest, but channelled it in such a way that it would produce public benefit. Unless

> you can show such orders of government as, like those of God in nature, shall be able to constrain this or that creature to shake off that inclination which is more peculiar unto it and take up that which it regards the common good or interest, all this is to no more end than to persuade every man in a popular government not to carve himself of that which he desires most, but to be mannerly at the public table, and give the best from himself unto decency and the common interest (Harrington, 1992, p. 22).

'Decency' can only be ensured by a complex set of institutions that direct human action to the common good. Some of these institutions relate to what Harrington called the 'goods of fortune' or property, which he identified with 'power'. He argued that the state must be an 'equal commonwealth', by which he meant that property must be so dispersed among the population that its power is balanced, thus avoiding the class antagonism that afflicted the late Roman Republic. In particular there must be a balance of power between the few and the many, one that is maintained by a 'perpetual law establishing and preserving the balance of dominion, by such distribution that no one man or number of men within the compass of the few or aristocracy can come to overpower the whole people by their possession in lands' (ibid., p. 33).

In addition to preserving this socio-political balance, the state should also maintain a balanced arrangement of offices, or a balance of 'authority'. This quality is a 'good of the mind', a product of the 'heavenly treasures of virtue', as distinct from the 'earthly treasures of power' (ibid., p. 19). Given humans' tendency to favour their own interests, the practice of virtue depends on 'orders of government' or fixed constitutional laws, not upon the wills of individuals. A properly ordered government forms an 'empire of laws, not men' (ibid., p. 8). In Harrington's account these laws specify a complex system of balloting designed to purge electoral outcomes of self-interest. They also impose a rigid separation between three governing functions: the senate debates, the popular assembly 'determines' or decides, while the execution of laws rests with 'magistrates'. This arrangement is presented in terms of a mixed constitution: 'the commonwealth consisteth of the senate proposing, the people resolving, and the magistracy executing, whereby partaking of the aristocracy as in the senate, of the democracy as in the people, and of monarchy as in the magistracy' (ibid., p. 25). Harrington believed that Machiavelli had placed insufficient positive emphasis on the 'gentry' or nobility, but like his Italian predecessors he associated elite leadership with 'natural' rather than hereditary aristocracy: it forms a senate of *authority*, not *power* (ibid., pp. 23, 15, 36).

Harrington's understanding of the lessons of ancient prudence has a strongly mechanical cast (Davis, 1981). States that are not subject to the 'empire of laws' must necessarily fall under the 'empire of men', a form of government that is incompatible with the proper exercise of political power. They exhibit not ancient prudence, but its debased and unstable modern counterpart, 'an art whereby some man, or some few men, subject a city or a nation, and rule it according unto his or their private interest' (Harrington, 1992, p. 9).

Separation of Powers in Eighteenth-Century and Early-Nineteenth-Century Political Theory: Montesquieu, Madison, Sièyes and Constant

A significant (and overt) expression of dissent from Harrington's judgement of the Venetian republic appeared in Montesquieu's *The Spirit of the Laws*, which was published to great acclaim in 1748. In this work Montesquieu bemoaned the position of the 'poor subjects' of the Italian republics. In these states, the same body of magistrates are possessed, as executors of the laws, of the whole power they have given themselves in [their capacity] ... of legislators. They may plunder the state by their general determinations; and as they have likewise the judiciary power in their hands, every private subject may be ruined by their particular decisions (Montesquieu, 1949, vol. i, p. 152).

This criticism rests on Montesquieu's belief that good government is incompatible with a unified source of power within the state, however this power is constituted. His position thus marks a shift from concern with a mixed constitution towards the idea of separation of powers.

Charles-Louis de Secondat Montesquieu (1689–1755)

Having trained as a lawyer, Montesquieu served as a legal official in the royal administration in Bordeaux. He had wide scientific, literary and political interests and travelled throughout Europe. On a visit to England in 1729 he conducted a close study of English political institutions, some of the results of which appeared in his widely acclaimed *The Spirit of the Laws* (1748).

Montesquieu's primary concern is with 'political liberty', that is, the 'right of doing whatever the laws permit' (ibid., p. 150). Political liberty exists only when each subject enjoys a 'tranquillity of mind arising from the opinion each person has of his own safety'. Consequently, 'when the legislative and executive powers are united in the same person, or in the same body of magistrates, there can be no liberty; because apprehensions may arise, lest the same monarch or senate should enact tyrannical laws, to execute them in a tyrannical manner' (ibid., pp. 151–2). In addition to stressing the importance of subjects' sense of security, Montesquieu also built requirements relating to efficiency into his account of properly constructed and regulated government. For example he insisted that legislative bodies are incapable of effectively executing law and must be restricted to formulating it (ibid., p. 155).

These goals can only be attained if distinctive functions are reserved for different institutions; they also necessitate a mixed social order of the kind promoted by other thinkers discussed in this chapter. Montesquieu identified three types of governmental power: the legislative or law-making power, the executive power as it applies to defence and external relations, and the executive in its internal and penal capacities. In free countries, those in which 'every man who is supposed to be a free agent is his own governor', legislative power 'should reside with the whole people' and be embodied in a representative assembly chosen by those whose attachment to a particular locale ensures an accurate representation of geographical and sectional interests (ibid., p. 154). Since members of the nobility have distinct interests and are likely to suffer at the hands of popular assemblies, they should form a separate assembly that cannot promote legislation but may reject that proposed by the elected chamber (ibid., p. 163). As noted above, the legislative body is ill-equipped to carry out executive functions. In any case, if it attempts to do so it will contravene the principle that the abusive exercise of power can only be avoided by separating functions. Consequently the legislative arm of government must be restricted to formulating law, scrutinising the actions of the executive and raising taxes.

Separation of powers prevents the executive (lodged in the monarch) from formulating or determining legal enactments. However Montesquieu thought that the monarch should possess a veto:

> If the prince were to have a part in the legislature by the power of resolving, liberty would be lost. But as it is necessary he should have a share in the legislature for the support of his own prerogative, this share must consist in the power of rejecting (ibid., pp. 159–60).

This stipulation highlights an important feature of Montesquieu's understanding of the conditions attached to the exercise of political power. While he insisted on a separation of powers to avoid legislative–executive tyranny, his account points to what in England was called the 'coordination of power'. That is, an arrangement stipulating that one branch cannot act positively without the agreement or 'coordination' of another (Hampsher-Monk, 1992, p. 238).

Aspects of Montesquieu's approach were reflected in the arguments advanced by various contributors to the *Federalist Papers* and were incorporated into the structure of the new American republic (see p. 176). The fact that this government is republican in form means there is no room for either a hereditary head of state or a hereditary aristocracy: all legislators and officeholders are chosen through systems of selection and election which reflect the state's popular basis. However the assumption of popular sovereignty does not eliminate the threat of tyrannical misuses of power. To the contrary, *Federalist* writers argued that it is still possible for officeholders to oppress the people and/or for some of the people to oppress others. The first of these threats can be avoided by an effective system of representation, but the second requires the sort of regulation that Montesquieu proposed. Separation *via* coordination means that members of legislative bodies can neither hold executive offices nor nominate other, and also that, while the president lacks legislative power he should possess a qualified veto. Similarly, while it is necessary to separate legislative and judicial functions at the federal level and to ensure the judicial independence of the executive by appointing judges for life, these officials are nominated by the president and their appointments must be confirmed by the senate (Hamilton *et al.*, 1942, pp. 256–60, 263–7).

However, as in Montesquieu's account of mixed government and the separation of powers, the avoidance of tyranny must not be achieved at the cost of efficient government. In the American case, efficiency was to be fostered by introducing an element of 'natural' aristocracy into a republican framework. Madison justified the federal system on the ground that it would ensure a degree of filtration, which would promote the popular election of the 'best' (see p. 177). In addition, while the direct and frequent reelection of members of the House of Representatives would give proper weight to the preferences of the people, the indirect election of senators by state legislatures and the imposition of a higher age and a longer residency qualification was meant to ensure that this part of the legislative branch would contain representatives of the most able sections of the population. The fact that the Senate's term was longer than that of the House, would give a degree of stability to the legislative body and help ensure that it would contain people with an extensive fund of relevant experience.

The *Federalist*'s rationale for the constitutional structure of the new American republic reflected the importance these writers ascribed to imposing constraints on the exercise of power within the state. Good government requires the establishment of a system of institutions and offices that avoid tyranny yet allow the talents of the most able members of the population to be harnessed to popular government. In the absence of a formal monarchy or aristocracy, the form of government that emerges in the wake of the revolution could be described as 'unmixed'. At the same time, however, the complex interdependence of actors and institutions exercising separate aspects of functionally defined powers, and the infusion of social forces into the processes through which officials are chosen, replicate many of the features that characterise conventional accounts of mixed government.

In revolutionary France, the new constitution of 1791 reflected aspects of mixture and balance that Montesquieu had identified with the British constitution. As the revolution progressed, however, the logic of Sièyes' dictum that the 'third estate is everything' was confirmed by abolition of the monarchy and aristocracy and adoption of a republican scheme to regulate the exercise of power. Towards the end of the 1790s, revulsion against the unchecked power of popular assemblies provided the opportunity for Sièyes to produce a complex constitutional structure that echoed a number of features of Harrington's 'orders of government'.

However, the role ascribed to the 'first consul', and the fact that this position was occupied by Napoleon Bonaparte (who possessed an independent power base in the army) negated its effectiveness. The new constitution merely provided an elaborate screen for the real head of state, one that turned the representative chambers into his corrupt cyphers.

The Emperor Napoleon was forced into exile in 1814, but on his return to France the following year he agreed to adopt the role of a constitutional monarch. Shortly after the promulgation of a new constitution in April 1815, Benjamin Constant (who had had a hand in drafting this document) published a work entitled *Principles of Politics Applicable to All Representative Governments*. In addition to presenting an implicit endorsement of Bonaparte's new position, Constant's book provided a detailed general account of a form of constitutional rule that was required in states based upon the principles of individual liberty and the rule of law.

Benjamin Constant (1767–1830)

A native of Switzerland, Constant was educated in Bavaria and Edinburgh. After serving at the court of Brunswick, Constant settled in Paris in 1795. He was actively engaged in French politics and supported the return of Napoleon as a constitutional monarch. His various political writings were brought together in a collection of volumes that began to appear in 1820.

Constant denied that the potentially overbearing weight of government could be moderated by a division of powers alone because it was quite possible for the various elements to form a despotic coalition. Consequently, Constant argued that the limitation of power 'will be ensured firstly by the same force which legitimates all acknowledged truths: by public opinion. Subsequently, it will be guaranteed more precisely by the distribution and balance of powers' (Constant, 1988, p. 183). In common with other writers discussed in this chapter, Constant stressed that these constraints on the exercise of power would not restrict the legitimate effectiveness of government.

Unlike his immediate predecessors in France and America, Constant looked to a constitutional monarchy to achieve these ends. His system incorporates an aristocracy, but in deference to contemporary developments in European political culture, it also recognises the principle of popular sovereignty; it thus marks a partial return to traditional notions of mixed government. Monarchy is valuable because it provides what

Constant called a 'neutral' power, an elevated and impartial element that maintains a balance between the representative power of public opinion located in an elected assembly, the executive power entrusted to nominated ministers, and the judicial power vested in the court system (ibid., p. 185). The Crown is assigned distinct functions – the right to dissolve the assembly when it threatens liberty, the nomination of ministers, the distribution of honours – but it also provides the state with an important psychological and symbolic element:

> It is ... the masterpiece of political organization, to have created, amidst those dissensions, without which no liberty is possible, an inviolable sphere of security, majesty, impartiality, which leaves those dissensions to develop without danger, provided they do not exceed certain limits, and which, as soon as some danger becomes evident, terminates it by legal constitutional means, without any trace of arbitrariness (ibid., p. 187).

The checking role of the monarch in relation to the popular assembly is reinforced by a separate chamber of hereditary legislators, the peers. In addition to providing a 'counterbalance' to the democratic forces located in the popular assembly, a hereditary chamber supports the monarch and reduces the distance between him and his subjects. This last point is underlined by reference to the naturally despotic aura of simple single-person rule in recent French experience: 'the elements of the government of one man, without a hereditary class are: a single man who rules, soldiers who execute and a people that obeys' (ibid., p. 198). While supporting and softening monarchy, a hereditary chamber also plays an important quasi-judicial role in relation to the executive. The purely 'private' crimes of ministers – including those involving a clear violation of citizens' rights – should be dealt with through the court system, but their 'public' misdemeanours – dereliction of duty, disregard for due process, actions tending towards arbitrary rule – should be investigated by a special tribunal of peers. This stipulation rests on the belief that the issues at stake in these cases involve a trial between 'executive power' and the 'power of the people'. Consequently they have to be heard by those who are independent of each of these interests, but share a general connection with them both (ibid., p. 234). The peers are an element in public opinion and thus have an interest in liberty. They also support the integrity of the constitutional structure upon which their own position depends. Moreover their social position, upbringing and experience gives them a special insight into the interests of the state, one that will help them to make the fine judgements necessary to determine complex cases arising in a political environment where conduct is subject to a range of influences that cannot be adequately specified in fixed and relatively simple legal codes.

Given the delicacy of these cases and the need to avoid besmirching the office of a minister in the course of investigating the conduct of its present and temporary occupant, the peers' tact, and 'mildness of manner' are also of considerable importance.

Finally, in order to give due weight to the principle of popular sovereignty, to give direct expression to prevailing public opinion, to look after the particular interests of ordinary members of the population and to prevent any tendency to despotic collusion on the part of the other powers in the state, legislative proposals must be discussed and approved by a popular, elected assembly. Electors must satisfy a modest property qualification and candidates also have to meet an age qualification. These conditions will ensure that electors possess 'the leisure indispensable for the acquisition of understanding and soundness of judgement', and that those elected by them include among their interests a 'love of order, justice and conservation' (ibid., pp. 214, 215).

Conclusion

Constant treated mixed government in relation to monarchical political systems. This application of the idea can be contrasted with the way that the doctrine was applied in the ancient world. Ancient political theory focused on the need to identify certain offices or institutions with monarchical, aristocratic and democratic qualities. These qualities were attached to the office or institution, not to membership of either hereditary or non-hereditary classes. In these theories, monarchy, aristocracy and democracy are primarily elements within the constitution.

Because mixed government has often been related to the requirements of hereditary monarchy, it has become irrelevant as Western states have either abandoned monarchy or transformed it in such a way that the democratic element comprises the dominant force within the state. The case is quite different with separation of power theories. As noted above, this doctrine focuses on functions, and does not allocate these to particular classes or legally defined sections of the population. Consequently this approach to regulating the exercise of political power is quite compatible with democratic forms of government. It has played an important role in the United States and in a number of other modern Western countries.

CHAPTER 10

Absolute Government

The theories discussed in the previous two chapters provide the conceptual and, to some degree, historical starting point for conceptions of absolute government. But while accounts of absolute government often incorporate ideas derived from natural law theory and stress the obligation of rulers to uphold natural law, they set these ideas in a framework that is distinguished by the supremacy of a sovereign power that is both absolute and unitary. Sovereigns hold *all* the agencies of government in their hands; they are the unquestioned and unquestionable source of law, and they claim the right to direct the lives of all those who are subject to them. To the extent that natural law directs and constrains the exercise of power, it only does so because sovereigns impose these obligations upon themselves. Their actions may be subject to divine regulation, but sovereigns cannot be regulated, judged or punished by those over whom they rule.

This feature of absolute government is underwritten by a sharp distinction between 'sovereigns' and 'subjects'. The former have the right to command, and the latter are under an obligation to obey; subjects possess no moral or legal attributes with which to challenge the sovereign's exercise of power. The distinction between sovereigns and subjects also serves to eliminate ideas about shared sovereignty, or what amounts to the same thing, mutual subjection. Theorists of absolute government argue that states are made up of two, mutually exclusive classes of persons – the sovereign and the subjects – and they adopt a unitary view of sovereign power that precludes arrangements by which power is separated and its elements allocated to discrete institutions and/or different sections of the population. This conception of sovereignty is incompatible with mixed government; indeed it is advanced as a critique of that system.

Theories of absolute government are closely related to the idea that the primary end of politics is to provide a system of regulatory order (see pp. 30ff). Many of those who understand politics in these terms believe that order can only be identified and sustained by a unitary orderer. It should be noted, however, that theories of order are conceptually distinct from theories of absolute government. While the former specifies the ends of politics, the latter deals with the structure of government and particularly with the relationship between subjects and sovereigns. In any case, many theories of order give rise to accounts of government that are incompatible with absolutism.

A number of proponents of absolute government believe that monarchy provides the most appropriate structure for this form of rule. It is important to remember, however, that there is no necessary connection between monarchy and absolute sovereignty. The crucial requirements – that sovereign power must be *absolute*, or finally determining for members of a particular state, and *unitary* – may be ideally satisfied under monarchy, but indivisible and absolute power may also be lodged in a collective body comprising a corporate sovereign power. Theories of absolute government may thus be applied to democratic, aristocratic or monarchical forms of rule, a point made quite clear by both Jean Bodin and Thomas Hobbes.

This chapter opens with an account of the equivocal role played by ideas of absolute government in medieval and early-modern political theory. A consideration of these theories will be followed by an examination of the more developed conceptions of absolute sovereignty formulated by Jean Bodin in France, by Thomas Hobbes in England, and by the German writer Samuel Pufendorf. The fourth section of the chapter will consider the distinctly monarchical theories of absolute government produced by Sir Robert Filmer and Jaques-Benigne Bossuet. The concluding section examines the role played by ideas of absolute sovereignty in eighteenth- and early-nineteenth-century utilitarianism.

Monarchical Supremacy and the Beginnings of Absolutism: Seyssel

Although the development of absolute conceptions of government was a feature of political thinking in early modern Europe, its earliest statements exhibit a significant degree of continuity with ideas that had been current in medieval political thought. Medieval kings were supreme heads of state, but they were part of institutional and normative structures that constrained their exercise of power. In particular, medieval ideas of kingship did not uphold the legislative supremacy of monarchs; to the contrary, their law-making powers were set within a framework of customary practice that made them the central but by no means the only partner in legislative processes. Moreover the lives of many of their subjects were regulated by systems of law that derived from custom rather than the commands of the king. These characteristics of medieval conceptions of sovereignty are illustrated in the writings of Claude de Seyssel, a figure who stood at the dividing line between medieval ideas of monarchical supremacy and the early modern theories of absolute government. Seyssel's account of French government highlights features of medieval constitutionalism that were to provide the critical starting point from which theories of absolute government were developed.

Claude de Seyssel (c. 1450–1520)

Seyssel, a native of Savoy in northern Italy, spent his adult life in the service of the French crown before retiring to his bishopric in Marseilles. His most important political work was the *Monarchy of France* (1519), a work that forms an important element in the transition between medieval constitutionalism and early-modern absolutism in French political thought.

Seyssel's *The Monarchy of France* (1519) presents an account of government that has some similarities with theories of mixed or limited government, although he assumed that power flowed downwards from the crown. While insisting upon royal supremacy, however, Seyssel placed great weight upon the fact that royal power formed part of a system containing advisors, 'parlements' (largely judicial rather than legislative bodies) and ecclesiastical institutions which constrained the exercise of power (Seyssel, 1981, pp. 49–57). These constraints were more like the friction created by a flywheel than the countervailing forces produced by systems of checks and balances. Seyssel likened them to 'bridles' on the monarchy. This image is particularly apposite because it conveys the idea that constitutional structures harnessed the power of a strong and competent monarch to produce the maximum benefit for the kingdom, but it would also support and guide weak rulers and restrain the headstrong or wicked. Seyssel's image of the bridled sovereign was shortly to be replaced by one that pictured him as a 'coachman' solely responsible for directing the state. The bridle was now placed on the subjects and organs of government rather than the monarch (Keohane, 1980).

This change in imagery reflected a crucial shift in the contemporary understanding of the nature of sovereignty, one that had important implications for attempts to specify the conditions under which power should be exercised, of the relationship between rulers and subjects, and of respective rights and duties. The early stages of this shift can be seen in the writings of a number of Seyssel's immediate successors. First developed by Jean Bodin in the late sixteenth century, the theory of absolute government underwent further refinement at the hands of the far less conventional, mid-seventeenth-century English thinker Thomas Hobbes. Hobbes' theory of absolute government was modified in important respects by Samuel Pufendorf in the latter part of the seventeenth century, and in this form ideas of absolute sovereignty played an important role in eighteenth-century political thinking. Although Hobbes' ideas were not generally popular in the eighteenth century, they were incorporated in command theories of law developed by eighteenth- and early-nineteenth-century utilitarians (see p. 271).

Legislative Supremacy and Absolute Government: Bodin

Bodin's focus on order can be explained by his experience of the dehabilitating effect of civil war in late-sixteenth-century France (see p. 30). This context is important to understanding many of the details of his theory of absolute government. Interestingly, this theory was not a product of Bodin's attachment to reactionary political or religious views. To the contrary, Bodin was, by contemporary standards at least, a proponent of moderate and generally tolerant solutions to the problems facing France. He supported extensive reform of the political and economic administration of the French state, and he thought the crown should adopt a policy towards its Protestant subjects that favoured toleration rather than persecution (Franklin, 1992, pp. xxii–xxiii). Paradoxically however, both these initiatives depended on strong, unified and legitimate government.

Bodin's theory of absolute government was designed to undercut the position of Catholic magnates who claimed to have independent power that allowed them to resist moves towards toleration. It also challenged Protestant claims that the crown's unwillingness to protect them constituted royal tyranny. In response to this abuse of political power, a number of Protestant writers argued that they had a right – embedded in institutions and particular offices – to engage in active resistance against the crown (see pp. 310ff). These pressing political concerns interacted with Bodin's interest in purely theoretical issues that arose from a consideration of the relationship between indivisible power and supreme authority in the state (ibid., p. xxiii). Having originally adopted a less than absolute view of supremacy, Bodin subsequently developed a fully fledged account of the necessarily absolute nature of sovereign power. The reasoning behind this was both logical and practical: less than absolute power would negate sovereignty, and it would leave the state prey to conflicting sources of authority. This state of affairs would produce anarchy and destruction rather than right order and general benefit.

In his *Six Books of the Commonwealth* Bodin defined sovereignty as 'the absolute and perpetual power of a commonwealth' (Bodin, 1992, p. 1). Perpetual power is irrevocable and has to be distinguished from power that is held by virtue of possession of an office conferred by someone else or under specified conditions. In each of these cases, the granter of the office possesses the capacity to revoke the grant and so power can not be said to be 'perpetual'. Absolute power is not subject to human regulation; it has 'no other condition than what is commanded by the law of God and of nature' (ibid., p. 8). Bodin made it clear that absolute power entails an untrammelled exercise of legislative supremacy: a sovereign must not

> be subject in any way to the commands of someone else and must be able to give law to subjects and to suppress or repeal disadvantageous laws and to replace them with others – which cannot be done by someone who is subject to the laws or to persons having command over him (ibid., p. 11).

The sovereign's law-making power is final: its products cannot be questioned authoritatively by any subjects, nor is the sovereign obliged to institute or restore any particular legal enactment. Bodin identified law with the 'will' of the sovereign, expressed through his commands, and he insisted that the nature of sovereignty means that a sovereign cannot be bound by customary law, by laws enacted by his predecessors, or by laws that he has promulgated. The first two types of law only acquire binding force when confirmed by the sovereign, in which case their legality is a consequence of an expression of his will. A sovereign's own laws cannot bind him precisely because they are an expression of his will:

> although one can receive law from someone else, it is impossible by nature to give one's self a law as it is to command one's self to do something that depends on one's own will. As the [Roman] law says ['*No obligation can exist that depends on the will of the person promising.*'] (ibid., p. 12).

Obligations are binding because they are upheld by someone other than those who are bound by them, and sovereigns are, by definition, subject to no other human being: if they were, they would not be sovereign.

Like his predecessors, Bodin stressed the sovereign's obligation to uphold natural law, but he reserved the right of enforcement to God alone, not to subjects. As far as the sovereign is concerned, the binding force of natural law is moral and self-imposed. Moreover, while Bodin clearly thought natural law to be important, he drew an unconventionally sharp distinction between positive and natural law. While the sovereign is under an overriding obligation to God to promulgate just positive laws and to administer them justly, Bodin regarded these laws as being made by the sovereign rather than being deductions from, or applications of, natural law. He also made it clear that the sovereign's law-making power does not depend on the consent of his subjects. Unlike medieval writers, who saw consent as completion of the sovereign's legislative actions, Bodin insisted that 'the main point of sovereign majesty and absolute power consists of giving the law to subjects in general without their consent' (ibid., p. 23). In addition to their emphatic but completely independent obligations to natural law, Bodin also stipulated that sovereigns are bound to adhere to certain 'fundamental laws'. In France these laws specified succession to the throne and regulated the monarch's control of his property, the 'royal domain'. Bodin believed that these laws cannot be seen as limiting sovereignty. Rather, sovereign power in a particular state is defined by reference to laws of this kind and cannot be enforced by subjects: acts that contravene fundamental laws are merely set aside at the death of any sovereign who has wrongfully ignored them (Franklin, 1994, p. 308).

The unquestionable right to create law was regarded by Bodin as one of the distinctive, exclusive and indivisible 'marks' or attributes of sovereignty. In discussing these marks Bodin went to great lengths to show that many political actors who exercise extensive and important powers do so with the authority of their sovereign. Sovereigns cannot grant irrevocable power to their subjects, and nor can they share sovereign attributes with them:

> the notion of a sovereign (that is to say, of someone who is above all subjects) cannot apply to someone who has made a subject his companion. Just as God, the great sovereign, cannot make a God equal to Himself because He is infinite and by logical necessity ... two infinities cannot exist, so we can say that the prince, whom we have taken as the image of God, cannot make a subject equal to himself without annihilation of his power (Bodin, 1992, p. 50).

A consequence of this stipulation is that generalised law-making power must be regarded as *the* definitive mark of sovereignty: 'all other rights are comprehended in it' (ibid., p. 58). Bodin argued, however, that the generality of this power makes it necessary to specify other marks of sovereignty. Although a range of functions may be performed by important subjects, the sovereign's standing in relation to these functions is unique. For Bodin, the distinctive position of the sovereign is shown by his independent possession of these rights, by the absence of legitimate control by other human beings or institutions, and by the derivative and dependent way in which these rights are held and functions performed by subjects. Marks of sovereignty include the right to make war and peace, to appoint officeholders or confirm appointments made by others, to provide final judgement and pardons, and to issue currency and regulate weights and measures. These rights are diverse, but they are essential attributes of a sovereign because they are necessary for the safety, prosperity and justness of the state (ibid., pp. 59, 67, 71, 73, 78, 80–1).

In addition to these largely practical rights, a sovereign also has the right to 'fealty and liege homage', 'faith and homage' (ibid., p. 78). In language that reflects a growing tendency to deify secular rulers, Bodin argued that a precise understanding of the status of the sovereign is necessary because, there being nothing 'greater on earth, after God, than sovereign princes', it is important that we 'respect and revere their majesty in complete obedience, and do them honour in our thoughts and in our speech. Contempt for one's sovereign prince is contempt toward God, of whom he is the earthly image' (ibid., p. 46). Like the other attributes of sovereignty, 'faith and homage' is not owed to non-sovereign figures (Bodin, n.d., p. 36). Given the importance of these various rights they must all be possessed exclusively by the sovereign; otherwise the sovereign's capacity to order the commonwealth and secure its peace, unity and prosperity will be seriously compromised. The end of government is such that it cannot be realised unless sovereigns are both absolute and perpetual rulers of their states.

Bodin's theory of sovereignty is open to criticism on the ground that it fails to distinguish between the *powers* of government – which he claimed should be indivisible – and the *need* for a coherent legal system to have a fundamental norm for conflict resolution. It also ignored the possibility that legislative and executive powers may be shared in ways that make sovereignty a function of their interaction (Franklin, 1992, pp. xx–xxi; King, 1974, pp. 271–3). Bearing in mind that Bodin believed that his account rested on the logic of sovereignty, these objections are well met. But in acknowledging this one should not lose sight of the particular considerations that led him to believe that government must be absolute. In the first place, it must be remembered that the traditional structure of government in early modern states was based on a variety of imprecise and inadequately analysed arrangements of powers. The lack of clarity that marked these arrangements was exacerbated by the practice of referring to monarchs as if they were absolute sovereigns, even when their exercise of power was constrained by the need to secure the cooperation of other actors and institutions (Franklin, 1992, p. xviii).

This point is illustrated by Seyssel's claim that the three 'bridles' of religion, justice and inherited law 'regulate' the absolute power of the King (see p. 251). For Bodin, of course, power that is regulated by human agency cannot be absolute, but the suggestion that it may be points to the intellectual confusion that proved positively dangerous in the unsettled

conditions existing in France in the mid to late sixteenth century. Moreover Bodin's understandable concern with order, and his desire to eliminate both conflicting sources of authority and systems of coordination
that could not be relied upon to produce effective government under the
prevailing conditions, led him to adopt a focus that emphasised unified
command and undercut the claims of those who tried to justify their
conduct by appealing to institutions and laws that were under
their control and seemed to give them immunity from the power of the
crown.

Bodin's concern with unified command is apparent both in his statement that 'the government of all commonwealths ... rests on the right of
command on one side, and the obligation to obey on the other' (Bodin,
n.d., p. 9), and in his argument that the family provides a 'model' of a
rightly ordered commonwealth, one in which the father's 'natural right of
command' is assumed by the sovereign (ibid., p. 12). This parallel trades
on conventional patriarchal conceptions of familial authority and allows
Bodin to raise the spectre of divided authority in the family: 'No household can have more than one head ... [because] if there was more than
one head there would be conflict of command and incessant family dis-
turbances' (ibid., p. 10). Like members of a family, the diverse range of
people who comprise a state can only form a unified and peaceful whole
if they are furnished with a unifying element:

> a ship is no more than a load of timber unless there is a keel to hold
> together the ribs, the prow, the poop and the tiller. Similarly a com-
> monwealth without sovereign power to unite all its several members
> ... is not a true commonwealth (ibid., p. 7).

Bodin believed that this unifying role can be fulfilled only if the powers
of government are themselves unified. Consequently he rejected theories
of mixed government on the grounds that they are conceptually incoherent and practically divisive: if one examines so-called mixed constitutions
it is evident that one group or element is really sovereign. However, since
this is not clearly recognised by participants, the result is a form of political disorganisation that involves the 'corruption of a state ... continually
agitated by the storms of civil sedition until sovereignty is wholly lodged
in one form or another' (Bodin, 1992, p. 105).

Bodin was aware that systems of absolute government might facilitate
the abuse of power by rulers, but he thought that this risk is one that
human beings must accept if they wish to have any reasonable prospect
of enjoying the benefits of good government. As he put it in the course of
a discussion of the possible abuse of parental power: 'Anyone who
wishes to abolish all those laws which were liable to give rise to difficulties would abolish all laws whatsoever' (Bodin, n.d., p. 14). Since the

family is the model for a rightly ordered commonwealth, this dictum presumably applies to sovereign as well as to parental power.

One reason why Bodin was sanguine about the benefits of absolute government was his insistence that the exercise of sovereign power is subject to a range of moral constraints that are central to the idea of the state as a 'right order':

> It ... is not the rights and privileges which he enjoys which makes a man a citizen, but the mutual obligation between subject and sovereign, by which, in return for the faith and obedience rendered to him, the sovereign must do justice and give counsel, assistance, encouragement, and protection to the subject (ibid., pp. 20–1).

Subjects' cannot enforce the performance of these duties, but Bodin believed that they will be taken seriously by any sovereign worthy of the faith and homage of his subjects. Moreover sovereigns are subject to natural law and are more closely bound to it than their subjects. Bodin's frequent references to the quasi-divine status of sovereigns serves to encourage subjects to revere them. It also emphasises Bodin's view that, because sovereigns have this status, they have a special relationship with God and are even more strongly bound to fundamental moral codes than other human beings:

> every prince on earth is subject to [divine and natural law] ... it is not in their power to contravene them unless they wish to be guilty of treason against God, and to war against Him beneath whose grandeur all the monarchs of this world should bear the yoke and bow the head in abject fear and reverence (Bodin, 1992, p. 13).

Although Bodin thought that tyrannical sovereigns cannot be resisted by their subjects, the language he used to describe them makes their dubious moral standing quite clear. 'Tyrannical monarchy is one in which the laws of nature are set at naught, free subjects oppressed as if they were slaves, and property treated as if it belonged to the tyrant', which is unsatisfactory for all those concerned (Bodin, n.d., p. 57). The welfare of subjects is jeopardised and tyrants are deprived of peace or any sense of security: they 'constantly tremble for their lives and harbour a thousand suspicions, envies, rumours, jealousies, desires for revenge, and other passions that tyrannize the tyrant more cruelly than he could tyrannize his slaves with all the torments he might imagine' (Bodin, 1992, p. 121).

In Bodin's view, therefore, the possession and exercise of absolute power must be distinguished from tyranny. Moreover he argued that a good sovereign will take measures to ensure that his rule is as just and efficient as possible. Many of these measures relate closely to the institutions that had been praised by earlier exponents of constitutionalism in France. Bodin urged rulers to maintain bodies of advisors and to take their advice seriously. They should utilise representative institutions such as 'estates' to provide them with advice, as well as an opportunity to reconsider and, if necessary, to revise their decisions if the interests of the state require it. Princes must also shun those who encourage them to exercise their power in inappropriate ways: 'those who uphold such opinions are even more dangerous than those who carry them out. They show the lion his claws and arm princes with a show of justice' (ibid., p. 39). It should be noted, however, that in Bodin's view advisors and representative institutions owe their standing to the sovereign. Since they have no right to impose their will upon him, they thus contribute to the proper exercise of power without undermining the principle of absolute government.

Bodin's account of a form of absolute government that owes its legal and moral force to the unifying, ordering presence of a sovereign possessing a range of indivisible powers was developed by his successors. Thus his young contemporary Charles Loyseau produced a detailed analysis of the process through which the kings of France disposed of honours and offices. Central to this account was the argument that the sovereign is the sole source of all offices and honours, including titles of nobility: 'the definition of nobility is that it proceeds "from possessing sovereign power"' (Loyseau, 1994, p. 92).

In France, Bodin's account of sovereignty and developments based upon it were authoritative throughout the *ancien régime*. Elsewhere in Europe, however, the theory of absolute government was formulated in very different terms. The most significant of these theories was produced by the English writer Thomas Hobbes in the mid seventeenth century. Like Bodin, Hobbes regarded the creation and maintenance of order as the primary goal of politics and he thought that order could only be ensured by an absolute sovereign. Unlike Bodin, however, Hobbes' account of absolute government did not rely on conventional notions of natural law, nor did it place any great reliance on the prescriptive force of Christianity.

Absolute Sovereignty: Hobbes' Leviathan

The core idea underlying Hobbes' defence of absolute sovereignty is that it provides the only means of ensuring that citizens will enjoy the security required for their self-preservation. This security depends ultimately on the combined powers of individuals, but Hobbes made it clear that this is not solely a matter of numbers: 'be there never so great a multitude; yet if their actions be directed according to their particular judgements, and particular appetites, they can expect thereby no defence, no protection, neither against a common enemy, nor against the injuries of another' unless the multitude is directed by a 'common power' (Hobbes, 1960, p. 110). Since uncertainty is an important source of insecurity, this common power must be continuous, not limited in time, or occasional. Hobbes' justification of such a power is related ultimately to his understanding of the characteristics of the state of nature, but he suggested that even without resort to this worst-case scenario, we can identify common human traits that render unregulated and unenforced order fragile and short-lived. Humans compete against one another for dignity and honour; they tend to prefer their private interests to those of a collective or public nature; their reason prompts them to challenge established practices and to disagree with their fellows, a tendency that is exacerbated by their capacity to communicate their ideas to others, and by their desire to show off their superiority (ibid., p. 111). These traits all mean that beneficial human interaction has to be forged and maintained by a single directing force that will curb humans' disruptive tendencies. This force can only be provided by an absolute sovereign, the 'Leviathan', or that

> *mortal god*, to which we owe under the *immortal God*, our peace and defence. For by this authority, given him by every particular man in the commonwealth, he hath the use of so much power and strength conferred on him, that by terror thereof, he is enabled to form the wills of them all, to peace at home, and mutual aid against their enemies abroad. And in him consisteth the essence of the commonwealth; which, to define it, is *one person, of whose acts a great multitude, by mutual covenants one with another, have made themselves every one the author, to the end he may use the strength and means of them all, as he shall think expedient, for their peace and common defence* (ibid., p. 112).

Hobbes thought that the process through which sovereignty is created is important in determining its distinctive characteristics. The transition from the state of nature to a 'civil' or political condition results from a contractual arrangement whereby individuals agree to forego their natural right to do anything they consider necessary for their preservation. The fact that individuals have freely contracted into this arrangement creates an obligation to obey the sovereign. It is important to note that Hobbes stressed that only subjects are parties to this contract. The sovereign is *created* by this arrangement. He receives power as a 'free gift' and he does not have a contractual relationship with those who become his subjects.

Hobbes describes the sovereign as an 'actor', meaning his actions are 'authorised' by subjects and belong to them. The fact that individuals 'authorise' the sovereign was important for Hobbes because it means that subjects are the 'authors' or originators of both the sovereign and his actions. Like lawyers who act for their clients, sovereigns act for their subjects and cannot have their actions set aside by them; the subjects are bound to regard the sovereign's actions as their own. The process through which sovereign power is created ensures that the sovereign possesses a number of rights that enable him to exercise power in ways that promote the 'common peace' and safety of those who have gifted him these powers. Hobbes identified two categories of 'rights of sovereigns'. First, he specified a number of negative rights that are designed to uphold sovereignty by insulating sovereigns from challenges by their subjects. Subjects cannot attempt to change the form of government by which they are ruled, because to do so would involve a breach of their covenant with one another and would also result in their being punished by the sovereign. Since the sovereign's actions 'belong to' the subjects they would thus be punishing themselves and contradicting the protective rationale that led them to create the sovereign power. The same considerations mean that sovereigns cannot be accused of treating their subjects unjustly:

> he that doth anything by authority from another, doth therein no injury to him by whose authority he acteth: but by this institution of a commonwealth, every particular man is author of all the sovereign doth: and consequently he that complaineth of injury from his sovereign, complaineth of that whereof he himself is author; and therefore ought not to accuse any man but himself; no nor himself of injury; because to do injury to one's self, is impossible (ibid., pp. 115–16).

Even if subjects act unanimously – thus eliminating any question of breaking the contractual agreement they have with each other – they will still have no right to change the form of government because they have given all their powers to the sovereign as a 'free gift', and will thus be taking from him what is rightfully his (ibid., pp. 113–14). Moreover, since there is no contract between subjects and sovereigns, the former cannot require the latter to forfeit their powers on the ground that they may have breached conditions attached to the transfer of power from subject to sovereign: without a contract there can be no conditions, and without conditions there can be no breach of them.

By insulating the sovereign's exercise of power from the judgement and control of subjects, these stipulations ensure that the sovereign is the absolute ruler of the state. In addition, Hobbes identified a range of positive rights that facilitate the exercise of this power. Sovereigns are solely responsible for matters of war and external defence, for judging what opinions should be circulated in the commonwealth and for determining property rights. They also have final powers of judgement and appointment, of apportioning punishment and reward and of determining honours and orders of precedence (ibid., pp. 116–18). Like Bodin, Hobbes insisted that these rights are indivisible and non-transferable: they 'make the essence of sovereignty; ... [they] are the marks, whereby a man may discern in what man, or assembly of men, the sovereign power is placed, and resideth' (ibid., p. 118). These rights are the marks of sovereignty because their exclusive possession by sovereigns provides the only satisfactory guarantee of the peace and safety of the subjects. If these rights are divided, then so too is the state: 'unless this division precede, division into opposite armies can never happen' (ibid., p. 119).

The power of sovereigns is expressed through commands, or laws. They are the *sole* source of law in the state and are not subject to the laws they have created. Laws that appear to owe their binding force to custom are, in fact, binding because they have received the explicit or tacit endorsement of the sovereign and have thus become *his* laws (ibid., pp. 174–5). Like the laws of nature, the laws of the commonwealth promote peace and safety. Once a commonwealth is created, however, natural laws that were originally mere precepts of reason acquire the status of civil law: they are the commands of the sovereign and it is sovereign power that obliges subjects to obey them (ibid., p. 174). One important effect of civil law is that it 'abridges' people's rights under the laws of nature; indeed this is why the commonwealth is created. Subjects may retain some liberty, but its extent will be defined by law, or, to be more precise, they have liberty 'where the law is silent ' (ibid., p. 143).

Hobbes thus maintained that the exercise of sovereign power must not be limited by institutional constraints, by law or by the oversight of those who are subject to it. Such limitations have the effect of dividing power and preventing the sovereign from bestowing unity and order on the state. Like Bodin, Hobbes maintained that the fixed and final resting place required of viable legal systems can only be achieved if all the various agencies and functions of government are placed in a single pair of hands. As in Bodin's case, however, this stipulation is not seen as a warrant for tyrannical government. The rationale of the state means that subjects' obligations to their sovereign cease if he poses an immediate threat to their lives, or even to their fundamental interests, or if he is unable to provide protection for them (ibid., pp. 144–5).

In addition, while the exercise of sovereign power is arbitrary in the sense that sovereigns' actions are neither regulated by law nor subject to the scrutiny of their subjects, Hobbes believed that it should accord with the rationale of government: order is important because it provides a greater degree of protection for individuals than they could reasonably hope to attain either in the state of nature or in those conditions of dissolution that resemble it in significant respects. Consequently Hobbes not only specified the *rights* of sovereigns but also their *duties*, all of which are subsumed in one overriding obligation:

> The office of the sovereign ... consisteth in the end, for which he was trusted with the sovereign power, namely the procuration of *the safety of the people*; to which he is obliged by the law of nature, and to render an account thereof to God, the author of that law, and to none but him (ibid., p. 219).

The law of nature in question here is that which enjoins gratitude: '*that a man which receiveth benefit from another of mere grace, endeavour that he which giveth it, have no reasonable cause to repent him of his good will*' (ibid., p. 99). Having received sovereign power as a gift from those who become his subjects, the ruler should not act in ways that cause his subjects to regret having bestowed this gift upon him. If he does misuse the gift there will be no basis for trust, voluntary assistance or reconciliation. The state will thus be deprived of the psychological underpinnings of secure and effective government, and the existence of sovereign power will not banish the spectre of war (ibid., p. 99).

Hobbes argued that the sovereign's obligations under the laws of nature relate not only to 'bare preservation, but also all the other contentments of life' (ibid., p. 219). Sovereigns must protect their subjects, instruct them in their duties towards their rulers and to one another, formulate good laws and ensure that they retain all the rights of sovereignty. These obligations cannot be enforced by subjects, but since they are backed by the laws of nature their binding force is as strong as that which morally compels subjects to submit to a sovereign and to remain loyal and obedient to him. There is thus a symmetry between the logic of subjection and the logic of sovereignty: while it is rational for subjects to obey sovereigns and proper for them to do so, it is no less reasonable and proper for sovereigns to exercise their power in ways that correspond to the rationale and conditions determining their creation. Given his contemporaries' predilection for disobeying their sovereigns, Hobbes laid particular stress on obedience: 'Take away in any kind of state, the obedience, and consequently the concord of the people, and they shall not only not flourish, but in short time be dissolved' (ibid., p. 222). However, while he clearly thought that *any* kind of sovereign power is better than none, he made it equally clear that obedience – and hence the attainment of both 'bare preservation' and 'contentments' – is far more likely to occur where the sovereign's exercise of absolute power makes a significant rather than a minimal contribution to the well-being of his subjects.

Paradoxically, the dependence of subjects on a Hobbesian sovereign may allow for a more significant degree of personal liberty than is afforded by some alternatives to absolute government. As noted above, the Leviathan's subjects are free in areas where the law is silent. In addition, while an absolute sovereign may regulate every aspect of his subjects' lives, he is under no obligation to do so. Unlike 'godly' rulers whose legitimacy depends on their imposing a specific form of order on the state, Hobbes' sovereign is under no such obligation. Sovereigns are under no obligation to impose particular patterns of religious profession or behaviour on their subjects and cannot be censured for failing to do so.

Hobbes has been described as having developed a theory of the state that equates it with a 'unified structure of will and power that incorporates and is independent of both rulers and the subjects' (Tully, 1991, p. xxxii). As subjects, subjects cannot lay a claim to sovereign power, but nor can the sovereign as sovereign divide his rights or alienate any of them; to do so would destroy both sovereignty and the state it defines and sustains. A similar conception of the state was advanced by Hobbes' contemporary, the German writer Samuel Pufendorf. However his understanding of the nature and implications of absolute government was designed to correct what he saw as unsatisfactory features of Hobbes' theory.

Natural Law, Sociability and Absolute Government: Pufendorf

Like Hobbes, Pufendorf equated ideas of shared sovereignty with confusion and disorder. Consequently he argued that an absolute sovereign is the only viable solution to the shortcomings of the state of nature, one that can be justified by an appeal to the laws of nature. As we have seen, however, Pufendorf derived these laws from the requirements of sociability rather than from the implications of the natural right to self-preservation (see p. 215). An important consequence of this aspect of Pufendorf's theory is that the state is seen a means of furthering the general purposes specified by the laws of nature and it derives its legitimacy from this: 'against those ills with which man in his baseness delights to threaten his own kind, the most efficient cure had to be sought from man himself, by men joining into states, and establishing sovereignty ' (Pufendorf, 1934, p. 959). States foster productive human intercourse by punishing those whose disregard for natural law undermines the advantages of sociability; they provide stable, secure environments in which the impact of public and family education can be most effectively applied to recalcitrant humanity, and where they can benefit from the civilising effect of social life. As Pufendorf put it, 'it is the first fruit of civil society, that in it men may accustom themselves to lead an orderly life' (ibid., p. 956; Tully, 1991, p. xxxi).

Samuel Pufendorf (1632–94)

A Saxon by birth, Pufendorf spent a large part of his life in the service of the Swedish crown. He wrote extensive histories of Sweden and a number of other European states. His most important political work, *Of the Laws of Nature and of Men* (1672), was a major contribution to the early-modern statements of natural law.

Paradoxically, Pufendorf rejected Hobbes' account of the formation of the state because he thought it yielded an insufficiently strong notion of sovereignty. The reason for this is that Hobbes failed to realise that since the covenant between natural beings is mutual, it will become void if any one individual fails to obey the sovereign. In order to deal with this problem, Pufendorf argued that the creation of political authority involves not merely one agreement and a gift, but two agreements and one decree (Pufendorf, 1991, pp. 135–7; Tully, 1991, p. xxxi). First, heads of families – the focus of sociability in the state of nature – create an association through a contractual agreement specifying that they will seek a form of common leadership that will ensure their safety. Secondly, the members of this association (or a majority of it) issue a decree stipulating the form of government they think will secure this end. The government so established may be absolute in the conventional sense, or it may be constrained by fixed or fundamental laws. Finally, the association enters into an agreement with a person or persons upon whom they confer sovereign power. Pufendorf insisted that unlike the free gift that empowers Hobbes' sovereign, this agreement is *reciprocal*. The subjects undertake to obey the sovereign and to be cooperative and respectful towards him; the sovereign undertakes to be responsible for the safety of the state and to exercise power in ways that conform to any constraints specified in the decree. Having promised, each party is bound by the laws of nature to maintain the unified structure they have created. Since sociability will be precarious without safety, and since security is impossible without sovereignty, it can be said that 'supreme sovereignty came from God as the author of natural law'. Even though sovereign power is created by human beings 'the command of God to establish states manifests itself through the dictates of reason, by which men recognised that the order and peace which natural law considers as its end, cannot exist without civil society' (Pufendorf, 1934, p. 1001).

Unlike Hobbes, Pufendorf did not believe that a reciprocal process of sovereignty formation left the sovereign open to the scrutiny of his subjects. Nor did it provide the basis for rebelling against him. The sovereign's immunity can be traced to the character of the rights that exist in a state of nature. Pufendorf maintained that since individuals in this condition lack the power to legislate or to punish, they cannot 'reclaim' these rights if they think the sovereign's conduct has nullified their agreement with him. Moreover, while the people form themselves into a union or association in their passage from the state of nature, this association does not possess supreme authority. To the contrary, authority of this kind only comes into being as a consequence of their agreement with the sovereign. Having never possessed supreme power, the people cannot be said to have delegated it to the sovereign. Consequently they cannot repossess it. Finally, since citizens are necessarily subject to their sovereign, there is no room for those accounts of mixed government that rest on the idea that citizens share sovereignty and subjection with rulers (Tully, 1991, p. xxxiv).

Pufendorf thus insulated the sovereign from the authoritative censure of his subjects by insisting that only the former possesses or has ever possessed *political* authority. As a consequence his sovereign is no less absolute than Hobbes' and his exercise of political power is free from the binding force of civil law or from the prospect that he may be liable to punishment at the hands of his subjects (Pufendorf, 1934, pp. 1055–6). However, while Pufendorf insisted on the supremacy of the sovereign, he allowed for two constraints on the exercise of sovereign power. It is significant that neither of these constraints can be traced to the possession of political authority by subjects. In the first place, individuals' natural right to self-defence may justify their resisting 'extreme and unjust' violence at the hands of their sovereign. However, since this right is a product of natural law and existed prior to the creation of the state, it is not a consequence of *political* authority. Secondly, Pufendorf argued that 'sovereign authority' may appear in either an 'absolute' or a 'limited' form:

> Absolute authority is said to be held by a monarch who can wield it according to his own judgement, not by following the rule of fixed, standing statutes, but as the actual condition of affairs seems to require, and who uses his own judgement in protecting the security of his country as its circumstances require (Pufendorf, 1991, p. 147).

In contrast, limited sovereign authority exists when the power conferred on a sovereign is defined by fixed limits specified in the decree that identifies the form of government the association has decided to adopt. Where these stipulations exist, they form part of the reciprocal agreement by which the association creates sovereignty by placing itself under a ruler. These limitations are particularly appropriate in relation to monarchy because 'the judgement of a single man is liable to error and his will may tend towards evil' (ibid., p. 147). Since the sovereign has promised to assume a form of supremacy that is subject to these limitations, he is obliged by the laws of nature to rule according to these terms. In circumstances in which these limitations threaten the safety of the state, the sovereign can only act after he has been authorised to do so by the people or its deputies. This stipulation is *pre*-political in the sense that it takes place in an environment that is conceptually equivalent to that in which the decree and second agreement were formulated. As is the case with the right to self-defence, these limitations were established prior to the creation of the state and can only be waived outside the state. Therefore they do not rest on the political authority of the subjects. Like Bodin's fundamental laws, these limitations are best seen as part of the definition of the state, and they do not impugn the supremacy of the sovereign.

Aspects of Pufendorf's theory of absolute sovereignty were utilised by a range of eighteenth-century German theorists who used it as the basis for a defence of absolute monarchy. In these formulations, however, the exercise of absolute power is related not merely to the protection of the subject, but also to their perfection. It is argued that human beings are endowed with natural freedom and natural rights so that they have the opportunity to realise their divinely implanted potentialities. However, their reason leads them to see that this end can only be realised if they enjoy the security and help that only an absolute ruler can provide. Individuals therefore transfer their rights to the prince, who now assumes responsibility for and possesses the coercive power to facilitate individuals' pursuit of perfection. This idea of kingship is often given a strongly patriarchal cast. As in earlier accounts of absolute rule, authority is limited conceptually by the purposes for which it was established, but these limitations have to be imposed by the monarch himself, not by any force external to him. All final responsibility for the state resides with the sovereign power. This power cannot be limited by those who have closed off this possibility by transferring their rights of independent action to the sovereign (Krieger, 1972, pp. 65–71).

Absolute Sovereignty and Divine Right Monarchy: Filmer and Bossuet

While Hobbes and Pufendorf regarded an absolute sovereign as a rational necessity, they allowed that power of this kind could be located either in a single person or in a corporate body made up of the few or the many. Their theories of absolute sovereignty can thus be contrasted with those produced by their contemporaries in England and France: Sir Robert Filmer and Jaques-Benigne Bossuet. These writers rejected the idea of natural freedom and denied that government is legitimated through a contract. They argued that the only appropriate form of government is one in which a monarch, endowed with power by divine right, exercises absolute control over his subjects. The use of the male pronoun is singularly appropriate in dealing with these writers since they considered the Bible to be the only legitimate source of political principles, and argued that according to the scriptures political authority must be patriarchal in both origin and form (see pp. 136–8). Although Filmer was critical of Hobbes' derivation of the state from 'a condition of natural freedom, he applauded his treatment of the rights of sovereignty because this is a central element of any viable conception of the exercise of political power and one that 'no man, that I know, hath so amply or judiciously handled' (Filmer, 1949, p. 239). Filmer was equally impressed with Bodin's thoughts on this subject and quoted him with approval and at great length (ibid., pp. 304ff). From Filmer's point of view, Bodin was particularly important because he identified political authority with the power that fathers exercise over their families.

Filmer identified monarchy as the only legitimate form of government, and argued that monarchs have an unquestionable right to exercise complete control over their subjects. He claimed, for example, that there is no scriptural warrant for either democracy or mixed government, and he argued that the weaknesses of these forms of government are clearly demonstrated by experience. Democracy has shown itself to be completely incompatible with order, or even with the semblance of good government, for the simple reason that 'the nature of all people is to desire liberty without restraint, which cannot be but where the wicked bear rule' (ibid., p. 89). Mixed government is hardly an improvement on this, because in such a case the exercise of sovereign power is subject to constraints imposed by 'the people', who must ultimately be in a position to judge their rulers in their individual capacities and according to their own consciences, a situation that necessarily gives rise to 'utter confusion, and anarchy' (ibid., p. 297).

For Filmer, ruling involves an exercise of will and this can only be effective if the will in question is single and unified. The will of the sovereign cannot be restrained by a law of which he is the sole human source, interpreter and enforcer (ibid., pp. 96, 106). Like Bodin, Filmer stressed the general obligation of absolute rulers under the laws of nature, a requirement he underlined by pointing to the implications of the patriarchal nature of political authority:

> As the Father over one family, so the King, as Father over many families, extends his care to preserve, feed, clothe, instruct and defend the whole commonwealth.... [A]ll the duties of a King are summed up in an universal fatherly care of his people (ibid., p. 63).

In performing his role, the sovereign may appoint judges and advisors and call parliaments. Filmer insisted, however, that these officers and

institutions are created by the sovereign, and must not be seen as imposing an external check on his absolute power. The sovereign's obligations
cannot be enforced by his subjects: sovereign power is ordained by God
and is subject to his control alone.

Although Filmer's account of absolute government has a general bearing, it is clear that his attack on what he saw as the novel and dangerous
ideas of natural freedom and mixed monarchy was directed in the first
instance at the problems facing the English crown in the mid seventeenth
century. In contrast Bossuet's *Politics Drawn from the Very Words of Holy
Scripture* explained and justified what he considered to be the admirable
system of government presided over by Louis XIV of France. Moreover,
while Bossuet thought that this regime conformed to a divinely created
and sanctioned model of absolute monarchy, he stressed the parallel
between the monarch and God rather than concentrating (as Filmer had
done) on the gift of power conferred on Adam by God and handed down
by him to his successors. Bossuet's procedure reflected language and imagery that were used by Louis XIV himself and by those who shared his
conception of government.

Jaques-Benigne Bossuet (1627–1704)

Although he was a bishop in the Catholic Church, Bossuet upheld the absolute power of the French crown against both its Protestant and papalist
rivals. Bossuet served as tutor to the heir to the French crown in the early
1670s. His major political work, *Politics Drawn from the Very Words of Holy
Scripture*, was published posthumously in 1709.

In a memoir written to prepare his heir for the position to which he
would succeed, Louis referred to the monarch as a 'human god'. Like a
deity, the monarch is an active creator of order within his kingdom and
keeps ceaseless vigil over its affairs (Louis was known as the 'Sun King',
a name that has less to do with splendour than with the life-giving and
invigorating oversight exercised by the king). In a very real sense the king
is the state; the government is merely an information gathering machine
that allows him to act in the best interests of his subjects (Keohane, 1980,
pp. 245–9). Bossuet endorsed this conception of royal power, but he buttressed it with a detailed analysis of the political significance of Holy
Scripture.

Although God created men as social beings, they can only benefit from
this condition if they are subject to the constraining force of government,
an agency that Bossuet described as a 'bridle of the passions' of humanity

(Bossuet, 1990, p. 14). In order to fulfil this role and to produce union and security, government must be in the hands of a figure who is endowed with the same authority over his subjects as God exercises over his creatures:

> Majesty is the image of the greatness of god in a prince.... The power of God can be felt in a moment from one end of the world to the other: the royal power acts simultaneously throughout the kingdom. It holds the whole kingdom in position just as God holds the whole world. If God were to withdraw his hand, the entire world would return to nothing: if authority ceases in a kingdom, all lapses into confusion (ibid., p. 160).

Like Filmer, Bossuet maintained that absolute monarchy is the ideal form of government, but while he related this to a paternal pattern, he stressed that it is modelled on God himself. The precedent of Adam upon which Filmer placed such importance was ignored. God was the first and true king, one who had himself exercised paternal government of his subjects: 'God having placed in our parents, as being in some fashion the authors of our life, an image of the power by which he made everything, he also transmitted to them an image of the power which he has over his works' (ibid., p. 41). The image in question is both monarchical and absolute: 'without this absolute authority, he [the monarch] can neither do good nor suppress evil: his power must be such that no one can hope to escape him; and, in fine, the sole defence of individuals against the public power, must be their innocence', a matter that is determined by the prince (ibid., p. 81). This claim serves to undercut theories of government (promoted at that time by a number of Protestant thinkers) which hold that the infringement of fundamental rights warrants defensive resistance on the part of subjects (see pp. 310ff). However, while Bossuet stressed that sovereigns are not accountable to human beings, he denied that this means that absolute government should be equated with *arbitrary* rule. To the contrary, absolute rulers must cherish the liberty of their subjects and protect their property. Unlike the arbitrary ruler, the power of the true sovereign is directed at the good of the subject, not at the good of the ruler. Bossuet's absolute monarch governs through stable and known laws. The formulation and administration of these laws is his exclusive prerogative, but he is under a strong moral and religious obligation to govern rationally and justly. This general obligation embodies the true interests of the prince; behind it lies the fear of God, the 'true counterweight to [human] power'. God 'lives eternally; his anger is implacable, and always living; his power is invincible; he never forgets; he never yields; nothing can escape him' (ibid., p. 101).

Absolute Sovereignty and Utilitarianism: Sainte-Pierre, Bentham and Austin

A previous chapter has described how a number of eighteenth- and early-nineteenth-century thinkers sought to reformulate the conventional idea that government should ensure the happiness of subjects, into a precise and scientific form that would make it a useful tool with which to gauge the effectiveness of various forms of government. This tool was meant to form the basis of ambitious programmes of administrative, legal and political reform (see pp. 108ff). An important aspect of these utilitarian conceptions of the ends of politics was that they were often married to conceptions of sovereignty that bore some similarity to early-modern accounts of absolute government.

An early example of this form of utilitarianism appeared in the writings of the Abbé Saint-Pierre in the first half of the eighteenth century. As noted above, Saint-Pierre's statement of utilitarianism differs from Jeremy Bentham's later formulations because it retains a place for religious sanctions (see p. 109). Despite this, however, Saint-Pierre believed that human agency has an important role to play in curbing people's destructive passions and ensuring that their understanding of their own interests can be fitted into a harmonious system that will maximise both individual and general happiness. Saint-Pierre placed a premium on peace and order – 'charity, concord, and tranquillity are greater goods than truth' (Keohane, 1980, p. 369) – and argued that this can only be attained if power is held and exercised by an absolute ruler. A unified source of authority will secure peace and use its power to encourage human beings to form habits that will produce utility-maximising behaviour.

Like Bodin, Saint-Pierre regarded divided authority as an impediment to good government, but he stressed that the effective exercise of absolute power depends on the rationality of the ruler. While earlier exponents of absolute monarchy in France sought to combine absolute rule with self-imposed restraints drawn from conventional constitutional theory, Saint-Pierre maintained that effective government is necessarily despotic. Ideally, therefore, the state should be ruled by an enlightened despot, one who combines unbridled power with highly developed rationality, wide-ranging information and expertise in ruling: 'when power is united to reason, it cannot be too great or too despotic for the greatest utility of society' (ibid., p. 370).

In addition to applying this idea to a traditional but enlightened monarch, Saint-Pierre suggested that the monarch could be placed within a system of government that does not depend on his personal qualities. This system takes the form of an administrative machine made up of laws and enforcement agencies that serve to harmonise the interests of individuals so as to maximise public utility. It also includes mechanisms designed to ensure that officials identify their interests with those of society. If these goals are achieved, there is no need to be concerned with limiting the exercise of power because the actions of officeholders will necessarily be conducive to the public good (ibid., pp. 370–2).

The details of what has aptly been described as Saint-Pierre's vision of government as 'a perpetual motion machine' reflect the distinctly eccentric cast of the mind of its creator. Nevertheless, later – less bizarre – formulations of utilitarianism incorporate the concern with absolute sovereignty that forms a central element in Saint-Pierre's theory of government. Thus in his *Fragment on Government* Jeremy Bentham dismissed both natural rights and the common law of England on the ground that they impede government's capacity to produce laws that maximise utility. According to Bentham, natural rights are part of an outmoded and essentially meaningless approach to politics that focuses attention on the origins of government and the basis of political obligation. For Bentham these are not important questions because government exists and subjects *are* in the habit of obeying their political superiors. The key issue is not the origin of political power, but the *tendency* of government (Francis, 1980). Good governments are those that promote the greatest happiness of the greatest number. Bentham maintained that this depends on the capacity of government to formulate laws that advance the cause of utility. Law provides a means of encouraging individuals to maximise utility and/or discouraging them from acting in ways that run counter to it (Bentham, 1967, pp. 281–435).

If laws are to provide an effective stimulus to utility-maximising behaviour, they have to be directed towards the good of the community. They also have to be formulated and enforced in ways that make them a rational and certain guide for human conduct, and an effective source of 'sanctions' (or punishments) that can be applied to those who infringe them. These requirements led Bentham to insist that laws must be clear and rational, so that they send unequivocal and consistent signals to those whose behaviour is regulated by them. These concerns are reflected in Bentham's demands that law be organised in a codified form, one that is quite at odds with the arcane, impenetrable and ramshackle features that distinguish the Common Law of England. In addition, however, Bentham argued that one of the major impediments to a clear, rational structure of law (and one of the primary causes of its practical and theoretical absurdity) is that it lacks any consistent and determinate source. English law at the time comprised an irrational and confusing mixture of parliamentary statutes, and variations on these formulated by judicial decisions that were based on precedent and judges' interpretations of the intention behind legislative enactments. These practices were a recipe for bewilderment; they failed to provide clear guidance on how individuals should behave. They also reflected a failure to grasp the nature of sovereignty and its implications. Bentham argued that both the logic of law and its practical effectiveness require the sovereign to be seen as the single legal authority and the absolute and final source of authority in the state. The sovereign is a definitive person or persons whose subjects are habitually obedient. Only this view of sovereignty will ensure that the law becomes what it ought to be, that is, an instrument for promoting the greatest happiness of the greatest number.

In making this point Bentham was not suggesting that *any* exercise of law-making power is acceptable. To the contrary, his strictures on codification and his stipulation that utility is the *only* proper end of government clearly indicate that an absolute sovereign (which could be a person, a group or the entire population) is only *one* requirement of good government. At times he even suggested that he did not think it necessary for sovereign power to be unlimited and indivisible (Bentham, 1967, pp. 98–9). Nevertheless he seemed to think that utility is most likely to be maximised if the sovereign is absolute: 'any limitation is in contradiction to the general happiness principle' (Bentham, 1843b, p. 119). The sovereign should not be constrained by other powers (as in theories of mixed government), nor should he be subject to rules (like those embodied in natural law) that constitute an overarching authoritative structure to which the actions and enactments of legitimate rulers are required to conform.

One implication that could be derived from Bentham's notion of sovereignty is that laws could be described as 'commands'. This position is associated with what has been called the 'command theory of law', which focuses on the capacity of sovereigns to impose their will through a system of commands embodied in law. As we have seen, a forceful statement of this position was advanced by Bentham's follower, the jurist John Austin, and by the twentieth-century writer Hans Kelsen. Both Bentham and Kelsen regarded the command theory of law as a necessary feature of any regime, including those based on democratic principles (see p. 37).

Conclusion

The assumption lying at the root of theories of absolute government is that effective systems of rule require a final arbiter. This figure, the sovereign, possesses exclusive responsibility for creating and enforcing bodies of law that are designed to sustain order and facilitate the pursuit of other goals. Historically, this theory has often been given a strongly monarchical cast. However, as both Bodin and Hobbes made clear, the logic of absolute sovereignty applies to all stable and effective forms of government. Early modern sovereignty theory incorporates both natural law and natural rights, but these are not thought to impose political constraints on sovereign power. Natural rights are used to explain the process through which sovereignty is created, but they do not play an authoritative role in regulating political power. Similarly, although natural law is held to be binding upon sovereigns, subjects are not entitled to police their sovereign's conduct. Sovereigns who act contrary to natural law will be judged and punished by God, not by the human beings who are subject to them.

While early modern theories of absolute government pay a great deal of attention to subjects' obligations to obey their sovereign, modern exponents of this doctrine generally ignore this issue. Utilitarians take the existence of government for granted, and focus on its tendency, or effects. The Hobbesian conception of sovereignty was valuable to these writers because it identifies the key requirement of an effective system of government. Law is seen as a way of issuing clear, unequivocal instructions to members of the community so as to ensure that their actions correspond to the dictates of utility. As we shall see in the next chapter, the idea of law as a command, and the assumption that government has a responsibility for directing the actions of subjects, has been challenged by those who argue that the exercise of political power should be set within a framework that makes government the servant – not the master – of law.

CHAPTER 11

The Rule of Law and Rule-Bound Orders

Theories of absolute government are formally authoritarian in the sense that they identify a single source of authority and order within the state. While these theories do not necessarily mean that an absolute sovereign will be harsh and oppressive, they imply that sovereign power can only ever be subjected to a system of self-regulation. This feature of absolute government is very apparent in Bodin's and Hobbes' insistence that legal regulations that *appear* to be independent of the sovereign owe their binding force to the fact that they have been recognised and upheld by the sovereign. As the source of law, the sovereign can only be subjected to the *directive* force of law, and is bound by it only to the extent that he chooses. Sovereigns exercise supreme power, and they alone are responsible for stipulating the legal framework through which they do so. These requirements are not accidental. As we have seen, theories of absolute government developed in an environment where contending sources of authority seemed to be undermining social order. The logical and practical imperative for an absolute conception of sovereignty was presented as a solution to this problem.

The development of this position involved a radical break with a long tradition of political thinking that sought to restrain the actions of governors by systems of law. Law defined the nature of the environment in which rulers acted and formed the framework within which they exercised power. Both the ideas on natural law and the theories of mixed constitutions that have been discussed in previous chapters served this general function, the first by identifying an objective standard to which human law has to conform, the second by stipulating arrangements of offices and/or powers that effectively regulate the conduct of particular political actors. But while there is some common ground between these ways of regulating the exercise of political power and those discussed in this chapter, the theories considered here are distinctive because they identify human law itself as the source of regulation.

The key idea here – that 'power ought to be exercised within institutionally determined limits' (Lloyd, 1994, p. 255) – is often expressed in terms of the 'rule of law'. That is, it is argued that political power must be exercised according to known, fixed rules, and that departures from these standards can be subject to legal challenge. These theories stress regularity and the importance of known conditions, and reject arbitrary or capricious exercises of power. Since the doctrine of the rule of law means that the law itself is supreme, it has a deeply ambivalent and in some cases an openly hostile relationship with theories of absolute government. These theories treat law as a product of sovereignty, not as something that regulates the way in which sovereign power is exercised.

A number of theories that give a prominent place to the regulatory and restraining role of human law will be discussed in this chapter. We shall first examine Plato's and Aristotle's views on the need for law to counteract the 'passions' to which even good rulers are liable. Aristotle's views on this issue are particularly important because they played a direct role in medieval accounts of the relationship between rulers and the law. In the late medieval and early modern periods ideas about the importance of law were often built up into theories of constitutional government that placed limits upon sovereign power and subjected it to legal constraints.

Bodin and Hobbes regarded these constraints as dangerous products of confused thinking and developed their theories of absolute sovereignty as alternatives to the views of their predecessors and contemporaries. Despite their efforts, conventional ideas of the rule of law continued to play a role in subsequent political thought. However, the most interesting developments focused on the *nature* of laws that provide the basis for the political order and regulate the exercise of political power within it. These developments gave rise to the idea that a properly regulated state comprises a 'rule-bound order' and to the requirement that political activity should be structured by these rules rather than by the commands or expressions of will of rulers. An important formulation of this position appeared in the writings of the eighteenth-century Scottish philosopher David Hume. The need to exercise political authority through systems of law also played a significant role in eighteenth- and early-nineteenth-century French and German thought. In the twentieth century these theories provided inspiration for Friedrich A. Hayek's conception of a rule-bound order. Hayek sought to revive the idea of the rule of law in the face of the dangers posed by widespread acceptance of theories that identified law with the determinations of those occupying positions of political authority. His critique was applied both to totalitarian conceptions of government and also to what he regarded as the authoritarian tendencies of modern democratic regimes.

The Rule of Law in Ancient Political Theory: Plato and Aristotle

The rule of law is central to the less-than-perfect state that is the focus of Plato's attention in *The Laws*. In this work Plato identified law with the maintenance of any political system: 'legislation should be directed not to waging war or attaining complete virtue, but to safeguarding the interests of the established political system, whatever that is, so that it is never overthrown and remains permanently in force' (Plato, 1980, p. 172). However, since most systems of law and most commonplace accounts of justice are designed to protect the interests of the dominant group within the state and ignore those of the rest of the population, they are inherently problematic. They do not produce stability because they are always being challenged by those members of the community whose interests are not protected by the existing legal structure, and they do not satisfy the requirement that the state exists for the benefit of *all* its members. As Plato put it:

> our position is that this kind of arrangement is very far from being a genuine political system; we maintain that laws which are not established for the good of the whole state are bogus laws, and when they favour particular sections of the community, their authors are not citizens but party-men; and people who say those laws have a claim to be obeyed are wasting their breath (ibid., p. 173).

Law compensates for the lack a class of philosophical rulers whose intellectual and moral qualities ensure they will always act in the interests of the whole community. If law is to compensate to some degree for this flaw, if it is to provide justice and remove grounds for seditious behaviour that will destroy the prospect of stability, it must be impartial in its provisions, and removed from the control of those who may be tempted to pervert it into an instrument that favours particular rather than general interests. In order to satisfy these requirements, Plato argued that the political structure of Magnesia, the regulations governing the allocation of offices and the conduct of officeholders must be subject to fixed provisions. Law must be sovereign:

> Where the law is subject to some other authority and has none of its own, the collapse of the state ... is not far off; but if law is the master

of government and government is its slave, then the situation is full of promise and men enjoy all the blessings that the gods shower on a state (ibid., p. 174).

The bulk of *The Laws* is devoted to identifying legal provisions that will ensure the state remains as free as possible from individual and class partiality. When the state is formed it must be provided with an extensive body of law that will regulate all its most important political, legal, educational, social and economic activities. A central feature of these arrangements are provisions for the selection of a special group – the 'guardians of the laws', who are charged with preserving the fundamental structure of the state and ensuring that any extensions of the legal code conform to the principles upon which the state is based (ibid., p. 227).

Aristotle's views on the rule of law form part of his treatment of rule by a single person, and like Plato's treatment of this topic in *The Laws*, they rest on the belief that when political authority is placed in the hands of people who are unable to satisfy the rigorous requirements of Platonic guardianship they must be subject to regulation. In his discussion Aristotle draws a distinction between an absolute ruler exercising 'regal' power, which is not circumscribed by law, and the leading figure in a 'political' constitution defined by law. In its pure and complete form, 'regal' government may capitalise on the intelligence and virtue of a superior human being. Aristotle recognised, however, that even those who are fit to be monarchs may be swayed by passions that cloud their judgement. This realisation means that a strong case can be made for a form of political monarchy that sets single-person rule within a framework of law. While the ruler is the supreme figure in the state, the law itself is really sovereign.

The advantages of such an arrangement depend to a considerable degree upon the character of the law. Aristotle argued that the laws in question must provide a 'neutral authority'; that is, they should be reasonable and impartial (Aristotle, 1958, pp. 147, 173). Such an authority is essential if the exercise of political power is to provide justice for the state.

He who commands that law should rule may ... be regarded as commanding that God and reason alone should rule; he who commands that a man should rule adds the character of the beast. Appetite has that character; and high spirit too, perverts the holders of office, even when they are the best of men (ibid., p. 146).

While the exercise of political authority is usually regulated through laws that are not of the sovereign's making, it is not possible to create a body of law that covers all cases. Law deals with general matters and cannot specify what might be appropriate in certain cases, or in particular circumstances. Aristotle thus sought to combine the regularity and impartiality of law with a degree of personal initiative that allows rulers to depart from the strict letter of the law when equity, justice and good sense require it. He therefore concluded that

> the one best man must be law-giver, and there must be a body of laws .... [T]hese laws must not be sovereign where they fail to hit the mark – though they must be so in all other cases (ibid., p. 142).

This stipulation applies to both written and unwritten codes of law, but Aristotle suggested that it is especially appropriate with respect to 'unwritten custom' (ibid., p. 147). Aristotle did not explain why he ascribed a special status to customary law, but he might have thought that the fact that these laws have been passed down from generation to generation means that they are communal rather than personal products. They are thus more likely to be impartial than laws that come from a determinate personal source.

Aristotle's preference for customary law was echoed by Cicero, although, as we have seen, he tended to justify this by treating custom as an expression of natural law (see p. 206). It also played a role in medieval and early modern conceptions of the relationship between rule and law. In formulating this position, medieval writers also availed themselves of Aristotle's distinction between 'regal' and 'political' forms of monarchy.

The Rule of Law in Medieval and Early Modern Political Theory: 'Bracton', Aquinas, Marsilius, Seyssel and Hooker

Because most medieval political thinking was premised on the superiority of monarchy and was created within monarchical contexts, issues having to do with legal constraints on the exercise of political power were necessarily framed by reference to the relationship between kings and law. Early medieval ideas of kingship drew upon Germanic conceptions that stressed the authority of customary law and the need for rulers' legislative innovations to be endorsed by representative mechanisms that signified their subjects' consent to these additions to, or departures from, customary law. This tradition was partially displaced by the ambiguous inheritance of Roman law doctrines that made the emperor the source of law (while stipulating that he should govern according to law), and by the role ascribed to natural law (Pennington, 1991, p. 426). It should be noted, however, that although the natural law provided an objective standard of 'right' law, it still left the problem of determining whether human law was consistent with it. Widely held beliefs about the need for kingly rule to provide the source of human law made it difficult to subject human rulers to law without challenging their sovereignty and undermining their capacity to ensure unity and order. The tensions between ideas of objective law, the need for rulers to uphold the law they had created, and the conceptual and practical dangers inherent in challenges to royal supremacy, meant that medieval political thought contained a number of strands that gave differing weights to each of these considerations. These theories could provide the basis for the development of either theories of absolute sovereignty, or constitutional theories that placed the exercise of sovereign power within a framework that subjected it to legal constraints. Nevertheless, in medieval and in much early modern thinking, there was a widely shared view that the exercise of political authority should be set within a normative framework, even when the responsibility for adhering to these standards was left to rulers themselves.

The dilemma posed by the interdependence of kingship and law were captured in a thirteenth-century English work:

> The king must not be under man but under God and under the law, because law makes the king. Let him therefore bestow upon the law what the law bestows upon him namely rule and power, for there is no [king] where will rules rather than [law] (Black, 1993, p. 153).

The unknown author of this work (which is conventionally ascribed to Henry Bracton, but is now known not to have been written by him) solved this dilemma by arguing that when kings do not impose the 'bridle' of law upon themselves, their most important subjects ('earls' and 'barons') should impose it upon them. This idea is obviously related to later constitutional conceptions, especially those promoting 'mixed' constitutions. Whatever its future importance, however, this formulation did not shed a great deal of light on the relationship between the ruler and the law. In particular, it failed to recognise the possibility that kings may stand in a complex relationship to the law such that they are in some respects bound by it, and in other respects able to go beyond, or 'dispense' from it.

Some medieval thinkers discussed this possibility with the help of Aristotle's distinction between 'regal' and 'political' rule. It was claimed that while kings should normally act as if they are bound by the laws they create, there may be occasions when they should act in a regal manner. When equity, mercy or dire necessity require it, the ruler may depart from the letter of the law. Significantly, it was claimed that these actions need not be seen as expressions of the 'will' of the monarch; they do not relate to his personal or partial interests, but rest upon impartial reason and gain their legitimacy from this. As Aquinas put it:

[if] will ... is to have the authority of law, [it] must be regulated by reason when it commands. It is in this sense that we should understand the saying that the will of the prince has the power of law. In any other sense the will of the prince becomes an evil rather than law (Aquinas, 1959, p. 111).

Some medieval theories were thus able to sustain the idea of an objective conception of law to which the 'will' of the ruler corresponds. Rulers exercise both 'regal' and 'political' rule, but the exceptional nature of the former means that the latter is the predominant pattern. In addition, the content of law is not reliant on the will of the ruler. Only when this latter stipulation could be set aside would a fully fledged theory of absolute government emerge, and an important step along this road was made in the second decade of the thirteenth century by Laurentius Hispanus, who argued that the 'will' of the prince 'is held to be reason'. This formulation made 'will' the measure of reason and thus broke with the conventional idea that reason is the measure of legitimate will. However, it still related princely will to the good of the public, and it coexisted with other ideas that drew rulers back within the confines of law (Pennington, 1991, pp. 427–8).

For example, a conception of royal supremacy in which ordinary exercises of power are subject to the constraining force of law, can be achieved by utilising a distinction between 'theocratic' and 'feudal' conceptions of kingship. Royal theocracy is unquestionable, but kings are also feudal overlords. As overlords, their relationships with their subjects are specified in a complex series of contractual arrangements that have all the force of law, and cannot be overridden by a declaration of will on the part of one of the parties (Ullmann, 1975, pp. 146–7). An important example of the application of these ideas occurred in England in 1215. In that year the major English barons utilised their feudal relationship with King John in order to gain his acceptance of the Magna Carta. This document signalled the king's recognition of the rights of his subjects and his willingness to adopt mechanisms to protect them, but it did so without calling his supremacy into question.

The fact that one of the chapters of the Magna Carta specified that certain forms of taxation could only be levied with the consent of the Great Council, means that this document can be seen as marking an important stage in the development of ideas of constitutional government. However constitutional theories focus on the relationship between different elements in the state, and only address the question of the relationship between law and political authority obliquely. In particular, theories of this kind do not necessarily deal with the question of whether exercises of political power should be subject to and confined by legal stipulations. In other words, while constitutional theories may specify *who* can make law, they do not necessarily relate law making to a preexisting body of rules.

In the late medieval period Marsilius of Padua drew upon Aristotle's ideas when presenting his case for the role of law in a just state:

> It is necessary to establish that in the polity that without which evil judgements cannot be made with complete rightness .... Such a thing is the law.... Therefore, the establishment of law is necessary in the polity (Marsilius, 1956, vol. ii, p. 37).

Law is free from 'perverted emotions'; it embodies the wisdom of past experience, and it gives government a degree of stability and peace because it reduces the risk of unjust and ignorant rule (ibid., pp. 38, 39–42). In making a case for the importance of law, however, Marsilius adopted the unusual step of advancing a strongly positivistic account of the source of human law, while maintaining that its content could be evaluated by an appeal to higher, non-legal norms (Canning, 1991, pp. 460–1). For the most part, late medieval–early modern thinkers tended to tread an uneasy path between upholding the legislative supremacy of rulers and assuming that law-making activity took place within a legal framework. This tendency appears quite clearly in Claude de Seyssel's analysis of the French monarchy (see p. 251). 'Concord' and 'unity' are only possible if subjects render complete obedience to the king, but the king himself is subject to the three 'bridles' of religion, justice and 'police'. Both justice and 'police' (dealing with social and economic order) rest on 'laws, ordinances and praiseworthy customs' (Seyssel, 1981, pp. 49–57). Bodin's definition of law in terms of the command of the sovereign was not endorsed by Seyssel or most of his contemporaries. In any case, even Bodin allowed that sovereigns' *private* transactions should be subject to legal provisions, and that they have no right to ignore those fundamental laws that define the extent of their state and their claim to rule it (see p. 254).

Marsilius of Padua (1275/80–1342/43)

Born and educated in Padua, where he trained as a physician, Marsilius subsequently practised medicine in Italy and taught at the arts faculty in Paris. His major political writing, *Defender of the Peace* (1324), was condemned as heretical and he was forced to seek refuge in Bavaria. He played an important role in the republic established in Rome during Lewis of Bavaria's expedition to Italy in 1327–30.

Seyssel's contemporaries took a variety of views on how far the framework created by the triumvirate of pre-existing 'laws, ordinances and praiseworthy customs' related to political supremacy. For example some writers thought that customary law (taken to embody the consent of the community) is supreme in republics but not in monarchies. Others argued that while custom is binding in private matters – those concerning 'contracts, wills, dues and obligations for landholding, inheritance practices' – the prerogative of the ruler might over rule it when the good of the public is at stake (Lloyd, 1994, pp. 267–9).

By the late medieval period the diversity of English customary law had largely given way to a more unified body of 'Common Law'. This law was held to be related to customary law because it had emerged out of the practice of the community. It was, as a later writer put it, 'so framed and fitted to the nature and disposition of this people, as we may properly say it is conatural to the Nation, so as it cannot possibly be ruled by any other Law' (Pocock, 1957, p. 33). A special status was accorded to the Common Law and even the actions of the king were subject to it. For the late-sixteenth-century writer Richard Hooker:

the best limited power is best, both for [kings] and for the people; the most limited is that which may deal in fewest things, the best that which in dealing is tied unto the soundest perfectest and most indifferent rule; which rule is the law. I mean not only the law of nature and of *God* but every national or municipal law consonant thereunto. Happier that people, whose law is their *King* in the greatest things than that whose *King* is himself their law (Hooker, 1989, p. 146).

Richard Hooker (1554–1600)

Hooker taught Hebrew, logic and theology in Oxford in the late 1570s and early 1580s. A Protestant critic of puritan influences in the Church of England, Hooker was the author of *Laws of Ecclesiastical Polity* (1593–7), often regarded as one of the most important early modern defences of the English church and state.

In early modern, as in late medieval, political thought the relationship between royal supremacy, unity and order, the status ascribed to natural law, and lingering notions of government by consent made it difficult to sustain both a strong conception of rule and an idea of law that was not reduced to the will of the sovereign. Bodin's tacit endorsement of some of the conventional wisdom concerning the role played by law in regulating the exercise of political power is testament both to the tenacity of these ideas, and to the complex and qualified ways in which they were formulated. The application of Thomas Hobbes' radical scepticism to the turmoil of the seventeenth century cut through these entanglements and produced an unalloyed statement of legislative sovereignty: rule had become the measure of law. However, the position Hobbes advanced coexisted with other theories (such as that produced by John Locke) that incorporated elements of late medieval–early modern thinking and conveyed ideas about the rule of law in traditional colours (see p. 216). Hobbes apart, this line of thinking was not challenged seriously until the middle of the eighteenth century, when the Scottish philosopher David Hume presented an account of politics that identified it with the determination and enforcement of rules possessing a distinctive character. In other words, while Hume insisted on the rule of law, he developed a new and significant account of the *nature* of law.

Hume's Rules of Justice

Hume's political thinking reflected a growing scepticism about religious truth that was the hallmark of the reorientation of European intellectual culture known as the 'Enlightenment'. The term was first employed by the French writer Voltaire, but enlightenment thinking in France was only one manifestation of a general European movement that sought to base human thinking and human society on a new, scientific basis. This endeavour corresponded with Hume's intellectual position, and particularly with his rejection of the intellectual status of Christianity. He was also interested in explaining the true basis of political society to his contemporaries so that they would not be led astray by the dangerous and erroneous doctrines that had played such a powerful role in recent European and British history (Forbes, 1975, pp. 91–101).

Hume thought that a scientific approach to politics necessitated the abandonment of perspectives on politics that were underwritten by what he described as 'two species of false religion', namely 'superstition' and 'enthusiasm'. These perspectives were not merely false (that is, conceptually incoherent and empirically untenable), they were also detrimental to human well-being. 'Superstition', a consequence of humans' 'weakness, ... melancholy, together with ignorance', was manifest in a desire to appease incomprehensible forces by resort to 'ceremonies, observances, mortifications, sacrifices, presents'. It threw government into the hands of religious tyrants and produced 'endless contentions, persecutions, and religious wars' rather than productive order (Hume, 1994, pp. 46, 49). In contrast 'enthusiasm' – a product of 'hope, pride, presumption, a warm imagination, together with ignorance' – gave rise to conflict, which sprang from individual self-assertion. Enthusiasts believed that they and they alone had a special relationship with superior powers and a duty to remake the world so that it corresponded to the individual's privileged view of the requirements of Christian virtue. Numerous exemplifications of the nature and consequences of enthusiasm can be seen in the history of the Protestant sectarians in the sixteenth and seventeenth centuries. Although the effects of enthusiasm were relatively short-lived, in its prime it produced a 'contempt for the common rules of reason, morality, and prudence' and gave rise to 'the most cruel disorders in human society' (ibid., p. 48).

The ill-consequences of both superstition and enthusiasm were a result of human beings' failure to develop a coherent account of the nature and purpose of government. For those in the grip of superstition, government was an authority that could only be explained in occult terms; for religious enthusiasts, political authority must be tailored to the needs of those whose self-ascribed sense of virtue placed a premium upon self-rule. Hume's reflections on the recent history of many European societies led him to the view that enthusiasts indulged their own fantasies at the expense of the rest of the community. In a sense however, this was not surprising since neither they, nor the devotees of superstition, were able to formulate a proper view of the ends of government. A coherent account of the state could not be produced by those who were in the grip of ignorance and incredulity.

The particular charges that Hume levelled against superstition and enthusiasm did not apply to other, less extreme, conceptions of politics, but these lacked philosophical coherence because they rested upon religious assumptions that could not stand up to rational scrutiny. In response to these inadequacies, Hume developed a theory of politics that was independent of Christianity and focused on the relationship between human interests, morality and political authority. There was a utilitarian dimension to Hume's thinking, but, as noted above, he did not think that the *direct* pursuit of happiness or pleasure could be seen as the ends of politics (see p. 109). Rather, politics was a means of promoting and protecting the public interest, which was made up of a combination of the interests held by members of a given society (Haakonssen, 1981, pp. 39–41). The public interest was specified by 'rules of justice' that were impartial in form, directed to the public good and enforced by government.

The starting point of Hume's theory is a series of arguments suggesting that fundamental moral notions such as 'justice' are 'artificial', not 'natural'; they are in fact necessary to make social life viable and generally beneficial. Hume argued that social life is a means by which human beings compensate for being unable adequately to satisfy their basic needs. Having compared the human condition with that of various animals, Hume ascribed to social life those attributes that enable humanity to match, and indeed excel over other species:

By society all his infirmities are compensated; and though in that situation his wants multiply every moment upon him, yet his abilities are still more augmented, and leave him in every respect more satisfied and happy than it is possible for him in his savage and solitary condition ever to become (Hume, 1962, p. 56).

An appreciation of the benefits of sociability encourages human beings to become aware of a correspondence between the general interest and their own interests. However, in order to ensure that the former is not undermined by a narrow and partial conception of the latter, humankind has developed rules of justice that make social intercourse stable and generally beneficial.

Formulation of these rules and development of a sense of justice and injustice that make them binding upon members of a given society are necessary if social life is to provide the means by which human beings can effectively pursue their own interests. Hume insisted that the idea of justice and the rules that specify its requirements are not natural. He could discern no natural motive impelling human beings to pursue the public interest: it is too remote a goal for practical purposes, and will not overcome the general and natural partiality that most human beings feel for their own interests (ibid., pp. 52, 58–9). Justice is an 'artificial' virtue, one that arose as a result of 'education and human conventions' rather than being an intrinsic characteristic of human beings (ibid., p. 54). Hume made it clear however, that the artificiality of justice does not in any way demean it. To the contrary,

I make use of the word *natural* only as opposed to *artificial*. In another sense of the word, as no principle of the human mind is more natural than a sense of virtue, so no virtue is more natural than justice. Mankind is an inventive species; and where an invention is obvious and absolutely necessary, it may as properly be said to be natural as anything which proceeds immediately from original principles, without the intervention of thought or reflection (ibid., pp. 54–5).

Hume traced the origin of ideas of justice to the problems produced by disputes over material possessions. Without fixed rules of property, and particularly without ways of specifying what belongs to whom and of preventing others from interfering with other peoples' possessions, social life would be virtually impossible. Justice originates in peoples' appreciation of the need for a general 'abstinence from the possessions of others'. This appreciation gives rise to an agreement about rules to realise this end and forms the basis of the ideas of justice and injustice (ibid., pp. 59–60). Hume regarded rules of justice as essentially negative. That is, they tell people what they ought not to do if their actions are to avoid

damaging the public interest (Haakonssen, 1981, p. 39). Actions that conform to the laws of justice may well be subject to other forms of moral
evaluation – for example a just action may not be benevolent – but these
considerations do not concern justice, and therefore fall outside the scope
of what can be enforced through legal mechanisms. All laws

> are general, and regard alone some essential circumstances of the case,
> without taking into consideration the characters, situations, and connec-
> tions of the person concerned, of any particular consequences which
> may result from the determination of these laws in any particular case
> which offers.... Public utility requires that property should be regu-
> lated by general inflexible rules; and though such rules are adopted as
> best serve the same end of public utility, it is impossible for them to
> prevent all particular hardships or make beneficial consequences result
> from every individual case. It is sufficient if the whole plan or scheme
> be necessary to the support of civil society, and if the balance of good,
> in the main, do thereby preponderate much above that of evil (Hume,
> 1962, pp. 277–8).

Although Hume thought that adherence to rules of justice is to the general advantage of all members of a given society and therefore serve all
their interests, he believed people may tend on occasion to act unjustly in
order to gain an immediate benefit. Rules of justice must therefore be
enforced, and government is the means by which this can be done. By
maintaining these rules, by settling disputes about what they entail, and
by ensuring that public goods are provided for, government thus serves
the interests of those it controls. Since it is impossible for the whole
population to directly and consistently equate their immediate interests
with upholding the laws of justice, society must be under the regulation
of those whose circumstances and situation ensure they have such an
interest. 'These are the persons', Hume writes,

> whom we call civil magistrates, kings and their ministers, our gover-
> nors and rulers, who, being indifferent persons to the greatest part of
> the state, have no interest, or but a remote one, in any act of injustice;
> and, being satisfied with their present condition and with their part in
> society, have an immediate interest in every execution of justice which
> is so necessary to the upholding of society (ibid., pp. 99–100).

Hume's view of the role of government as the upholder of laws of justice
may be contrasted with the constructive and particular interests pursued
by those in the grip of both superstition and enthusiasm. Rather than
restricting themselves to maintaining a system of artificial rules, these
people regard government as an embodiment of natural sentiment (Whe-

lan, 1985, p. 354). In Hume's view, however, natural sentiments cannot provide the basis for pursuing the public interest. They necessarily involve the pursuit of partial and private interests that are fatal to the idea of social life and prevent human beings from reaping its benefits.

While Hume thought that the particular principles upheld by government reflect the value system adhered to by a given society (Haakonssen, 1981, p. 43), he maintained that their general form must relate to a conception of public benefit. When Hume applied this idea of benefit to contemporary society he sought to identify forms of legal regulation that would contribute to the growth of 'civilization', by which he meant the development of the material, cultural and scientific capacities that contribute to a higher degree of public utility than had been attained in less developed conditions. The essential requirement is that systems of law and political regulation should produce certainty and security; that is, they should conform to the general structure of rules of justice rather than being arbitrary and uncertain impositions. Hume thus identified the rise of what he called the 'arts and sciences' with governments based on systems of law that regulate the conduct of both subjects and rulers: 'from law arises security: From security curiosity: And from curiosity knowledge' (Hume, 1994, p. 63). The first stage in this process – the development of law as the regulator of social interaction – cannot take place under despotic or 'barbarous' monarchies 'where the people alone are restrained by the authority of the magistrates, and the magistrates are not restrained by any law or statute' (ibid., p. 63). Hume argued, however, that monarchies can adopt the legal practices that first appeared in republics and thereby provide an environment where civilisation is able to flourish. In 'civilised monarchy',

> the prince alone is unrestrained in the exercise of his authority.... Every minister or magistrate, however eminent, must submit to the general laws, which govern the whole of society, and must exert the authority delegated to him after the manner, which is prescribed. The people depend on none but their sovereign, for the security of their property. He is so far removed from them, and is so much exempt from private jealousies or interests, that this dependence is scarcely felt. And thus a species of government arises, to which, in a high political rant, we may give the name of *Tyranny*, but which, by a just and prudent administration, may afford tolerable security to the people, and may answer most of the ends of political society (ibid., p. 69).

In other words, the rule of law incorporating rules of justice may exist within a variety of constitutional frameworks. The crucial issue is whether government is conducted on the basis of known, impartial and certain rules that provide security both from other individuals and from government itself. If these conditions are satisfied, people can be assured that political power is being exercised in a way that is conducive to public benefit. Hume believed that constitutional regimes such as that which existed in England provide the best security against the misuse of political authority, but he thought that government can be absolute without being arbitrary. The fact that power is exercised through legal means is more important than the fact that it is in the hands of an absolute ruler.

The Rule of Law in Eighteenth- and Early-Nineteenth-Century French and German Theory: Montesquieu, Constant and the *Rechsstaat*

Hume's idea that detailed formulations of rules of justice reflect the value systems prevailing in particular societies means that legal structures that regulate the conduct of subjects and their relationship with rulers will vary from place to place and time to time. A similar point was made by Hume's French contemporary, Baron de Montesquieu. Although Montesquieu adopted some aspects of conventional natural law theory, he stressed the distinctive features of systems of positive law: 'Law in general is human reason ... the political and civil laws of each nation ought to be particular cases of the application of human reason'. These cases should take account of the nature and principles of different systems of government, the physical characteristics of the people, their history and even the geographical and climatic features of their country (Montesquieu, 1977, p. 177).

Starting from this presupposition, Montesquieu identified a range of laws that he considered fundamental. These laws concern the form of government, the liberty of subjects in relation to the constitution ('political liberty') and their liberty as subjects. Political liberty exists where 'no one is compelled to do what is not made obligatory by law' and is most effectively secured by a system of constitutional checks that prevent, or at least minimise, the risk of misuse of political power (ibid., p. 244). While political liberty is a purely legal matter, the liberty of the subject rests on a broader basis made up of laws, 'manners, customs or received examples'. It consists in 'security, or the opinion that people have of their security' (Montesquieu, 1949, vol. i, p. 183).

For Montesquieu, therefore, the rule of law is supported by public opinion and other non-legal constraints that ensure that the conduct of governments is both reasonable and legal. Important aspects of Montesquieu's general position were incorporated in the theory of constitutional monarchy developed by his successor Benjamin Constant (see p. 158). Constant stressed that constitutional government must give clear legal recognition of the liberty of the subject, and must protect it through legal procedures that lie beyond the control of those holding political office. The goal is to establish what Constant called a 'union of men under the empire of laws', an arrangement that precludes arbitrary applications of either political or judicial power (Constant, 1988, p. 292).

This ambition also lies behind the idea of a *Rechtsstaat* (the 'state of law'), which was developed by Constant's German contemporaries. Given the variety of forms of government that existed in early-nineteenth-century Germany, it is not surprising that the idea of the *Rechtsstaat* has not been tied to any particular set of political institutions. The doctrine has been applied to any form of government that acts upon *all* its citizens through general laws. Unlike the negative conception of law developed by Hume, the laws upheld by a *Rechtsstaat* are capable of being given a strongly positive bearing and can provide a structure for the pursuit of social goals by an active state (Krieger, 1972, p. 260). To the extent that this application of the idea of law produces regularity and uniformity, it marks an improvement on the arbitrary conduct of despotic rulers.

Because of its positive implications however, the doctrine of the *Rechtsstaat* lent itself to the idea of the *Kulturstaat*, that is, a state dedicated to the development of a particular way of life. One reason for this development was that early-nineteenth-century accounts of the *Rechtsstaat* did not contain clear specifications of the generality of law: they merely specified that laws should be applied equally to all subjects. The issue of the character of acceptable forms of law found its most sophisticated formulation in the writings of F. A. Hayek.

Hayek's Rules of Justice

Hayek was of Austrian origin, although most of his major political writings were written in English and were first published in Britain and/or the United States. Hayek's work in political theory was closely related to his primary role as an economist. For example, many aspects of his political thought were influenced by his understanding of the type of order that emerges as a result of the free exchange of goods and services in a market economy. Hayek thought of himself as working in the tradition in which Hume played an important role, but his conception of rules was applied much more directly and overtly to developing strictures concerning the exercise of political power. Hayek's understanding of the rules of justice involved very restricted limits being set on legitimate political regulation, restrictions that went far beyond more conventional constitutional or rule-of-law doctrines. For Hayek the rule of law meant the rule of a *particular type* of law, not mere adherence to legally prescribed standards.

Friedrich von Hayek (1899–1992)

An Austrian by birth, Hayek taught economics in England, Germany and the
United States and he was awarded the Nobel Prize for his contributions to
that discipline in 1974. Hayek's political writings (the most important of
which was *The Constitution of Liberty*, 1960) argue for individual freedom, the
rule of law and the value of the free market, and caution against attempts to
use the state to achieve 'social justice'.

Hayek's arguments on this point were developed in overt opposition to
the 'constructionist rationalist' tradition that he identified with Hobbes,
Austin, Bentham and Kelsen, and with the command theory of law to
which these writers subscribed (see pp. 37–8). He also claimed, however,
that their way of thinking about law has tainted the theory and practice
of modern democratic politics. The key element of Hayek's critique of
these traditions is that they rest on the erroneous assumption that order
must be created through the commands of political superiors, whether
these be monarchical sovereigns or popularly elected sovereign legislative
chambers.

This critique does not doubt that some sort of order can be created
and sustained through a command system of law, but it rejects the
possibility that it will be either efficient, generally beneficial or morally
acceptable. For Hayek, these values are intimately related to individual
freedom because this helps to mitigate the limited knowledge that any
individual possesses about the expectations of other human beings and
about the unintended consequences of their actions. Hayek thought
human knowledge to be necessarily limited, and he argued for the
adoption of systems of social organisation that allow the maximum
amount of human freedom. Free individuals can respond quickly and
reasonably sensitively to the demands of their fellows, and to the
unknowable consequences produced by the infinite number of transactions that take place in a complex society. An order created by commands simply cannot maximise the benefits of human interaction; when
it attempts to do so it gives rise to unproductive uncertainty, inefficiency and arbitrary oppression. For Hayek the paradoxical nature of
attempts to create order through the commands of a sovereign is shown
by the tendency for such regimes to be as oppressive as Hobbes'
Leviathan, and yet to reproduce many of the deprivations that
characterise his 'state of war'. Hayek supported this claim by reference
to the history of communist states in Russia and Eastern Europe. However, he also pointed to the dangers lurking behind the more benign
facade of Western welfare states. These regimes oppress their subjects to

a greater or a lesser degree, they impede technological and material development, and they also inhibit the processes of spontaneous experimentation, which are the key to human progression.

These outcomes result from attempts to create and sustain a beneficial order through the actions of an all-powerful political figure. For an order created through commands to satisfy this requirement, it is necessary to presuppose either an impossibly extensive degree of knowledge on the part of the orderer, or endless regulation so as to channel and/or repress humans' expectations and control their behaviour. If one cannot *know* what humans want then one must *make* them conform to a pattern that can be known. In short, a created order is utopian in aspiration and must be oppressive and unproductive in practice. To use political power for these purposes is therefore unacceptable. Hayek's idea of a 'spontaneous' order was advanced as the only viable alternative to the forced, inefficient and endlessly oppressive model promoted by Hobbes and his followers, practised unconsciously by modern social democrats and epitomised in the history of the 'command economies' of the communist states of Eastern Europe.

Spontaneous orders are the unintended product of past action. They make possible a wide range of individually willed and executed actions. Hayek developed this conception of a spontaneous order by direct reference to the series of expectation-driven and want-satisfying actions that characterise a pure market economy. But he believed that economies of this kind are only one example of a wide variety of maximally beneficial orders that are found throughout human life, and indeed in nature as well.

For Hayek the distinguishing characteristic of spontaneous order is that the behaviour of its constituent elements can be *explained* by reference to a system of rules. In many cases, however, a spontaneous order is created and sustained through the interaction of constituent elements who are not conscious of the existence of an order, or of the patterns of regular interaction that make up the order. To some degree this feature is discernable in human orders, but the rules that apply to complex entities such as the modern state take on a conscious and prescriptive character. Hayek argued that the key problem in political thought is to identify the distinctive characteristics of these rules and to arrive at a clear understanding of the sort of order they produce.

The political implications of this approach are explored most fully in Hayek's major work in political theory, *The Constitution of Liberty* (1960), and are restated in his later writings. The critical aspects of this work built upon Hayek's earlier exploration of rational constructionism, and particularly its totalitarian consequences, in *The Road to Serfdom* (1944). In *The Constitution of Liberty* Hayek's belief that he was making a contribution to a long tradition in political thinking that focused on the need to subject political authority to the regulatory force of fixed law, was signalled by his use of mottos drawn from a wide range of historical thinkers. These include one taken from a work attributed to the medieval writer Henry Bracton (see p. 278). Significantly, this motto draws attention to the dangerous implications of unspecified obligations:

> that is an absolute villeinage from which an uncertain and indeterminate service is rendered, where it cannot be known in the evening what service is to be rendered in the morning, that is where a person is bound to whatever is enjoined to him (Hayek, 1960, p. 133).

'Bracton's' comment refers to feudal bondage, and Hayek argued that unlimited political authority produces a form of servitude in the modern state that is as harmful to freedom as that exercised by feudal lords over their 'villeins'.

Hayek called the rules in question 'rules of law' or 'rules of just conduct'. Unlike rules that explain the behaviour of natural phenomena, or those customary ones that form part of the framework of the human mind, individuals

> may have to be made to obey [rules of law], since, although it would be in the interest of each to disregard them, the overall order on which the success of their actions depends will arise only if these rules are generally followed.

Such rules are 'normative'; they tell individuals what 'they ought and ought not to do' (Hayek, 1982, vol. i, p. 45). Hayek insisted, however, that the need for rules of this kind does not detract from the spontaneous nature of the order in question: 'its particular manifestation will always depend on many circumstances which the designer of these rules did not and could not know' (ibid., p. 46). The overall order is thus *facilitated* by rules of law rather than *created* directly by them. Moreover Hayek argued that the rules of law that are most productive of beneficial spontaneity are themselves the product of spontaneous order rather than legislative enactment. Unlike Hobbes 'Leviathan', who is empowered to create order, the government in Hayek's spontaneous order merely enforces, and in some cases 'improves', rules that have already shown themselves to be beneficial (ibid., p. 51).

The purpose of rules of justice is to delineate a private sphere where individuals are protected from coercion by other individuals or by the government itself. Hayek maintained that the range and content of this private sphere can only be specified in general terms; a greater degree of specificity would itself be coercive. Consequently he argues for the need for general rules that govern the conditions under which objects or circumstances become part of the protected sphere of a person or persons. The acceptance of such rules enables each member of a society to shape the content of his protected sphere and all members to recognize what belongs to their sphere and what does not (Hayek, 1960, p. 140).

These rules have a negative cast and must be distinguished from 'commands'. Commands are *directive*; they are addressed to particular individuals, and are intended to produce a state of affairs that is determined by the person issuing the command. In contrast general rules are 'directed to unknown people, . . . abstracted from all particular circumstances of time and place and refer only to such conditions as may occur anywhere at any time' (ibid., p. 150).

When acting in a framework made up of general rules, individuals must satisfy the largely negative conditions specified by them. Provided they do so, they are free to act as they choose. Since these rules inhibit the actions of others, they provide individuals with a degree of certainty about the behaviour of others that they can take into account when deciding how they will act. As Hayek put it, general rules are 'instrumental, they are means put at his disposal, and they provide part of the data which, together with his knowledge of particular circumstances of time and place, he can use as the basis for his decisions' (ibid., p. 152). When people obey commands they pursue other people's ends, but when they act within the laws of justice they follow their own. For this reason Hayek argued that the idea of law as a command is appropriate only in systems of regulation that are applied to administrators and government officials: it is necessary to direct the conduct of these individuals so that they can perform their assigned task. By the same token however, if this model is applied to citizens at large, they are reduced to the status of unpaid servants of the state.

The idea of the rule of law has important implications for the exercise of political power because it limits the power of government. Private individuals can only be coerced in order to enforce known law; such law must, of course, take the form of a general rule. As a consequence, except when it is applied to public servants, the exercise of political power must be confined within the limits specified by just laws. Governments that use their coercive powers for other, more extensive purposes are acting beyond the limits of their legitimate competence and are embarking on a path that is conceptually indistinguishable from that which leads to 'arbitrary tyranny' (ibid., p. 206). This position is based on the erroneous and dangerous assumption that whatever the government does is right and legal. Hayek believed that in the late nineteenth and early twentieth centuries a long and sound tradition based on ideas of the rule of law was being undermined by conscious or unconscious proponents of the view of law developed by Hobbes. The wide recognition accorded to legal positivism in British and American legal circles, the perversion of the *Rechtsstaat* into the *Kulturstaat* in late-nineteenth- and early-twentieth-century Germany, the imposition of communism in Russia and Eastern Europe, and the acceptance, of ideas of distributive justice in Western democracies were all underwritten by rejection of a substantive notion of the rule of law.

Hayek's account of the role that 'rules of law' play in sustaining a spontaneous order was developed in direct opposition to command theories of law. These theories presuppose that viable human life can only develop in an order that is created by a known and distinctive orderer (ibid., p. 73). Hayek denied that command theory is compatible with a very limited degree of direction. It is not likely, for example, that the sovereign will create and maintain a system of minimal order while leaving space for spontaneous action by the subject. The reason for this is that command theory rests on an assumption that beneficial human arrangements are *due* to human intention; as we have seen, Hayek rejected this position. Many features of a spontaneous order are themselves the product of spontaneity. Command theory ignores this, and operates on the fatally flawed assumption that beneficial order is created through the foreknowledge of the orderer. For Hayek, foreknowledge must necessarily be imperfect, and when humans try to create systems of order they produce inefficiency and oppression rather than general benefit.

Conclusion

Hayek set his notion of a law-bound order within a tradition that constrains political power within a legal framework. This tradition has a long pedigree in the history of political thought, but ancient and early-modern exponents of the idea of the rule of law did not attempt to provide strict specifications of legitimate law. Arguments about the rule of law stress the importance of the consistency of human law, and the need for it to be applied in a regular and non-arbitrary manner. Hayek's theory incorporates these ideas, but it adds to them the stipulation that the scope of law is necessarily limited. Natural law theorists thought that rulers should retain a considerable amount of discretion, and they did not restrict the directive scope of legitimate laws. Their main concern was to establish the principle that the exercise of political power must further the common good, not merely the particular good of rulers.

In contrast Hayek insisted that laws are only legitimate if they take the form of 'rules of justice'. Building on Hume's argument about the artificial nature of ideas of justice, Hayek produced a conception of a just legal order that conforms to his understanding of the role that legal rules should play within modern societies. Rules of this kind are particular reflections of the general principle that good laws serve the general interests of all members of society. In the past, these interests have been threatened by monarchical and aristocratic forms of government. In the modern world, however, they are threatened by democratic forms of government that provide opportunities for more extensive, but still limited, sections of the population to exercise power in ways that ignore the interests of other members of the community.

PART IV

Challenging Political Authority

The theories of absolute sovereignty discussed in Chapter 10 were originally developed in response to prevailing ideas concerning the need to limit government, either by means of internal constitutional constraints or by setting up an external standard of natural law. Both of these mechanisms can be seen as part of the normal structure of government, and to the extent that these institutions and norms ensure that government actually fulfils the purposes for which it exists, they eliminate the grounds upon which the exercise of political power can be challenged. Proponents of natural law or mixed government are no less concerned with stability and order than those who espouse doctrines of absolute sovereignty, but they differ on how this end can be attained.

However, while the concern to maintain stability and order has played an important role in the history of political thought, it has long been recognised that this goal will not always be achieved. Constitutional safeguards may be circumvented through the corrupt application of human ingenuity, or they – and the legal system of which they form a part – may fail to produce substantive justice through the accidental or wilful myopia of those charged with framing law. Ignorance, or indifference to the sanction of divine disapproval, which underwrites natural law, may also make this an ineffective means of regulating the conduct of governors. In response to these problems a number of writers have developed theories to justify resistance to specific acts by rulers who abuse their position. In addition to these defensive responses to the corruption of generally acceptable systems of institutional and normative regulation, there has also appeared a range of theories with overtly revolutionary implications. These theories rest on the claim that the realisation of fundamental values necessitates the destruction of existing forms of political authority and the reconstitution of the state.

The theories considered in this part of the book all imply that particular exercises of political power and/or certain forms of government lack 'legitimacy'. That is, the thinkers discussed here argue that the acts or systems in question do not conform to standards of rightness that are acceptable to those who are subject to them, and that they fail to satisfy the requirements of good government. As we shall see, challenges to the legitimacy of systems of political authority provide the basis for theories that promote resistance to unjust rulers, or for more fundamental claims about the need for a revolutionary transformation of political relationships.

Arguments questioning the legitimacy of exercises or systems of political authority often focus on one or more of the following issues. First, they question whether political power has been acquired and exercised in accordance with formal or informal established rules. Second, the rules in question have to be justified by reference to widely shared beliefs about the qualities expected of rulers and the outcomes of the proper exercise of political power. Finally, those who question the legitimacy of rulers or systems of government frequently argue that acceptable relationships of subordination and superiority should be consented to by those who occupy subordinate positions (Beetham, 1991, pp. 16–19). Rules, beliefs and modes of consent may be culturally specific, but in some cases they may be seen as local applications of universally valid standards.

For example, as noted above (see pp. 201ff), the legitimacy conferred on governments and/or rulers who uphold natural law reflects assumptions about the relationship between human enactments and universally binding rules that are not a matter of human determination. Whatever the specificity of the procedures and standards that confer legitimacy, the lack of it is due to a serious failure to adhere to them. When such failure occurs, the person or persons who possess political power, and in some cases the systems through which this power is exercised, are delegitimated to a greater or lesser degree, and may be subject to challenge. On the one hand it is argued that rulers and/or systems of rule no longer have a claim on the allegiance of their subjects, while on the other hand it is argued that it is right for subjects to challenge them. Issues pertaining to the nature of rules, supporting beliefs and the basis of consent are central to the theories discussed in this part of the book. Questions about the basis for distinguishing minor failures from serious ones are also important, although some theorists argue that the nature of certain forms of government can never be legitimate.

The problem of legitimacy may be related to that of 'political obligation'. Theories of political obligation consider the object of obligation ('to whom or what do I have political obligations?'), the extent and limit of these obligations and the justification of them (Horton, 1992, pp. 12–13), and it seems clear that the latter two of these issues have a direct bearing on whether a particular government is seen as legitimate. In particular, ideas of legitimacy and political obligation both hinge on questions concerning beliefs about the rightful forms, sources and purposes of political authority. While recognising this point, however, it is important to note that ideas of legitimacy are more closely tied to the exercise of political power than those arising from questions of political obligation. These obligations not only relate to obedience and rightful subjection but may extend to duties of a moral rather than a legal nature. Moreover political obligation is often set in the context of a 'political community', an entity of which government is merely a part. An important implication of this wider relationship is that while political obligation often has to do with obedience to those in positions of political authority, this need not necessarily be the case. In some cases, as we shall see in the chapters that follow, people's obligations to their political community may oblige them to disobey a particular law, or even actively to seek to depose rulers, or to replace one system of government with a more acceptable alternative (ibid., pp. 166–7). In other words, issues of political obligation may undermine the legitimacy of a given form of rule and may compel subjects to seek more satisfactory alternatives to them.

The first chapter in Part IV examines a range of arguments that justify resistance to unjust rulers, but do not challenge the general validity of a particular form of government. In medieval and early-modern political thought, this approach gave rise to arguments that focused on the question of how subjects should react to rulers who corrupt kingly government into 'tyranny'. Medieval and early-modern theories were invariably set within a religious framework that identified justice with divine commands, and in this respect at least they are similar to those produced by modern writers working within the Islamic tradition (see pp. 383–6). Theories of *revolution* differ from theories of *resistance* because they promote the overthrow of a *system* of government, rather than seeking merely to regulate rulers' conduct, or in some cases, justify their deposition. Some early-modern theories of resistance may imply revolutionary conclusions, but developed and overt theories of revolution are a feature of the modern world. They have played a prominent role in nineteenth- and early- twentieth-century conceptions of anarchism and socialism, and in anticolonial movements in Africa and Asia. The final challenge to authority that will be discussed here involves various forms of 'civil disobedience'. Some of these theories were developed by revolutionary movements for national independence, but they differ from more conventional theories of revolution because they promote non-violent processes of radical change.

CHAPTER 12

Resisting Unjust Rulers

Resistance theories address four sets of issues bearing on the legitimisation of challenges to established authority. They justify resistance by reference to the *rationale* of government, they specify the *conditions* under which it may take place, they stipulate the *form* it may take and they identify *the person or persons* entitled to undertake it. The refutation of claims that resistance is never justified is central to this enterprise, and so too is the need to identify the circumstances in which there is no obligation to obey a ruler. The theorists discussed below offer a range of views about who may resist: some restrict this right to limited sections of the population, while others argue that in certain circumstances the right to resist is possessed by all or most of the population.

Considerations of these issues relate closely to ideas about the ends of government, the location of political authority and the exercise of political power. For those who regard order as the end of politics, resistance is necessarily problematic; much the same can be said of those who identify the proper exercise of political power with notions of absolute sovereignty. In any case, since resistance may jeopardise the continued existence of the state, it is not surprising to find that even critics of absolutism tread very carefully on this issue. These writers are no more enamoured of anarchy than Hobbes or Filmer. Indeed they go to great lengths to show that resistance to unjust rulers may be necessary to strengthen the political order, thus making resistance an obligation that individuals have to their political community. In these cases theories of resistance imply a distinction between the larger purposes served by membership of a political community, the way that power is exercised within it, and the relationship between subjects and rulers.

Although resistance always has important political implications, it is useful to distinguish between theories that see resistance as *extra-political* and those that locate it *within* the structure of the state. Many medieval theories fall into the first category because resistance is portrayed as a corrective device that is applied *to* politics. In contrast the early modern period saw the development of theories of resistance that identified sources of resistance to the gross misconduct of rulers that were part of the structure *of* the state. These theories are often described as 'constitutional' because they assume that legitimate forms of government incorporate institutions and office holders endowed with the right to curb the excesses of princes. In other words, mechanisms of resistance are legal and political; they are *part* of the structure of the state rather than external to it. Rulers may lack legitimacy but this does not undermine the position of other members of the political system, provided they play the role assigned to them according to rules that rest upon the beliefs of the political community.

Resistance in Medieval Political Theory: Aquinas, John of Salisbury, William of Ockham and Marsilius

In the early medieval period Germanic ideas of kingship gave rise to a relatively straightforward and non-contentious understanding of appropriate responses to the abuse of political authority. Germanic kingship depended on popular acceptance and was expressed through acclamation and the paying of homage. In cases where a king acted in a clearly unjust manner this endorsement was withdrawn; he was deprived of his authority by the whole community or by a significant part of it, and a successor was nominated and acclaimed in his stead (Franklin, 1969b, p. 11). However, later developments in medieval ideas of Christian kingship, together with the growing complexity and sophistication of political society, meant that this approach to resistance was no longer appropriate. In particular the stress placed on 'peace and union' as primary political goals and identification of the state with the king meant that resistance (carrying with it the risk of discord, bloodshed and 'tumults') was seen as highly problematic. This point was underlined by the importance ascribed to biblical injunctions to 'obey the powers that be' because they owe their position to divine choice and hold it through divine sanction. It was also buttressed by St Augustine's idea that depraved members of the earthly city should be subject to strict authority and are liable to suffer injustice on account of their flawed characters and sinful conduct (see p. 28). It should be noted that in these cases the legitimacy of rulers does not depend on the consent of their subjects. Rather, subjects are under a general obligation to obey those who have been placed in authority over them.

These conceptions of the source and function of political authority leave little or no room for legitimate resistance to princely injustice. At the same time, however, it was recognised that rulers may abuse their position to such an extent that they undermine the rationale of the state. The coexistence of these potentially incompatible ideas means that medieval arguments about resistance were marked by a certain degree of equivocation. Nevertheless a number of influential writers cautiously endorsed resistance to unjust rulers, they specified the circumstances in which such action may be undertaken, and they identified those entitled to undertake it. These theories usually focus on the issue of how subjects should respond to 'tyranny', or the consistent, extreme and widespread misuse of political authority, involving contempt for the law and cruelty. Such conduct is illegitimate because it ignores established rules and runs contrary to accepted beliefs about the role of governors. Consequently any idea that government is based on consent is undermined.

The medieval position is reflected in Aquinas' injunction that subjects have a general obligation to obey secular rulers. This obligation is emphasised by a parallel that Aquinas drew between rulers in human society and God's role in the government of the universe:

> In the same way as in the natural order created by God, the lower must remain beneath the direction of the higher, in human affairs inferiors are bound to obey their superiors according to the order established by natural and divine law (Aquinas, 1959, p. 177).

Aquinas stressed that this obligation is not incompatible with humans' religious obligations or with the idea of Christian liberty. Because human beings 'are freed by the grace of Christ from the defects of the soul, but not from those of the body' (ibid., p. 179), secular governors are necessary to regulate 'external' conduct. Aquinas insisted however, that obedience to secular rulers is limited. For example Christians are not obliged to obey human commands that conflict with God's commands, nor can their 'interior acts' be subject to regulation by other human beings. In addition, because all humans are 'equal in nature', rulers cannot presume to regulate them in the performance of such natural functions as those concerning reproduction (ibid., p. 177).

Aquinas did not discuss these particular limitations of obedience in terms of resistance, nor did he do so when he argued that subjects should disobey commands that produce vice rather than virtue. Although these commands are incompatible with the rationale of authority, the appropriate response is what Aquinas called 'passive disobedience', not resistance. Subjects should refuse to obey a particular command, but they should not make a direct attempt to correct a ruler's conduct, or to challenge his general authority. The model that Aquinas employed in his discussion of passive disobedience was that of 'holy martyrs who suffered death rather than obey the impious commands of tyrants', not active resistance (ibid.,

p. 183). Nevertheless Aquinas believed that resistance may be justified in some circumstances.

Aquinas' discussion of this question rests upon a distinction (one that was to become a common feature of later resistance theory) between 'usurpers' and 'tyrants'. A usurper has no legitimate claim to authority and cannot establish a just system of authority: 'whoever possesses himself of power by violence does not truly become lord or master' (ibid., p. 183). While questions of public safety may make it expedient to obey a usurper, he may be resisted and killed if circumstances allow (ibid., pp. 179, 185). Aquinas adopted a similar approach to abuse of authority, or 'tyranny' in the conventional sense. Tyranny is unjust because it places the private good of the ruler above the welfare of his subjects. It is thus contrary to the rationale of the state and resistance to tyranny is not 'seditious'. To the contrary, it is the tyrant who has compromised the peace and safety of the community and those who resist injustice are merely acting in response to the misuse of political authority. Like unjust laws that are not proper laws, unjust rulers are not to be regarded as authentic sources of political authority. Their legitimacy is undermined because their actions do not correspond to those required by rulers acting on the basis of widely accepted beliefs about the nature of the common good.

The fact that Aquinas' discussion of resistance focuses on the problem of tyranny reflects his belief that the obligations imposed on human beings by natural law mean that authority is shared by both the king and other members of the community. In most circumstances this arrangement makes resistance difficult to justify, but the fact that the laws of a tyrant are not true laws because they are not directed towards the good of the community cuts through these complexities. It was thus argued that a tyrant can be resisted on the same grounds that justify coercive protective action against any other kind of outlaw. As we shall see, a variation on this position plays an important role in early-modern resistance theories.

The idea that obedience to just rulers is compatible with Christian liberty was given a more positive cast by a medieval English philosopher known as 'John of Salisbury'. In his *Policraticus* (1159) John glossed the biblical claim that 'wherever there is the spirit of God, in that place there is liberty' with the comment that 'servility to fear and assent to vice exterminates the Holy Spirit' (John of Salisbury, 1990, p. 27). Good rule promotes both security and liberty. The latter is necessary if human beings are to develop a sense of virtue by having the opportunity to choose between good and evil. Justice lies at the mean point between rigid control and chaotic laxity, (Nederman, 1990, p. xxiv). Tyrannical rulers are unjust because they treat their subjects with undue severity in order to further their own interests rather than those of the community (John of Salisbury, 1990, pp. 49–50). In other words, severity and the consequent curtailment of liberty are necessary features of tyranny pre-cisely because of the corrupt aims of tyrants. Since tyrants ignore the common good they have to depend on forced compliance extracted through cruel means, rather than on the consent of their subjects.

John of Salisbury (1115/20–80)

After studying in Paris, John served on the staff of the papacy and of two archbishops of Canterbury. He was Bishop of Chartres from 1176. His most important political work was *Policraticus* (1159).

In considering how subjects should respond to tyranny, John made it clear that both tyrants 'with title' and usurpers may legitimately be resisted and killed by their oppressed subjects: subjects are under no obligation to obey those who are systematically unjust, or those who lack entitlement to rule (ibid., p. 25). He later suggested that tyrannicide and lesser forms of resistance and correction may be used against *all* unjust rulers. By ignoring the claims of justice, tyrants are guilty of perverting a gift of power that has been bestowed upon them by God: 'As the image of the deity, the prince is to be loved, venerated and respected; the tyrant, an image of depravity, is for the most part even to be killed' (ibid., p. 191). It is important to note, however, that although John thought that tyrannicide could be justified, he insisted that tyrannicides act as *agents of God* rather than as *members of a political community*. In other words, they are not subjects of those they slay; they stand outside the state (Lewis, 1954, vol. i, p. 249).

Unlike 'constitutional' resistance, which will be discussed below, strictly speaking the theory advanced by John of Salisbury is not a politi-cal one. Agents of God are not part of the political community and their relationship to it does not involve issues of political obligation. The pri-vate status of John's resisters, and the fact that they are authorised by God, reflects his belief that disregard for justice is blasphemous. Given this view, it is more accurate to speak of a *duty* of resistance derived from humans' obligations to God rather than a *right* of resistance belonging to subjects. As we shall see, one of the important developments in early modern resistance theory was a move away from a conception that made resistance a religious duty with political implications, towards one that gave rise to political conceptions of resistance. These theories were devel-oped in the sixteenth and seventeenth centuries, but aspects of them were foreshadowed in works by two medieval thinkers, William of Ockham and Massilius of Padua.

> **William of Ockham (1280/85–1349)**
>
> William, who was a member of the Franciscan Order, taught in Oxford before a dispute with the pope in Avignon over elements of his writings encouraged him to seek the protection of Lewis of Bavaria. For most of the rest of his life he attacked what he saw as the pretensions of the papacy. A renowned logician and theologian, his major political work was *A Short Discourse on the Tyrannical Government of Things Divine and Human* (1346).

Ockham's *A Short Discourse on the Tyrannical Government of Things Divine and Human, but Especially Over the Empire* focused on papal claims to temporal supremacy over the Holy Roman Emperor and asserted the right of the latter to resist the spurious and unjust claims of the former. In arguing this case, however, Ockham developed a conception of resistance that could be applied to other political relationships. Ockham denied that any ruler has a claim to absolute power over his subjects because such a relationship is incompatible with Christian liberty. 'Christ's law' enjoins human freedom and specifies that subjection to human superiors can only be justified if it promotes the good of subjects (William of Ockham, 1992, pp. 25–8). Ockham thought that in many cases sovereignty is created by human enactment, and he argued that this means that political power can be resisted by those who establish it. While sovereigns are entitled to exercise *'regular* superiority' over their subjects, gross breach of justice provides grounds for reversing this relationship. That is, subjects can assume occasional supremacy over their (putative) superiors to ensure that power is exercised for the common good of the community (ibid., p. 112).

An important feature of Ockham's theory of resistance is that it recognises a popular basis for this right. In considering the appropriate response to imperial heresy, Ockham allowed that the right to judge in such a case lies with the pope because of his acknowledged spiritual supremacy. However the right to punish a heretical emperor lies not with the Holy See, but with the electoral princes who collectively form the 'senate' of the Holy Roman Empire. If this body is negligent in supervising the correction of the emperor, the duty to punish devolves to 'the people' because they are the original source of imperial power and also of the power of imperial supervision (ibid., pp. 159–60). In this case at least, Ockham identified a *legal* and *constitutional* basis for popular resistance that makes it part of the structure of the state. This position is echoed in a far less equivocal form in Marsilius of Padua's *The Defender of the Peace* (1324).

Marsilius was unusual among medieval writers because he identified 'peace and order' with republics rather than monarchies (see p. 173). In Marsilius' republic the supreme ruler is subject to laws made by a popularly elected assembly. (Marsilius, 1956, vol. ii, p. 45). This body has the right to regulate the conduct of the ruler and to correct, punish or depose him if he acts contrary to the law:

> since the ruler is a human being, he has understanding and appetite, which can receive other forms (than those of the law), like false opinion or perverted desire, or both, as a result of which he comes to do the contraries of the things determined by the law. Because of these actions, the ruler is rendered measurable by someone else who has the authority to measure or regulate him, or his unlawful actions, in accordance with the law (ibid., p. 87).

For Marsilius, action in conformity with law is the key requirement for legitimate political action and so the power of rulers must be curtailed when they ignore this stipulation.

Marsilius' formulation prefigured later resistance theories because it rests on the idea that illegal behaviour by rulers may be resisted through legal mechanisms that embody the principle of popular sovereignty. The people are thus both the *source* of law and (through their elected representatives) the *means* of judging and correcting unjust rulers. A feature of this type of theory is that it does not, strictly speaking, justify resistance to governors. Rather, what is involved is a reaction by one part of the government (the legislative) against another, the ruler. This process is analogous to the interaction of elements within a mixed constitution, a point that emerged quite clearly in early modern theories of 'constitutional resistance'.

Resistance in Early Reformation Political Theory: Luther and Calvin

The Protestant Reformation raised questions about resistance to political authority because, both in supranational entities such as the Holy Roman Empire and unified states such as England, France and Scotland, the adoption of reformed religion was not universal. In these circumstances the religious views of sovereigns did not always coincide with those of all their subjects. When rulers sought to impose their conceptions of 'true' religion on their subjects, questions were raised about whether the latter were entitled to resist measures that ran contrary to fervently held, religiously based conceptions of justice. Two distinctive perspectives on resistance were developed in the period when the politics of European states were most severely affected by the political implications of the Reformation, that is, during the sixteenth century and much of the seventeenth century. The first position was largely religious in orientation. It concerned the way in which Protestants should respond to rulers who sought to impose unacceptable religious doctrines and practices upon them. These impositions clashed with people's perception of their obligations to God and led them to question the legitimacy of rulers who used their power in such a way. Consideration of this issue sometimes raised the question of whether obedience should be owed to heretical princes, that is, those who remained attached to Roman Catholicism and obedient to the pope. This question implied that adherence to a 'true' conception of Christianity was a necessary condition for political legitimacy.

In addition to these issues concerning the political implications of humans' obligations to God, the Reformation period also saw the emergence of a perspective on resistance that focused on the conduct of rulers and considered the response that subjects were entitled to make to rulers who failed to exercise power in ways that secured justice for their subjects. This line of enquiry eventually led to the formulation of theories of resistance that related obedience to the implications of membership of a political community, and withheld legitimacy from regimes and rulers whose characteristics and actions were incompatible with them.

Approaches to these questions were influenced by the circumstances faced by different groups in various European states. In particular they reflected their conception of the problems and possibilities facing reformers at particular stages in the process of reformation and counterreformation. An important issue was the degree of support that reformers enjoyed among elites and the general population. These contextual considerations help to explain why many statements on resistance were marked by a high degree of ambivalence, and were formulated in equivocal terms. Even allowing for this, however, a number of distinct positions can be identified. The first of these appears in the writings of Martin Luther and Jean Calvin, two of the fathers of the Reformation; their ideas provide a benchmark against which later and more radical statements from Germany and France can be compared.

In *On Secular Authority* (1523) Luther confronted the threat posed to the Reformation by political authorities (in this case the emperor) by advancing a doctrine of toleration that rests on a distinction between the jurisdiction of secular and spiritual governments (Hopfl, 1991, p. xviii). The fact that Luther identified discrete spheres of authority rather than establishing a standard that relates to the power of rulers and the religious duties of subjects, means he was able to reject imperial claims without undermining his general hostility to resistance. Luther's support for established political authorities and his emphasis on the need for regulation reflect his aversion to the chaotic potentialities of popular action. Luther believed that God had created secular authority in order to check anarchic tendencies in human society, and he regarded non-resistible sources of human authority as necessary to the attainment of this end. Like later proponents of absolute sovereignty, Luther stressed the personal nature of rule (ibid., p. xiv), and insisted that subjects are obliged to render complete obedience to their sovereigns. Both the argument of *On Secular Authority* and Luther's subsequent endorsement of the justification of resistance issued by the city of Madelburg in 1546, rest on a distinction between resistance by princes and semi-sovereign corporate entities against the emperor, and popular resistance against princely and corporate authorities. As far as the ordinary population is concerned, questions about the rightful source of political authority and the way in which it should be used are subsumed by an overriding obligation to live an orderly existence by observing unquestioning obedience to 'the powers that be'.

Martin Luther (1483–1546)

Luther, a native of Saxony, studied and taught theology at the University of Wittenberg and took monastic orders. His public rejection of the theological basis of Catholicism in 1517 marked the beginning of the division of Western European Christians into Roman Catholics and Protestants. In the course of grappling with the political implications of this division, Luther wrote a number of political tracts, including *On Secular Authority* (1523).

Luther's hostility to popular resistance was given a new sense of urgency by the Peasants' Revolt of 1525, a movement that challenged the authority of Protestant princes and produced a number of emphatic rejections of Luther's doctrine. For example the author of *To the Assembly of the Common Peasantry May 1525* argued that while political authority is necessary to regulate the impious and protect the pious – 'the torturing punishments of hell are never so terrible that they would drive us from evil if there were no temporal fears and punishments' (Anon, 1991, p. 105) – it is only legitimate if it is a genuinely *Christian* authority. Authority of this kind is possessed only by a ruler who 'truly protects brotherly love, zealously serves God, his lord, and paternally tends to the flock of Christ' (ibid., p. 106). This stipulation stresses both the spiritual and temporal interests of the community, and promotes the idea that legitimate rule is based on the concept of stewardship. It entails a rejection of claims to power that are based on spurious assumptions of superiority and are exercised largely for the aggrandizement of rulers:

All the popes, kings, etc. who puff themselves up in their own estimation above other pious poor Christians, claiming to be a better kind of
human being – as if their lordship and authority to rule others was
innate – do not want to recognise that they are God's stewards and
officials. And they do not govern according to his commandments to
maintain the common good and brotherly unity among us. God has
established and ordained authority for this reason alone, and no others.
But rulers who want to be both lords for their own sake are all false
rulers, and not worthy of the lowest office among Christians. (ibid., pp.
107–8).

Faced with the corruption of political authority, subjects have a duty to
engage in defensive resistance. They are entitled to depose ungodly tyrants who, by failing to acknowledge their obligations to their subjects,
breach their obligations to God and thereby negate the moral basis of
their political supremacy.

Luther's hostility to these radical ideas of popular resistance was
echoed by Jean Calvin. In his *Christian Institutes* (1559) Calvin built a strict
doctrine of non- resistance upon his theory of the necessity for political
authority and stressed its application to 'private men', that is, ordinary
individuals as distinct from office holders. He assumed that subjects owe
complete obedience to their rulers, regardless of the way in which power
is used; only God has the right to punish those who abuse political
authority. After citing many examples of divine punishment, Calvin
enjoined princes to 'hear and be afraid', but he also issued a stern warning to subjects:

> As for us, ... let us take the greatest possible care never to hold in
> contempt, or trespass upon, the plentitude of authority of magistrates
> whose majesty it is for us to venerate ... even when it is exercised by
> individuals who are unworthy of it and do their best to defile it by
> their wickedness. And even if the punishment of unbridled tyranny is
> the Lord's vengeance, we are not to image, that it is we ourselves who
> have been called upon to inflict it (Calvin, 1991, p. 82).

At the same time, however, Calvin allowed that resistance may be appropriate in systems of government where popularly elected magistrates are
duty-bound to restrain unjust rulers (ibid., p. 82). This concession is based
on the assumption that since these magistrates are part of the structure of
authority, rulers are not, strictly speaking, being resisted by their subjects.
Rather, one element of a system of rule is being opposed by another of its
elements. In such cases popular magistrates are elements of government,
and so resistance to a supreme ruler is part of the operation of the system, rather than a challenge to it. Resistance by popular magistrates does

not call the legitimacy of government into question; it merely utilises one element of government to redress wrongs perpetrated by another and is essentially restorative.

Calvin's treatment of this issue illustrates the ambiguities of Reformation statements on resistance, but it also marks the beginning of a line of argument that incorporates resistance within mixed government. To the extent that Calvin upheld the right of nominally subordinate magistrates to challenge their superiors, he laid the foundation for the less-guarded theories of resistance produced by writers associated with his French followers, the 'Huguenots'.

Resistance Theory in the Late Sixteenth Century: Beza, Hotman and Mornay

The equivocation that marked Calvin's statements on resistance resulted from his unyielding adherence to the idea that political authority is divinely ordained; even unjust rulers are often agents employed by God to punish his particularly unworthy subjects. Calvin's position also reflected widespread fears of the threat to the orderly reformation of society posed by radical, popularist sectaries attempting to take the process of reformation, and the ongoing government of a reformed, 'Godly' society, into their own hands. In Calvin's native France the Huguenots were a minority group, but they were led by members of the high nobility and harboured hopes that their faith might be tolerated by Catholic monarchs. These factors strengthened the hand of those urging caution and moderation in practice, and a degree of theoretical equivocation in advancing their political claims. From time to time, however, the pressure of events forced Huguenot thinkers to take a clear stand on the issue of resistance. The outbreak of military hostilities between Catholics and Protestants in 1562, the increasingly important role played by a violently anti-Huguenot faction led by the noble house of Guise, and traumatic events such as the St Bartholomew's Day Massacre of 1572 made it essential for the Huguenots to identify grounds for resisting a government that seemed prepared to countenance their destruction. Significantly the French governments of this period were fortified both by religious ideas and by theories of absolute government. As we have seen, these theories place unquestioning obedience at the centre feature of the relationship between subjects and their sovereigns (see pp. 249ff). The rationale for this form of rule was thought to be so compelling that it overcame all the conventional qualms about legitimacy.

In the course of confronting these difficulties, a number of writers with Huguenot connections developed important resistance theories. These statements avoided the extreme popularism current within some of the

German sects, and they have gained a significant and lasting foothold in the history of political thought. Developments in France were paralleled by those made by writers working in the still fraught, but less consistently and overwhelmingly hostile environments of contemporary England and Scotland. However, the work of various Huguenot writers is of particular importance because they developed a distinctly *political* conception of resistance. Their theories focus increasingly on the relationship between human subjects and temporal rulers, and do not treat either sovereignty or subjection as consequences of prior obligations to God. Resistance comes to be seen as a response to a breach in a contractual relationship forged by human beings; it is a *right* that belongs to human beings by virtue of their role in creating political authority, not a *duty* owed by Christians to God. Questions of obedience are thus set within a framework of *political* obligation, and beliefs about the exercise of power are considered in relation to people's understanding of the duties they owe to their political community.

Four main lines of argument can be identified within the complex and often hesitating process through which a fully fledged conception of resistance emerged. The first of these arguments draws on theories that treat resistance as a right of self-defence, one that is justified by an appeal to private-law conceptions of individual rights. The second builds upon the role ascribed by Lutheran theory to 'inferior magistrates', that is, to public officials who owe general obedience to a prince, but also exercise authority over ordinary members of the population. The role of inferior magistrates may be contrasted with ideas about 'ephoral' authority, which lies at the heart of the third line of argument. 'Ephors' (the term derives from the ancient Spartan constitution) are officials or assemblies that are constituted by the people rather than ordained by God for religious ends. The final argument utilises Catholic conceptions of natural law to formulate a contractual account of the state, and it makes this the basis of both obligation and resistance. These theories justify resistance on the grounds that the abuse of political authority implies a breach of faith that may be punished by correction or deposition of the sovereign by his putative subjects (Skinner, 1978, vol. ii, pp. 319–21).

The appeal to private law rests on the assumption that victims of illegal aggression by rulers are entitled to activate a right to self-defence that is more commonly evoked when individuals are attacked by their fellows. It is claimed, for example, that the actions of an emperor who exceeds his jurisdiction are those of a felonious private individual rather than a legitimate sovereign (ibid., pp. 197–201). Although this theory has radical implications for determining who may resist, the individualistic conclusions that can be derived from it are usually evaded by arguments showing that the agent of self-defence is not the individual, but an inferior official or a corporate body representing the entire community.

This line of argument was used by moderates associated with Luther – thus imperial aggression is to be resisted by princes who are normally subject to the emperor – but more radical versions of it were developed by Scottish and English writers. For example, in response to Queen Mary's persecution of English Protestants, Christopher Goodman came to the conclusion that it is 'lawful for the people, yea even it is their duty' to ensure that 'every rotten member' is cut off and that the law of God is imposed 'as well upon their own rulers and magistrates as upon others of their brethren' (ibid., p. 235). In Goodman's case, and in that of the leading Scottish Calvinist John Knox, this argument is supported by reference to a 'covenant' or agreement between God and his subjects. In this line of argument, resistance is seen as a *duty* owed to God, rather than a *right* possessed by human beings (ibid., p. 236). Lutherans and Calvinists thus look to established authorities, not private people, to undertake acts of resistance.

An advantage of this move is that it avoids the dangerous implications of private resistance and conforms with the privileged position conventionally accorded to the 'powers that be'. Resistance by inferior magistrates utilises God-ordained powers to punish those whose particular and extensive wrongdoing undermines their claims upon the loyalty of both their subjects and those magistrates who are usually subordinate to them. According to Luther's associate Martin Bucer, Christian magistrates are duty-bound to uphold God's expressed commands against ordinary subjects and recalcitrant superior magistrates (ibid., pp. 205–6). This argument was elaborated by John Knox, who drew a distinction between the 'person' and the 'office', and argued that resistance to the former does not undermine the authority of the latter. A significant point about Knox's use of this distinction is that it challenges the Augustinian idea that tyrants are ordained by God to punish sinners: it is now possible to claim that while the *office* of ruler is divinely ordained, occupants of this position who ignore God's intentions should be resisted (ibid., pp. 225–6).

In both its original and modified formulations, the role ascribed to inferior magistrates does not depart from the conventional idea that rulers of all degrees are ordained by God. This is also true of those theories that ascribe a central role to 'ephoral' authorities. However, theories of this kind have provided the most fertile soil for the development of accounts of resistance that rest not on the idea of the divine ordination of sovereigns, but on popular sovereignty. A tentative and restricted statement of the role that popularly elected assemblies can play in resisting rulers' unjust impositions was advanced by Calvin in the *Christian Institutes* (see p. 309). This theory was attractive to Calvin's Huguenot successors because it allowed them to appeal to non-Protestant elements in the French nobility who resented absolute tendencies in French government. The key figures in the development of Huguenot theories of resistance in the latter part of the sixteenth century were François Hotman, Philippe Mornay and Theodore Beza.

François Hotman (1524–90)

Hotman was a French convert to Protestantism and lived in exile in Switzerland during the last third of his life. His best-known political work is *Francogallia* (1573).

In *Francogallia* (1573) Hotman presented an account of Biblical, European and French history that emphasises the role played by representative assemblies in curbing tyrannical monarchs. Hotman stressed that reliance on assemblies of this kind limits the danger of destabilisation because it avoids a *direct* appeal to the general population. For example, he pointed out that the resort to armed force against Louis XI in the 'War of the Commonweal' of 1460 was initiated and guided by a 'lawful assembly of citizens', the Estates General. It was emphatically not a result of the spontaneous action of the 'whole people' (Hotman, 1972, p. 443). But while they were eager to deny a right of resistance to what Mornay called that 'many-headed monster' the people, Calvin's French successors insisted that tyranny should not be tolerated. As Beza put it in *The Right of Magistrates* (1574):

> I detest seditions and disorders of all kinds as horrible monstrosities, and I agree that in affliction most of all we should depend on God alone. I admit that prayers united with repentance are proper and necessary remedies to tyranny since it is most often an evil or scourge sent by God for the chastisement of nations. But for all this, I deny that it is illicit for peoples oppressed by notorious tyranny to make use of lawful remedies in addition to repentance and prayers (Beza, 1969, pp. 104–5).

This statement captures Beza's determination to allow resistance while admitting the force of conventional objections to it. It also points the way to the essentially legal and constitutional conception of resistance that characterises late-sixteenth-century Huguenot treatments of this issue. This last point is underlined in a somewhat paradoxical manner by Beza's insistence that while suffering and patience are the only legitimate response to religious persecution, resistance to tyranny – that is, 'confirmed wickedness involving general subversion of the political order and of the fundamental laws of the realm' – is founded on 'human institution' (ibid., pp. 132, 103). In *Vindiciae contra tyrannos* (1579) Mornay made a very similar point, but he grounded his argument on a distinction between two different forms of contract: one between God, princes and their subjects, the other involving only human subjects and sovereigns. The first contract, the object of which is obligatory 'religious piety', is enforced by God alone. The second, designed to secure earthly justice, must be enforced by human agency (Mornay, 1969, p. 181).

Theodore Beza (1519–1605)

Beza, a disciple of Calvin, followed his master from France to Geneva and succeeded him as leader of the Reformed Church in Geneva in 1564. His political ideas are expounded most fully in *Of the Law of Magistrates* (1574).

Beza and Mornay not only differentiated religious and political abuses of princely power, they also argued that it is necessary to distinguish between usurpation and tyranny. The crucial point is that, since there is no contract between usurpers and their victims, there is no question of the latter being obliged to obey the former: they are not part of the same political community and have no right to exercise political authority. Usurpers can be resisted by *any* individual because they pose a threat to the existence of a civilised community. In this case resistance is necessary to preserve the basis of human life (Franklin, 1969b, p. 34). Mornay's statement of this position was particularly clear and forceful. He argued that tyrants 'without title' are merely invaders. They may therefore be resisted on the grounds of self-defence as recognised in the universal law of nations. Usurpation is also contrary to civil law precisely because it involves rule without title. Resistance to such affronts to the constitutional and legal basis of political authority is not a *right*, for there can be no rights where there is no compact, no relationship based on collective recognition. There is, however, a *duty* to resist usurpers because they threaten the basis of beneficial and orderly human interaction. The usurper

> does violence to that association to which we owe everything we have, because he subverts the foundations of the fatherland to which we are bound – by nature, by the laws, and by our oath. Therefore, if we do not resist, we are traitors to our country, deserters of human society, and contemners of the law (Mornay, 1969, p. 188).

Mornay insisted, however, that the very grounds that make it obligatory for individuals to resist tyrants without title make it illegitimate for them to resist the gross abuse of political authority by legitimately established rulers. He argued that tyrants *with* title are part of a legal and constitutional structure because there is a compact between them and their subjects that establishes the legitimacy of the ruler's claim to power. Since private individuals are not assigned power within this structure, they can have no right or duty to resist tyrannical rulers: 'private persons have no power, discharge no magistracy, and have no dominion ... or right of punishment' (ibid., p. 154). Because individuals do not possess the 'sword of magistracy' God cannot require them to use it. But while private individuals have neither a right nor a duty to resist tyrants in their personal capacities as subjects, they are obliged to follow magistrates who resist abuses of power by their princes. Mornay underlined the impotence of private persons within a constitutional structure by noting that where magisterial initiatives are not forthcoming, ordinary subjects face the choice of self-imposed exile or silent suffering. The sole exception that he allowed to this prohibition concerns those extraordinary occasions where individuals receive a special 'call' from God. In such cases they became *God's agents* (not private persons) and are endowed with the sword by Him. Mornay was aware that this exception could be abused and so he warned of the dangers of self-deception, and laid down strict criteria for identifying an authentic call from God (ibid., pp. 155–6).

Phillipe Duplessis Mornay (1549–1623)

Mornay, a leading political figure among French Protestants, is thought to have been the author of the *Vindiciae contra tyrannos* (1579).

The role ascribed to magistrates in Mornay's account of resistance and that which appears in Beza's *The Right of Magistrates*, rest upon a constitutional theory of resistance, and upon a related set of assumptions about the nature of the state, the purpose of sovereignty and the structure within which power is exercised. Both writers maintained that the state exists to further the common good. Legitimate sovereignty must be exercised for the welfare of the subjects, and is, indeed created by them for this purpose. Whatever the mode of succession, the authority of princes depends on the consent of the people, a point that is both signified and confirmed by devices such as coronation oaths, which indicate that there

is 'pact' or covenant between subjects and their sovereign. Like all contractual arrangements, those between subjects and sovereigns
stipulate conditions that must be fulfilled and the means by which
performance is monitored and, if necessary, enforced. In politics the
central obligation is to secure justice by upholding a just system of law.
As Mornay put it,

> law is like an instrument, divinely given.... A king who finds obedi-
> ence to the law demeaning is ... as ridiculous as a surveyor who
> considers the rule and compass and other instruments of skilled
> geometers to be disgraceful and absurd (ibid., pp. 169–70).

He argued that since sovereignty and law are produced by the community they can only be effectively regulated and upheld through corporate
(as opposed to individual and private) means that embody its interests.
'The people' does not refer to the 'entire multitude, that many headed
monster', but to 'the people collectively', or, 'those who receive authority
from the people, that is, the magistrates below the king who have been
elected by the people or established in some other ways' (ibid., p. 149).
As representatives of the community, these magistrates are endowed with
the exclusive right to resist the misuse of power by the sovereign. They
alone have responsibility for ensuring that the terms of the compact are
upheld, and that sovereign power is directed towards the ends for which
it has been created.

A variation of this argument is presented by Beza. He distinguished
between lesser magistrates who may resist, but not depose, a tyrant, and
the more extensive powers belonging to representative 'estates' or assemblies. These powers are a consequence of the fact that particular sovereigns receive their authority directly from the estates, who have been
given this responsibility by the people: 'those who have the power to
give ... [princes] their authority have no less power to deprive them of it'
when the conditions attached to the grant are breached grossly (Beza,
1969, pp. 114, 123). In Mornay's formulation, magistrates and assemblies
are described as 'coprotectors' of the kingdom; in normal circumstances
they are subject to the sovereign, but when a ruler becomes a tyrant they
have a duty to resist him (Mornay, 1969, pp. 191–2). As coprotectors,
magistrates and estates possess powers that are independent of the sovereign but are part of the *sovereignty* of the state. They are, as Franklin puts
it, 'not isolated' from the structure of the state; they provide the ultimate
guarantee of a set of particular controls upon authority that are 'implicit'
in the act of election (Franklin, 1969b, p. 37).

Late Huguenot theories of resistance are, therefore, both constitutional
and popular. However, for reasons of safety and efficiency it was thought
necessary to use representative assemblies to transform 'the people' from

a mass of individuals into a corporate whole. When these ideas were applied to the problem of how tyrants should be resisted, they identified constitutional bodies as the appropriate agencies for checking the abuse of power. In so doing, they gave rise to an understanding of the on-going exercise of political power that embraced many of the assumptions underlying mixed constitutions. As Mornay put it:

[A]s a well-constructed kingdom contains all the advantages of the other good regimes, tyranny contains all the evils of the bad ones. A kingdom resembles aristocracy in that the best men are invited to the royal council, whereas tyranny resembles oligarchy in inviting the worst and most corrupt.... A kingdom also resembles constitutional democracy ... in that there is an assembly of all the orders to which the best men are sent as deputies to deliberate the affairs of the commonwealth. Tyranny resembles lawless democracy, or mob-rule ... because, in so far as it cannot prevent assemblies, it bends every effort, uses every device of electioneering and deception, to insure that the worst of men are sent to them. Thus does the tyrant affect the posture of a king, and tyranny, the appearance of a kingdom (Mornay, 1969, pp. 186–7).

Beza and Mornay introduced a number of arguments that played an important role in the subsequent development of resistance theory. Despite their attachments to the Huguenot cause their approach was largely secular, or at least non-sectarian, and could thus be utilised by those who were not concerned with the defence of a Protestant minority (Skinner, 1978, vol. ii, p. 321). Moreover both these writers dealt with resistance in distinctly political terms, relating it not only to religious persecution, but to more widespread injustices that undermine the rationale of the state. This point was signalled quite clearly by Mornay's emphatic statement that tyranny concerns the *bilateral* relationship between sovereigns and subjects, not the *trilateral* one that embraces God, rulers and subjects. Tyranny is wrong because it runs counter to the conditions governing membership of a political community, not because it disrupts humans' fulfilment of their obligations to God. Of course Huguenot writers thought of justice as a divinely ordained feature of human relationships, and in this sense their theory of resistance cannot be divorced from their religious views. At the same time, however, their political treatment of resistance meant that it could provide the basis for later accounts that recognised the right of individuals to resist. Beza and Mornay avoided this radical conclusion by insisting that although sovereignty has a popular basis, 'the people' play no role in either the ordinary administration of the state or the corrective processes that are brought to bear against tyrants. In addition, while these writers traced sovereignty to a creative act of the people, their stress on the incorporation of the community into particular historical institutions meant they did not need to make definitive statements about the original role of individuals, the nature of the conceptual environment from which the state emerged, or about the relationship between the community's right to resist and the moral status of those who had created it. Huguenot writers were thus able to insulate the right to resist from the dangerously popularist potentialities of a theory that traced this to popular sovereignty. However, features of their approach to resistance could serve as the foundations of a far more radical account of the implications of popular sovereignty, such as that developed by the English writer John Locke in the closing decades of the seventeenth century.

Popular Sovereignty and Resistance: Locke

Locke's *Second Treatise* was written in the early 1680s, but was only published in 1689 following the deposition of James II from the thrones of England, Scotland and Ireland. The last chapter of this work, 'On the Dissolution of Government', raised issues concerning the effects of tyrannous rule upon the legitimacy of government. In his treatment of these questions Locke produced an account of sovereignty as a form of *trusteeship*, and he argued that when the terms of this relationship are breached the bonds of civil society are dissolved. For Locke there was no such thing as illegitimate *political* rule; when the conduct of rulers or the structure of government does not correspond to the requirements of good government, the relationship between subjects and rulers ceases to be a political one and assumes a non-political form, most commonly that of slavery. Dissolution frees subjects from their obligations to their sovereign and allows them to resist demands made upon· them by one who no longer has any claim to their allegiance. Locke regarded resistance as an individual right, but he also thought that individuals have a *duty* to resist unjust governors. But since resistance takes place in a situation where government has already been dissolved, the duty to resist is one that individuals impose on themselves.

Like his predecessors among the Huguenots, Locke treated resistance as a legitimate response to the exercise of power without, or 'beyond', right. However, he extended this idea from the conventional categories of usurpation and tyranny to include certain forms of foreign conquest. In considering this last issue Locke distinguished between cases where conquest is legitimate, that is, where the invader's action is to punish a breach of his rights or some other serious transgression of the laws of nature, and those instances where invasion constitutes a violation of rights. An invader who acts legitimately is entitled to subject transgressors to despotic rule, but Locke stressed that this is part of a regime of punishment; it should not be regarded as a *political* relationship since this involves subjects and sovereigns, not transgressors and those who punish them. In the latter case, despotic rule is legitimate and cannot be rightfully resisted. However, if the conqueror acts unjustly, that is, if he attacks those who do not deserve to be punished, they become subject only to his *power*, not to his *authority*, and they do not owe obedience to him (Locke, 1967, pp. 412–13). Any promise of obedience exacted through fear is void, and since the relationship between the conqueror and his victims has no basis in right, the conquered may overthrow their conquerors when the chance arises. As is the case with resistance to a usurper,

> that shaking off a Power, which Force, and not Right hath set over any one, though it hath the Name of *Rebellion*, yet is not an offence before God, but is that, which he allows and countenances, though even Promises and Covenants, when obtained by force, have intervened (ibid., pp. 414–15).

Strictly speaking, conquest and usurpation do not produce political relationships because power is not legitimised by the consent of those who are subject to it; as noted above, consent plays a central role in Locke's account of legitimate political authority. The case of tyranny is different because the tyrant misuses power that has been acquired legitimately. Tyranny involves 'the exercise of power beyond right' in ways that are detrimental to the interests of the subject. As Locke put it, '*where-ever Laws end, Tyranny begins*, if the Law be transgressed to another's harm' (ibid., p. 418). Locke allowed that it might occasionally be necessary for a ruler to act extra-legally, but he insisted that this is acceptable only if it is in the interests of the subject. In all other cases 'the exercise of power beyond right' is tyrannical because it involves a breach of trust on the part of the ruler and runs contrary to the rationale of *political* authority. Tyrants may thus be opposed, as may 'any other Man, who by force invades the right of another' (ibid., pp. 418–19).

Locke's statements on resistance are far less equivocal than those of his French predecessors, because they are tied to his idea that rulers hold power in trust for those who are ordinarily subject to them:

> *Who shall be Judge* whether the Prince or the Legislative act contrary to their trust? ... *The People shall be Judge*; for who shall be *Judge* whether his Trustee or Deputy acts well, and according to the Trust reposed in him, but he who deputes him, and must, by having deputed him have still a Power to discard him, when he fails in his Trust? (ibid., pp. 444–5).

In addition, while Locke thought that subjects should be prepared to tolerate both 'minor mismanagement' and isolated 'great mistakes', stressed the need to pursue legal avenues of redress and warned of the human and divine punishment that can be visited on those who engage in unnecessary resistance, he allowed that subjects have a right to embark upon what might be termed 'anticipatory resistance'. They may resist the impositions of rulers whose actions show they intend to create a system of absolute and arbitrary rule (ibid., pp. 423, 429). Locke responded to the possibility that his position might be seen as a warrant for anarchy by pointing out that 'the people' are usually very slow to respond to significant injustice, and by arguing that unjust sovereigns are the real rebels because their behaviour threatens the peace of the community and involves a disregard for the laws of nature. (ibid., pp. 433–4).

As with other theorists considered in this chapter, Locke's treatment of resistance places considerable emphasis on its defensive nature. That is, while allowing that resistance may result in changes both to personnel and to the structure of government, he offset the radical implications of this position by implying that many acts of resistance are directed towards restoration of the existing constitution, rather than to the creation of a new form of government (ibid., p. 432). In these respects he treated resistance in relationship to the existing constitutional structures. At the same time, however, his theory highlights the extent to which even constitutional accounts of resistance have an extrapolitical dimension because rulers who abuse their powers cease to be 'true' sovereigns.

This point emerges from Locke's account of the difference between 'dissolution of society' and 'dissolution of government'. The former occurs when foreign invasion reduces subjects to a position of virtual slavery and breaks up the union of society, thus causing the dissolution of political society or government:

> That which makes the Community ... into *one Politik Society*, is the Agreement which every one has with the rest to incorporate, and act as one Body, and so to be one distinct Commonwealth (ibid., p. 424).

In addition, however, dissolution of government can also occur when the bonds of society – the agreement of each person to combine with their fellows – remains intact. Forced alteration of the legislative body, the core of the commonwealth, or the abdication of the supreme executive dissolves government by stripping those in power of legitimate authority. It leaves the people free to form a new government and/or appoint new officers of state. Since society is not dissolved, this process may be smooth and may involve no significant disruption of the general benefits that the state confers upon its members. While this possibility removes the threatening alternative that confronts the subjects of Hobbes' 'Leviathan', it endows the whole issue of challenge to rulers with an ambivalent political and constitutional status. Since political authority no longer exists, resistance takes the form of extraconstitutional responses to the void created by the disappearance of legitimate power. However, these responses come not from isolated individuals in a natural condition, but from 'the people', that is, from members of the collective entity formed by an agreement to pool individual powers and place them in the hands of a sovereign. Seen from this point of view, resistance takes place within a social framework that forms an essential component of the state, albeit one that temporarily lacks the distinctive political quality of voluntary submission and legitimate rule.

The radicalism of Locke's theory of resistance is evident in his argument that 'the people' have the right to judge the actions of their rulers and to determine whether resistance is necessary (ibid., p. 445). The fact that Locke's stipulation is not hedged by a reference to the role of inferior magistrates, signals a move beyond the constitutional conception of resistance advanced by earlier French thinkers. Locke argued that if rulers refuse to accept the judgement of the people, the political relationship between them is destroyed: 'Force between either Persons, who have no known Superior on earth, or which permits no Appeal to a Judge on Earth, being properly a state of war, wherein the Appeal lies only to Heaven, and in that state the *injured Party must judge* for himself' (ibid., p. 445). Individuals cannot take legislative power into their hands while government still exists, but this power devolves to them when government is dissolved. The dissolution of government thus makes it impossible for resistance to be reserved for those inferior magistrates who play such an important role in French resistance theory. When, 'by the Miscarriages of those in Authority (legislative power) is forfeited ... *it reverts to the Society*, and the People have a Right to act as Supreme, and continue the Legislative in themselves, or erect a new Form, or under the old form place it in new hands, as they think good' (ibid., p. 446).

While aspects of Locke's theory deal with forms of resistance that do not necessarily result in the creation of a new form of government, his belief that the dissolution of government can provide the opportunity to establish a new political structure means that it could be used to justify a revolutionary transformation of the state. At the same time, however, it is important to bear in mind that for Locke, as for his French predecessors, resistance is essentially defensive: that is, it involves a reaction against the unjust exercise of power by office holders. Except in the case of his general prohibition of absolute and arbitrary government (see p. 80), Locke did not develop an argument that equates the attainment of desirable political ends with the rejection of certain forms of government and the creation of a new and distinctive political and social environment. This type of challenge to the exercise of political power forms the core of the theories of revolution that will be discussed in the next chapter.

Conclusion

Like his medieval and early-modern predecessors, Locke treated resistance as a response either to the unjust exercise of power by office holders, or, in the case of usurpation, to the illegitimate possession of political power. While tyrants exercise power 'beyond right', usurpers exercise it 'without right'. Theories permitting resistance to usurpers reflect a widely held assumption that those who seize power illegitimately are unlikely to use it in an acceptable way. They also rest on an understanding of the conditions that must be satisfied by *political* relationships. Political society comprises a sovereign and his subjects; the former has a right to rule that is accepted by the latter, and may in some cases be explained by reference to ideas of consent. Moreover the sovereign's legitimacy depends upon the way in which, and the ends for which, power is exercised. For the most part the sovereign should rule in a law-like manner because the purpose of human government is to create and uphold systems of law that give clear guidance on the implications of natural law. Where the laws are silent, or in exceptional cases, rulers may go beyond the law, but since their actions must be directed towards the common good they conform to the substance if not the form of legitimate government.

Acts of resistance have important political implications, but they have not always been seen as part of a political process. Theories that see resisters as agents of God, and those that present resistance as a duty individuals owe to God, may be contrasted with those that treat resistance in strictly political terms. In the former case, resistance is external to political relationships: it is applied to them. In contrast the constitutional theories developed by Huguenot theorists treat resistance in relation to the institutions of government: parts of the constitutional structure are responsible for resisting the improper exercise of political power. Resistance is seen as a corrective mechanism designed to ensure the survival of a generally legitimate structure. This feature of resistance theory distinguishes it from the revolutionary theories that will be discussed in the next chapter.

CHAPTER 13

Revolutionary Political Thought

There is a significant difference between the theories of resistance discussed in the last chapter and the types of revolutionary political thinking that will be dealt with in this one. Resistance theories deny legitimacy to rulers who act improperly, but they do not deny that subjects have an obligation to obey their rulers when they act in accordance with the letter or spirit of what are seen as legitimate systems of government. In contrast revolutionary thinkers argue that subjects are under no obligation to accept the authority of those whose claim to rule is derived from an unjust political structure. The purpose of revolutionary political thought is to identify the weaknesses of existing political structures, and to show that these weaknesses can only be avoided by establishing a radically different social and political order. In these cases, resistance is a challenge to the state. In contrast the fact that many theories of resistance have a constitutional basis means that claims to resist are part of the structure of a state. The extralegal nature of revolutionary change, and the fact the revolutions are intended to bring about a fundamental alteration to the structure of the state and the distribution of political power within the community, means that revolutionary theory usually assumes the need for a violent challenge to an existing political system and to those who wield power within it.

The following discussion will begin with a brief account of ancient, medieval and early-modern treatments of revolution. Subsequent sections of the chapter will look in some detail at revolutionary political thinking in late-eighteenth-century America and France, and at a range of Marxist theories of revolution and anarchist responses to them. The chapter will conclude with an account of an important example of revolutionary thinking set within the context of postwar anticolonial movements.

Ancient, Medieval and Early-Modern Theories of Revolution: Plato, Aristotle, Radical Protestants and Levellers

Revolutions have been a recurring feature of the history of political societies, but self-consciously revolutionary theories were not developed until relatively recently. Although Plato and Aristotle discussed revolutions, they had no intention of promoting them. Plato treated revolutions as a consequence of the moral corruption of the population, a process that inaugurated lawless mob rule and ended in tyranny (see p. 128). Aristotle attributed them to the desire of certain sections of the population – especially the rich few and the numerous poor – to press their unjust claims for exclusive power in the state. He also related revolutions to changes in the socioeconomic structure of the *polis* (Aristotle, 1958, p. 213). In these circumstances, and in others where the claims of certain sections are completely ignored, there may be a sense in which revolutions can be justified. However, Aristotle's political instincts were conservative so he generally viewed the disruption caused by revolutions with a jaundiced eye. His perspective is reflected in the observation that while only the virtuous few really have a claim to seize power, their sense of virtue, and presumably their awareness of the destabilising effects of revolutionary activity, means that they will not press their claims (ibid., p. 204). Polybius and Machiavelli also discussed revolution, but in their thought, as in that of Plato and Aristotle, the focus is very much on keeping the threat of revolutionary action at bay. For these writers revolution was part of a process of political change that they associated with the corruption of the state and its degeneration to a less acceptable form.

Revolutionary political theory, which can hardly be said to have existed in the ancient and medieval worlds, made its first direct appearance among some radical Protestants during the Reformation. Although mainstream Protestant thinkers only moved very tentatively towards developing theories that would justify resistance on constitutional grounds (see pp. 310ff), some of their radical coreligionists posed a revolutionary challenge to the existing political order. For example the unknown author of *To the Assembly of the Common Peasantry*, written at the time of the Peasants Revolt in Germany in 1525, rejected the idea of a hereditary right to rule on the ground that it is incompatible with Christianity. He argued that such 'false' rulers should be deposed and that Christians should seek to establish new forms of political authority that are compatible with their faith (Anon, 1991). Arguments of this kind assume that when individuals are faced by forms of rule that are incompatible with Christianity they are freed from any obligation to unjust superiors and are entitled to reconstruct their political institutions according to their own – God-infused – lights.

Religious justification for political revolution also played a role in mid-seventeenth-century England when the long-running conflict between the king and parliament came to a head. While many of those who opposed the king did so because they merely wished to restore the constitutional arrangements that had been undermined by the crown and its agents, others developed distinctly revolutionary positions. In the early stages of the Civil War members of some Protestant sects thought that the clash between parliament and the king marked the 'last days' in a struggle between the forces of Christ and those of the Antichrist. Consequently they looked forward to the millenarian transformation that had been foretold in the Bible. The coming of the millennium would inaugurate a reign of justice and prosperity presided over by Christ himself, or by his saints (Wootton, 1994, pp. 421–2). This expectation was underwritten by radical Protestantism, but while religious considerations were almost always central to the political thinking of those engaged in the English Revolution, two sets of developments in the period had more distinctively political implications. These developments emerged in the course of discussions about how the kingdom should be 'settled'.

The struggle against the king resulted in his execution, in rejection of the monarchy and hereditary aristocracy and in the establishment of a republic. Although many proponents of republicanism were conservative in other respects, the change from monarchy to republic was a revolutionary one. The same point may also be made about some of the ideas produced by the Levellers (see p. 174). Some Levellers argued for electoral rights on the basis of natural rights rather than the conventional property qualification, and they also claimed that an elected assembly that rests on the ultimate sovereignty of the people should have supreme authority in the state (ibid., p. 412). It is significant that these proposals were not presented as an attempt to restore a corrupted constitution; they involved a revolutionary departure from the ideas and practices of contemporary government.

From the late 1640s the ideas of the Levellers served as a constant, oft-evoked warning of the dangers of radical politics. When their ideas finally began to get a sympathetic airing, tentatively in the early-nineteenth-century writings of William Godwin and more fulsomely in the works of later socialist thinkers, they did so in an environment in which revolutionary political thinking had become self-conscious, unequivocal and relatively widespread. This development owed much to the French Revolution of 1789, an event that marked the establishment of the modern idea that revolutions involve innovations that ensure a previously excluded and oppressed minority will take their rightful place in the state. In some significant cases, it was also underwritten by a range of economic and social theories that related oppression to the interaction of unjust economic and political structures.

Natural Rights and Revolutionary Political Theory in late-Eighteenth-Century America and France: Otis, Sièyes and Babeuf

Those who resisted attempts by the British parliament to impose taxes on the North American colonies frequently based their claims on an appeal to historical constitutional principles. This meant that aspects of the American Revolution reflected the old idea that revolutions restore a preexisting and preferred state of affairs. In some respects however, both the establishment of a republican United States of America and the arguments used to justify rejection of the authority of the British parliament, meant that the breach between Britain and its colonies constituted a revolution in the modern, innovatory sense of that term. This possibility was inherent in John Locke's theory of resistance, and in the appeal to rights that were derived from 'nature' rather than from law or custom (see p. 318). In addition, however, aspects of the debates on the relationship between the parliament at Westminster and the North American colonies pointed to more deep-seated socioeconomic grounds for a political rupture between Britain and its colonies.

The first point can be illustrated by the writings of James Otis. Although Otis' position was not overtly revolutionary, he insisted that the colonists were entitled to uphold their natural rights even if this necessitated a fundamental change in their system of government. In arguing this point Otis advanced a straightforward justification for resistance on Lockean grounds: 'whenever the administrators ... deviate from truth, justice and equity, they verge towards tyranny, and ought to be opposed; and if they prove incorrigible, they will be deposed by the people' as they were in England by the Glorious Revolution of 1688–89 (Otis, 1766, pp. 21–2). Subjects' right to resist is a consequence of the natural freedom that they enjoyed in a state of nature, and of the requirement that legitimate government must be based upon consent. It thus follows that individuals are free to choose the form of government to which they will be subject: 'The form of government is by *nature* and by *right* so far left to *individuals* of each society, that they may alter it from a simple democracy ... to any other form they please. Such alteration may and ought to be made by express consent' (ibid., p. 16).

In addition to affirming the contractual source of government and the right of the people to depose their rulers and establish a new form of government, some of those involved in defence of the rights of the American colonists argued that the development of the colonies had undercut the basis of their subservience to British government. These writers argued that since legitimate government is directed towards the 'common good' of society, the control of one society by another cannot be justified if they no longer possessed a common sense of interest. In the 1760s this line of argument was used to delegitimate British government and provide the foundation for a reconstitution of political authority in North America on the basis of the natural rights of those residing there. The issue of distance played a role in divorcing the interests of the colonists from those of Britain, but this process was also seen as a consequence of the economic and social development of the colonies. They had now become distinct societies, and their interests could no longer be included within the conception of the common good adhered to by political elites in Britain. In this situation a revolutionary breach with Britain was the only appropriate response (Miller, 1994).

The equivocation that marked political debates on the government of North America in the 1760s and 1770s gave way in the 1790s to new and unequivocal expressions of revolutionary political theory. As noted above, Thomas Paine rejected monarchy and aristocracy and argued that only representative democracy is compatible with the rights of man. Given the structure of contemporary British government, Paine's position was unmistakeably revolutionary. The same can be said of the Abbé Sièyes' response to the crisis that confronted French government and society in the late 1780s and 1790s. In *What is the Third Estate?* Sièyes argued that the distinction that had traditionally been made between the three estates (the 'third', the 'noble' and the 'clerical') was unsustainable because there was now only *one* estate in France. Sièyes argued that the third estate *was* the 'nation', that is, an equal union of individuals formed by a voluntary engagement. Since the feudal structure from which the nobility had derived its functions and its rationale no longer existed, it was redundant and had no claim to a distinct political status. The union of equals that embodied the 'common will' of the nation left no room for privileged classes in the political system (Sièyes, 1963, p. 58).

Emmanuel Joseph Sièyes (1748–1836)

Sièyes was educated at the Sorbonne and ordained in 1772, after which he held a number of clerical appointments in prerevolutionary France. He published *What is the Third Estate?* early in 1789, and was subsequently elected to the Estates-General, where he framed the resolutions that transformed that body into the National Assembly. Sièyes played a prominent role in the politics of the 1790s and worked with Napoleon to establish the Consulate, which paved the way for the emergence of the Empire. Having played a role in the condemnation of Louis XVI Sièyes was forced into exile when the Bourbons were restored in 1815.

In rejecting the political claims of the nobility and the clergy, Sièyes was proposing a revolutionary transformation of French government. The effect of this change was intensified by his claim that 'the nation' should establish a political structure appropriate to the realisation of its interests. This structure, one that must maintain and develop citizens' natural and civil rights, and assign political rights in a way that would serve these ends, was to be created by a constituent assembly. Furthermore, while Sièyes thought that there was a role for monarchy in representative government, he did not think of it in traditional terms. For him monarchy was valuable because it avoided the inherent dangers involved in placing all executive and legislative functions in a single chamber. Consequently Sièyes proposed that ministers should be chosen by the monarch, but should be answerable to parliament, not to the king. The king would not be answerable to this body, rather he would be accountable to the constituent assembly from which he derived his power (Forsyth, 1987, pp. 176–9). Monarchs, like the other organs of government, were created by the people and were answerable to them.

The implications that Sièyes drew from his identification of the third estate with the nation involved a radical transformation of the structure of the French state. The revolutionary character of his political thinking was also clearly apparent in his assumption that human beings are able to take it upon themselves to recreate their political institutions. In making his case Sièyes appealed to the principles of 'reason' and 'equity' to provide the basis for a new order embodying immutable standards of truth and justice. This aspiration, which was common among revolutionary figures in contemporary France, was expressed most forcefully by Maximilien Robespierre (a leading figure in the radically anti-aristocratic Jacobin group) in a speech made to the National Assembly in late 1789: 'Eternal Providence has summoned you alone since the origin of the world to re-establish on earth the empire of justice and liberty.' In

Robespierre's view, this task involved the regeneration of institutions and of human nature itself. In the past, human character had been corrupted by the oppressive and unjust influences of non-egalitarian forms of government. It was now necessary to substitute 'all the virtues and miracles of the Republic for all the vices and puerilities of the monarchy' (Tholfsen, 1984, pp. 64, 69–70).

At a later stage in the Revolution, however, Gracchus Babeuf and his followers argued that a merely political revolution was incomplete and precarious (see p. 189). Babeuf maintained that the new constitution of 1794 marked a retreat from the true principles of the revolution because it abandoned universal male suffrage in favour of a relatively high property qualification for voters. In response to this he argued for thoroughgoing democracy, and for the use of the power of a democratised state to eliminate the gross inequalities that undermined the formal equality recognised by the French Republic. As Babeuf put it, 'The first and basic prerequisite of human association is the recognition of an implicit right to improve the social and political system in order to promote the happiness of its members. This right is usually unwritten, but it is absolutely inalienable' (Babeuf, 1972, pp. 35–6).

Babeuf's 'conspiracy of the equals' was exposed before action could be taken to realise its objectives, but the idea that the attainment of liberty and equality necessitates both social and political revolutions became a key feature of socialist political thought in the nineteenth century. Socialists portrayed existing society as inherently unjust, and they sought to replace inegalitarian and oppressive social and political institutions with a variety of arrangements that would make liberty and equality a reality for all members of society. In addition to pursuing revolutionary goals, a number of nineteenth-century socialist thinkers believed that violent action would be necessary to attain these ends. The most significant examples of this strand of socialist theory in the nineteenth century were produced by Marxist and anarchist thinkers.

Marxist Theories of Revolution: Marx and Engels, Kautsky, Lenin, Stalin, Trotsky, Gramsci and Mao Tse-tung

In common with a number of his contemporaries, Marx wished to promote a radical transformation of human society that would make human emancipation a reality rather than a dream. Marx thought that the development of humanity's productive capacities meant it was now possible to satisfy material needs, but he believed that these benefits could only be realised if human beings were integrated within a social framework that would free them from the oppressive inequalities that disfigured all existing and previous social and political structures. The distinctive characteristics of a free society would be classlessness and statelessness. Revolutionary Marxists thus called for the abolition of private property and the state, as well as for the communal control of material resources and the establishment of a system of distribution directed towards the fulfilment of human needs.

Marx and Engels believed that they had established a scientific basis for understanding both capitalism and the revolutionary process that would destroy it. As noted above, this theory rested on an analysis of the implications of the historical development of European societies that was informed by Marx and Engels' conception of historical materialism (see p. 92). They argued that the nature of capitalism and the direction of historical change could only be fully understood by reference to the process thro·igh which this mode of production had developed.

The capitalist class had emerged from the previous feudal mode of production through successful expropriation of the labour of those who lacked access to capital. Over time this process had produced a social structure that contained two major classes: the capitalists, or *bourgeoisie*, and the *proletariat*, a propertyless class who were obliged to sell their labour power in order to secure a minimal level of material well-being.

The growth of the bourgeoisie as an economic class had underwritten its emergence as the dominant political class within modern society. This process, marked by revolutionary outbreaks (in England in the seventeenth century and France in the late eighteenth century), transformed the social and political structures of those societies. The English and French revolutions signalled the demise of feudal elites and their displacement by a class that controlled the key productive resource of modern societies, that is, capital. Capitalism had broken free from the constraints imposed on it by feudal society and established political institutions that, in more or less overt ways, ensured that the state had become a 'committee for managing the common affairs of the whole bourgeoisie' (Marx, 1973, p. 69).

Marx and Engels' historical account provided the basis for identifying developmental tendencies inherent in the capitalist mode of production. Their analysis focused on the rationale of the capitalist mode of production, its implications for the class structure of modern society and for the development and eventual demise of capitalism itself. In their efforts to maximise the productivity of capital and labour, the capitalist class had developed the productive capacities of society to such an extent that it was now possible to satisfy humanity's fundamental material needs.

Under capitalism, however, this aspiration was not being realised. In fact the development of capitalism had given rise to a large, impoverished class of exploited, propertyless workers, exploitation being facilitated by the erosion of medieval regulations and conventions governing employer–employee relationships, by the increase in population stimulated by economic growth, and by the utilisation of machinery. These developments deprived the working class of traditional forms of protection and weakened their bargaining position in an unregulated labour market; they resulted in fierce competition between workers and a reduction in wages to the lowest level necessary to sustain human life. To these material forms of impoverishment had been added those produced by desperate overwork, by the tendency to make the labour of human beings subservient to the superhuman capacities of machines, and by the impoverishment of the human spirit that results from a system of production that makes human activity, the satisfaction of human needs and social interaction the source of misery rather than benefit (ibid., pp. 70–6).

By producing a way of life that was intolerable to large sections of the population, by sharpening and simplifying class antagonisms, and by failing to benefit anything more than an increasingly small class, capitalism would generate from within itself the forces that would destroy it. Foremost among these forces would be a large and increasingly disaffected proletarian class that was deprived of the material benefits of economic and technological development, and is subjected to the dehumanising conditions of life and labour that characterise the capitalist mode of production. The threat posed to capitalism by this revolutionary proletariat would be augmented by failures in its internal workings. For example, increasingly intense competition between capitalists would produce commercial crises that would have the effect of destroying capital. A system of production that enshrines private property as the legal form of capital periodically destroys property itself:

> the productive forces at the disposal of society no longer tend to further the development of the conditions of bourgeoisie property; on the contrary, they have become too powerful for these conditions, by which they are fettered, and so soon as they overcome these fetters, they bring disorder into the whole of bourgeois society, endanger the existence of bourgeois property. The conditions of bourgeois society are too narrow to comprise the wealth created by them (ibid., p. 73).

The growth of a radically disenchanted proletariat with no positive attachment to capitalism, and the self-defeating outcomes of capitalism's internal operation, would provide the basis for its destabilisation and eventual demise.

One result of Marx and Engels' analysis was that revolutionary action was given a strongly positive bearing. Revolution had become necessary for the progressive development of human society, and for the universal benefit of humanity. Capitalism had divided humanity into two classes with distinctive interests and favoured those of the dominant capitalist class. Under capitalism the proletariat had been stripped of all of their particular interests, leaving them nothing but their humanity. The cause of the proletariat was thus the cause of humanity, and so Marx and Engels could argue that its emancipation would entail the emancipation of humanity.

By relating revolution to developments taking place within capitalist society, Marx and Engels were able to specify the conditions under which a proletarian revolution would be possible. The key requirements were the full development of capitalism so that it would form the dominant mode of production on a global, not merely a national scale, and conversion of the proletariat into an effective revolutionary force. If these requirements were not satisfied,

> [if] these material elements of a complete revolution are not present (namely, on the one hand the existing productive forces, on the other the formation of a revolutionary mass, which revolts not only against separate conditions of society up till then, but against the very 'productive life' till then, the 'total activity' on which it was based), then, as far as practical development is concerned, it is absolutely immaterial whether the idea of this revolution has been expressed a hundred times already; as the history of communism proves (Marx and Engels, 1968, pp. 29–30).

In their earliest writings Marx and Engels suggested that if these conditions were satisfied a proletarian revolution would become an inevitable 'historical necessity'. This expectation rested on their evaluation of the unstable nature of capitalism in the 1840s, and on the role they ascribed to *absolute* as opposed to *relative* impoverishment. Later, however, in light of their awareness of capitalism's apparent capacity for recovery, they placed increasing reliance on relative poverty and on the tendency of capitalism to veer towards crisis, rather than on the immediate prospect of a complete collapse of capitalist economies. These reformulations appeared to weaken those parts of Marxist theory that pointed to the inevitability of a successful overthrow of capitalism by the proletariat. In some respects, however, this idea played a role in Marx and Engels' later theory. They continued to explain capitalism by reference to large-scale processes of historical development, and they insisted that the only way to resolve the tensions of capitalist society was through a revolutionary transformation (Maguire, 1978, pp. 160–8).

However, in their later work, Marx and Engels' understanding of the revolutionary process underwent significant change. The *Communist Manifesto* of 1848 focused on the seizure of state power by the proletariat and the use of this power to establish the conditions necessary for the evolution of a classless, stateless society:

the first step in the revolution ... is to raise the proletariat to the position of ruling class, to win the battle of democracy.

The proletariat will use its political supremacy to wrest, by degrees, all capital from the bourgeoisie, to centralise all instruments of production in the hands of the state, i.e., of the proletariat organised as the ruling class, and to increase the total productive forces as rapidly as possible. . . .

When, in the course of development, class distinctions have disappeared, and all production has been concentrated in the hands of a vast association of the whole nation, the public power will lose its political character. . . . If the proletariat ... sweeps away by force the old conditions of production, then it will, along with these conditions, have swept away the conditions for the existence of class antagonisms and of classes generally, and will thereby have abolished its own supremacy as a class.

In place of the old bourgeois society, with all its classes and class antagonisms, we shall have an association, in which the free development of each is the condition for the free development of all (Marx, 1973, pp. 86–7).

Marx later refined this account. He argued that the proletariat would not merely seize hold of a ready-made state apparatus, but would need to transform it into a truly democratic system of government. Thus in his late reflections on the Paris Commune of 1870–71 he made much of 'working', as opposed to the merely 'parliamentary' character of the Commune. The Commune provided a model for genuine government of the nation by the nation: 'The Communal Constitution would have restored to the social body all the forces hitherto absorbed by the State parasite feeding upon, and clogging the freer movements of, society' (Marx and Engels, 1973, vol. ii, p. 222). While earlier revolutionaries had mistakenly attempted to seize control of the existing machinery of government and perfect its operation, the Communards sought to transform it into a vehicle for radical social and political change (ibid., p. 224). The conventional, bourgeois state was a class instrument and control of it was not part of a viable revolution. To the contrary, Marx saw revolution as a process that transcended class interests; it was therefore necessary to create a radically democratic structure that would direct political power to the attainment of universal ends.

The impact of Marx and Engels' theory was felt most immediately in Germany, where a large, electorally successful Marxist party, the Social Democratic Party (SDP), came into being. In 1891 this party adopted the 'Erfurt Programme', a step that marked its self-definition as a revolutionary rather than a 'reformist' party. In his commentary upon this programme Karl Kautsky contrasted 'reformism' (attempts to alleviate the problems of capitalism from within the existing structure) with the revolutionary stance adopted by the SDP (Kautsky, 1971, p. 89). However, while Kautsky embraced Marxist ideas about the inevitability of the revolutionary goal of the abolition of private property, he argued that the pursuit of this goal might involve a number of stages. Moreover he insisted that if social reform were to be seen in the context of an ultimately revolutionary struggle, it could form part of a viable socialist programme. Reform would provide partial and temporary relief for the working classes; it might stimulate economic development, and it might also hasten the onset of the revolution by speeding up the demise of small and increasingly marginalised sectors of capitalism (ibid., p. 184).

Karl Kautsky (1854–1938)

Born in Prague and educated at the University of Vienna, Kautsky gravitated from radical Czech nationalism to socialism in the late 1870s. Originally associated with the Austrian Socialist Party, Kautsky later became a leading member of the German Social Democratic Party. Kautsky's *The Dictatorship of the Proletariat* (1918) signalled a clear rift between his conception of the revolutionary process and that promoted by Lenin, the Russian communist leader.

In making these points Kautsky offered a challenge to those contemporary Marxist thinkers who argued that working class attempts to pursue social and political objectives within the structure of a capitalist society were inherently contradictory. To the contrary, he argued that the organisational and educational gains of involvement in trade union activity could enhance the political effectiveness of the proletariat. This point was of great importance to Kautsky since he believed that an active, politically conscious proletariat could use the parliamentary system to advance its revolutionary aspirations. For example he maintained that if a party representing the proletariat were to gain control of a state through electoral means, a revolutionary change in society could be brought about by parliamentary action. In an implicit departure from Marx's position on the Paris Commune, Kautsky argued that proletarian participation in electoral politics could transform the character of parliament and greatly increase the workers' political effectiveness:

> Whenever the proletariat engages in parliamentary activity as a self-conscious class, parliamentarianism begins to change its character. It ceases to be a mere tool in the hands of the bourgeoisie. This very

participation ... proves to be the most effective means of shaking up the hitherto indifferent divisions of the proletariat and giving them hope and confidence. It is the most powerful lever that can be utilized to raise the proletariat out of its economic, social and moral degradation (ibid., p. 188).

Ten years after the publication of Kautsky's commentary, the position he had advanced in this work was challenged implicitly in a manifesto issued by V. I. Lenin, a leading member of the Bolsheviks, which at the time was a relatively insignificant Russian Marxist party. In *What is to be Done?* (1905) Lenin claimed that the revolutionary potential of the proletariat would be fulfilled only if their actions were directed by a theoretically informed elite who focused on the 'political' rather than the 'economic' aspects of the struggle against capitalism. This elite must overthrow the state rather than merely try to extract economic concessions from the capitalist class. Lenin's arguments on this point involved a critique of working-class activism. He claimed that the spontaneous activity of the working classes would only produce a limited 'trade union consciousness'. 'Class political consciousness can be brought to the workers *only from without*, that is, only from outside the economic struggle, from outside the sphere of relations between workers and employers' (Lenin, 1975, vol. i, pp. 152–3). This position was quite at odds with Kautsky's belief that a working-class consciousness could develop throughout the labour movement. Kautsky believed that the scientific details of Marxism had to be derived from intellectuals, but he insisted that there was no need for a socialist, revolutionary consciousness to be imported from outside the economic struggle (Kautsky, 1994).

The conflict between Lenin's and Kautsky's positions came to a head in 1917 as a result of Lenin's attempt to apply his ideas to the revolution that broke out in Russia. After the Bolsheviks seized power in October of that year, Lenin found himself having to relate Marxist ideas about revolution to a situation where the major revolutionary force was a peasantry committed to retaining its recently acquired landholdings, rather than a proletariat committed to the transformation of society. Lenin's and Kautsky's divergent understanding of the socialist revolution caused an open breach between them in the years 1917–18. In *State and Revolution* (1918) Lenin launched an attack on 'Kautskyism', claiming that Marxists of this stamp 'omit, obscure or distort the revolutionary side of this theory, its revolutionary soul' (Lenin, 1975, vol. ii, p. 240). In opposition to this alleged neutralisation of Marxism, Lenin insisted on the need for a violent revolution that would destroy the apparatus of bourgeois state power, and replace it with a new, but still coercive, set of institutions possessing both the power and the will to advance the interests of the oppressed masses (ibid., pp. 243–4). The bourgeois state must be stripped of its distinctive bureaucratic, military and political structures and be replaced by a new form of truly democratic administration modelled on the Paris Commune. This new political entity – no longer the 'state proper' – would reflect the will of the previously oppressed majority and pursue its interests. The revolutionary state would thus realise what Lenin claimed was the essence of revolutionary Marxism, namely extension of the prerevolutionary class struggle into a post-revolutionary dictatorship of the proletariat. This period would inevitably be marked by an

> unprecedently violent class struggle in unprecedently acute forms, and consequently, during this period the state must essentially be a state that is democratic *in a new way* (for the proletariat and the propertyless in general) and dictatorial *in a new way* (against the bourgeoisie) (ibid., p. 262).

Lenin's account of the structure and purpose of this new form of democracy reflected his awareness of the numerical weakness of the revolutionary proletariat in contemporary Russia. It also recognised the extent to which Russia fell short of the level of economic development that Marx regarded as a precondition for the emergence of revolutionary communism. In these circumstances Lenin identified a leading role in the dictatorship of the proletariat for its revolutionary vanguard, the Communist Party. Rejecting anarchist claims that revolutionary social transformation required a transformation of human nature, Lenin insisted that

> we want the socialist revolution with people as they are now, with people who cannot dispense with subordination.... The subordination, however, must be to the armed vanguard of all the exploited and working people, ie to the proletariat.... *We*, the workers shall organise large scale production on the basis of what capitalism has already created, relying on our own experience as workers, establishing strict, iron discipline backed up by the state power of the armed workers.... This is *our* proletarian task, this is what we can and *must start* with in accomplishing the proletarian revolution (ibid., p. 273).

Lenin linked these draconian measures to the beginning of the post-revolutionary process and set them within the context of utopian visions of the ultimate revival of 'primitive democracy', under which 'the *mass* of the population will rise to taking an *independent* part, not only in voting and elections, *but also in the everyday administration of the state*' (ibid., p. 324). He also envisaged a time when even democracy itself, being a form of rule, would wither away (ibid., p. 303). In the immediate future, however, the process of social revolution must be fostered by the vanguard of the proletariat. This body would eliminate the bourgeois class, and impose coercive direction on the entire population.

Lenin's conception of the revolutionary process was strenuously rejected by Kautsky. In *The Dictatorship of the Proletariat* (1918) Kautsky reiterated his earlier arguments about the possibility of non-violent revolution, and confirmed the role that even bourgeois parliamentarianism could play in the organisation of the working class organisation and in fostering consciousness (Kautsky, 1983, pp. 101, 114). He also argued that Lenin's idea of the dictatorship of the proletariat was incompatible with the socialist conception of the nature of revolutionary change. Socialism involved the abolition of 'every form of exploitation', including those proposed by Lenin. Kautsky claimed that Marx had used the term 'dictatorship of· the proletariat' to refer a *state of affairs* that necessarily arose whenever the proletariat attained political power, while Lenin had transformed it into a *form of government* in which a party rules on behalf of a class (ibid., pp. 114, 116). This system of rule was totally incompatible with the conditions necessary to ease the transformation to socialism.

> A state of chronic civil war, or its alternative under a dictatorship, the complete apathy and despondency of the masses, renders the construction of a socialist system of production well nigh impossible. And yet the dictatorship of a minority ... necessarily gives rise to civil war and apathy (ibid., p. 120).

In response to what he regarded as an erroneous and dangerous conception of revolutionary change, Kautsky stressed the need to distinguish between 'social revolution', 'political revolution' and 'civil war'. Civil war, a consequence of Lenin's theory and a goal promoted by Kautsky's German contemporary Rosa Luxemburg and her colleagues in the revolutionary Spartacus League (Luxemburg, 1971, pp. 371–3), would positively hinder the revolutionary process. While Kautsky acknowledged that 'political revolution' might involve some violence, he insisted that except in cases where the bourgeoisie refused to accept the legitimate measures of a democratic parliament, the danger of civil war could be largely avoided by a process of 'social revolution'. That is,

> a profound transformation of the whole structure brought about by the creation of a new mode of production. It is a protracted process which can last for decades.... The more peaceful the manner in which it is

carried out the more successful it will be. Civil and foreign war are its mortal enemies (Kautsky, 1983, p. 121).

The implication of this is that social revolution would only be truly revolutionary in its final stage and in the long term, not in the immediate or the middle term. Kautsky thought that a cautious approach was in order because the eventual triumph of socialism would depend on the enlightenment of the general population, and this process could not be hurried.

Lenin's political ideas focused on the distinctive problems facing Russian Marxists. They also dealt with a post- revolutionary situation. In some respects, however, the seizure of power by the representatives of the oppressed masses had to be seen as merely the first move in a process that would result in attainment of the final goal of revolutionary Marxism – a communist society. For these reasons, Leninism can be seen as a theory of development as well as a theory of revolutionary politics, a point that also applies to Lenin's successors (Kautsky, 1994). The attainment of communism required the development of Russia's economic infrastructure and the growth of a universal proletarian consciousness. The first of these tasks meant that the Communist Party had to utilise the labour of the peasantry in order to feed the population and to provide surpluses with which to fund industrial and infrastructural developments.

Post-Leninist thought saw the abandonment, or at least the postponement, of the international dimensions of the proletarian revolution. This point was confirmed by Joseph Stalin's adoption of 'socialism in one country', a doctrine that was first developed by Nicolai Bukharin in an attempt to legitimise a process of economic and political development that would utilise Russian resources alone. Having tacitly accepted this doctrine by 1924, Stalin advanced a forceful statement of it in his *Problems of Leninism* (1926). 'Socialism in one country' rested on the

> possibility of the proletariat assuming power and using that power to build a complete socialist society in one country with the sympathy and support of the proletariat of other countries, but without the preliminary victory of the proletarian revolution in other countries (Stalin, 1934, vol. i, p. 300).

Stalin, who succeeded Lenin as leader of the Communist Party, maintained that this doctrine was in accord with the thought of his illustrious predecessor. This claim is very dubious (McClellan, 1979, p. 123). In any case Stalin's position clashed with the idea of 'permanent revolution' promoted by his rival, Leon Trotsky.

Joseph Stalin (1879–1953)

Stalin succeeded Lenin as head of the communist government of the Soviet Union and maintained his hold on the country until his death. His enemies (imagined and real) were ruthlessly purged from positions of influence and most were executed; these elite purges were part of a systematic terror that claimed millions of lives. *Problems of Leninism* (1926) was Stalin's major statement of his version of Marxism.

Trotsky has been credited with having produced the most 'radical restatement, if not a revision, of the prognosis of Socialist revolution undertaken since Marx [and Engels'] *Communist Manifesto*' (Deutscher, 1954, p. 150). He argued that the peculiar conditions prevailing in Russia – the uneven development that had produced an advanced but geographically and numerically limited group of industrial capitalist enterprises dependent upon an autocratic state; a relatively small but cohesive urban proletariat; a large, amorphous, disgruntled and exceedingly backward peasantry; and a virtually non-existent independent bourgeoisie – made it very likely that a revolution would occur. This revolution could be led most effectively by the proletariat: they would establish a system of 'permanent revolution' that would eliminate feudal and bourgeois elements, develop the economic base of society, and foster a socialist consciousness among the bulk of the population. Although the proletariat would originally ally themselves with the peasantry, their policies would eventually bring them into conflict with the peasantry and other backward elements in society. Since the proletariat were numerically weak, the revolution could only survive if it had external support. In other words, permanent revolution necessarily had an international dimension:

> Without the direct support of the European proletariat the working class of Russia cannot remain in power and convert its temporary domination into a lasting socialist dictatorship (Trotsky, 1969, p. 105).

The circumstances facing Russia in the mid-1920s made socialism in one country the only plausible approach, and Trotsky tacitly acknowledged this. However, he remained a stern critic of the way the revolution was being conducted by his political rivals. He warned that failure to eradicate bureaucracy would lay Russia open to the danger of sliding towards capitalism, and he accused Stalin of creating a system of 'Soviet Bonapartism' that rested on a new form of party aristocracy (McLellan, 1979, p. 139). These tendencies needed to be reversed by a *political* revolution that would restore the proletariat to their proper position in a revolutionary social order. Paradoxically this critique displayed an attitude towards the political dimensions of revolution that was not markedly different from that which had first appeared in France in the 1790s.

The fact that the Russian Revolution was the first successful seizure of power by a revolutionary Marxist party meant that it provided a focal point to encourage, guide and in some cases direct Marxist revolutionaries in other countries. As a consequence, twentieth-century theorists working within the Marxist tradition have sought to relate their positions both to Marx's views and to the Russian experience. An important feature of post-Leninist theories of revolution has been the attempt to determine the theoretical and tactical implications of the distinctive circumstances of the Russian case, and to gauge the extent to which it has been necessary to produce varieties of revolutionary Marxist theory that differ from those developed by Lenin and his Russian successors.

This aspect of twentieth-century Marxist thought is apparent in the writings of the two leading figures in non-Russian revolutionary politics, the Italian Antonio Gramsci, and Mao Tse-tung, who dominated the Chinese communist movement. Gramsci stressed that the complex nature of the political, economic and cultural structures of Central and Western European societies meant that the straightforward insurrectionary tactics employed in Russia in 1917 would not be appropriate in these areas (Sassoon, 1987, pp. 65–6). Mao too drew attention to the distinctive circumstances faced by revolutionary communists in the Chinese context.

Gramsci's major contributions to revolutionary political thought were his development of the idea of 'hegemony', his analysis of the implications of this idea for the revolution as a process in which politics plays an important role, and his attempt to relate the responses of a revolutionary party to the concrete reality of a given capitalist society. Building on Lenin's idea that the proletariat needs to weld a range of anticapitalist elements into an effective revolutionary force, Gramsci developed the idea of hegemony into a general theory. One the one hand, it explains how different classes are able to sustain their dominant position without total reliance on force. For example Gramsci argued that in the context of Western democracies,

> the 'normal' exercise of hegemony ... is characterised by the combination of force and consent, which balance each other reciprocally without force predominating excessively over consent. Indeed, the attempt is always made to ensure that force would appear to be based on the consent of the majority expressed by the so-called organs of public opinion – newspapers and associations – which therefore, in certain situations, are artificially multiplied (Gramsci, 1971, p. 80).

On the other hand, this theory also plays a crucial role in setting the agenda for revolutionary activity. Gramsci rejected deterministic explanations of revolutionary change, arguing that it is necessary for the hegemony of bourgeois society to be challenged by a proletarian counterhegemony embodying true social interests. Revolution is a *process* rather than an *event*, one that requires a counterhegemony forged by the interaction of intellectuals and workers within the framework of a revolutionary party.

Antonio Gramsci (1891–1937)

Gramsci, the leading Marxist theoretician of Italian communism, served as general secretary of the Italian Communist Party and was elected to parliament. He was imprisoned by the fascists in 1926 and remained in prison until his death. Gramsci's most important work, the *Prison Notebooks*, written between 1929 and 1935 and published posthumously, sought to reemphasise the importance of intellectual and political action within the Marxist tradition.

A distinctive feature of Gramsci's notion of hegemony, one that appears in his analysis of pre-, counter- and post-revolutionary hegemonies, is the importance he ascribed to ideological and cultural elements. He thus argued that the development of a hegemonic revolutionary force requires the development of a proletarian *culture*. This requirement can only be satisfied if the party interacts with a range of organisations and activities in which the bulk of the working class are engaged.

> First of all, [the party] contains within it the best part of the working class, a vanguard tied directly to non-party proletarian organisations, which the communists frequently lead. Secondly, because of its experience and authority, the party is the only organisation able to centralise the struggle of the proletariat and thus to transform the political organisations of the working class into its own coordinating organs. The party is the highest form of class organisation of the proletariat (Sassoon, 1987, p. 81).

The variety of these interactions, and the fact that they necessarily take place within a fluid environment, means that the party is an evolving entity rather than a rigidly fixed structure. The party is charged with a political educational role that requires it to adopt an internal structure that will facilitate interaction and participation rather than centralised direction. The need to develop the basis for a proletarian hegemony thus has important implications for both the internal structure of the party and for the ways in which its members interacted in the wider working-class culture.

The idea of hegemony also plays a role in Gramsci's understanding of the post-revolutionary situation. In common with other Marxists, Gramsci believed that the seizure of state power is an important stage in the revolutionary process. He also stressed the need to employ the power of the state to transform the social relations of production, and to develop further the cultural hegemony of the proletariat. This process will result in the creation of a new type of state (ibid., p. 132).

Here, as elsewhere in his theory, Gramsci drew attention to the complex nature of the reality that confronts the revolutionary party. This consideration also plays a role in determining the course of the struggle that concludes with the seizure of state power by the revolutionary party. In discussing revolutionary tactics Gramsci developed a distinction between a 'war of movement or manoeuvre' and a 'war of position'. The first of these engagements involves a direct attack. According to Gramsci, this is only possible in societies such as tsarist Russia where the state lacks the support of a well-entrenched civil society buttressed by a hegemonic bourgeoisie. In more developed societies a 'war of position' – a long-run process involving a search for favourable positions *vis-à-vis* the dominant bourgeois state and development of a counterhegemonic structure that will eventually undermine it – is more appropriate.

Gramsci's distinction between approaches to revolutionary transformation is underwritten by his identification of two sorts of crisis, each of which provides different opportunities for aggressive action. *Organic* crises signal a breach between a society's social structure and superstructure as a result of deep-seated dislocations within the ruling hegemony. Crises of this kind open the way for wars of manoeuvre and thus differed from what Gramsci called *conjectural* crises, which result from temporary tensions within a dominant class or from loss of confidence in particular members of the political elite. Conjectural crises frequently produce changes of ruling personnel, but they do not threaten the hegemony of the dominant class. At most they provide the opportunity to engage in wars of position, but in so doing they may serve to promote a counter-hegemony that will provide the basis for future revolutionary action (Gramsci, 1971, pp. 232–38).

Emphasis on concrete circumstances is an important aspect of Gramsci's theory of revolution, and this idea also plays a central role in Mao's conception of the revolutionary process. Mao was openly disdainful of intellectuals, and much of his theorising takes the form of injunctions formulated for the guidance of the Chinese Communist Party in its prolonged military and political struggles against a range of enemies. Mao maintained that the essence of Marxism, its 'living soul', is 'the concrete analysis of concrete conditions' (Mao, 1967, pp. 93–4). Consequently, while he acknowledged the inspirational and theoretical importance of the Russian Revolution, he warned that the pursuit of communism in China must take account of the distinctive circumstances confronting revolutionaries in that country. Of central importance was the relative strength of the revolutionary forces *vis-à-vis* their various opponents, the extent to which China had been reduced to semicolonial status by the Western powers and the Japanese, and the unevenness of Chinese political and economic development. The last of these considerations is of cardinal importance for the conventional Marxist model. Where a weakly developed capitalist economy coexists with a largely semifeudal agrarian economy, a revolution cannot take place under the guidance or control of a classical Marxist proletariat. Of course this issue had also confronted Russian Marxists, but while they continued to cling to the idea that the revolution must be made by the proletariat, Mao focused on the significant (but theoretically ambiguous) revolutionary potential of the rural masses. During the various armed conflicts in which the Chinese communists were engaged from the early 1920s, the countryside served as both a major theatre of war and as the source of recruits for the Red Army. This body was led by the Communist Party, but it had originated in revolutionary agrarian responses to both feudal and capitalist exploitation. Mao regarded the Red Army as the major instrument of revolutionary change in China.

Mao Tse-tung (1893–1976)

Following his conversion to Marxism in 1927, Mao played a prominent role in the military struggle against the nationalist leader Chiang Kai-shek and then against the Japanese. Until his death Mao was the dominant figure in the Chinese Communist Party. His political ideas were presented in a large number of essays and speeches addressing the military and political problems facing the Communist Party in its attempt to seize power and establish a communist society.

Every Communist must grasp the truth 'Political power grows out of the barrel of a gun.' Our principle is that the Party commands the gun, and the gun must never be allowed to command the Party. Yet, having guns we can create Party organisations.... We can also create cadres, create schools, create culture, create mass movements.... All things grow out of the barrel of a gun. According to the Marxist theory of the state, the army is the chief component of state power. Whoever wants to seize and retain state power must have a strong army (ibid., pp. 274–5).

Even at that time Mao stressed the political opportunities that military success would open up, and in his later formulations the emphasis on superstructural elements became more marked. This position was closely related to Mao's belief that if the peasantry could be organised and led by the party they would possess great revolutionary potential.

Mao originally regarded the Chinese revolution as a *stage* in the progression to socialism, one that would ultimately result in the creation of a genuine democratic republic. In the early 1950s, however, he argued that the transition to socialism had already begun and that it was being carried out under the direct control of the party. The fact that Mao now discounted the significance of the backward condition of Chinese society and implicitly rejected the conventional Marxist view that socialism follows the triumph of democracy, made it necessary for him to reformulate his account of the class characteristics of contemporary Chinese society and the role of the class struggle within it. These issues were addressed in *On the Correct Handling of Contradictions Among the People*. In this work Mao argued that the political victory of the forces of socialism in China meant that the 'people's government' could be the directing force for a revolutionary transformation of Chinese society. The state could resolve the real but non- antagonistic contradictions that still persisted between the surviving classes in Chinese society. Mao expected that these contradictions would be overcome as society progressed towards socialism. In his later writings Mao portrayed this as a permanent process that would stimulate the revolutionary enthusiasm of both party cadres and the masses (Mao, 1957). He insisted however, that this stimulation should be controlled by the upper echelons of the party, and he gave increasing prominence to the role played by ideas of personal leadership. Mao's theory of leadership is based on the dictum that 'all correct leadership' is necessarily 'from the masses to the masses'. However, the role he ascribed to the party and the individual leadership in drawing in, refining and then disseminating these ideas, means that his political theory echoes some of the key themes of traditional Chinese thought by pointing to a patriarchal mode of government set within a strongly hierarchical system of social and political authority (Deutscher, 1966, p. 112).

Revolutionary Anarchism and the Critique of Marxism: Bakunin and Kropotkin

Social anarchists promoted a vision of a classless, stateless future that was similar to the end-point of revolutionary Marxism. These anarchists

were intensely critical of the material and moral implications of capitalism, and they believed that its overthrow would come about through a
process of international revolution carried out by the working classes
and the oppressed peasantry. Like other revolutionary socialists, anarchists thought that the French Revolution provided both inspiration and
warning. In particular the events of the early 1790s highlighted the
limitations of purely formal conceptions of liberty and equality, a point
that was driven home by the unsuccessful outcome of Babeuf's conspiracy (see p. 189).

The primary anarchist target was authority in general, and in particular
that source of supreme authority that was located in the state. They
regarded the impositions of capitalism as part of a generalised system of
oppression that was centred in the state and spread into various economic, social and religious outworks. The purpose of anarchist revolution
was to destroy the state and those oppressive institutions that were maintained by it and also gave it legitimacy.

While leading figures in nineteenth-century social anarchism believed
that a revolutionary change was imminent, their views on the cause and
nature of revolution varied significantly. Proudhon, for example, relied on
social transformation through non-political initiatives, and was not a proponent of violent revolution. He believed that the time was ripe for such
a change because the level of injustice in contemporary society had risen
to a level where it was stimulating individuals to overcome selfish
impulses and develop their capacity for cooperation. In contrast Bakunin
and Kropotkin made the idea of revolution a central component of their
anarchism. Although these thinkers regarded the advent of anarchism as
a consequence of the deep-seated historical processes that were coming to
fruition in the nineteenth century, neither of them adopted Marx's theory
of historical materialism. Bakunin regarded anarchism as the outcome of
a development of human consciousness from a condition where authority
is a regrettable but necessary evil, to one in which it is both unnecessary
and regressive. For example, when explaining the universality of the false
idea of a 'supreme being' or God, Bakunin wrote that it must be an idea
that is an 'outcome of ourselves, ... an error historically necessary in the
development of humanity' (Bakunin, 1973, p. 122).

Kropotkin's account of anarchism was framed in clear evolutionary
terms. As we have seen, he regarded mutual aid as a natural and beneficial pattern of interaction that accounts for both animal and human
development (see p. 99). Kropotkin treated authority, oppression and the
state as aberrations in a process of development that is underwritten by
moral ideas that make anarchism the next stage in the evolution of
human society. Within the framework of evolutionary development Kropotkin identified a series of conflicts between two traditions: the 'Roman'
tradition of authoritarian and imperial rule, and a 'popular' tradition of

federalism and libertarianism that reflects the influence of the mutual aid principle (Kropotkin, 1903, p. 41). Since mutual aid is the key to human progress it has not been completely stifled even within capitalist societies. However the main features of capitalism – its denial of equality and its reliance on a coercive state to maintain a system of economic and social oppression – are incompatible with the mutual aid principle. Progress requires the destruction of both capitalism and the state, and the establishment of a system of free federating communes that will make the ideals of the French Revolution – liberty, equality and fraternity – a reality. Given the coercive capacities of the state and its close relationship with capitalism, it is unlikely that such a radical change can be inaugurated without revolutionary action.

In their accounts of the revolutionary process both Bakunin and Kropotkin ascribed a great deal of importance to people's instinctive sense of justice and their natural aversion to the imposition of authority. These drives mean that revolutions are a consequence of spontaneous outbursts of popular indignation reflecting a deep-seated spirit of revolt that has survived the stifling oppression of conventional political structures. An important consequence of this position was that nineteenth-century anarchist thinkers rejected the reliance on a conspiratorial elite that had formed the cornerstone of Blanqui's conception of revolution (see p. 165). They were also hostile to what they saw as the authoritarian aspects of the Marxian tradition of revolutionary socialism, claiming that it would pervert the course of the revolution and merely create a new political order. These fears played an important role in the history of late-nineteenth and early-twentieth-century revolutionary socialism because they gave rise to a series of vigorously contested ideological confrontations between the Marxists and the anarchists. In the course of these debates there emerged a number of important divergences between revolutionary Marxism and revolutionary anarchism.

In the first place, both Bakunin and Kropotkin questioned the scientific standing of Marx's theory. They claimed that Marx's materialism had no empirical basis and that it had been applied in a dogmatic and mechanical manner. In particular, Bakunin resisted the idea that the development of a revolutionary consciousness requires the development of capitalism. According to Bakunin, revolutionary consciousness is instinctive and perpetual, and does not have to await the development of a particular form of oppression.

Bakunin linked these shortcomings in the basis of Marxism to its authoritarian political implications. He argued that true science starts from the facts of human existence and then sets up systems of ideas that explain and order these facts. When this approach is applied to politics, it places a premium on the actual aspirations, feeling and knowledge of the populace – these are political facts – and discounts the preconceived ideas of self-appointed intellectual leaders. Unlike Marxism, anarchism rests on

> the broad popular method, the method of real and total liberation, accessible to anyone and therefore truly popular. It is the method of the *anarchist* social revolution, which arises spontaneously within the people and destroys everything that opposes the broad flow of popular life so as to create new forms of free social existence out of the depths of the people's existence (Bakunin, 1990, p. 133).

According to Kropotkin, the scientific studying of Marxism was comprised by Marx's neglect of emprical data and his failure to take account of the lessons of evolutionary theory (Kropotkin, 1970, p. 152).

Bakunin contrasted his general approach with that found in the writings of Marx and his followers. Having identified an ideal social order the Marxists have to impose this on the general population: a Marxist revolution cannot liberate humanity because it is rooted in ideas that are divorced from human aspirations, experiences and interests. In contrast the anarchist conception of revolution reflects the popular instinct for liberty, equality and fraternity, and recognises that the realisation of popular aspirations has to come about through the development and application of the consciousness of the population itself. The key insight of anarchism is the

> belief that [as] the masses bear all the elements of their future organisational norms in their own more or less historically evolved instincts, in their everyday needs and their conscious and unconscious desires, we seek that ideal within the people themselves (Bakunin, 1990, p. 135).

Kropotkin made a similar point when he claimed that anarchism owes 'its origins to the constructive creative activity of the people, by which all institutions of communal life were developed in the past' (Kropotkin, 1970, p. 149).

Although much of Bakunin's revolutionary career was devoted to setting up hierarchical revolutionary organisations, he did not think that these bodies would take a leading or directive role in the revolutionary process. For example he dismissed radical attempts to educate the Russian peasantry. Despite appearances, these well-meant gestures involved the imposition of elites upon the people. Bakunin insisted that the only role that elites can play is to incite 'the people' to independent action and to open their eyes to the possibility of their liberation (Bakunin, 1990, p. 200). The role that Bakunin ascribed to an enlightened intelligentsia is quite different from that promoted by the Marxists. In place of spontaneous organisation 'from below', the Marxists had cast themselves as both instigators and 'managers of all popular movements' (ibid., p. 136). The Marxists' presumption explains why their ideas had so little appeal among the masses in Italy and Spain, where the spirit of revolt was still strong. In other parts of Europe, however, Marx's ideas were at the forefront of socialism and posed a serious threat to the revolutionary process. Marxists saw the revolution as a means of destroying the capitalist order, but they wrongly insisted that

> on the morrow of the revolution a new social organisation must be created not by the free union of popular associations, communes, districts, and provinces from below upward, in conformity with popular needs and instincts, but solely by means of the dictatorial power of this learned minority, which *supposedly* expresses the will of all the people (ibid., p. 136).

Both Bakunin and Kropotkin argued that proletarian dictatorship results in the establishment of a new form of state, one that cannot discern or embody the real interests of the population in whose name it presumes to rule. Even given the best of intentions, and ignoring the inevitable tendency for power to corrupt those who wield it, a proletarian state is still a state. It will thus suffer from all the evils inherent in a form of political and social organisation that is imposed on the population rather than being a genuine expression of its aspirations and interests. Revolutionary anarchists maintain that the Marxist theory of revolution is dangerously misguided because it fails to take account of the inherently oppressive nature of all forms of political organisation.

Decolonisation and Revolutionary Political Theory: Fanon

Given the role that Marx ascribed to imperialism – that is, a strategy to sustain the profitability of capitalism by securing new markets and new areas of investment – it is not surprising that opponents of colonisation have often adopted insights derived from Marx's writings. One example of this has been touched upon in the discussion of Mao's theory. As noted there, Mao maintained that the development of a revolutionary movement in China must take account of the fact that the masses were being exploited by native capitalists *and* external forces who were treating China as an informal annexe of their colonial and imperial possessions (see p. 343). In the wake of the Second World War, the declining influence of the colonial powers of Western Europe gave a fillip to pre-existing indigenous movements in Africa, the Middle East and South-East Asia. Beginning in the late 1940s, there had appeared a number of independence movements committed to the expulsion of colonial powers from these regions. Since these movements had to contend with the coercive power of local and imperial governments, and since the struggle for independence was accompanied by a desire radically to restructure the political, social and economic organisation of the state, the pursuit of independence necessitated the development and propagation of revolutionary programmes. In some states, most notably India, liberation and revolutionary transformation were pursued largely through non-violent means and gave rise to a distinctive set of theories (see pp. 360ff).

Elsewhere, however, decolonisation was thought to necessitate violent revolutionary action. The discussion that follows will consider the ideas of Franz Fanon, who was closely involved with the attempt by Algeria to free itself from the domination of France and the presence of long-established settlers of French origin. While Mao treated imperialism as one generalised source of exploitation, Fanon's theory draws attention to the relationship between the settler culture and that of the indigenous people. In particular he emphasised the degree to which the combination of direct external and internal domination gives rise to a general dehumanisation of life within colonial society. The repossession of humanity requires the end of colonial domination. It also necessitates the restructuring of social, economic and political life within former colonies so that human beings can develop a capacity to enjoy a way of life that is free from *all* forms of domination. Although Fanon's understanding of this goal was informed by his study of Marx's writings, he thought that indigenous cultures contain the seeds from which this way of life can grow. Consequently he was a stern critic of the tendency towards party and personal control that had played an increasingly prominent role in both the theory and the practice of revolutionary Marxism.

Frantz Fanon (1925–61)

Fanon was born in Martinique and trained in medicine and psychiatry in France. He served in a hospital in Algeria during the uprising against French colonial rule, and his experience of this particularly brutal conflict led him to become a spokesman for the Algerians. Fanon's most important political writings, *The Wretched of the Earth* (1961) and *Towards the African Revolution* (1964), examined the requirements for human liberation in colonial and post-colonial settings. To some degree Fanon's political thought was indebted to Marx, but it also incorporated insights into the conditions of human well-being that he had gained during his psychiatric training and practice.

Fanon offered three revisions to conventional Marxist accounts of the revolutionary process. In the first place, he argued that the relationship between the dominant and subordinated classes in colonial society differs significantly from those described by Marx in his accounts of capitalist or even precapitalist societies. There is no dominant bourgeois and no identifiable proletariat in colonies, and nor can these societies be described by reference to conventional accounts of precapitalist modes of production. In precapitalist Europe the dominant classes were legitimated by culturally embedded ideas (such as divine right) that reflected a widely accepted belief in the moral unity of humanity. In contrast colonial societies are characterised by a sharp and unbridgeable distinction between the dominant elites (who come from outside the indigenous culture) and the native population, whom they openly and systematically exploit. As a consequence the attributes that determine class membership in both capitalist and precapitalist societies have no bearing in colonial society:

> In the colonies, the foreigner coming from another country, imposed his rule by means of guns and machines. In defiance of his successful transplantation, in spite of his appropriation, the settler remains a foreigner. It is neither the act of owning factories, nor estates, nor a bank balance which distinguishes the governing class. The governing race is first and foremost those who come from elsewhere, those who are unlike the original inhabitants, 'the others' (Fanon, 1967, p. 31).

Secondly, the alien nature of settler domination and its reliance on violence means that the process of liberation necessitates the expulsion of the colonialists and reclamation of the colony and its resources by the indigenous inhabitants. Revolutionary violence is a spontaneous product that develops in reaction to the experience of colonisation, and does not need to be fostered by an elite: 'To wreck the colonial world is ... a mental picture of action which is very clear, very easy to understand and which may be assumed by each one of the individuals which constitute the colonized people' (ibid., p. 31).

Thirdly, because colonies exist in a precapitalist twilight they lack a conventional proletariat and can only be liberated through a revolution based on the rural masses. Although Fanon's views on the issue are similar to those adhered to by Mao in the 1930s and 1940s, he did not see the creation of bourgeois democracy as the appropriate goal of revolutionary activity. To the contrary, he believed that revolution to free a colony from the shackles of colonialism is merely the first step in a continuous process of human liberation that does not conform to the conventional Marxist model. Fanon claimed that since ex-colonies lack a genuine bourgeoisie, they tend to veer towards economic stagnation and political repression. To avoid these outcomes it is necessary to use the struggle for national independence as the launching pad for a process of cultural and political revolution that will inaugurate a form of liberation resembling that which Marx identified with true democracy. For Fanon, however, this goal can be achieved by incorporating traditions of social interaction that are embedded in the popular culture of the rural areas of the colonised society.

In Fanon's analysis, the exploitation that characterises colonial societies is the most overt manifestation of the dehumanising nature of colonisation. Decolonisation is necessary to shake off this incubus and to establish the conditions needed to create what Fanon called 'new men': 'the "thing" which has been colonized becomes man during the same process by which it frees itself' (ibid., p. 28). Fanon's understanding of revolution as a process has important implications for the way in which it is carried out. Anticolonial revolutions should aim at total destruction of the relationships of colonial society – 'the last shall be first and the first last' (ibid., p. 28) – and of the ideological superstructure, imported by the colonists and adopted by some colonised elites and privileged members of the subordinated classes (ibid., p. 36).

The actions and utterances of indigenous (but largely Westernised) elites tend to develop a momentum among the mass of the population that quickly outstrips the limited (and largely self-interested) intentions of those who occupy leading positions in nationalist political parties. These politicians seek compromises with their colonial overlords to preserve their own positions and that of their urban supporters, and they attempt to use outbreaks of mass violence as instruments in this process. Fanon insisted, however, that the rural population forms the true core of the revolutionary movement:

> The starving peasant, outside the class system, is the first among the exploited to discover that only violence pays. For him there is no compromise, no possible coming to terms; colonization and decolonization are simply a question of strength. The exploited man sees that his liberation implies the use of all means, and that of force first and foremost (ibid., pp. 47–8).

In his treatment of wars of independence, and also in his strictures on the need to continue the revolutionary process in the post-colonial period, Fanon stressed the positive effect of the process of struggle on the consciousness of the rural masses: the 'mobilisation of the masses ... introduces into each man's consciousness the ideas of a common cause, of national destiny and of collective history' (ibid., p. 73). Fanon thought that this arises from social values that still hold sway in the countryside, but have been abandoned by those who have moved to the cities. Popular attachment to these values is revitalised by the experience of revolution. Revolutionary action is a way of expelling the colonial power and purifying people's present existence so as to provide the basis for further development of a collective, revolutionary consciousness within the newly liberated state (ibid., p. 105).

Fanon warned, however, that this process of liberation may be threatened by the persisting political, economic and ideological influence of the former colonial power, and also by potentially exploitative elements within the indigenous culture, the 'national bourgeoisie'. Within the context of Western capitalism, the bourgeoisie play an important role, but the 'national bourgeoisie' of the post-colonial world have no claims to dominance other than those springing from their corrupt interaction with self-interested and self-perpetuating military and political elites:

> In under-developed countries ... no true bourgeoisie exists; there is only a sort of little greedy caste, avid and voracious, with the mind of a huckster, only too glad to accept the dividends that the former colonial power hands out to it. This get-rich-quick middle class shows itself incapable of great ideas or of inventiveness. It ... imperceptibly ... becomes not even a replica of Europe, but its caricature (ibid., p. 141).

This tendency to set up a caricature of Europe extends to the sort of single-party state that is spawned by subversion of the process of national and human liberation. Many post-colonial states subvert democracy while claiming to maintain it, and give a prominent role to an irremovable leader. While presenting themselves as an embodiment of the general interest of the community, these figures pursue particular interests expressed in racial and tribal terms. They use the party machine to manipulate the rural population and reduce them to the status of a passive, marginalised group that is of little more consequence in the independent state than it was in its colonial predecessor (ibid., pp. 115–18).

As an alternative to single-party governments of conventional Third World democracy (see p. 195), Fanon promoted mass participation in a grass roots party that is the tool of the people, not of a new governing class. He insisted that this party must not dominate the state administration, and that the latter should be radically decentralised, dynamic and sensitive to the expressed preferences of the local population. While retaining faith in a single revolutionary party, Fanon wished to prevent it from directly dominating the state or forming a source of authoritarian control:

> For the people, the party is not an authority, but an organism thorough which they as the people exercise their authority and express their will. The less there is of confusion and duality of powers, the more the party will play its part of guide and the more surely it will constitute for the people a decisive guarantee (ibid., p. 149).

Fanon regarded the beneficial interaction between locally based systems of administration (a 'bottom-up' party) and the rural population as natural developments of the locally based initiatives that provided the driving force for the first stage of the revolutionary process. Post-colonial societies must capitalise on the experiences of the struggle for independence in order to further the goals of the revolution. These goals include development of the economic and human resources of the countryside. However, Fanon insisted that the material benefits of national revolution must be set within a framework of human liberation. In pursuing this goal, revolutionaries must build upon a sense of collective interest that incorporates ordinary members of the population so that they become the source of economic and political initiatives. The key to fostering this approach to the transformation of human life is to expose the public to an interactive and participatory programme of political education:

> To educate the masses politically does not mean, cannot mean making a political speech. What it means is to try, relentlessly and passionately, to teach the masses that everything depends on them; that if we stagnate it is their responsibility, and that if we go forward it is due to them too, that there is no such thing as a demiurge, that there is no famous man who will take responsibility for everything, but that the demiurge is the people themselves and the magic hands are finally only the hands of the people (ibid., p. 159).

Although Fanon's theory of revolution started with the promotion of struggles for national independence, it is significant in that it endorses the ethical goals of Marxism as a means of advancing universal human goals: 'Individual experience, because it is national and because it is a link in the chain of national existence, ceases to be individual, limited and shrunken and is enabled to open out into the truth of the nation and the world' (ibid., p. 161). For Fanon, therefore, the development of national consciousness is a significant but temporary step along the road to universal liberation.

Conclusion

Resistance theorists identify general standards to which rulers are expected to conform. They assume that existing regimes are capable of embodying these standards and believe that they are usually endorsed by both rulers and subjects. In contrast revolutionary thinkers believe that the realisation of fundamental human aspirations is incompatible with both the values and practice of conventional politics. Those individuals and classes who frustrate human progress must be removed from positions of power, and political and/or social relations must be radically restructured so that they can be used to promote the realisation of what are taken to be the true ends of politics.

Revolutionary theories identify fundamental failings in existing political structures, promote more satisfactory alternatives, and seek to determine the tactics necessary to realise revolutionary goals. Revolutions are often seen as a way of creating the preconditions for social change, but some forms of modern revolutionary thinking are distinctive because they emphasise the interdependence of social and political structures. As a result it is argued that substantive political change requires radical changes in the social structure, particularly in the distribution of material resources that have a bearing on power relationships within society.

The connection between social and political revolution is a notable feature of the Marxist tradition, but this idea has also played an important role in revolutionary anarchism and in anticolonial theories such as those formulated by Fanon. In addition to seeing revolutions as both social and political events, these writers stress their universal significance. While early American and French revolutionary ideas rested on appeals to the 'rights of man' that were focused on particular states, Marxists, anarchists and theorists of anticolonial revolution challenge systems of oppression that are seen as international in form and scope.

CHAPTER 14

Theories of Civil Disobedience and Non-Violent Resistance to Political Authority

The ideas discussed in this chapter are frequently grouped together as theories of 'civil disobedience'. The distinctive character of the type of actions that are promoted and justified by ideas of civil disobedience is captured in their designation as forms of 'principled' disobedience. This term draws attention to the fact that acts of disobedience are directed by a desire to resist political injustice and to produce a change in the exercise of political authority, not – as is the case with conventional law breaking – to gain some personal advantage (Harris, 1989). 'Civil disobedience' is related to, but must be distinguished from, the idea of 'passive resistance', which played a role in medieval political theory. 'Passive resistance' refers to a refusal to obey unjust commands; it generally precludes challenges to rulers, and does not necessarily involve a concerted attempt to change their conduct or modify the structures within which they operate.

The absence of any overt and systematic critique of the exercise of political authority distinguishes the responses discussed in this chapter from other historical examples of principled disobedience, such as that by the Hebrew midwives, as recounted in the book of Exodus, by Antigone in Greek tragedy and by Sir Thomas More in his relationship with King Henry VIII. Although the term civil disobedience will be used here as a general label, it should be noted that one important proponent of non-violent resistance regarded the idea of civil disobedience as too negative.

As we shall see, Mahatma Gandhi preferred to describe his doctrine as one of 'civil resistance'. He did so in order to signal his desire for a positive transformation of politics so that political authority would once again become legitimate.

Three theories of civil disobedience or non-violent resistance will be discussed in this chapter. The mid-nineteenth-century American writer Henry Thoreau was largely concerned with preserving the moral integrity of the just individual in the face of governmental injustice. Thoreau's notion of civil disobedience can be contrasted with the ideas on non-violent resistance developed by Mahatma Gandhi in India. Gandhi's theory was developed in the context of a movement dedicated to expelling the British from the subcontinent and to promoting a radical restructuring of Indian politics and society. Gandhi's revolutionary use of non-violence differs significantly from that promoted by the Reverend Martin Luther King in the middle years of the present century. King developed his version of civil disobedience during the course of a campaign to end legally sanctioned discrimination against blacks. For King, civil disobedience was a way of bringing pressure to bear on liberal-democratic governments in order to make them subscribe to the moral, and in some cases legal, standards that are claimed to be inherent to this sort of regime.

Moral Integrity and Civil Disobedience: Thoreau

Thoreau's 'Resistance to Civil Government', which was first delivered as a lecture in 1848 and published the following year, is often regarded as the first modern statement of a doctrine of civil disobedience. Thoreau's essay was referred to by Gandhi, and it is widely noted in contemporary treatments of civil disobedience. It seems clear, however, that Thoreau's position differed significantly from that employed by later theorists who treated resistance in the context of the reform of democratic institutions. Moreover, unlike both Gandhi and King, Thoreau was not opposed to the use of violence in some circumstances. The act of disobedience that provided the focus of 'Resistance to Civil Government' was non-violent, but in a later work he wrote in support of Captain John Brown, an extremely militant member of the movement to abolish slavery in the United States (Thoreau, 1996, pp. 139–40).

In his essay Thoreau sought to justify his refusal to pay a poll tax levied by the Commonwealth of Massachusetts, an action that unequivocally breached state law. Thoreau made it quite clear that he had no intention of complying with the law, and as a consequence he was imprisoned. Although he was quite prepared to serve his full sentence he spent only one night in prison because his poll tax obligations were settled without his approval by a member of his family.

Thoreau's refusal to pay the poll tax stemmed from his abhorrence of
US aggression in the Mexican–American war of 1846–8 and the
persistence of slavery in the United States. Imperialist adventures and
slavery were fundamentally unjust, and refusing to pay the tax was a
way of drawing attention to this and separating himself from a
government that was grossly infringing the rights of its neighbours
and subjects. In some passages of 'Resistance to Civil Government'
Thoreau indicated that he was motivated by a desire to correct the
conduct of federal and state governments. For example he appealed
to his readers to deny the authority of the US government: 'Let your
life be a counterfriction to stop the machine' (Thoreau, 1992, p. 233). He
also remarked that if actions such as his became widespread they
would 'clog' the whole machinery of government: if all just men had to
be imprisoned, the state would give up slavery immediately (ibid., p.
235).

However, these largely instrumental explanations of civil disobedience
seem incidental to Thoreau's general and more consistently stated
position. This argument is laid down in the opening passage of the essay
where, having alluded to his preference for anarchism – 'That government
is best which governs not at all' (ibid., p. 226) – he pleaded in the
short term for 'better government' and urged his fellow citizens to 'make
known what kind of government would command [their] respect'. He
expected that his gesture of non-compliance with the poll tax law would
be 'one step towards obtaining' such a government (ibid., p. 227). It
should be noted, however, that Thoreau was not talking of a *system* of
government, but of the *attitude* towards it by citizens and office holders
alike. For the most part his appeal focused primarily on *citizens* rather
than *governors*, and was meant to encourage the former to signal their
commitment to a standard of justice to which they expected office holders
to adhere.

Thoreau thought that ideas of justice had their roots in the uncorrupted consciousness of ordinary human beings, and he insisted that it was this – rather than the demands of governors, or the voice of the majority, or the idea that individuals had a primary obligation to smooth the path of government – that provided the standards for individual moral and collective political responsibility. In response to the question 'must the citizen ever for a moment, or in the least degree, resign his conscience to the legislator?', Thoreau observed that 'we should be men first, and subjects afterwards' (ibid., p. 227). He argued that a state that tolerated slavery or engaged in aggressive wars was acting in disregard of justice and was not worthy of the respect or obedience of its citizens.

It is significant, however, that Thoreau's account of his response to the unjust actions of American government focused primarily on the maintenance and observance of moral integrity among upright individuals, not upon reforming the system of government, or even correcting the conduct of those who currently controlled it. Thoreau claimed that association with the present government of the United States involved such 'disgrace' that 'I cannot for an instant recognise that political organisation as *my* government which is the slaves government also' (ibid., p. 229). He justified his act of civil disobedience on the ground that there was a lack of correspondence between the actions of government and the moral stance required by the demands of justice. Consequently Thoreau argued that his refusal to pay the poll tax should be seen as a 'deliberate and practical denial' of the government's authority. It signalled to other upright individuals that he would not lend himself to the wrong he condemned (ibid., p. 233).

The fact that Thoreau was prepared to suffer imprisonment did not imply acceptance of the penalties of the law and the state that lay behind it. To the contrary, his removal from society was a consequence of his general rejection of the legitimacy of an unjust state:

> Under a government which imprisons any unjustly, the true place for a just man is also a prison. The proper place to-day, the only place which Massachusetts has provided for her free and less desponding spirits, is in her prisons, to be put out and locked out of the State by her own act, as they have already put themselves out by their principles (ibid., p. 235).

Even if those who Thoreau called 'abetters' of the state were to pay a protester's tax and secure his release from prison, this would not undermine the position of the 'just man'. He would still remain separate from the state and would have done nothing to compromise his relationship with it.

Thoreau's notion of resistance thus hinges on the determination of just individuals to separate themselves from an unjust state. He made it clear, however, that when civil disobedients divorce themselves from the state they are not engaging in an act that is part of a conventional political process. Unlike the casting of a vote, which merely expresses a hope that 'right will prevail' but leaves this up to the majority to determine , an act of civil disobedience removes the individual from the state's moral ambit (ibid., p. 230). Thoreau adhered to a notion of 'democratic individualism', which means that the conscience of individuals cannot be represented through the outcome of electoral processes. Democratic communities are made up of individuals who retain responsibility for their own sense of moral rightness. Civil disobedience is an expression of one's duty to be a good member of such a community (Rosenblum, 1996, pp. xxv–xxvi). For Thoreau, therefore, disobedience is a *human* act based on an appeal to a higher law of justice that lies beyond the reach of the state, but which should be upheld by it. It is emphatically not a tactic to win the state over to a particular point of view: 'I simply wish to refuse allegiance to the State, to withdraw and stand away from it effectually' (Thoreau, 1992, p. 241).

Insofar as this act appeals to other upright individuals, the net effect of a number of such withdrawals may be to create enough 'friction' to 'clog' the machinery of the state. Thoreau insisted, however, that this possibility should not be the determining factor of whether civil disobedience is appropriate. To the contrary, he argued that individuals owe allegiance to an authority that is far higher than the state, and must adhere to it even when this action has no discernable effect on the state's conduct. It is not the individual who has to seek the approval of the state, but rather the state must recognise that it is the individual who is the arbiter of justice: 'There will never be a really free and enlightened State, until the State comes to recognise the individual as a higher and independent power, and treats him accordingly' (ibid., p. 245).

In twentieth-century political theory the term 'civil disobedience' is frequently used to describe irregular and in some cases illegal actions that bring pressure to bear on the operation of the democratic state. Sit-ins, obstructive demonstrations and the flouting of unjust laws, are meant to hinder the operation of government, to draw legislators' and voters' attention to alleged injustice by appealing to the shared sense of justice that is thought to underwrite a democratic community. It should be noted that this position differs from that of Thoreau. Thoreau's civil disobedient separates himself from the state and his imprisonment epitomises this separation. Moreover, as noted above, Thoreau regarded the individual as the source of ideas of justice, and argued that the best the state can do is to recognise this and avoid transgressing a standard that is independent of it and cannot be related positively to its existence. Even the most democratic states are only incidently concerned with justice because their main decision-making mechanism – the will of the majority – leaves justice to chance. Since the individual is the repository of ideas of justice, the state can have no effect on an individual's sense of moral responsibility to a higher power, to a perpetually higher authority. According to Thoreau, *all* political authority is conditional; there is no such thing as an obligation to submit to government (Rosenblum, 1996, p. xxv).

This doctrine presents a potentially revolutionary challenge to the conventional democratic state because it sees political obligation as a source of danger to the moral conscience. When such dangers materialise, individuals are under an obligation to sever their ties with the state and to stand up against its unjust measures. Thoreau's individual does not have to justify civil disobedience; rather the state must make itself worthy of the necessarily conditional obedience of the individual. In Thoreau's theory, therefore, the conscience of the upright individual provides a permanent source of challenge to those who exercise political power. If they wish to secure the obedience of those nominally subject to them, they must act in ways that conform to the dictates of their subjects' conscience. For Thoreau, the obligation of subjects' to their political superiors is always conditional; indeed it is so conditional that one could almost say that those in political authority have to ensure that their actions are worthy of the obedience of those over whom they wish to exercise such authority.

Non-Violent Resistance and Anticolonialism: Gandhi

Thoreau's essay provided a source of inspiration for Mahatma Gandhi, the leading figure in the Indian independence movement in the first half of the twentieth century. But while Gandhi admired Thoreau's stance, he produced a theory of non-violent resistance to unjust authority that differed in significant respects from that of his American predecessor. Gandhi's goal was a distinctly revolutionary one because he sought the liberation of India and other Third World countries from colonial domination. Non-violent resistance was thus meant to provide the basis for a programme of political action rather than being restricted to expressing the moral integrity of just individuals. In developing his theory Gandhi made it clear that its key idea – '*satyagraha*' – differed from Thoreau's notion of civil disobedience.

Gandhi first enunciated this concept in response to specific acts of injustice committed by colonial authorities in the South African state of Natal in the early decades of the twentieth century. Later, however, it was applied more generally to the entire struggle for independence in the Indian subcontinent. Pursuit of this goal necessitated the rejection of various schemes mooted in the 1920s and 1930s for power sharing, for 'dominion' status like that enjoyed by predominantly white settler colonies in Australia, Canada and New Zealand, or for any measures that stopped short of complete independence from Great Britain. As Gandhi wrote in 1930, it was not a question of determining 'how much power India should or should not enjoy, but ... [of considering] ways and means of framing a scheme of complete independence' (Gandhi, 1986, vol. iii, pp. 103–4).

This demand was based on a general critique of the authority of imperial rulers, and a particular rejection of British rule in India. Gandhi argued that however well intentioned individual officials might be, the British system of rule was inherently autocratic and unjust. The British policy of 'divide and rule' encouraged communal antagonism between ethnic and religious groups within India and made the need for outside intervention part of a self-fulfilling prophecy (ibid., p. 281). The patronage of their British masters allowed local elites ruthlessly to exploit the rest of the community, and provided an important element in a system of rule that subjugated Indian interests to those of the British. The boasted *pax Britannica*, the guarantor of stability and order, epitomised the illusory benefits of colonial domination:

It has as much value to India as the slave dwellers have in an estate, whose owner keeps the slaves from fighting one another, protects the estate from foreign inroads and makes the slaves work with a regularity that is just enough to keep the estate going in his, the owner's interest (ibid., p. 595).

Mohandas Karamchand Gandhi (1869–1948)

Gandhi, an Indian-born, English-trained lawyer, originally formulated his concept of non-violent resistance while engaged in a campaign against anti-Indian racial discrimination in the South African colony of Natal. This theory was refined during the course of Gandhi's subsequent involvement in the long struggle to free India from British rule. In the course of this campaign (concluded successfully in 1947) Gandhi acquired the status of a special political and spiritual leader, hence the title 'Mahatma', or 'Great Soul'.

Although Gandhi developed his ideas on civil resistance in an Indian context, he regarded the independence movement there as part of a more widespread struggle against colonialism. In India and elsewhere in the Third World, this struggle was directed in the first instance at the liberation of these countries from the direct political, economic and moral effects of imperialism. In addition, however, it was also meant to be applied to the more deep-seated corruption that disfigured colonial countries and impeded their development into viable, morally acceptable societies. As Gandhi put it in 1928, 'My ambition is much higher than independence. Through the deliverance of India, I seek to deliver the so-called weaker races of the earth from the crushing heels of exploitation in which England is the greatest partner' (ibid., p. 255). This goal required alien Western values to be shaken off. In light of the programme that Gandhi developed it is also significant that he believed the struggle for independence would bring Englishmen and other Europeans to an understanding of the evils they had inflicted on their colonies, and that this would encourage them to abandon imperialism throughout the world (ibid., p. 255). This aspiration played a central role in Gandhi's belief that the most effective and morally acceptable form of anticolonialism should be based on the principle of non-violent resistance.

One reason why Gandhi promoted non-violent resistance was that his experiences in South Africa had convinced him of its practical advantages. In Natal, Gandhi had headed a minority movement that was in confrontation with the colonial administration and white settlers, and the large indigenous population who were played off against the Indian minority. In these circumstances violent resistance was bound to fail; if anything it would strengthen the hand of the colonial government in their dealings with the Indian population. Later, in India, the proponents of independence had to contend with an extensive, highly militarised colonial government backed by one of the world's most significant naval and military powers. They also faced a situation where a deliberately fragmented society was frequently torn apart by outbreaks of 'communal' violence fuelled by ethnic and religious antagonism. In addition to his awareness of the practical futility of armed resistance, Gandhi's preference for non-violence was based on his conviction of its moral futility: violence debases and dehumanises those who resort to it; it limits their capacity to appeal to the moral sense of others; and it would also corrupt the outcome of the struggle for independence.

Identification of a genealogy of proponents of non-violence in both the Indian and Western traditions played an important justificatory role in Gandhi's theory. The Western tradition included figures from the ancient world (Socrates), the Bible (Daniel) and near contemporaries such as Thoreau and the English suffragettes. Although Gandhi regarded this tradition as an important source of inspiration and legitimation, his attitude towards it was in some respects critical. In the course of formulating this criticism Gandhi distinguished a range of attitudes towards non-violence. In the first place he rejected contemporary understandings of 'passive resistance', an idea that he associated with the suffragettes. Gandhi argued that since some suffragettes employed violence they could hardly be described as being engaged in passive resistance. In addition, however,

Gandhi rejected the idea of passive resistance because he wanted to establish modes of non-violent action that were strongly active rather than passive. It was important for proponents of independence to act with a full sense of their own personal and collective strength: non-violence was not the refuge of the weak, but a tactic employed by those who were strong in numbers, determination and moral rectitude (ibid., pp. 44–5).

Although at times Gandhi seemed to endorse Thoreau's form of civil disobedience, he eventually rejected both the term itself and the approach it described. In its place he developed a doctrine that he thought could best be encapsulated in English by the term 'civil resistance'. Unlike civil disobedience, civil resistance was more than just an expression of moral abhorrence; it entailed active resistance directed not merely against particular injustices, but at a system that was inherently unjust. Resistance was meant to discredit the *status quo* and usher in a distinctive and positive alternative to it. The expulsion of the British had to be seen as part of a process that would forge a new, just order that would be free from the incubus of materialistic and individualistic Western culture. Finally, the use of the term 'civil' underlined the non-violent character of resistance:

> the current phrase was 'passive resistance'. But my way of resistance or the force I had in mind was not passive. It was active, but 'active' might also mean violent. The word 'civil' suggests nothing but non-violence. I, therefore, joined it with resistance (ibid., p. 112).

Gandhi's conception of civil resistance was part of a wider doctrine known as *satyagraha*, which incorporated reinterpretations of a number of precepts that were common currency among Hindus. *Satya*, which refers to the primacy of truth and is usually given an individualistic cast that relates to individual self-perfection, was endowed by Gandhi with a strongly social connotation. In *satyagraha* the pursuit of truth became a key element in a programme of radical political and social transformation (Bondurant 1965, pp. 109–110). In place of the conventional and largely negative meaning of *ahimsa* (non-violence or the avoidance of injury to others), Gandhi envisaged a positive force that was integral to the pursuit of social and political truth and involved a revolutionary challenge to British rule and conventional revolutionary ideas (ibid., p. 112). Finally, Gandhi incorporated in his doctrine the idea of *tapasya* (self-sacrifice), but he related this to the realisation of a revolutionary social and political programme.

A central point of this reformulation of conventional Hindu concepts was that non-violence was given a positive rather than a negative connotation, and in particular the concept was extended to incorporate a genuine concern for the well-being of opponents. This feature of Gandhi's position was reflected in his refusal to engage in strike action during the heat of the day, or when Britain was at war with Germany and Japan. It also lay behind his attempt to incorporate conventional means of protest – sit-down demonstrations (*dharna*) and strikes (*hartel*) – into a more extensive process of discovering the truth and having this accepted by opponents (ibid., pp. 118–19).

Moreover, while *satyagraha* was a weapon forged in the face of a hostile and overwhelming military capacity for mass oppression, it was not seen as a weapon of the weak. Rather it was possessed by those who recognised a moral right that was superior to the coercive power held by the colonial authorities. The attractiveness and flexibility of this characteristic of *satyagraha* may be illustrated by its adoption by the Pathans, a tribe from the north-west frontier region with a highly developed militaristic ethos and a long tradition of retributive conduct involving extreme violence. The Pathans are Muslims, so the development of an ethic of non-violent resistance among them involved an appeal to Islamic values, and particularly to the stress on peace in the Koran. It also required a transformation of ideas about strength and courage so that emphasis was placed on the pursuit of peace through moral rather than physical force, and on the necessity for endurance in the face of provocation and injury. Endurance was not a sign of helpless weakness. To the contrary, it rested on a form of courage that was infinitely superior to that exhibited by the perpetrators of violence (ibid., pp. 131–44).

Suffering was a product of strength because it enabled the sufferer to change the conduct of the apparently powerful. When victims failed actively to resist the suffering imposed on them they inhibited the actions of their oppressors; their power seemed to be negated. In addition Gandhi maintained that the victims' suffering sparked a sympathetic response among many of those who had supported imperial rule. This sympathy undermined their feelings of hatred for their opponents and thus increased the prospect of arriving at a mutual recognition of fundamental truths about the inherent injustice of the colonial system. This expectation was derived from Gandhi's understanding of the role that *satyagraha* played in identifying truth and gaining general acceptance of it.

Gandhi held that non-violent action was the most appropriate form of resistance because it allowed the search for truth, and hence the realisation of the injustice of colonialism, to be a cooperative endeavour. In the course of this search the participating parties, both oppressors and oppressed, might modify or even abandon pre-existing ideas. The process of resistance began with an invitation to pursue truth, and even when it gave rise to direct action avenues for dialogue were left open. *Satyagraha* thus required a humble and open-minded desire to search for truth, a sincere effort to understand the position of others and sincere goodwill towards them (Parekh, 1989, pp. 143–4). These requirements flowed from the conclusion that Gandhi had drawn from observing the intractable positions that had emerged in debates between colonial elites and proponents of independence. Violence was often seen as the only way of breaking the impasse but Gandhi maintained that violence was incompatible with the discovery and mutual acceptance of truth: it was non-rational, it assumed that agreement was impossible, it implied a debased view of one's opponents and it created hatred rather than goodwill. In order to avoid these counterproductive outcomes, it was necessary to adopt a view of rationality that recognised the need to appeal both to the heart and to the head of one's opponents, to take account of their legitimate interests, and to ensure that trenchant resistance did not deprive the resisters of sympathy for their misguided opponents. As Parekh neatly puts it, *satyagraha*

> combined the patience and persuasive power of reason with the urgency and energy of violence. It respected and reconciled the integrity of the parties involved, tapped and mobilised their moral and spiritual energies, and paved the way for a better mutual understanding .... [I]t did not replace but complemented reason (ibid., p. 148).

In practice *satyagraha* worked through a number of stages. A clear statement and defence of objectives was followed by popular agitation to convince the authorities of the seriousness of the situation. The resisters then issued an ultimatum, and finally they resorted to direct mass action. At each stage the door to resolution remained open. Gandhi stressed that one should be flexible in one's acceptance of compromise solutions to particular issues because the immediate outcome was secondary to the benefits produced by the general process.

Gandhi's later formulation of *satyagraha* described it as a way of exerting pressure on supporters of colonial rule, one that recognised the extent to which the powerful depended ultimately on the cooperation of their apparently powerless subjects. Non-violent action withdrew cooperation and thus weakened the power of dominant elites (ibid., pp. 153–6). To the extent that this development involved the application of pressure as a form of force, it tended to weaken the exclusively moral character of Gandhi's position. It remained true, however, that this pressure was merely a tactic in a struggle that was seen in moral terms. In addition the application of pressure awakened the imperial power to the precarious nature of its position and helped ensure the minimalisation of violent counterresistance. It thus increased the prospect of a non-violent transition to independence, something that would be especially hard to achieve in an environment where communal conflict was an ever-present threat to human life and the pursuit of collective goals.

Civil Disobedience and Just Democracy: King

Gandhi applied the idea of civil resistance to a system of rule that he regarded as fundamentally flawed: non-violent resistance was a means of freeing India (and other colonised countries) from the domination of colonial powers. It was also part of a programme that would result in the creation of a just political order. These features of Gandhi's theory limited its application to Western states. Western governments were already democratic; they possessed mechanisms that regulated the exercise of power and ensured that officeholders would act as the agents of those who elected them. In a sense, the members of a democratic state were both rulers and the ruled. It is worth recalling, however, that Thoreau's ideas had been developed in a democratic context, and he had denied that the mere existence of democratic government made civil disobedience either unnecessary or illegitimate. Seen from this point of view, Thoreau's defence of principled disobedience formed part of a tradition of thinking that has played an important role in the recent history of the United States.

Modern American arguments about civil disobedience have treated it in relation to values that are seen as fundamental to democratic government in the United States. It is assumed that governments that uphold these values are legitimate. Members of the community are therefore under an obligation to uphold the system of government, and to abide by the laws produced by it. Some of these arguments treat disregard for the law as a tactic designed to exert pressure on conventional political processes. Others, however, are more in sympathy with Thoreau's advocacy of civil disobedience as a way of protesting about fundamental injustices. The difference is that many modern writers are more sanguine than Thoreau about the relationship between democracy and justice, and more importantly they assume that people have positive obligations to democratic systems of government. In recent times the doctrine of civil disobedience has been most closely identified with Dr Martin Luther King.

King was a leading civil rights activist in the late 1950s and early 1960s. The civil rights movement campaigned for an end to racial discrimination, which was widespread in the United States, and particularly to discrimination that gave rise to racial segregation in education, public transport and public facilities in the southern United States. In some cases segregation was sanctioned by state and municipal law; in others it was not outlawed by local legislation even when it had been deemed unconstitutional by the United States Supreme Court. It is important to recall that these institutionalised forms of racial discrimination were common in political systems that were, nominally at least, fully democratic.

Martin Luther King (1929–68)

Born into a family of black clerics in Atlanta, Georgia, King overcame his reservations about the overly emotional appeal of fundamentalist Christianity and was ordained. His subsequent career as a pastor in the Baptist Church was combined with an increasingly prominent role in black community politics and in the civil rights movement. King was a member of the National Association for the Advancement of Coloured Peoples and was the leading figure in protest activities directed against racial discrimination in the southern United States. His later career also embraced the anti-Vietnam War movement, and he won the Nobel Peace Prize in 1964. He was assassinated by a white extremist in 1968 while campaigning in Memphis. King's 'Letter from Birmingham Jail' presents his views on non-violent civil resistance.

King and his supporters challenged discriminatory practices by launching a range of protests, most notably demonstrations, sit-ins and attempts to gain access to segregated services. Some of these actions were contrary to state laws and local ordinances, and resulted in the imprisonment of protesters. In 1963 King and a number of his supporters were imprisoned by the authorities in Birmingham, Alabama. While serving his prison term King published a 'Letter From Birmingham Jail' in which he both explained and justified civil disobedience. This letter was addressed to members of the local clergy, who had claimed that King's conduct had been 'unwise and untimely'. The idea that gross injustice justified a challenge to both the form of the law, and the way in which it was administered, was central to King's rejection of the accusations made against him.

King identified four steps that characterise a morally legitimate campaign of non-violent civil disobedience: identification of a significant injustice, negotiation to resolve it, self-purification to ensure the moral purity of any future action, and finally protest action itself. Direct action becomes necessary when those who perpetrated injustice refuse to adjust their conduct and/or the legal regulations that uphold it. Acts of civil disobedience are meant to produce what King regarded as a creative, non-violent tension between the demands of those seeking recognition of civil rights and their segregationist opponents. This tension takes a direct political form, but it also draws in those whose economic interests may be compromised by protest action. King was more open than Gandhi in his recognition that civil disobedience involves coercion, but he denied that this gives it a violent character. To the contrary, Gandhi's ideas had had a marked impact on King's views of political action (Ansbro, 1983, pp. 3–7), and he insisted that if civil rights activists uphold the necessary connection between the morality of their ends and the morality of the means through which these ends are pursued, they must avoid violent forms of protest. Consequently he denied that the force generated by civil disobedience is violent: it does not produce physical harm, nor does it deprive people of their legitimate economic and political rights. Rather it opens up the prospect of *supporters of injustice* being made to suffer as a consequence of actions carried out in response to their own intransigence. Civil disobedience is a response to injustice that conforms to the principles of justice. (King, 1989, p. 70).

Both conservative and radical critics rejected King's appeal to non-violence on the grounds that it was inconsistent with the revolutionary character of his aspirations. They also argued that his strategy ignored the intractably hostile nature of the political, social and economic environment in which he worked (Storing, 1989, p. 76). For King however, non-violent civil disobedience was justified because it was directed at the realisation of values that lay at the heart of American politics. Consequently his answer to his critics among the clergy of Birmingham addressed four important implications of this relationship.

First, he attempted to justify the involvement of outsiders like himself in what the Birmingham clergy portrayed as a local issue. These critics implied that what happened in Birmingham concerned only the residents of that city; national campaigns of protest were an unwarranted interference in the affairs of others. In response to this charge, King claimed that particular acts of injustice are matters of *universal* concern: 'the interrelatedness of all communities and states' means that 'injustice anywhere is a threat to justice everywhere'. This threat is partly practical – the unjust will promote injustice elsewhere – but it is also a consequence of the idea that a political community marked by injustice in some of its component parts cannot be regarded as just; justice is an absolute. Consequently King argued that he should not

> sit idly by in Atlanta [his place of residence] and not be concerned about what happens in Birmingham.... We are caught in an inescapable network of mutuality, tied in a single garment of destiny. Whatever affects one directly, affects all indirectly. Never again can we afford to live with the narrow, provincial 'outside agitator' idea. Anyone who lives inside the United States can never be considered an outsider anywhere within its bounds (ibid., p. 58).

While this argument established a general obligation to oppose particular injustices, King's second response dealt with the claim that civil disobedience is inappropriate in a democratic environment. This objection rests on the grounds that since democracies contain mechanisms for correcting injustice, and since democratic laws are based on the consent of those who are bound by them, there can be no grounds for wilful disregard of the law (Harris, 1989, pp. 22–3). King insisted that this argument could not be applied in the present context because Alabama was not a truly democratic state. Since blacks were prevented from registering as voters, the legislative body that enacted Alabama's segregation laws could not be said to represent all the inhabitants of the state: 'can any law enacted under such circumstances be considered democratically structured?' (King, 1989, p. 62).

Thirdly, King drew a distinction between 'evading' or 'defying' the law on the one hand, and conscientiously and openly breaking it on the other. Evasion or defiance of the law – for example when segregationists disregarded federal laws upholding the right to peaceful assembly and protest – is not acceptable because it will result in anarchy. In contrast the law-breaking of civil disobedients is done 'openly, lovingly, and with a willingness to accept the penalty' (ibid., p. 63). It is intended to awaken the moral consciousness of the community to the injustice of a law or practice, not to perpetuate an injustice by evading just law, or, as in the case of ordinary criminality, to gain a personal advantage.

The distinction between just and unjust law formed the fourth and final strand of King's defence of non-violent civil disobedience. He argued that the laws broken by civil disobedients are unjust and he appealed to St Augustine's dictum that 'an unjust law is no law at all' (ibid., p. 61). For King, as for Augustine, just laws are those that are in harmony with moral and divine law; they 'uplift human personality'. In contrast, 'any law that degrades human personality is unjust' (ibid., p. 62). Unlike Augustine, however, King maintained that unjust laws have no legitimate hold on those to whom it is applied (see p. 78). King argued that since the constitution of the United States recognises God-given rights, laws that are incompatible with these rights have no place in the American legal system. Consequently, from both a constitutional and a fundamental perspective, laws supporting racial segregation are illegitimate. Challenges to them must be seen as the most recent attempts to realise the fundamental principles underlying the American system of government: 'the goal of America is freedom. Abused and scorned though we may be, our destiny is tied up with America's destiny' (ibid., p. 69). From this point of view, it may be said that civil disobedients show their respect for the principles of American democracy by openly challenging unjust laws and willingly accepting the penalties annexed to them. Unjust suffering in the cause of justice was regarded by King as a way of signalling acceptance of the principle of law when appealing to the consciences of other members of the community.

Unlike Thoreau, King does not seem to have regarded civil disobedience as a way of insulating upright individuals from a morally dubious political culture. To the contrary, his account suggests that civil disobedience is justified because it involves an appeal to values that underwrite American democracy. This appeal is designed to ensure that the American government conforms to these standards. Civil disobedience is a corrective mechanism applied to a potentially just system of government. It should therefore be seen as a civil act, one that is directed towards the moral good of the political community.

Conclusion

Because Thoreau did not develop a theory of non-violence – violence played no role in his account – his ideas were of very limited use to Gandhi. Indeed, to the extent that Thoreau's notion of civil disobedience emphasised its defensive and reactive features, it was not, as Gandhi himself realised, an appropriate model for his followers to adopt. Gandhi's theory of non-violence reflected his understanding of the necessary connection between political effectiveness and moral veracity. Non-violence was designed to achieve objectives that had conventionally been pursued by violent means, without falling prey to the moral and practical shortcomings of this approach.

The fact that Gandhi saw non-violent resistance as part of a revolutionary programme meant that his position differed significantly from that of both Thoreau and King. Neither Thoreau nor King wished to promote a general transformation of American society. Rather they sought to appeal against particular acts that ran contrary to conceptions of justice that they identified with American democracy. King did not question conventional notions of political obligation, but Thoreau's stance was underwritten by a conception of citizenship that made obligation conditional on a correspondence between the actions of government and the conscience of the individual.

The difference between these positions is apparent in King's remarks on democracy. While King argued that citizens were not obliged to obey Alabama's segregation laws because of the corruption of its electoral machinery, Thoreau denied that it was possible for the conscience of the individual to be represented through democratic procedures. Since King would not have accepted legalised segregation even if it had been endorsed by legitimate democratic procedures, this contrast should not be pushed too far. The fact remains, however, that King's remarks on democracy did not rest on the conception of democratic individualism to which Thoreau adhered. Moreover, while King regarded acts of civil disobedience as part of the practice of democratic politics, Thoreau viewed them primarily as a way of sustaining the moral independence of the individual.

CHAPTER 15

Conclusion: Some Contemporary Themes

In accordance with the historical focus of this book, the preceding chapters have not ventured beyond the middle decades of the twentieth century. To have done so would have launched us into a complex and rapidly expanding body of literature that could not be canvassed adequately within the space available. It is worth noting, however, that the end-point of the discussion coincides with the dividing line between the modern and 'postmodern' worlds. What has been described as the postmodernist 'turn' embraces a range of critical perspectives on a number of features of the modern world. In particular, the 'postmodern problematic' focuses on what Stephen White has described as 'the increasing incredulity towards metanarratives, the growing awareness of new problems wrought by societal rationalisation, the explosion of new informational technologies and the emergence of new social movements' (White, 1991, p. 4). All these phenomena have important political implications, and the first of them has a bearing on the history of political thought.

This point is illustrated in the work of the French thinker Jean-Francois Lyotard. Like other postmodernists, Lyotard associates modernity with a stress on science and rationalism. This way of thinking has provided the basis for the grand narratives that are claimed to have characterised post-enlightenment political thinking and has also played a formative role in the later stages of the early modern period. As Lyotard put it:

Societies which anchor the discourses of truth and justice in the great historical and scientific narratives ... can be called modern. The French Jacobins don't speak like Hegel but the just and the good are

371

always found caught up in a great progressive odyssey (Sarup, 1988, p. 132).

Hegel and Marx are seen as archetypical creators of metanarratives reflecting enlightenment aspirations for the universalistic conceptions that have underwritten large-scale programmes of social and political reconstruction. These programmes and their intellectual supports were, it is argued, inherently oppressive since they rested on unitary conceptions of 'truth'. The distinctive feature of the postmodern world, however, is that their basis has been undermined by social, economic and political changes, and their intellectual preeminence has been challenged by those who seek to identify stances that are appropriate in a fragmented postmodern condition. In response to these developments postmodernist thinkers reject universalism, they adopt an ironic stance towards truth claims, and they promote localised action resting on difference and particularity rather than identity and universalism. A central element of the postmodern response to the 'discourse of truth' is the attempt to unveil the truth of the unitary, rational, essential self of liberalism and to reveal it as a fictional subject.

While aspects of this critique appear to echo the rejection of universality found in the writings of Burke and Hayek (ibid., p. 133), postmodernism has underwritten distinctive departures in contemporary political thinking. These include feminist arguments about the significance of difference (see p. 380), and attempts to seek an understanding of the postmodern condition by exploring the implications of 'globalisation', or forms of interdependence and interpenetration that extend beyond the geographical, cultural and intellectual boundaries of nation states in general and the Western world in particular (Rengger, 1992, p. 570). Postmodernism has also prompted a revaluation of the ideas of historically significant thinkers in order to relate their ideas to the conceptions of rationality and metanarrative that postmodernists identify with the modern world (Connolly, 1988; Shankman, 1994). The last two endeavours open up areas of interpretation that lie beyond the scope of an introductory text, but the first can be included in the brief glance at a very restricted range of recent works with which this book concludes. The purpose of the discussion that follows is to assess the extent to which some of the issues discussed in the preceding chapters continue to play a role in contemporary political thinking.

The issues in question touch upon contemporary perspectives on virtue, happiness and freedom as ends of politics, and on human rights. An important aspect of contemporary political thinking has been the application of feminist ideas to problems that have generally been discussed in supposedly neutral but generally male-oriented terms. Given the generally liberal-democratic cast of modern Western political cultures, most of the discussion will focus on ideas about politics that are set within this framework. However, because recent developments in revolutionary thought involve the rejection of many Western values, the chapter will conclude with a brief discussion of a distinctive form of revolutionary theory that has developed within Islamic fundamentalism.

Virtue and Politics

A central feature of liberal-democratic politics is the stress placed on notions of tolerance and the related idea that individuals should have the opportunity to frame and pursue their own goals, provided this does not impinge on other people's formulation and pursuit of goals. To the extent that this position is agnostic about the routes individuals may take to moral perfection, it has a general affinity with the position advanced by John Stuart Mill in his essay *On Liberty*. It rests upon a largely secular conception of human well-being and entails the rejection of 'moral objectivism', or of the idea that it is possible to identify standards of conduct that correspond to human nature and provide the basis for conceptions of human perfectibility. In making this point, however, it is important to note that moral objectivism continues to play a limited role in modern political thinking, and lies behind conceptions of politics that rest on religious fundamentalism. These theories define virtue in religious terms and justify certain political structures and practices on the ground that they promote it. This approach has had a profound impact on politics in Islamic countries, and it also plays a marginal role in Christian fundamentalism in some Western liberal-democratic cultures.

In addition to these modern survivors of traditional approaches, other arguments about virtue and politics have recently begun to play a role in contemporary debates. For the most part, however, the recent revival of what is known as 'virtue politics' focuses either on the relationship between virtue and human flourishing as a problem of ethics, or, in its more directly political manifestations, on the extent to which the maintenance of modern liberal-democratic regimes requires the development of certain virtues among the citizen body. A consideration of the last of these issues has assumed pressing importance in light of the democratisation of countries that were formerly part of the communist bloc. In these countries, and in the West, it has been asked whether liberal-democratic societies need to be based on 'virtuous citizens and not just on institutions that artfully average competing interests?' (Galston, 1992, p. 1). Consideration of this question has produced attempts to identify the virtues necessary to sustain a liberal-democratic political culture (Macedo, 1992). It should be noted, however, that this line of thinking rests on the assumption that while particular virtues may be necessary to maintain these cultures, they can hardly be said to be the *end* of politics, rather, virtue is a means of sustaining political systems that are valued for reasons other than their capacity to promote virtue.

Moral and Political Utilitarianism

It was noted in an earlier chapter that utilitarianism has become commonplace in modern political thinking (see p. 121). The significance of this development has been remarked upon by Stuart Hampshire. Hampshire's remark focuses on British experience, but it is equally applicable to other liberal-democratic societies. Hampshire argues that utilitarianism has become

> part of the furniture of the minds of enlightened persons, who criticise institutions, not from the standpoint of one of the Christian churches, but from a secular point of view.... The utilitarian philosophy, before the First World War and for many years after it, ... was still a bold, innovative, even a subversive doctrine, with a record of successful social criticism behind it (Hampshire, 1978, p. 1).

Since Hampshire believes that contemporary utilitarianism has become narrow and obstructive, his remark has a valedictory tone. It is probably true to say, however, that some of the assumptions underlying classical utilitarianism – its secular focus, its emphasis on the interests of ordinary members of the population and its concern with their perception of these interests – still underwrite Western conceptions of the ends of politics.

As a field for detailed speculation and prescription, the recent career of utilitarianism has been marked by vigourous disputes over the viability of 'action' as opposed to 'rule' applications of the doctrine. While some writers have argued that utilitarians should act on the basis of *rules* that tend to maximise happiness, others adhere to formulations that are close to Bentham's idea that good *actions* are those that directly promote utilitarian outcomes (Barrow, 1991, pp. 107–23). In many respects these disputes focus on the 'ethical' rather than the more strictly 'political' dimensions of utility. That is, utilitarianism has become a 'code of personal conduct' that guides individuals in the stance they should take on issues of public debate such as war, punishment or abortion. Used in this way, the doctrine is open to a number of objections. Critics raise questions about the impersonality of utilitarianism, its stress upon calculation, its focus on consequences and its crassness. It has recently been argued, however, that these objections do not apply to utilitarianism as a *public* doctrine, designed (as Bentham intended) to guide legislators and citizens in their attempts to find the best solutions to problems of public or political conduct (Goodin, 1995, pp. 7–10). While there is some justification for seeing this approach as marking a return to Bentham's position, it should be noted that this application of the principle of utility makes it an *instrument* rather than an end.

Liberty, Individualism and Communitarianism

One of the objections that modern thinkers have raised against utilitarianism is that its reliance on an aggregative principle denies the 'separateness' of individuals, and thus it is hostile to liberty. Hence John Rawls argues that

> Whenever a society sets out to maximize the sum of intrinsic value or the net balance of the satisfaction of interests, it is liable to find that the denial of liberty for some is justified in the name of this single end (Rawls, 1973, p. 211).

Robert Nozick makes a similar point when he argues that utilitarians must necessarily endorse the violation of *some* individual rights, even while seeking to minimise rights violations in general (Nozick, 1974, pp. 28–9).

As an alternative to utilitarianism, Rawls has developed a theory that holds that rational individuals will see that the best way to maximise the satisfaction of their interests is to establish forms of political organisation and systems of rules that conform to the idea of 'justice as fairness'. Such systems would emerge from a contractual process carried out behind what Rawls calls a 'veil of ignorance', that is, a situation in which individuals lack knowledge of their particular interests. A political order that satisfies these conditions will recognise two principles: each person should have an equal right to the most extensive liberty that is compatible with a similar liberty being enjoyed by others; and social and economic inequalities are only justified when they produce the greatest benefit to the least advantaged, and are attached to offices and positions that are open to all by virtue of equality of opportunity. Rawls maintains that the first of these principles has priority over the second, and that 'liberty can be restricted only for the sake of liberty' (Rawls, 1973, p. 302). The emphasis on liberty appears in an even more uncompromising form in Nozick's work. He starts with a conception of human beings as bearers of inviolable 'natural' rights, and argues that only those forms of political activity that adhere to strict standards concerning the non-violability of rights can be regarded as legitimate. Although their positions differ significantly, both Rawls and Nozick believe that utilitarianism is likely to produce outcomes that are hostile to the protection and (in Rawls' case at least) promotion of human freedom.

Rawls' and Nozick's insistence on preserving the separateness of individuals is closely related to their concern with liberty. Both writers think that it is important for individuals to have the opportunity to formulate and pursue their own goals, subject, of course, to the proviso that they recognise a like freedom on the part of others. This line of argument has played an important role in the history of Western political thought. As noted above, however, there is a strand within this tradition that anchors freedom to the social dimensions of human personality, and stresses the implications of *social* membership for individual action (see pp. 84ff). In contemporary political philosophy the relationship between these two positions has been revisited in the context of a debate between 'liberals' and 'communitarians'.

In large measure this debate was sparked off by Rawls' and Nozick's work. Despite the differences in their accounts of the *source* of individual rights – Nozick regards them as being fundamental, while Rawls derives them from a contractual process conducted behind a 'veil of ignorance' – both writers have been portrayed by their communitarian critics as proponents of 'primacy-of-right theories' (Taylor, 1992, p. 30). The general implication derived from such theories is that political institutions and practices must not impede the free action of right-bearers. These theories may thus be seen as modern expressions of the idea that individual freedom sets limits to the scope of politics, and that it has important implications for the ways in which political power can be exercised (see p. 74).

In contrast the communitarian response to modern liberalism incorporates a *social* conception of freedom that has affinities with that found in the theories of Rousseau, Hegel and the British Idealists (see pp. 86–90). The parallel with Hegel's position has been made quite explicit in the work of and commentaries on the Canadian philosopher Charles Taylor (Avineri and de-Shalit, 1992, p. 2). Like Hegel, communitarians believe that ethical principles are embedded in the ideas and institutions of a given society. They argue, moreover, that societies must be seen as *communities*, as pre-existing structures of institutions, sympathies and ideas, not as contractually based aggregations of individuals. Communitarians contrast the notion of what Michael Sandel calls the 'unencumbered self' of modern liberalism with the 'embedded self' that is produced by membership of a community. Liberal theory rests upon a conception of the individual, and of the relationship between individuals, that is empirically false and normatively unsatisfactory. The idea of the 'unencumbered self' – the individual as possessor of a personality that is forged by acting upon the choices made possible by the possession of rights – fails to take account of the extent to which people's conception of themselves is a consequence of their location within a community.

In Taylor's formulation, communities are thought to possess common cultures; integration within a culture is a precondition for any meaningful conception of moral autonomy. Taylor contrasts his view with that implied by primacy-of-right theories: this position wrongly assumes that individuals can develop their distinctly human attributes 'outside of society or outside a certain sort of society' (Taylor, 1992, p. 35). In Sandel's writings, arguments about the empirical falseness of the liberal view of personality are related closely to claims concerning the intrinsic benefits of conceptions of social and political life that are embedded in distinctive communities. These conceptions point to ideas of individual flourishing that are set in the context of a common good. Membership in a community in which 'moral ties' are 'antecedent to choice ... engage the identity as well as the interests of the participants, and so implicate its members in a citizenship more thorough-going than the unencumbered self can know' (Sandel, 1992, p. 19). For Michael Walzer, the very idea of a state requires the idea of the common good: 'states don't only preside over a piece of territory and a random collection of individuals; they are also the political expression of a common life' (Walzer, 1992, p. 78). While these statements conjure up a positive image of the embedded individual that is reminiscent of Rousseau, Hegel and the British Idealists, another communitarian, Alasdair MacIntyre, gives a Hobbesian account of the implications of a liberal conception of politics. MacIntyre argues that the liberal denial of community undermines the possibility of consensus or a common communal view. The result is that

> modern politics is civil war carried on by other means.... [G]overnment does not express or represent the moral community of the citizens, but is instead a set of institutional arrangements for imposing a bureaucratized unity on a society which lacks genuine moral consensus (MacIntyre, 1992, pp. 62–3).

It is important to note that the communitarians' opponents do not necessarily accept the implications that are imputed to them. For example Will Kymlicka has argued that liberalism can retain its integrity without denying the importance of collective endeavours. He claims that communitarians have failed to distinguish 'collective action' from 'political action', and have consequently ignored the extent to which liberal values uphold rights that protect the former against the latter. For example freedom of speech and association (two of Mill's fundamental liberties) are rights ascribed to *individuals*, but they are essential if they are to formulate and pursue *collective* goals (Kymlicka, 1992, p. 175). According to this view (which is unconscious echo of Paine's position – see p. 222) community reflects natural social interaction and does not need, and in fact may well be hindered by, political prescriptions that distort 'normal processes' of voluntary cooperation.

In addition to arguing that liberal conceptions of politics do not preclude communal values, proponents of the liberal position have argued that communitarianism is conservative and morally relativistic: it overemphasises existing values and attachments, and it denies the validity of universal standards. Michael Sandel's appeal to the idea of 'civic republicanism' has been questioned on both these grounds. For Sandel, civic republicanism is 'implicit within our [the United States] tradition'. As Amy Gutmann put it, however, would one want to revive those aspects of the tradition that 'excluded women and minorities, and repressed most significant deviations from white, Protestant morality in the name of the common good?' (Gutmann, 1992, p. 132). Gutmann's remark is directed specifically at communitarian appeals to tradition, but her reference to the exclusion of women reflects the impact of a major development that both builds upon and challenges the entire history of Western political thought.

Liberal Feminism

The fact that the preceding chapters contain only a few brief references to the role ascribed to women in the Western tradition of political thought is a consequence of the overwhelmingly male-oriented character of this tradition. A large and growing body of scholarly commentary has been devoted to this issue, and has explored the gender bias of various thinkers and traditions. While the extent and richness of this literature precludes the possibility of providing an adequate summary of it here, it is useful to make brief reference to two themes that relate to the approach to the history of political thought adopted in this book. Unlike issues raised by radical and socialist feminists, those dealt with here present a challenge that remains within a broadly liberal-democratic framework. They raise important questions that bear on conceptions of the ends of politics and also on the location of political power.

One of the focal points of contemporary feminist accounts of historical political theory is the degree to which politics has been conceptualised in gender terms. In particular it has been argued that although political values and modes of behaviour are frequently based on claims about *human* nature, they are generally construed in *male* terms. A related point is that this approach to politics ignores the possibility that there might be values and interests that are distinctly female. Such criticisms have important implications when considering the ends of politics. It can be argued, for example, that the conceptions of order, virtue, freedom and happiness, which have played an important role in the history of political thought, have actually been firmly based on the assumed male superiority that is endemic in Western culture. In some cases, for example in Filmer's theory of patriarchal order and in a long Christian tradition that has upheld female inferiority, these assumptions are quite overt. But they can also be discerned in theories that do not have any obvious gender bias. It has thus been argued that although Plato rejected conventional claims concerning women's natural incapacity to rule, he did so on the basis of an argument that discounted the political significance of any distinctly female attributes (Annas, 1981). Similarly, while a number of writers have asserted that humans are naturally free in a prepolitical condition, they have tacitly assumed that this applies only to males. Consequently the social contract has been conceived of as an exclusively and distinctly male transaction (Pateman, 1988). Finally, it has been noted that many of the putatively 'human' attributes that are assumed in a range of historical accounts of politics – for example the notion of the unencumbered, rational individual of liberal theory, and the related assumption of self-seeking individuals whose interests have to be incorporated within an orderly framework – are at best derived from historically specific conceptions of male values and do not correspond to roles ascribed to females (Lloyd, 1984). These arguments have played an important role in modern feminist theory, and they all have serious implications for arguments relating to the ends of politics.

Feminist theorists have also raised important questions that bear on the conception of rule by the many. They argue that conventional conceptions of democratic politics have not eliminated the bias against women that has been such a persistent feature of the Western tradition of political thinking. In particular, it is argued that the liberal distinction between a 'public' and political sphere, which is subject to scrutiny and control by the state, and a 'private' sphere of voluntary actions between autonomous beings, conceals the reality of the persistent influence of patriarchal power (Millett, 1970; Siltanen and Stanworth, 1984, pp. 185–208). One of the tasks of contemporary liberal feminist political theory has been to expose the ways in which male domination of the private sphere impinges on the effective exercise of women's political rights and thus undermines the credibility of modern democracy. Two aspects of this line of argument will be discussed here. The first concerns the effect of private constraints upon political participation, while the other raises questions about the gender requirements of authentic democratic political practice.

Private constraints that have a bearing on female participation spring from a lack of equality within the family. Feminist writers argue that the unequal division of domestic labour within the family increases the relative costs of political activity for women. Further, it is claimed that women's inferior earning capacity and the structure of power within the family discourage women from participating politically because their perception of their capacity to be politically effective is lower than that of men. The impact of these inequalities is exacerbated by the norms that govern politics. It has been observed that participatory occasions tend to be structured according to male values and are biased towards the more effective participation of men (Mansbridge, 1980, pp. 105–7).

In response to these problems, feminist writers argue that the attainment of true political equality requires a reduction in the cost of participation borne by women (through the provision of services that meet their needs and the sharing of domestic responsibilities), as well as the adoption of institutional strategies such as women's cauci that preclude male domination and facilitate the development of a stronger sense of political efficacy in women. These measures are intended to make female participation more likely and more effective, to erode the male-dominated power structure, and to contribute to the development of the skills and sense of efficacy that are necessary for future participation in other areas of politics. In addition to the measures outlined above, some feminists argue that since the public and private spheres are not as distinct as conventional liberal theory implies, it is necessary to adopt political practices that take account of this. An important implication of the integration of the personal and the public is that private experiences – as conveyed, for example, through 'personal disclosure' – are appropriate in political contexts. Further, it is argued that if political action is to advance the liberation of women, then it is necessary for it to be practised in ways that promote 'prefigurative forms' of attitude, behaviour and language that are consistent with this goal and discourage those that are not (Phillips, 1991, pp. 113–14).

These strategies are designed to make liberal democracy live up to its name; to ensure, in other words, that the patterns of domination that underwrite modern society are eliminated and that political equality is not merely formal but also substantive. Without the elimination of deep-seated forms of domination along gender lines, 'the rule of the many' will remain, at best, 'the rule of the many who are male'. As long as this situation continues to prevail, the universalistic claims made for democracy, the insistence that all should be treated equally, that differences should be ignored and that everybody should be subjected to the same rules applied in the same manner, will merely serve to perpetuate male domination of both public and private spheres.

One feminist response to this problem is to argue for the abandonment of the pseudo-universality that is applied in liberal democracy. In its place, it is necessary to adopt structures and procedures that take account of the *special* (and neglected) interests and needs of sections of society (including, but not limited to, women) whose oppressed status is merely confirmed if they are treated as if they are already equal with others. It is argued that the universal ideal ignores differences in an arbitrary and unfair way; in fact it ignores some interests (those important to women) and promotes others (identified with men) while pretending that these interests are really universal ones. In practical terms, special interests can be given recognition by granting special rights to members of disadvantaged groups. These rights are necessary to counteract and overcome the injustices and inequalities that are built into existing institutions and practices and that will be perpetuated if everybody is merely granted the same rights. Examples of these special rights include affirmative action and equal opportunity programmes, the provision of targeted facilities and services, and structuring political organisations so that they recognise the special rights accorded to some of their members (Young, 1990).

Natural Rights, Human Rights and Legal Rights

Feminist claims for special rights involve rejection of the universalistic assumptions underlying theories of liberal democracy. However, to the extent that these rights are seen as part of a corrective process designed to create conditions where equal rights become meaningful, they are not necessarily incompatible with the conceptions of natural rights discussed above. Unlike many historical conceptions of natural rights however, and unlike that advanced by Nozick, many modern theories of what are described as 'human rights' have a strongly positive cast. Governments must not merely refrain from infringing the rights of their subjects, they must also make positive contributions to securing their well-being. For example the United Nations Declaration of Human Rights imposes an obligation upon governments to secure minimal material and educational provisions.

Unlike the natural rights of historical theory, human rights are not seen as expressions of God's will. Rather, these rights belong to individuals by virtue of their humanity (Gewirth, 1981, p. 119). However, while both historical and contemporary theorists treat natural rights as fixed and universally valid, many authors of accounts of human rights think they may be subject to change – for example new rights may emerge – and prioritise existing rights on the basis of circumstantial considerations. At times some rights may have to give way to others, and not all human rights can be recognised in all situations (Pennock, 1981, p. 7). An important feature of contemporary thinking about human rights is that they are often seen to extend beyond the bounds of the state and to give rise to more wide-ranging obligations to ensure that the rights in question are recognised within the international community. In other words, human rights have both a national and an international bearing. They are accepted in principle as a basis for fundamental legal enactments within states, and they are also recognised as a matter of international concern (Henkin, 1981, pp. 258–9). In the latter case, questions arise about the content of human rights and the ways in which they can be upheld effectively. Apart from practical problems of enforcement in an international environment that recognises the sovereignty of nation states, the idea of human rights runs the risk of universalising standards that are only adhered to in certain (usually Western) cultures. One way round this difficulty is to restrict ideas of human rights to *political* contexts. It has recently been argued that, despite wide cultural divergences, humans face general problems that relate to control of political power. As a result, ideas of human rights that focus on matters such as eliminating torture, arbitrary imprisonment and censorship do have a universal bearing (Ingram, 1994, pp. 199–200).

Claims for human rights play a significant role in modern arguments about the rule of law. In addition to the conventional stress on legal regularity and procedural justice, rule-of-law theory incorporates ideas about the reach and content of law. Enactments such as bills of rights enshrine fundamental claims, and often do so by reference to international standards. As we have seen, a concern with the nature of law is central to Hayek's arguments for rule-bound orders.

As in other aspects of contemporary political thought, liberal feminism has important implications for conceptions of the rule of law. A number of feminist theorists have argued that the patriarchal attitudes that underwrite traditional political argument also play a role in the formulation and administration of law. For example it has been claimed that the judicial attitudes of the United States Supreme Count continue to reflect assumptions about women's natures and capacities that result in the perpetuation of *legally* sanctioned discrimination against them (MacKinnon, 1989; Okin, 1992, pp. 272–3). Issues concerning the deficiencies in the legal entitlements of women are related to arguments about the implications of human rights for women. Conventional conceptions of human rights have been seen as male-centred constructions that do not address women's needs. Moreover it has been argued that human rights have been seen in purely public terms; if they are to protect women's interests they must be extended into the private sphere and be applied to forms of discrimination that have their roots there. Finally, if claims to human rights are to be applied effectively to women, it is necessary to understand the cultural variety of forms of discrimination and also to recognise the extent to which incidents of violence are gender-based (Bunch, 1995; Cook, 1994).

Although these and other aspects of feminism have potentially radical implications for politics, it still operates for the most part within the general parameters of liberal-democratic conceptions of politics and does not pose an overtly revolutionary challenge to existing forms of government. For the time being at least, the formulation of revolutionary conceptions of politics has moved outside the ambit of Western cultures, and in one of its most important manifestations involves rejection of the secular, liberal-democratic and feminist assumptions that have played such an important role in contemporary Western political theory. This point can be illustrated by a brief survey of a doctrine that has been developed by proponents of a revolutionary Islamic approach to politics in Iran.

Revolutionary Fundamentalism

Although Fanon's theory of revolutionary anticolonialism involved a rejection of some Western values and stressed the importance of recovering and extending aspects of indigenous culture, his endorsement of the general goals of Marxism meant that his view of the revolutionary process was both modern and secular. This aspect of Fanon's position stands in stark contrast to the type of revolutionary doctrine espoused by recent proponents of Islamic revolutionary movements, particularly by the Ayatollah Khomeini, the leading figure in the Iranian Revolution.

The context of Iranian anticolonialism differed from that faced by Fanon because imperialist influences in that country were either applied indirectly through western, multinational corporations, or were mediated by the traditional ruling house following their cooption into the sphere of first British and then American imperialism. Consequently the struggle against imperialism involved an attempt either to rid the traditional system of government of corrupting Western influences, or to depose the shah and create a new state based on indigenous Islamic values and practices. The latter of these strategies was adopted by Khomeini and finally bore fruit in 1979 when the shah was overthrown. However, the significance of this move, and an understanding of the theoretical implications of the system of government that has since been established in Iran, must be set in the context of earlier responses to the domination of the Iranian government by forces that were not only exploitative but also ran contrary to a variety of interpretations of economic, social and political requirements of the Islamic faith.

Throughout the twentieth century significant elements in the *Shía* clergy have tried to use an appeal to Islamic tradition as the basis for resistance to imperialist influences within Iran. Despite the potentially revolutionary implications of such an appeal, this tendency has been marked by a thoroughgoing conservatism in religious, economic, social and political matters that blunted its impact. This conservative form of anticolonialism has been challenged by two modernising tendencies within Islam. The first of these is associated with the 'constitutionalists', who sought to create a generally liberal and constitutional state, albeit one that recognised Islam as the supreme religious and moral authority within the political and social culture. Islamic constitutionalism rests on an unstable combination of Western ideas about the supremacy of constitutionally prescribed representative bodies, traditional Islamic notions that the authority of Islam and the clergy are only directly enforceable in moral and religious matters and are not a necessary part of a system of political authority, and recognition of the importance of clerical oversight of secular authority. For example the constitutional structure created in 1906–7 specified that 'All laws necessary to strengthen the foundations of the State and the Throne and set in order the affairs of the Realm and the establishment of the Ministries, must be submitted for approval to the National Consultative Assembly'. It also required that 'at no time must any legal enactment of the Sacred National Consultative Assembly ... be at variance with the sacred principles of Islam' and sought to reconcile these requirements by instituting a system that subjected the activities of the assembly to the general supervision of clerical jurists (Lahidji, 1988, pp. 140–1).

The second major modernising element within revolutionary Islam rests on a synthesis of Islamic and socialist principles and is overtly hostile to both conservative and constitutionalist movements. Within this tradition the ideas of Ali Sharíati and the Mujahedin are particularly significant. Although Sharíati rejected the 'first' (atheistic) and the 'third' (political) aspects of Marx, he accepted his contributions as a social scientist and particularly his identification of laws of historical development. He insisted, however, that adaptation of aspects of Western economic development must be grounded in national cultures and particularly in their religious dimensions. Consequently he argued that the process of development in Iran necessitated two revolutions: the first to be directed against imperialism and towards revitalisation of the national culture; and the second to involve a process of social transformation that would eliminate poverty and lay the basis for a classless society. Sharíati's revolutionary doctrine was marked by a strong element of anticlericalism. He claimed that Islam was inherently egalitarian and revolutionary, and castigated the *Shíite* clergy for having corrupted Islam into a rigidly institutionalised doctrine that served the interests of the middle classes and ignored those of the lower classes. The corruption of clerical culture meant that the revolution would have to circumvent the clergy's baneful influence. Sharíati looked to the progressive intelligentsia to provide guidance and leadership (Abrahamian, 1988, pp. 292–6).

The Mujahedin's position was similar in many respects to that of their predecessor. Members of this movement espoused a democratic, egalitarian, and socialistic doctrine that drew on Marx's economic analysis and made class struggle a part of the Islamic tradition. The Mujahedin saw

God as the first mover of the laws of historical development, and Mohamad as the prophet who provided guidance on their implications. They argued that advancement of the goals of Islam required destruction of the existing, exploitative social system. In an analysis that was influenced by Fanon's writings, Mohamad Hanifrejad (the chief ideologue of the movement) stressed the extent to which exploitation in countries such as Iran was tied up with its subordination to the interests of imperialist powers. Like Shariati, Hanifrejad was strongly anticlerical. As one of his followers put it, 'the most dangerous of all forms of oppression are laws, and restrictions forcibly imposed on the people in the name of religion' (Omid, 1994, p. 53). The goal of the Islamic revolution was to create a universal society that was classless, indifferent to national boundaries and united by a monotheistic religion. It was claimed that these ends could only be realised through a revolutionary organisation that could ensure the clergy would assume an authentic, revolutionary role. As religious rather than political authorities, the clergy would assume a moral and inspirational role rather than a directive one. This stipulation was underlined by the Mujahedian's development of martyrdom as a mode of revolutionary action: martyrdom is a religious action in pursuit of a just cause, but it can be embarked upon at the volition of the revolutionary. It does not need the authorisation of a clerical intermediary (ibid., p. 49).

Khomeini's theory of Islamic revolution was developed in reaction to Western influences in Iran and to the doctrines outlined above. In contrast to these arguments, Khomeini's position was strongly elitist, clerical and anti-Marxist. At the same time, however, it also involved rejection of the traditional idea that political authority should be divorced from the moral and religious authority of Islamic clergy and jurists. Khomeini produced what has been termed 'revolutionary traditionalism', which was used to underwrite a political *and* religious revolution within the Iranian state, and the creation of a theocratic system of government that was foreign both to traditional and to modernising Islam (Arjomand, 1988, p. 192).

The key element of this theory is identification of the right to rule by a supreme religious figure. This ignores the traditional idea that such a figure only possesses specific types of authority; it requires the elimination of any duality of religio-legal and political authority. It also involves redefinition of the conventional view of juristic pluralism so that it corresponds to the type of unitary theocratic leadership created by the Islamic revolution of the late 1970s and early 1980s (ibid., p. 194). As one of the participants in this process put it, 'This revolution is the integration of religion and politics, or better put, it is the refutation of the colonialist idea of "separation of religion from politics."' (ibid., p. 195). The product of this integration is the notion of *vali-yi faqih*, or rule by a wise religious male leader. In this system there can be no female *faqih*, and any arrangements for consultation with elected institutions is subsidiary to and directed by the leadership (Omid, 1994, pp. 59–60).

An important indication of the revolutionary dimensions of the new Islamic Republic of Iran is that not only does the right to direct the political life of the state rest with the *vali-yi-faqih*, but obedience to this figure is also a religious obligation. As one of Khomeini's supporters put it, 'political activity is an incumbent ... duty. Today, one of the most important acts of devotion ... is political activity because without politics our religiosity ... will not last' (Arjomand, 1988, p. 202). Thus while Khomeini stressed the importance of traditional Islamic values as the basis for life within the Islamic state, he and his followers produced a theory of government that transformed traditional patterns of authority within Islam, and in doing so promoted a radical restructuring of the ideological and administrative character of the Iranian state.

Further Reading

The volumes of the *Cambridge History of Political Thought* listed in the Bibliography (Burns, 1991, and Burns with Goldie, 1994) are invaluable sources for scholarly and accessible treatments of political thought before 1700. Volumes on the eighteenth, nineteenth and twentieth centuries are in preparation. The following list contains works dealing with thinkers discussed in this book and is designed to supplement the secondary works referred to in the text and listed in the second part of the Bibliography.

Ancient and Medieval Periods, c. 400 BC–1500 AD

Barker, Ernest, *The Political Thought of Plato and Aristotle* (New York: Dover, 1959).

Barnes, Jonathan (ed.), *The Cambridge Companion to Aristotle* (Cambridge: Cambridge University Press, 1995).

Bathory, P. D., *Political Theory as Public Confession: the social and political thought of Augustine of Hippo* (New Brunswick, NJ: Transaction Books, 1981).

Bluestone, N. H., *Women and the Ideal Society: Plato's Republic and modern myths of gender* (Amherst, Mass.: University of Massachusetts Press, 1987).

Brookes, E. H., *The City of God and the Politics of Crisis* (Westport, Conn.: Greenwood Press, 1980).

Cross, R. C. and Woozley, A. D., *Plato's Republic: a philosophical commentary* (London: Macmillan, 1971).

Deanne, Herbert, *The Political and Social Ideas of Saint Augustine* (New York: Columbia University Press, 1963).

Fuhrmann, Manfred, *Cicero and the Roman Republic* (Oxford: Basil Blackwell, 1992).

Hall, R. W., *Plato* (London, Allen & Unwin, 1981).

Johnson, C. N., *Aristotle's Theory of the State* (London: Macmillan, 1980).

Kenny, Anthony (ed.), *Aquinas: a collection of critical essays* (London: Macmillan, 1969).

Keyt, David, *A Companion to Aristotle's Politics* (Oxford: Basil Blackwell, 1991).

Kraut, Richard (ed.), *The Cambridge Companion to Plato* (Cambridge: Cambridge University Press, 1992).

Markus, R. A., *Saeculum: history and society in the theology of Saint Augustine* (Cambridge: Cambridge University Press, 1970).

Morrall, J. B., *Aristotle* (London: Allen & Unwin, 1977).

O'Connor, D. J., *Aquinas and Natural Law* (London: Macmillan, 1967).

On, Bat-Ami Bar, *Engendering Origins: critical feminist readings of Plato and Aristotle* (Albany, NY: State University of New York Press, 1994).

Rawson, Elizabeth, *Cicero, a portrait* (London: Allen Lane, 1975).

Reeve, C. D. C., *Philosopher-Kings: the argument of Plato's Republic* (Princeton, NJ: Princeton University Press, 1988).

Seung, T. K., *Plato Rediscovered: human value and social order* (Lanham MD: Rowman & Littlefield, 1996).

Smalley, B. (ed.), *Trends in Medieval Political Thought* (Oxford: Basil Blackwell, 1965).

Tierney, Brian, *Religion, Law, and the Growth of Constitutional Thought (1150–1650)* (Cambridge: Cambridge University Press, 1983).

White, N. P., *A Companion to Plato's Republic* (Indianapolis, IA: Hackett, 1979).

Early Modern Period, c. 1500–1800 AD

Ayling, S. E., *Edmund Burke: his life and opinions* (New York: St Martin's Press, 1988).

Baumgold, Deborah, *Hobbes' Political Theory* (Cambridge: Cambridge University Press, 1988).

Bock, Gisela *et al.* (eds), *Machiavelli and Republicanism* (Cambridge: Cambridge University Press, 1990).

Chappell, V. C., *The Cambridge Companion to Locke* (Cambridge: Cambridge University Press, 1994).

Church, W. F., *Constitutional Thought in Sixteenth-Century France* (New York: Octagon, 1969).

Claeys, Gregory, *Thomas Paine* (Boston: Unwin Hyman, 1989).

Courtney, C. P., *Montesquieu and Burke* (Oxford: Basil Blackwell, 1963).

Cullen, D. E., *Freedom in Rousseau's Political Philosophy* (DeKalb, Ill.: Northern Illinois University Press, 1993).

Dietz, Mary (ed.), *Thomas Hobbes and Political Theory* (Lawrence: University of Kansas Press, 1990).

Donaldson, P. S., *Machiavelli and the Mystery of State* (Cambridge: Cambridge University Press, 1988).

Dunn, John, *Locke* (Oxford: Oxford University Press, 1984).

Dyck, Ian (ed.), *Citizen of the World: essays on Thomas Paine* (New York: St Martin's Press, 1988).

Eisenbach, E. J., *Two Worlds of Liberalism: religion and politics in Hobbes, Locke and Mill* (Chicago, Ill.: University of Chicago Press, 1981).

Franklin, J. H., *Jean Bodin and the Rise of Absolutism* (Cambridge: Cambridge University Press, 1973).

Freeman, Michael, *Edmund Burke and the Critique of Political Radicalism* (Oxford: Basil Blackwell, 1980).

Goldsmith, M. M., *Hobbes' Science of Politics* (New York: Columbia University Press, 1966).

Grant, R. W., *John Locke's Liberalism* (Chicago, Ill.: University of Chicago Press, 1987).

Hampsher-Monk, Iain, *The Political Philosophy of Edmund Burke* (London: Longman, 1987).

Johnston, Daniel, *The Rhetoric of Leviathan* (Princeton, NJ: Princeton University Press, 1986).

Lee, K., *The Legal-Rational State: a comparison of Hobbes, Bentham and Kelsen* (Aldershot: Avebury, 1990).

Macpherson, C. B., *Burke* (Oxford: Oxford University Press, 1980).

Masters, R., *The Political Philosophy of Rousseau* (Princeton, NJ: Princeton University Press, 1968).

Parry, Geraint, *John Locke* (London: Allen & Unwin, 1978).

Philp, Mark, *Paine* (Oxford: Oxford University Press, 1989).

Rapacznski, A., *Nature and Politics: liberalism in the philosophy of Hobbes, Locke and Rousseau* (Ithaca, NY: Cornell University Press, 1987).

Rogers, G., and Ryan Alan, (eds), *Perspectives on Thomas Hobbes* (Oxford: Clarendon Press, 1988).

Shelton, George, *Morality and Sovereignty in the Philosophy of Hobbes* (New York: St Martin's Press, 1992).

Shklar, J. N., *Men and Citizens: a study of Rousseau's social theory* (Cambridge: Cambridge University Press, 1969).

Shklar, J. N., *Montesquieu* (Oxford: Oxford University Press, 1987).

Tuck, Richard, *Hobbes* (Oxford: Oxford University Press, 1989).

Wokler, Robert, *Rousseau* (Oxford: Oxford University Press, 1994).

Modern Period, 1800–

Adamson, W. L., *Hegemony and Revolution: a study of Gramsci's political and cultural theory* (Berkeley, CA: University of California Press, 1980).

Avineri, Shlomo, *Hegel's Theory of the Modern State* (Cambridge: Cambridge University Press, 1972).

Avineri, Shlomo, *The Social and Political Thought of Karl Marx* (Cambridge: Cambridge University Press, 1968).

Avrich, Paul, *Anarchist Portraits* (Princeton, NJ: Princeton University Press, 1988).

Barry, Norman, *Hayek's Social and Economic Philosophy* (London: Macmillan, 1979).

Beiner, Ronald and W. J. Booth (eds), *Kant's Political Philosophy: the contemporary legacy* (New Haven, CT: Yale University Press, 1993).

Beiser, F. C. (ed.), *The Cambridge Companion to Hegel* (Cambridge: Cambridge University Press, 1993).

Brooker, Paul, *The Faces of Fraternalism: Nazi Germany, fascist Italy and imperial Japan* (Oxford: Clarendon Press, 1991).

Cahm, C., *Kropotkin and the Rise of Revolutionary Anarchism* (Cambridge: Cambridge University Press, 1989).

Carter, April, *The Political Theory of Anarchism* (London: Routledge & Kegan Paul, 1971).

Carver, Terrell (ed.), *The Cambridge Companion to Karl Marx* (Cambridge: Cambridge University Press, 1991).

Collaiaco, J. A., *Martin Luther King jr: apostle of militant nonviolence* (New York: St Martin's Press, 1988).

Collini, Stefan, *Liberalism and Sociology: L. T. Hobhouse and political argument in England 1880–1914* (Cambridge: Cambridge University Press, 1979).

Crowder, George, *Classical Anarchism* (Oxford: Clarendon Press, 1991).

Curtis, Michael, *Three Against the Republic: Sorel, Barrès and Maurras* (Princeton, NJ: Princeton University Press, 1959).

Dalton, Dennis, *Mahatma Gandhi: nonviolent power in action* (New York: Columbia University Press, 1983).

Dodge, G. H., *Benjamin Constant's Philosophy of Liberalism* (Chapel Hill, NC: University of North Carolina Press, 1990).

Elster, Jon, *An Introduction to Karl Marx* (Cambridge: Cambridge University Press, 1986).

Elster, Jon, *Making Sense of Marx* (Cambridge: Cambridge University Press, 1985).

Femina, J. V., *Gramsci's Political Thought* (Oxford: Clarendon Press, 1981).

Freeden, Michael, *The New Liberalism: an ideology of social reform* (Oxford: Clarendon Press, 1978).

Gay, Peter, *The Dilemma of Democratic Socialism: Edward Bernstein's challenge to Marx* (New York: Columbia University Press, 1953).

Gendzier, I. L., *Frantz Fanon: a critical study* (London: Wildwood House, 1973).

Gray, John, *Hayek on Liberty* (Oxford: Basil Blackwell, 1984).

Gray, John, *Mill on Liberty: a defence* (London: Routledge & Kegan Paul, 1983).

Greary, Dick, *Karl Kautsky* (Manchester: Manchester University Press, 1987).

Green, Martin, *The Origins of Nonviolence: Tolstoy and Gandhi in their historical setting* (University Park, PA: Pennsylvania University Press, 1986).

Green, Martin, *Gandhi: voice of a new age revolution* (New York: Continuum Books, 1993).

Greengarten, I. M., *T. H. Green and the Development of Liberal Democratic Thought* (Toronto: University of Toronto Press, 1981).

Hansen, Emmanuel, *Frantz Fanon: social and political thought* (Columbus, Ohio: Ohio State University Press, 1977).

Harding, Neil, *Lenin's Political Thought*, 2 vols (London: Macmillan, 1977–81).

Jinadu, L. A., *Fanon: in search of the African Revolution* (London: KPI, 1986).

Kelly, G. A., *The Humane comedy: Constant, Tocqueville, and French Liberalism* (Cambridge: Cambridge University Press, 1992).

Kolakowski, L., *Main Currents of Marxism*, 3 vols (Oxford: Oxford University Press, 1978).

Lebrun, R. A., *Joseph de Maistre: an intellectual militant* (Kingston and Montreal: Queens-McGill University Press, 1988).

McLellan, David, *Karl Marx* (London: Fontana, 1986).

Paterson, R. W. K., *The Nihilistic Egoist: Max Stirner* (London: Hull University Press, 1971).

Pelcznski, Z. A., *The State and Civil Society: studies in Hegel's political philosophy* (Cambridge: Cambridge University Press, 1984).

Perinbam, M. B., *Holy Violence: the revolutionary thought of Frantz Fanon* (Washington DC: Three Continents Press, 1982).

Pierson, Stanley, *Marxist Intellectuals and the Working-Class Mentality in Germany* (Cambridge, Mass.: Harvard University Press, 1993).

Plant, Raymond, *Hegel* (London: Allen & Unwin, 1973).

Ransome, Paul, *Gramsci: a new introduction* (London: Harvester Wheatsheaf, 1992).

Ritter, Alan, *The Political Thought of Pierre-Joseph Proudhon* (Princeton, NJ: Princeton University Press, 1969).

Schram, Stuart, *The Thought of Mao Tse-Tung* (Cambridge: Cambridge University Press, 1989).

Singer, Peter, *Hegel* (Oxford: Oxford University Press, 1983).

Singer, Peter, *Marx* (Oxford: Oxford University Press, 1980).

Teeple, G., *Marx's Critique of Politics 1842–1847* (Toronto: University of Toronto Press, 1984).

Tudor H., and J. M. Tudor (eds), *Marxism and Social Democracy* (Cambridge: Cambridge University Press, 1988).

Vandem Bossche, C. R., *Carlyle and the Search for Authority* (Columbus, Ohio: Ohio State University Press, 1991).

Vincent, Andrew and Raymond Plant, *Philosophy, Politics and Citizenship: the life and thought of the British Idealists* (Oxford: Basil Blackwell, 1984).

Vincent, S. K., *Pierre-Joseph Proudhon and the Rise of Republican Socialism* (Oxford: Oxford University Press, 1984).

Williams, H. L. (ed.), *Essays on Kant's Political Philosophy* (Chicago, Ill.: University of Chicago Press, 1992).

Womack, Brantly, *The Foundations of Mao Zedong's Political Thought* (Honolulu: University Press of Hawaii, 1982).

Woodcock, George, *Gandhi* (London: Fontana, 1972).

Bibliography

This Bibliography contains the primary and secondary works referred to in the main body of the text. Primary works are listed by original author even when they appear in anthologies or selections. The dates listed here are the dates of the editions consulted; the original date of publication and/or composition are noted in the chronological charts (see pp. 7–8, 9–10).

Primary Works

Anon, (1991) *To the Assembly of the Common Peasantry 1525*, in Michael Baylor (ed.), *The Radical Reformation* (Cambridge: Cambridge University Press).

Aquinas, St Thomas (1959) *Selected Political Writings*, ed. A. P. D'Entreves, trans. J. G. Dawson (Oxford: Basil Blackwell).

Aristotle (1958), *The Politics*, ed. and trans. Ernest Barker (Oxford: Clarendon Press).

Aristotle (1975) *Ethica Nicomachea*, ed. and trans. W. D. Ross (Oxford: Oxford University Press).

Augustine (1972) *City of God*, ed. David Knowles (Harmondsworth: Penguin).

Austin, John (1995) *The Province of Jurisprudence Determined*, ed. Wilfred E. Rumble (Cambridge: Cambridge University Press).

Babeuf, Francois-Noel (1972) *The Defence of Gracchus Babeuf*, ed. and trans. John Anthony Scott (New York: Schocken Books).

Bakunin, Michael (1970) *God and the State*, ed. Paul Avrich (New York: Dover).

Bakunin, Michael (1973) *Selected Writings*, ed. Arthur Lehning (London: Jonathan Cape).

Bakunin, Michael (1990) *Statism and Anarchy*, ed. and trans. Marshall S. Shatz (Cambridge: Cambridge University Press).

Beccaria, Cesare (1995) *On Crimes and Punishments and Other Writings*, ed. Richard Bellamy, trans. Richard Davis (Cambridge: Cambridge University Press).

Bentham, Jeremy (1843a) *Anarchical Fallacies*, ed. John Bowring, *The Works of Jeremy Bentham*, 10 vols (Edinburgh: William Tait), vol. ii.

Bentham, Jeremy (1843b) *Constitutional Code*, John Bowring ed., *The Works of Jeremy Bentham*, 10 vols (Edinburgh: William Tait), vol. ix.

Bentham, Jeremy (1952–4) *Economic Writings*, 3 vols (London: Allen & Unwin, 1952–4).

Bentham, Jeremy (1967) *A Fragment on Government with An Introduction to the Principles of Morals and Legislation*, ed. Wilfred Harrison (Oxford: Basil Blackwell).

Bernstein, Eduard (1972) *Evolutionary Socialism*, trans. Edith C. Harvey (New York: Schocken Books).

Beza, Theodore (1969) *The Right of Magistrates* in J. H. Franklin (ed. and trans.), *Constitutionalism and Resistance in the Sixteenth Century: three treatise by Hotman, Beza & Mornay* (New York: Pegasus).

Bodin, Jean (n.d.) *Six Books of the Commonwealth*, ed. and trans. M. J. Tooley (Oxford: Basil Blackwell).

Bodin, Jean (1992) *On Sovereignty. Four chapters from The Six Books of the Commonwealth*, ed. and trans. Julian H. Franklin (Cambridge: Cambridge University Press).

Bosanquet, Bernard (1899) *The Philosophical Theory of the State* (London: Macmillan).

Bossuet, Jaques-Benigne (1990) *Politics Drawn from the Very Words of Holy Scripture*, ed. and trans. Patrick Riley (Cambridge: Cambridge University Press).

Bunch, Charlotte (1995) 'Transforming Human Rights from a Feminist Perspective', in Julie Peters and Andrea Wolper (eds), *Women's Rights, Human Rights. International Feminist Perspectives* (London: Routledge), pp. 11–17.

Burke, Edmund (1834) *Works*, 2 vols (London: Holdsworth & Bell).

Burke, Edmund (1969) *Reflections on the Revolution in France*, ed. C. C. O'Brien (Harmondsworth: Penguin).

Calvin, Jean (1950) *Institutes of the Christian Religion*, ed. John T. McNeill, trans Ford Lewis Battles, 2 vols (Philadelphia, PA: The Westminster Press).

Calvin, Jean (1991) *De politica administrione*, in Harro Hopfl (ed.), *Luther and Calvin on Secular Authority* (Cambridge: Cambridge University Press).

Carlyle, Thomas (1980) *Selected Writings*, ed. Alan Shelston (Harmondsworth: Penguin).

Chateaubriand, François. (1816) *Monarchy According to the Charter* (London).

Cicero (1970) *De Re Publica and De Legibus*, trans. C. W. Keyes (Cambridge Mass.: Harvard University Press).

Cobbett, William (n.d.) *Cobbett's Political Works*, 6 vols (London).

Cole G. D. H. (1935) *The Simple Case for Socialism* (London: Victor Gollancz).

Coleridge, S. T. (1990) *Coleridge's Writings. Volume I: On Politics and Society*, ed. John Morrow (London: Macmillan).

Condorcet, Antoine-Nicolas de (1955) *Sketch for a Historical Picture of the Progress of the Human Mind*, trans. June Barraclough, ed. Stuart Hampshire (London: Weidenfeld & Nicolson).

Constant, Benjamin (1988) *Political Writings*, ed. and trans. Biancamaria Fontana (Cambridge: Cambridge University Press).

Cook, Rebecca J. (1994) 'Women's International Human Rights Law: The Way Forward', in Rebecca J. Cook (ed.), *Human Rights of Women. National and International Perspectives* (Philadelphia, PA: University of Pennsylvania Press), pp. 3–36.

Diderot, Denis (1992) *Political Writings*, ed. and trans. John Hope Mason and Robert Wokler (Cambridge: Cambridge University Press).

Fanon, Frantz (1967) *The Wretched of the Earth*, trans. Constance Farrington (Harmondsworth: Penguin).

Fanon, Frantz (1970) *Toward the African Revolution*, trans. Haakon Chevalier (Harmondsworth: Penguin).

Filmer, Sir Robert (1949) *Patriarcha . . . and Other Political Works*, ed. Peter Laslett (Oxford: Basil Blackwell).

Galston, William A. (1992), 'Introduction' in J. W. Chapman and Willam A. Galston (eds), *Virtue, Nomos*, vol. xxxiv (New York: New York University Press) pp. 1–23.

Gandhi, Mahatma (1986) *The Moral and Political Writings of Mahatma Gandhi*, 3 vols, ed. Raghava Iyer (Oxford: Clarendon Press).

Gewirth, Alan (1981) 'The Basis and Content of Human Rights', in J. Roland Pennock and John W. Chapman, *Human Rights, Nomos XXIII* (New York: New York University Press), pp. 119–47.

Godwin, William (1969) *An Enquiry Concerning Political Justice*, 3 vols, ed. F. E. L. Priestley (Toronto: University of Toronto Press).

Goldman, Emma (1911) 'Anarchism: What It Really Stands For', in Emma Goldman, *Anarchism and Other Essays*, second edn (New York: Mother Earth), pp. 53–73.

Goodin, Robert E. (1995) *Utilitarianism as a Public Philosophy* (Cambridge: Cambridge University Press).

Gramsci, Antonio (1971) *Selections from the Prison Notebooks*, ed. and trans. Quinton Hoare and Geoffrey Nowell Smith (London: Lawrence and Wishart).

Green, T. H. (1986) *Lectures on the Principles of Political Obligation and Other Political Writings*, eds Paul Harris and John Morrow (Cambridge: Cambridge University Press).

Grotius, Hugo (1738) *The Rights of War and Peace in Three Books* (London: W. Innys).

Guicciardini, Francesco (1994) *Dialogue on the Government of Florence*, ed. and trans. Alison Brown (Cambridge: Cambridge University Press).

Gutmann, Amy (1992) 'Communitarian Critics of Liberalism', in Shlomo Avineri and Avner De-Shalit (eds), *Communitarianism and Individualism* (Oxford: Oxford University Press), pp. 120–37.

Hamilton, Alexander, John Jay and James Madison (1942) *The Federalist* (London: J. M. Dent).

Hampshire, Stuart (1978) 'Morality and Pessimism', in Stuart Hampshire (ed.), *Public and Private Morality* (Cambridge: Cambridge University Press), pp. 1–22.

Harrington, James (1992) *The Commonwealth of Oceana and A System of Politics*, ed. J. G. A. Pocock (Cambridge: Cambridge University Press).

Hayek, Friedrich A. (1960) *The Constitution of Liberty* (Chicago, Ill.: University of Chicago Press).

Hayek, Friedrich A. (1982) *Law, Liberty and Legislation*, 3 vols (London: Routledge).

Hazlitt, William (1819) *Political Essays* (London).

Hegel, G. W. F. (1991) *Elements of the Philosophy of Right*, ed. Allen W. Wood, trans. H. B. Nisbet (Cambridge: Cambridge University Press).

Henkin, Louis (1981) 'International Human Rights as "Rights"', in Roland J. Pennock and John W. Chapman, *Human Rights, Nomos XXIII* (New York: New York University Press), pp. 257–80.

Hitler, Adolf (1969) *Mein Kampf,* trans. Ralph Manheim (London: Hutchinson).

Hobbes, Thomas (1960) *Leviathan, or the Matter, Forme, Power of a Commonwealth Ecclesiastical and Civil,* ed. Michael Oakeshott (Oxford: Basil Blackwell).

Hobhouse, L. T. (1909) *Democracy and Reaction,* 2nd edn (London: T. Fisher Unwin).

Hobhouse, L. T. (1990) *Liberalism and Other Writings,* ed. James Meadowcroft (Cambridge: Cambridge University Press).

Hooker, Richard (1989) *Of the Laws of Ecclesiastical Polity,* ed. Arthur Stephen McGrade (Cambridge: Cambridge University Press).

Hotman François (1972) *Frangiogallia,* trans. J. H. M. Salmon (Cambridge: Cambridge University Press).

Hume, David (1962) *Moral and Political Philosophy,* ed. Henry D. Aiken (New York: Hafner).

Hume, David (1987) *Essays. Moral, Political and Literary,* ed. Eugene F. Miller (Indianapolis, IA: Liberty Press).

Hume, David (1994) *Political Essays,* ed. Knud Haakonssen (Cambridge: Cambridge University Press).

Huxley, T. H. (n.d.) 'Struggle for Existence', in Peter Kropotkin, *Mutual Aid* (Boston, Mass.: Extending Horizon Books).

Ingram, Attracta (1994) *A Political Theory of Rights* (Oxford: Clarendon Press).

John of Salisbury (1990) *Policraticus,* ed. Cary J. Nederman (Cambridge: Cambridge University Press).

Kant, Immanuel (1971) *Political Writings,* ed. Hans Reiss, trans. H. B. Nisbet (Cambridge: Cambridge University Press).

Kant, Immanuel (1972) *Groundwork of the Metaphysic of Morals,* trans. H. J. Paton (London: Hutchinson).

Kant, Immanuel (1975) 'Conjectural Beginning of Human History' in Lewis White Becker (ed.), *Kant: On History* (Indiannapolis, Bobbs-Merrill.).

Kautsky, Karl (1971) *The Class Struggle,* ed. Robert C. Tucker, trans. William E. Bohn (New York: W. W. Norton).

Kautsky, Karl (1983) *Selected Political Writings,* ed. and trans. Patrick Goode (London: Macmillan).

Kelsen, Hans (1949) *General Theory of Law and State,* trans. Anders Wedburgh (Cambridge, Mass.: Harvard University Press).

King, Martin Luther (1989) 'Letter from Birmingham Jail', in Paul Harris (ed.), *Civil Disobedience* (Lathan, MD: University Press of America).

Kropotkin, Peter (n.d.) *Mutual Aid* (Boston, Mass.: Extending Horizon Books).

Kropotkin, Peter (1903) *The State: Its Historic Role* (London: Freedom Press).

Kropotkin, Peter (1970) *Revolutionary Pamphlets,* ed. Roger N. Baldwin (New York: Dover).

Kropotkin, Peter (1971) *In French and Russian Prisons* (New York: Shocken Books).

Kymlicka, Will (1992) 'Liberal Individualism and Liberal Neutrality', in Shlomo Avineri and Avner De-Shalit (eds), *Communitarianism and Individualism* (Oxford: Oxford University Press), pp. 165–85.

Lenin, V. I. (1964) *Collected Works,* 45 vols (Moscow: Progress Publishers).

Lenin, V. I. (1971) *Selected Works* (Moscow: Progress Publishers).

Lenin, V. I. (1975) *Selected Writings*, 3 vols (Moscow: Progress Publishers).

Lloyd, Genevieve (1984) *The Man of Reason* (Minneapolis, MA: University of Minnesota Press).

Locke, John (1967) *Two Treatise of Government*, ed. Peter Laslett (Cambridge: Cambridge University Press).

Loyseau, Charles (1994) *A Treatise of Orders and Plain Dignities*, ed. and trans. Howell A. Lloyd (Cambridge: Cambridge University Press).

Luther, Martin (1991) *On Secular Authority*, in Harro Hopfl (ed.), *Calvin and Luther on Secular Authority* (Cambridge: Cambridge University Press).

Luxemburg, Rosa (1971) 'What does the Spartacus League Want?', *Selected Political Writings of Rosa Luxemburg*, ed. Dick Howard (New York: Monthly Review Press).

Macaulay, T. B. (1984) 'Mill's Essay on Government: Utilitarian Logic and Politics', in Jack Lively and John Rees (eds), *Utilitarian Logic and Politics* (Oxford: Clarendon Press), pp. 97–130.

Macedo, Stephen (1992) 'Charting Liberal Virtues', in J. W. Chapman and William Galston (eds), *Virtue, Nomos*, vol. xxxiv (New York: New York University Press), pp. 204–33.

Machiavelli, Niccoló (1975) *The Discourses of Niccoló Machiavelli*, 2 vols, trans. Leslie J. Walker (London: Routledge).

Machiavelli, Niccoló (1988) *The Prince*, ed. Quentin Skinner and Russell Price (Cambridge: Cambridge University Press).

MacIntyre, Alasdair (1992) 'Justice as a Virtue: Changing Conceptions', in Shlomo Avineri and Avnar De-Shalit (eds), *Communitarianism and Individualism* (Oxford: Oxford University Press), pp. 51–64.

MacKinnon, Catherine À. (1989) *Towards a Feminist Theory of the State* (Cambridge, Mass.: Harvard University Press).

Maistre, Joseph de (1965) *The Works of Joseph de Maistre*, ed. and trans Jack Lively (New York: The Macmillan Company).

Mao, Tse-tung (1957) *On the Correct Handling of Contradictions Among the People* (Peking: Foreign Languages Press).

Mao, Tse-tung (1967) *Selected Military Writings* (Peking: Foreign Language Press).

Marsilius of Padua (1956) *The Defender of the Peace*, 2 vols, trans. Alan Gewirth (New York: Columbia University Press).

Marx, Karl (1973) *The Revolutions of 1848*, ed. David Fernbach (Harmondsworth: Penguin).

Marx, Karl (1975) *Early Writings*, ed. Lucio Colletti, trans. Rodney Livingstone and Gregor Benton (Harmondsworth: Penguin).

Marx, Karl and Friedrich, Engels (1968) *The German Ideology*, ed. R. Pascal (New York: International Publishers).

Marx, Karl and Friedrich, Engels (1973) *Selected Works*, 3 vols (Moscow: Progress Publishers).

Maurras, Charles (1971a) 'Dictator and King', in J. S. McClelland (ed.), *The French Right from de Maistre to Maurras* (London: Jonathan Cape) pp. 215–380.

Maurras, Charles (1971b) 'Romanticism and Revolution', in McClelland, *The French Right*, op. cit., pp. 239–63.

Maurras, Charles (1971c) 'The Politics of Nature', in McClelland, *The French Right*, op. cit., pp. 264–94.

Mill, James (1984) 'Essay on Government', in Jack Lively and John Rees (eds), *Utilitarian Logic and Politics* (Oxford: Clarendon Press), pp. 53–130.

Mill, John Stuart (1983) *Utilitarianism, On Liberty and Considerations on Representative Government*, ed. H. B. Acton (London: Dent).

Mill, John Stuart (1989) *On Liberty, with the Subjection of Women and Chapters on Socialism*, ed. Stefan Collini (Cambridge: Cambridge University Press).

Millett, Kate (1970) *Sexual Politics* (Garden City, NY: Doubleday).

Mo Tzu (1963) *Basic Writings*, trans. Burton Watson (New York: Columbia University Press).

Mo Tzu (1973) *The Ethical and Political Works of Mo Tzu*, trans. Yi-Poa Mei (Westport, Conn.: Greenwood Press).

Montesquieu, Charles (1949) *The Spirit of the Laws*, 2 vols, trans. Thomas Nugent (New York: Hafner).

Montesquieu, Charles (1977) *The Political Theory of Montesquieu*, ed. Melvin Richter (Cambridge: Cambridge University Press).

Mornay, Phillipe (1969) *Vindiciae contra tyrannos*, in J. F. Franklin (ed. and trans.), *Constitutionalism and Resistance in the Sixteenth Century: three treatise by Hotman, Beza & Mornay* (New York: Pegasus).

Mosca, Gaetano (1939) *The Ruling Class*, trans. Hannah D. Kahn (New York: McGraw-Hill).

Müller, Adam (1955) 'Elements of Politics', in H. S. Reiss (ed.), *Political Thought of German Romantics* (Oxford: Basil Blackwell).

Mussolini, Benito (1935) 'The Doctrine of Fascism', in Benito Mussolini, *Fascism. Doctrines and Institutions* (Rome: Ardita).

Nietzsche, Friedrich (1967) *Beyond Good and Evil*, trans. Marianne Cowan (Chicago: Henry Regnery).

Nietzsche, Friedrich (1968) *The Will to Power*, trans. Walter Kaufmann and R. J. Hollingdale (New York: Vintage Books).

Novalis (1996) *Faith and Love*, in Frederick C. Bieser (ed. and trans.), *The Early Political Writings of the German Romantics* (Cambridge: Cambridge University Press).

Nozick, Robert (1974) *Anarchy, State, and Utopia* (Oxford: Basil Blackwell).

Otis, James (1766) *The Rights of the British Colonies Asserted and Proved* (London).

Owen, Robert (1991) *A New View of Society and Other Writings*, ed. Gregory Claeys (Harmondsworth: Penguin).

Paine, Thomas (1976) *The Rights of Man*, ed. Henry Collins (Harmondsworth: Penguin).

Paley, William (1803) *The Principles of Moral and Political Philosophy*, 2 vols, 14th edn (London: R. Faulder).

Pareto, Vifredo (1966) *Sociological Writings*, ed. S. E. Finer, trans. Derick Mirfin (London: Pall Mall Press).

Pateman, Carole (1988) *The Social Contract* (Stanford, CA: Stanford University Press).

Phillips, Anne (1991) *Engendering Democracy* (Cambridge: Polity Press).

Pizan, Christine de (1994) *The Book of the Body Politic*, ed. and trans. Kate Langdon Forham (Cambridge: Cambridge University Press).

Plato (1960) *The Gorgias*, trans. Walter Hamilton (Harmondsworth: Penguin).

Plato (1970) *The Republic*, trans. M. D. P. Lee (Harmondsworth: Penguin).

Plato (1980) *The Laws*, trans. T. J. Saunders (Harmondsworth: Penguin).

Plato (1991) *Protagoras*, trans. C. C. W. Taylor, revised edn. (Oxford: Clarendon Press).

Polybius (1979) *The Rise of the Roman Empire*, ed. F. W. Walbank, trans. Ian Scott-Kilvert (Harmondsworth: Penguin).

Proudhon, P.-J. (1923) *General Idea of the Revolution in the Nineteenth Century*, trans. John Beverley Robinson (London: Freedom Press).

Proudhon, P.-J. (1979) *The Principle of Federation*, trans. Richard Vernon (Toronto: University of Toronto Press).

Pufendorf, Samuel (1927) *The Two Books on the Duty of Man and Citizen According to the Natural Law*, trans. Frank Gardner Moore (New York: Oxford University Press).

Pufendorf, Samuel (1934) *On the Law of Nature and Nations, Eight Books*, trans. C. H. Oldfather and W. A. Oldfather (Oxford: Clarendon Press).

Pufendorf, Samuel (1991) *On the Duty of Man and Citizen*, ed. James Tully, trans. Michael Silverthorne (Cambridge: Cambridge University Press).

Rawls, John (1973) *A Theory of Justice* (Oxford: Oxford University Press).

Ritchie, D. G. (1894) *Natural Rights* (London: Allen and Unwin).

Ritchie, D. G. (1902) *Studies in Social and Political Ethics* (London: Swan Sonnenschein).

Rosenberg, Alfred (1971) *Selected Writings*, ed. Robert Pois (London: Jonathan Cape).

Rousseau, Jean-Jacques (1987) *The Basic Political Writings*, trans. Donald A. Cress (Indianapolis, IA: Hackett).

Sandel, Michael (1992) 'The Procedural Republic and the Unencumbered Self', in Shlomo Avineri and Avner De-Shalit (eds), *Communitarianism and Individualism* (Oxford: Oxford University Press), pp. 12–28.

Sattler, Michael (1991) *The Schleitheim Articles* in Michael B. Baylor (ed.), *The Radical Reformation* (Cambridge: Cambridge University Press), 172–80.

Schlegel, F. (1964) *Die Entwicklung Der Philosophie In Zwolf Buchern*, in *Philosophische Vorlesungen*, ed. Jean-Jacques Ansttett, *Kritsche Friedrich-Schlegel-Ausgabe*, vol. 13 (Munich: F. Schoningh).

Seyssel, Claude de (1981) *The Monarchy of France*, ed. Donald A. Kelly, trans. J. H. Hexter (New Haven, CT: Yale University Press).

Sidgwick, Henry (1874) *The Methods of Ethics* (London: Macmillan).

Sidgwick, Henry (1891) *The Elements of Politics* (London: Macmillan).

Sièyes, Emanuel Joseph (1963) *What is the Third Estate?*, trans M. Blondel, ed. S. E. Finer (London: Pall Mall Press).

Siltanen, Janet and Michelle Stanworth (1984) 'The politics of private woman and public man', in Janet Siltanen and Michelle Stanworth (eds), *Women and the Public Sphere* (London: Hutchinson), pp. 185–208.

Stalin, Joseph (1934) *Leninism*, 2 vols (Moscow and Leningrad: Co-operative Publishing Society).

Stirner, Max (1995) *The Ego and Its Own*, ed. David Leopold (Cambridge: Cambridge University Press).

Suàrez, Francisco (1856–78) *De Opere Sex Dierum*, in Suarez, *Opera Omnia*, 27 vols, ed. Carolus Berton (Paris: Apud Ludovicum Vives), vol. iii.

Suàrez, Francisco (1944) *De Legibus, ae Deo Legislatore*, in Francisco Suàrez, *Selections from Three Works*, ed. J. B. Scott, trans. G. L. Williams *et al.* (Oxford: Clarendon Press), vol. ii.

Taylor, Charles (1992) 'Atomism', in Shlomo Avineri and Avner De-Shalit (eds), *Communitarianism and Individualism* (Oxford: Oxford University Press), pp. 29–50.

Taylor, Harriet (1993) *The Enfranchisement of Women*, in Marie Mulvey Roberts and Tamae Mizuta (eds), *The Disenfranchised. The Fight for the Suffrage* (London, Routledge/Thoemmes Press; Tokyo: Kinokuniya).

Thompson, Willam and Anna Wheeler (1993) *Appeal of One Half of The Human Race, Women, Against the Pretensions of the Other Half, Men*, in Marie Mulvey Roberts and Tamae Mizuta (eds), *The Reformers. Socialist Feminism* (London: Routledge/Thoemmes Press; Tokyo: Kinokuniya).

Thoreau, Henry D. (1992) *Walden and Resistance to Civil Government*, ed. William Rossi (New York: W. W. Norton).

Thoreau, Henry D. (1996) *Political Writings*, ed. Nancy L. Rosenblum (Cambridge: Cambridge University Press).

Thucydides (1968) *The History of the Peloponnesian War*, trans. Richard Crawley (London: Dent).

Tocqueville, Alexis de (1945) *Democracy in America*, 2 vols, trans. Henry Reeve (New York: Vintage Books).

Trotsky, Leon (1969) *The Permanent Revolution and Results and Prospects*, 3rd edn (New York: Labour Publications).

Tucker, Benjamin (1970) 'State Socialism and Libertarianism', in Irving L. Horowitz (ed.), *The Anarchists* (New York: Dell), pp. 169–82.

Walzer, Michael (1992) 'Membership', in Shlomo Avineri and Avner De-Shalit (eds), *Communitarianism and Individualism* (Oxford: Oxford University Press), pp. 65–84.

Warren, Josiah (1970) 'True Civilization and Personal Liberty', in Irving L. Horowitz (ed.), *The Anarchists* (New York: Dell), pp. 321–9.

Webb, Beatrice (1948) *Our Partnership* (London: Longman).

Webb, Sidney (1889) 'Historic', in G. Bernard Shaw (ed.), *Fabian Essays in Socialism* (London: The Fabian Society), pp. 30–61.

Weber, Max (1994) *Political Writings*, eds Peter Lassman and Ronald Spiers (Cambridge: Cambridge University Press).

William of Ockham (1992) *A Short Discourse on the Tyrannical Government of Things Divine and Human, but Especially Over the Empire*, ed. A. S. McGrade, trans. John Killkullen (Cambridge: Cambridge University Press).

Wollstonecraft, Mary (1790) *A Vindication of the Rights of Men* (London: J. Johnson).

Wollstonecraft, Mary (1983) *Vindication of the Rights of Women*, ed. Miriam Brody (Harmondsworth: Penguin).

Wollstonecraft, Mary (1995) *A Vindication of the Rights of Men and A Vindication of the Rights of Women*, ed. Sylvana Tomaselli (Cambridge: Cambridge University Press).

Woodhouse, A. S. P. (ed.) (1951) *Puritanism and Liberty* (London: Dent).

Young, Iris Marion (1990) 'Polity and Group Difference: A Critique of Universal Citizenship', in Cass R. Sunstein (ed.), *Feminism & Political Theory* (Chicago, Ill.: University of Chicago Press), pp. 117–42.

Secondary Works

Aalders, G. J. D. (1975) *Political Thought in Hellenistic Times* (Amsterdam: Hakkert).

Abrahamian, Ervand (1988) 'Ali Shari'ati: Ideologue of the Iranian Revolution', in Edmund Burke III and Ira M. Lapidas (eds), *Islam Politics and Social Movements* (Berkeley, CA: University of California Press), pp. 289–97.

Akhavi, Shahrough (1990) *Religion and Politics in Contemporary Iran* (Albany, NY: University of New York Press).

Anderson, Olive (1981) 'The Feminism of T. H. Green: A Late Victorian Sucess Story?', *History of Political Thought*, vol. 12, pp. 671–194.

Allen, J. W. (1951) *A History of Political Thought in the Sixteenth Century* (London: Methuen).

Annas, Julia (1981) *An Introduction to Plato's Republic* (Oxford: Clarendon Press).

Ansbro, John J. (1983) *Martin Luther King Jnr.: The Making of a Mind* (New York: Orbis Books).

Ansell-Pearson, Keith (1994) *An Introduction to Nietzsche as Political Thinker* (Cambridge: Cambridge University Press).

Arjomand, Said Amir (1988) 'Ideological Revolution in Shi'ism', in Said Amir Anjomand (ed.) *Authority and Political Cultural in Shi'ism* (Albany, NY: State University Press of New York), pp. 178–212.

Avineri, Shlomo and Avner, De-Shalit (eds) (1992) *Communitarianism and Individualism* (Oxford: Oxford University Press).

Baker, Keith Michael (1975) *Condorcet: From Natural Philosophy to Social Mathematics* (Chicago, Ill.: The University of Chicago Press).

Barrow, Robin (1991) *Utilitarianism: a contemporary statement* (Aldershot: Edward Elgar).

Bax, Ernest Belfort (1911) *The Last Episode of the French Revolution* (London: Grant Richards).

Beetham, David (1991) *The Legitimation of Power* (London: Macmillan).

Beiser, Frederick, C. (1992) *Enlightenment, Revolution & Romanticism. The Genesis of Modern German Thought* (Cambridge, Mass.: Harvard University Press).

Bernstein, Samuel (1972) *Auguste Blanqui and the Art of Insurrection* (London: Lawrence & Wishart).

Black, Anthony (1993) *Political Thought in Europe 1250–1450* (Cambridge: Cambridge University Press).

Bodde, Derk and Clarence, Morris (1967) *Law in Imperial China* (Cambridge, Mass.: Harvard University Press).

Bondurant, Joan V. (1965) *Conquest of Violence. The Gandhian Philosophy of Conflict* 2nd edn (Berkeley, CA: University of California Press).

Bottomore, T. B. (1966) *Elites and Society* (Harmondsworth: Penguin).

Brooker, Paul (1985) 'The Nazi *Fuehrerprinzip*: A Weberian Analysis', *Political Science*, vol. 37, no. 1, pp. 50–71.

Burgess, Glen (1992) *The Politics of the Ancient Constitution. An Introduction to English Political Theory, 1603–1642* (London: Macmillan).

Burns, J. H. (ed.) (1991) *The Cambridge History of Medieval Political Thought c. 350–c. 1450* (Cambridge: Cambridge University Press).

Burns, J. H. with Mark Goldie (eds) (1994) *The Cambridge History of Political Thought 1450–1700* (Cambridge: Cambridge University Press).

Carroll, John (1974) *Break-out from the Crystal Palace: the anarcho-psychological critique; Stirner, Nietzsche, Dostoevsky* (London: Routledge).

Chapman, J. W. and Galston, William (eds) (1992) *Virtue, Nomos*, vol. xxxiv (New York: New York University Press).

Claeys, Gregory (1989) *Citizens and Saints. Politics and anti-politics in early British Socialism* (Cambridge: Cambridge University Press).

Collini, Stefan (1977) 'Liberalism and the Legacy of Mill', *Historical Journal*, vol. 20, pp. 337–54.

Connolly, William E. (1988) *Political Theory & Modernity* (Oxford: Basil Blackwell).

Coole, Diana H. (1988) *Women in Political Theory. From Ancient Misogyny to Contemporary Feminism* (Brighton: Wheatsheaf).

Copleston, F. C. (1975) *Aquinas* (Harmondsworth: Penguin).

Davis, J. C. (1968) 'The Levellers and Democracy', *Past and Present*, vol. 40, pp. 174–80.

Davis, J. C. (1981) 'Pocock's Harrington: Grace, Nature and Art in the Classical Republicanism of James Harrington', *Historical Journal*, vol. 24, pp. 683–97.

Davis, J. C. (1994) 'Utopianism', in Burns with Goldie, *The Cambridge History of Political Thought*, pp. 329–46.

Deutscher, Isaac (1954) *The Prophet Armed: Trotsky, 1879–1921* (New York: Oxford University Press).

Deutscher, Isaac (1966) 'Maosim – its Origins and Outlook', in Isaac Deutscher, *Ironies of History. Essays on Contemporary Communism* (Oxford: Oxford University Press), pp. 88–120.

Detwiler, Bruce (1990) *Nietzsche and the Politics of Aristocratic Radicalism* (Chicago: University of Chicago Press).

Dinwiddy, J. R. (1993) 'Early-Nineteenth-Century Reactions to Benthamism', in Parekh, *Jeremy Bentham*, vol. i, pp. 255–76.

Dunbabin, Jean (1991) 'Government', in Burns, *The Cambridge History of Medieval Political Thought*, pp. 477–519.

Dunn, John (1984) *The Politics of Socialism* (Cambridge: Cambridge University Press).

Dunn, John (ed.) (1992) *Democracy. The Unfinished Journey, 508BC to AD 1993* (Oxford: Oxford University Press).

Enayat, Hamid (1983) 'Iran: Khumayni's Concept of the "Guardianship of the Jurisconsult"', in James P. Piscatori (ed.), *Islam in the Political Process* (Cambridge: Cambridge University Press), pp. 160–80.

Farrar, Cynthia (1992) 'Ancient Greek Political Theory as a Response to Democracy', in Dunn, *Democracy*, pp. 17–40.

Finnis, John (1980) *Natural Law and Natural Rights* (Oxford: Clarendon Press).

Fontana, Biancamaria (1992) 'Democracy and the French Revolution', in Dunn, *Democracy*, pp. 107–24.

Forbes, Duncan (1975) *Hume's Philosophical Politics* (Cambridge: Cambridge University Press).

Forsyth, Murray (1987) *Reason and Revolution. The Political Thought of the Abbé sièyes* (Leicester: Leicester University Press).

Francis, Mark (1980) 'The Nineteenth-Century Theory of Sovereignty and Thomas Hobbes', *History of Political Thought*, vol. 1, pp. 517–40.

Francis, Mark and John Morrow (1994) *A History of English Political Thought in the Nineteenth Century* (London: Duckworth).

Franklin, J. H. (ed. and trans.) (1969a) *Constitutionalism and Resistance in the Sixteenth Century: three treatise by Hotman, Beza & Mornay* (New York: Pegasus).

Franklin, J. H. (1969b) 'Introduction', in Franklin, *Constitutionalism and Resistance*.

Franklin, J. H. (1992) 'Introduction', in Bodin (1992) *On Sovereignty*.

Franklin, J. H. (1994) 'Sovereignty and the mixed constitution: Bodin and his critics', in Burns with Goldie, *The Cambridge History of Political Thought*, pp. 299–328.

Fritz, Kurt von (1954) *The Theory of the Mixed Constitution in Antiquity* (New York: Columbia University Press).

Gilby, Thomas (1958) *Principality and Polity: Aquinas and the Rise of State Theory in the West* (London: Longman).

Green, Philip (1985) *Retrieving Democracy* (London: Methuen).

Grogan, Susan K. (1992) *French Socialism and Sexual Difference. Women and the New Society, 1803–44* (London: Macmillan).

Gunn, J. A. W. (1983) *Beyond Liberty and Property. The Process of Self-Recognition in Eighteenth-Century Political Thought* (Kingston and Montreal: McGill-Queen's University Press).

Haakonssen, Knud (1981) *The Science of a Legislator. The Natural Jurisprudence of David Hume & Adam Smith* (Cambridge: Cambridge University Press).

Haakonssen, Knud (1985) 'Hugo Grotius and the History of Political Thought', *Political Theory*, vol. 13, pp. 239–65.

Haakonssen, Knud (1993) 'The Structure of Hume's political theory', in David Fate Norton (ed.), *The Cambridge Companion to Hume* (Cambridge: Cambridge University Press), pp. 182–221.

Halevy, Elie (1972) *The Growth of Philosophical Radicalism* (London: Faber).

Hampsher-Monk, Iain (1991) 'John Thelwall and the Eighteenth-Century Radical Response to Political Economy', *Historical Journal*, vol. 34, pp. 1–20.

Hampsher-Monk, Iain (1992) *A History of Modern Political Thought. Major Political Thinkers from Hobbes to Marx* (Oxford: Basil Blackwell).

Hampson, Norman (1991) *Saint-Just* (Oxford: Basil Blackwell).

Harding, Neil (1992) 'The Marxist Leninist Detour', in Dunn, *Democracy*, pp. 155–88.

Harris, Paul (ed.) (1989) *Civil Disobedience* (Latham, MD: University Press of America).

Hart, H. L. A. (1982) *Essays on Bentham. Jurisprudence and Political Theory* (Oxford: Clarendon Press).

Havelock, Eric A. (1964) *The Liberal Temper in Greek Politics* (New Haven, CT: Yale University Press).

Hillerbrand, Hans, J. (ed.) (1968) *The Protestant Reformation* (New York: Harper & Row).

Hopfl, Harro (1981). 'Introduction' in Harro Hopfl (ed.), *Luther and Calvin on Secular Authority* (Cambridge: Cambridge University Press).

Horowitz, Irving, L. (1954) *Claude Helvetius: philosopher of democracy and enlightenment* (New York: Paine-Whitman).

Horton, John (1992) *Political Obligation* (London: Macmillan).

Hsiao, Kung-chuan (1979) *A History of Chinese Political Thought. Volume 1: From the Beginnings to the Sixth Century A.D.*, trans. F. W. Mote (Princeton, NJ: Princeton University Press).

Hsu, Leonard Shihlien (1932) *The Political Philosophy of Confucius* (London: Routledge).

Hume, L. J. (1993) 'Bentham as Social and Political Theorist', in Parekh, *Jeremy Bentham*, vol. iii, pp. 482–500.

Hutton, Patrick H. (1981) *The Cult of the Revolutionary Tradition. The Blanquists in French Politics, 1864–1893* (Berkeley, CA: University of California Press).

Jessop, Bob and Charlie Malcolm-Brown (eds) (1990) *Karl Marx's Social and Political Thought. Critical Assessments*, 4 vols (London: Routledge).

Jones, A. H. M. (1957) *Athenian Democracy* (Oxford: Basil Blackwell).

Kautsky, John H. (1994) *Karl Kautsky. Marxism, Revolution & Democracy* (New Brunswick, NJ: Transaction Publishers).

Kelidar, Abbas (1981) 'Ayatollah Khomeini's Concept of Islamic Government', in Alexander S. Cudsi and Ali E. Hillal Dessouki (eds), *Islam and Power* (London: Croom Helm), pp. 75–92.

Keohane, Nannerl O. (1980) *Philosophy and the State in France. The Renaissance to the Enlightenment* (Princeton, NJ: Princeton University Press).

Khilnani, Sunil (1992) 'India's Democratic Career', in Dunn, *Democracy*, pp. 189–205.

King, Preston (1974) *The Ideology of Order. A Comparative Analysis of Jean Bodin and Thomas Hobbes* (London: George Allen and Unwin).

Klosko, George (1986) *The Development of Plato's Political Theory* (London: Methuen).

Krieger, Leonard (1972) *The German Idea of Freedom* (Chicago, Ill.: University of Chicago Press).

Lalidji, Abdol Karim (1988) 'Constitutionalism and Clerical Authority' in Said Amir Arjomand (ed.), *Authority and Political Culture in Shi'ism* (Albany, NY: State University of New York Press, pp. 133–58.

Leopold, David (1995) 'Introduction' in Max Stirner, *The Ego and its Own*, ed. David Leopold (Cambridge: Cambridge University Press).

Lewis, Ewart (1954) *Medieval Political Ideas*, 2 vols (London: Routledge & Kegan Paul).

Lichtheim, George (1968) *The Origins of Socialism* (London: Weidenfeld & Nicolson).

Lively, Jack (1965) *The Social and Political Thought of Alexis de Tocqueville* (Oxford: Clarendon Press).

Lively, Jack and John Rees (eds) (1984) *Utilitarian Logic and Politics* (Oxford: Clarendon Press).

Lloyd, Howell A. (1994) 'Constitutionalism', in Burns with Goldie, *The Cambridge History of Political Thought*, pp. 254–97.

Lyons, David (1973) *In the Interests of the Governed. A Study of Bentham's Philosophy of Utility and Law* (Oxford: Clarendon Press).

Macpherson, C. B. (1965) *The Real World of Democracy* (Toronto: CBC).

Maguire, John M. (1978) *Marx's Theory of Politics* (Cambridge: Cambridge University Press).

Maier, Charles S. (1992) 'Democracy Since the French Revolution', in Dunn, *Democracy*, pp. 125–4.

Mansbridge, Jane J. (1980) *Beyond Adversary Democracy* (New York: Basic Books).

Markus, R. A. (1991) 'The Latin Fathers', in Burns, *The Cambridge History of Medieval Political Thought*, pp. 92–122.

McLellan, David (1979) *Marxism After Marx: An Introduction* (London: Macmillan).

Meisel, James H. (1962) *The Myth of the Ruling Class: Gaetano Mosca and the Elite* (Ann Arbor, Mich.: University of Michigan Press).

Miller, David (1981) *Hume's Political Thought* (Oxford: Clarendon Press).

Miller, David (1984) *Anarchism* (London: J. M. Dent).

Miller, Peter N. (1994) *Defining the common good. Empire, religion and philosophy in eighteenth-century Britain* (Cambridge: Cambridge University Press).

Miller, Richard W. (1984) *Analysing Marx: Morality, Power and History* (Princeton, NJ: Princeton University Press).

Morrow, John (1990) *Coleridge's Political Thought. Property, Morality and the Limits of Traditional Discourse* (London: Macmillan).

Mulgan, R. G. (1977) *Aristotle's Political Theory* (Oxford: Clarendon Press).

Murphy, Jeffrie G. (1970) *Kant: The Philosophy & Right* (London: Macmillan)

Nederman, Cary J. (1990) 'Introduction', in John of Salisbury, *Policraticus*, ed. Cary J. Nederman (Cambridge: Cambridge University Press).

Nelson, Janet (1991) 'Kingship and Empire', in Burns, *The Cambridge History of Political Thought*, pp. 211–50.

Neumann, F. (1944) *Behemoth: The Structure and Practice of National Socialism, 1933–1944* (London: Victor Gollancz).

Nicholson, Peter (1990) *The Political Philosophy of the British Idealists* (Cambridge: Cambridge University Press).

Nursey-Bray, Paul (1983) 'Consensus and Community: the theory of African one-party democracy', in Graeme Duncan (ed.), *Democratic Theory and Practice* (Cambridge: Cambridge University Press), pp. 96–114.

Okin, Susan Mollor (1992) *Women in Western Political Thought* (Princeton, NJ: Princeton University Press).

Omid, Homa (1994) *Islam and the Post-Revolutionary State in Iran* (London: Macmillan).

Parekh, Bhikhu (ed.) (1973) *Bentham's Political Thought* (London: Croom Helm).

Parekh, Bhikhu (1989) *Gandhi's Political Philosophy. A Critical Examination* (London: Macmillan).

Parekh, Bhikhu (ed.) (1993) *Jeremy Bentham: Critical Assessments*, 4 vols (London: Routledge).

Parry, Geraint (1970) *Political Elites* (London: George Allen and Unwin).

Pennington, K. (1991) 'Law, legislative authority and theories of government, 1150–1450', in Burns, *The Cambridge History of Medieval Political Thought*, pp. 424–53.

Pennock, J. Roland (1981) 'Rights, Natural Rights, and Human Rights – A General Overview', in Pennock and Chapman, *Human Rights*, pp. 1–28.

Pennock, J. and John W. Chapman (1981) *Human Rights*, Nomos xxiii (New York: New York University Press).

Plamenatz, John (1949) *The English Utilitarians* (Oxford: Basil Blackwell).

Plummer, Alfred (1971) *Bronterre* (London: Allen and Unwin).

Pocock, J. G. A. (1957) *The Ancient Constitution and the Feudal Law* (Cambridge: Cambridge University Press).

Pocock, J. G. A. (1975) *The Machiavellian Moment* (Princeton, NJ: Princeton University Press).

Pocock, J. G. A. (1985) *Virtue, Commerce and History* (Cambridge: Cambridge University Press).

Quillet, Jeannine (1991) 'Community, counsel and representation', in Burns, *The Cambridge History of Medieval Political Thought*, pp. 520–72.

Rengger, N. J. (1992) 'No Time Like the Present? Postmodernism and Political Theory', *Political Studies*, vol. xl, no. 3, pp. 561–70.

Rosen, Allan D. (1993) *Kant's Theory of Justice* (Ithaca, NY: Cornell University Press).

Rosen, F. (1993) 'Jeremy Bentham and Democratic Theory', in Parekh, *Jeremy Bentham*, vol. iii, pp. 573–92.

Rosenblum, Nancy L. (1996) 'Introduction' in Henry D. Thoreau, *Political Writings*, ed. Nancy L. Rosenblum (Cambridge: Cambridge University Press).

Rowen, Herbert H. (1980) *The King's State. Proprietary Dynasticism in Early Modern France* (New Brunswick, NJ: Rutgers University Press).

Rubin, Vitaly A. (1979) *Individual and State in Ancient China*, trans. Stephen I. Levine (New York: Columbia University Press).

Salvador, Massimo (1979) *Karl Kautsky and the Socialist Revolution, 1880–1938*, trans. Jon Rothschild (London: New Left Books).

Sarup, Madan (1988) *Post-Structuralism and Postmodernism* (London: Harvester Wheatsheaf).

Sassoon, Anne Showstack (1987) *Gramsci's Politics*, 2nd edn (London: Hutchinson).

Schofield, T. P. (1993) ' "Economy as Applied to Office" and the Development of Bentham's Democratic Thought', in Parekh, *Jeremy Bentham*, vol. iii, pp. 868–78.

Scott, Jonathan (1988) *Algernon Sidney and the English Republic 1623–1677* (Cambridge: Cambridge University Press).

Shankman, Steven (ed.) (1994) *Plato and Postmodernism* (Glenside, PA: Aldine Press).

Sigmund, Paul E. (1971) *Natural Law in Political Thought* (Cambridge, Mass.: Winthrop).

Sinclair, R. K. (1988) *Democracy and Participation in Athens* (Cambridge: Cambridge University Press).

Sivan, Emmanuel (1985) *Radical Islam. Medieval Theology and Modern Politics* (New Haven, CT: Yale University Press).

Skinner, Quentin (1978) *The Foundations of Modern Political Thought*, 2 vols (Cambridge: Cambridge University Press).

Skinner, Quentin (1992) 'The Italian City Republics', in Dunn, *Democracy*, 1992, pp. 57–70.

Schochet, Gordon J. (1975) *Patriarchalism in political thought: the authoritarian family and political speculation and attitudes especially in seventeenth-century England* (Oxford: Basil Blackwell).

Spitzer, Alan B. (1970) *The Revolutionary Theories of Louis Auguste Blanqui* (New York: AMS Press).

Storing, Herbert J. (1989) 'The Case Against Civil Disobedience' in Paul Harris (ed.), *Civil Disobedience* (Latham, MD: University Press of America) pp. 73–90.

Tholfsen, Trygve R. (1984) *Ideology and Revolution in Modern Europe. An Essay in the History of Ideas* (New York: Columbia University Press).

Thomas, William (1985) *Mill* (Oxford: Oxford University Press).

Tooley, M. J. (n.d.) 'Introduction', in Jean Bodin, *Six Books of the Commonwealth*, ed. and trans. M. J. Tooley (Oxford: Basil Blackwell).

Tuck, Richard (1979) *Natural Rights Theories: Their Origin and Development* (Cambridge: Cambridge University Press).

Tuck, Richard (1984) 'Thomas Hobbes: the sceptical state', in Brian Redhead (ed.), *From Plato to Nato* (London: Ariel Books).

Tuck, Richard (1993) *Philosophy and government 1572–1651* (Cambridge: Cambridge University Press).

Tully, James (1991), 'Introduction' in Samuel Pufendorf, *On the duty of man and citizen according to natural law*, ed. James Tully (Cambridge: Cambridge University Press).

Ullmann, Walter (1975) *Medieval Political Thought* (Harmondsworth: Penguin Books).

Webb, Beatrice (1948) *Our Partnership* (London: Longman).

Whelan, Frederick G. (1985) *Order and Artifice in Hume's Political Philosophy* (Princeton, NJ: Princeton University Press).

White, S. K. (1991) *Political Theory and Postmodernism* (Cambridge: Cambridge University Press).

White, Stephen, John Gardner and George Schopflin (1982) *Communist Political Systems* (London: Macmillan).

Wood, Allen W. (1991) 'Introduction', in G. W. F. Hegel, *Elements of the Philosophy of Right*, ed. Allen W. Wood, trans. H. B. Nisbet (Cambridge: Cambridge University Press).

Wood, Ellen Meiskins and Neal Wood (1978) *Class Ideology and Ancient Political Theory: Socrates, Plato and Aristotle in Social Context* (Oxford: Basil Blackwell).

Wood, Gordon S. (1992) 'Democracy and the American Revolution', in Dunn, *Democracy*, pp. 91–106.

Wood, Neal (1988) *Cicero's Social and Political Thought* (Berkeley, CA: University of California Press).

Wootton, David (1992) 'The Levellers', in Dunn, *Democracy*, pp. 71–90.

Wootton, David (1994) 'Leveller Democracy and the Puritan Revolution', in Burns with Goldie, *The Cambridge History of Political Thought*, pp. 412–42.

Index of Personal Names

Index of Subjects

absolute government   200, 215, 218,
219, 249ff, 278–9, 288, 321
  aristocracy and   250
  democracy and   250, 267
  God's oversight of   257, 269
  Holy Scriptures and   267, 268
  fundamental law and   264, 266
  law and   252–3, 261, 265, 269, 271–1,
287–9
  medieval kingship and   250–1
  mixed government and   249, 256,
267, 268
  monarchy and   250, 251, 266, 267–9,
270–1
  moral constraints on   257–8, 269
  natural law and   249, 257, 258, 262–
6, 267
  natural rights and   265
  order and   249–50, 252, 261
  parental power and   256
  patriarchal model of   267
  rationality and   270,
  resistance to   252, 264, 300
  self-preservation and   258–9, 261–3
  sovereign(ty) and   249, 250, 251–73
  subjects and   249, 255, 257, 262–3,
264–5
  unified command and   256
  utility and   270–2
alienation   92–3
anarchism   18, 19, 20, 46–8, 75, 94–103,
104, 344–8
anarchist revolutionary theories
344–9, 354

  capitalism in   345, 346
  critique of Marxism in   345, 346–8
  dictatorship of proletariat in   348
  evolutionary aspects of   345–6
  federation in   346
  historical dimensions in   345
  idea of God in   345
  mutual aid in   345–6
  popular instincts in   346–7
  revolutionary elites in   347
  revolutionary goals in   345
  science in   346–7
  spontaneity in   346–8
  state in   345, 348
anti-colonial revolutionary
theories   348–53, 354, 383
  capitalism in   350
  classes in   350, 352
  colonised elites in   351
  cultural and political aspects
of   350–1
  development in   353
  general liberation in   349, 353
  indigenous cultures in   349, 351
  Marxism and   348–50, 353
  national bourgeoisie in   352
  non-violence in   349
  parties in   349, 352–3
  political education in   353
  post-revolutionary world in   351–2
  rural masses in   350–1
  settlers in   350
  spontaneous action in   350
  Third World Democracy in   352

410